Martin Luther King, Jr.

Peter Ling's acclaimed biography of Martin Luther King, Jr. provides a thorough re-examination of both the man and the Civil Rights Movement, showing how King grew into his leadership role and kept his faith as the challenges facing the movement strengthened after 1965. Ling combines a detailed narrative of Martin Luther King's life with the key historiographical debates surrounding him and places both within the historical context of the Civil Rights Movement.

This fully revised and updated second edition includes an extended look at Black Power and a detailed analysis of the memorialization of King since his death, including President Obama's 50th anniversary address, and how conservative spokesmen have tried to appropriate King as an advocate of color-blindness.

Drawing on the wide-ranging and changing scholarship on the Civil Rights Movement, this volume condenses research previously scattered across a larger literature. Peter Ling's crisp and fluent style captures the drama, irony, and pathos of King's life and provides an excellent introduction for students and others interested in King, the Civil Rights Movement, and America in the 1960s.

Peter J. Ling is Professor of American Studies in the Department of American and Canadian Studies at the University of Nottingham. His previous works include the edited collection, *Gender and the Civil Rights Movement* (2004), a history of the Democratic Party (2004), and a biography of John F. Kennedy (2013).

ROUTLEDGE HISTORICAL BIOGRAPHIES

Series Editor: Robert Pearce

Routledge Historical Biographies provide engaging, readable and academically credible biographies written from an explicitly historical perspective. These concise and accessible accounts will bring important historical figures to life for students and general readers alike.

Bismarck by Edgar Feuchtwanger (second edition 2014)
Calvin by Michael A. Mullett
Neville Chamberlain by Nick Smart
Oliver Cromwell by Martyn Bennett
Edward IV by Hannes Kleineke
Elizabeth I by Judith M. Richards
Franco by Antonio Cazorla-Sanchez
Gladstone by Michael Partridge
Henry VII by Sean Cunningham
Henry VIII by Lucy Wooding
John F. Kennedy by Peter J. Ling
John Maynard Keynes by Vincent Barnett
Lenin by Christopher Read
Louis XIV by Richard Wilkinson
Martin Luther King Jr. by Peter J. Ling
Martin Luther by Michael A. Mullet (second edition 2014)
Mao by Michael Lynch
Marx by Vincent Barnett
Mary Queen of Scots by Retha M. Warnicke
Mary Tudor by Judith M. Richards
Mussolini by Peter Neville (second edition 2014)
Nehru by Benjamin Zachariah
Emmeline Pankhurst by Paula Bartley
Richard III by David Hipshon
Trotsky by Ian Thatcher

Forthcoming:

Churchill by Robert Pearce
Cranmer by Susan Wabuda
Gandhi by Benjamin Zachariah
Henry VI by David Grummitt
Khrushchev by Alexander Titov
Stalin by Christopher Read
Wolsey by Glenn Richardson

Martin Luther King, Jr.

Second edition
Peter J. Ling

 Routledge
Taylor & Francis Group

LONDON AND NEW YORK

First published 2015
by Routledge
2 Park Square, Milton Park, Abingdon, Oxon OX14 4RN

and by Routledge
711 Third Avenue, New York, NY 10017

*Routledge is an imprint of the Taylor & Francis Group, an informa
business*

British Library Cataloguing in Publication Data
A catalogue record for this book is available from the British
Library

Library of Congress Cataloging in Publication Data
Ling, Peter J. (Peter John), 1956-
Martin Luther King, Jr. / Peter J. Ling. – Second edition.
pages cm. – (Routledge historical biographies)
Includes bibliographical references and index.
1. King, Martin Luther, Jr., 1929-1968. 2. African Americans–
Biography. 3. Civil rights workers–United States–Biography. 4.
Baptists–United States–Clergy–Biography. 5. African Americans–
Civil rights–History–20th century. 6. Civil rights movements–
United States–History–20th century. I. Title.
E185.97.K5L55 2015
323.092–dc23
[B]
2014033643

ISBN: 978-1-138-78161-0 (hbk)
ISBN: 978-1-138-78163-4 (pbk)
ISBN: 978-1-315-73151-3 (ebk)

Typeset in Garamond
by Taylor & Francis Books

Contents

Chronology   ix

1 Introduction   1

2 Junior: Becoming Martin Luther King,
   1929-55   10

3 Loving Your Enemies: Montgomery,
   1955-59   29

4 Finding His Way, 1960-62   65

5 Let The Children Come To Me: Birmingham,
   1963   105

6 Along A Tightrope, 1963-64   141

7 Across A Bridge Of Mistrust: Selma To Montgomery,
   1964-65   180

8 King's Call: Organizing And Mobilizing Chicago,
   1965-66   212

9 Shrinking Options: "Black Power" And Vietnam,
   1966-67   247

10 Going For Broke: Memphis, 1968   278

11 Epilogue: *In Memoriam* – Remembering King   313

   Glossary of Organizations   339
   Guide to Further Reading   341
   Select Bibliography   354
   Index   368

Chronology

Date	Personal events	National events	International events
1929	(January) King's birth registered as Michael King (15th).	(October) Wall Street crash.	
1930			Gandhi's Salt March
1933		Franklin D. Roosevelt becomes President.	Adolf Hitler comes to power in Germany.
1934	After visit to Germany King Sr. changes his and his son's name to Martin Luther King.		
1936		New Deal coalition, including African Americans, reelects FDR.	
1939			German invasion of Poland starts World War II.
1940		FDR wins unprecedented third term by promising to keep US out of the war.	
1941		Threatened mass black March on Washington prompts FDR to establish a Fair Employment Practices Committee.	Japanese bomb US Naval Base at Pearl Harbor in Hawaii. US enters the war.
1943		Racial tensions produce major riots in Harlem and Detroit.	

(continued)

Date	Personal events	National events	International events
1944	King enters Morehouse College (aged 15).	US Supreme Court outlaws all-white primary elections. Gunnar Myrdal publishes *An American Dilemma*. FDR wins fourth term.	D-Day landings.
1945		FDR's death catapults Harry S. Truman of Missouri into the presidency.	Germans surrender. Atomic bombs dropped on Hiroshima and Nagasaki. Japanese surrender. Winston Churchill delivers his "Iron Curtain" speech.
1946	Protest letter by King published in *Atlanta Constitution*.	Returning black veterans face violence as they try to register to vote.	Communists take power in Hungary. US–Soviet tensions increase.
1947	King graduates from Morehouse and enters Crozer Theological Seminary near Philadelphia.	President's Committee on Civil Rights' report. Loyalty tests for federal workers as part of Cold War domestic anti-communism.	
1948	King ordained as his father's assistant at Ebenezer Baptist Church.	Desegregation of US armed forces ordered. Black votes help Truman win surprise election victory.	Gandhi assassinated in India.
1949			Communist victory in China and Soviet explosion of nuclear bomb intensify US anti-communism.
1950		Senator J. McCarthy heads domestic anticommunist witch hunt. US Supreme Court requires graduate school desegregation.	Korean War, the first conflict for US desegregated armed forces, adds to Red Scare at home.
1951	King graduates from Crozer with high academic honors and begins doctoral study at Boston University.		

Date	Personal events	National events	International events
1953	King marries Coretta Scott in Marion, Alabama.	Dwight D. Eisenhower becomes President. Republicans also control Congress.	Korean War ends. Soviet leader Stalin dies.
1954	King becomes pastor of Dexter Avenue Baptist Church in Montgomery.	US Supreme Court's Brown decision rules segregated schools are unconstitutional. White Citizens Councils organized to resist desegregation.	
1955	(March) Arrest of teenager Claudette Colvin raises bus segregation issue during Montgomery municipal election. (April) King finishes his doctoral thesis. (November) King's first child Yolanda Denise born.	(May) Implementation ruling or "Brown II" orders school desegregation in the South "with all deliberate speed." (July) Alabama passes "pupil placement law" to evade school desegregation. Southern politicians increasingly fight to represent the segregationist vote. (November) US Supreme Court uses Brown precedent to outlaw segregation of public parks, playgrounds, golf courses, and beaches.	(May) Bandung Conference of so-called nonaligned nations like India condemns the Cold War.

(continued)

Date	Personal events	National events	International events
1956	(January) White city leaders try to undermine and intimidate King who experiences a spiritual awakening (27th) that enables him to preach nonviolence when his home is bombed (30th). (February) MIA sues for desegregation and city retaliates with 115 indictments under state anti-boycott law. Outside experts, Bayard Rustin and Glenn Smiley, explain nonviolence to King. (June) Federal district court rules 2 to 1 in favor of the MIA. King skillfully diffuses potential scandal over alleged MIA misuse of donations.	(March) Nineteen US Senators and eighty-one Congressmen sign the "Southern Manifesto" against the *Brown* decision. (May) Black Baptist minister C.K. Steele leads Tallahassee Bus Boycott in Florida. (June) Alabama state law banning NAACP typifies increasing legal harassment. To sustain civil rights protests in Birmingham, Reverend Fred Shuttlesworth founds the Alabama Christian Movement for Human Rights.	Tunisia and Morocco secure independence from France, as does the Sudan from Great Britain. Nelson Mandela and other African National Congress activists are charged with treason by South African authorities.

Date	Personal events	National events	International events
			(October) US embarrassed by Anglo-French attempts to secure the Suez Canal, which had been nationalized by Egyptian President Nasser. Soviets take advantage to put down the Hungarian revolt.
	(November) US Supreme Court affirms desegregation ruling at the same time that state court bans the MIA's car pool.	(November) Eisenhower wins second term with increased Southern support due to his perceived reluctance to force desegregation.	
	(December) Boycott ends, but white sniper attacks prompt city to suspend evening bus services.	(December) Shuttlesworth survives bombing that destroys his Birmingham home.	
1957	(January) Despite the bombing of several Montgomery black churches, the SCLC is founded in Atlanta with King as President.	Eisenhower's focus on foreign policy is evident in the so-called "Eisenhower Doctrine" allowing US military intervention in the Middle East.	
	(March) King attends Ghana's independence celebrations.		(March) Treaty of Rome establishes the European Economic Community (EEC).
	(May) King delivers his "Give Us the Ballot" speech at the Prayer Pilgrimage in Washington, DC.		

(continued)

(continued)

Date	Personal events	National events	International events
	(June) Meets with Vice-President Richard Nixon.	(September) Congress passes its first Civil Rights Act since the Reconstruction period ended in 1877. Weakened by strong Southern opposition, it only vaguely strengthens federal power to protect voting rights. After State Governor Orval Faubus fails to support a federal court order, President Eisenhower sends US troops to protect nine black children at the newly desegregated Central High School in Little Rock, Arkansas.	
	(September) King is photographed next to a known communist at the Highlander Folk School. Later, the photo is used to prove his "Red" links.		
			(October) Soviets launch "Sputnik," the first satellite in space. It arouses US fears that they are falling behind in the space race.
1958	(January) Veteran activist Ella Baker arrives to organize SCLC offices in Atlanta.	White segregationists use increasing economic intimidation to deter civil rights protests.	(January) US satellite, "Explorer I" orbits the Earth.
	(February) King launches a largely unsuccessful Southern voter registration drive, the "Crusade for Citizenship."		

(continued)

Date	Personal events	National events	International events
		(July) Eisenhower establishes the National Aeronautics and Space Administration (NASA).	(July) US Marines intervene in Lebanon.
	(September) King is seriously wounded by a deranged woman at a Harlem book signing.		
1959			(January) Cuban Revolution brings Castro to power.
	(February–March) King visits India.		
	(April) Ella Baker returns to try to improve SCLC efficiency.		
	(November) King resigns from Dexter Avenue to return to Atlanta.		
1960	(February) King arrested for tax evasion in Alabama.	(February) Protest in Greensboro, North Carolina sparks wave of sit-ins across the South.	Eisenhower administration considers plans to oust Castro in Cuba and to support anti-communist regimes in Southeast Asia.
			(March) Sharpeville massacre in South Africa leaves sixty-seven protesters dead.

(continued)

Date	Personal events	National events	International events
		(April) Using SCLC money, Ella Baker organizes Raleigh conference at which SNCC is formed. A new Civil Rights Act slightly improves the Justice Department's ability to protect voting rights.	
	(May) Acquitted by all-white jury.		
	(June) King meets presidential hopeful John F. Kennedy.		(June) Belgian Congo declares independence, but is engulfed by civil war.
	(August) Wyatt Walker replaces Ella Baker as SCLC executive director.		
	(October) King imprisoned for his part in Atlanta sit-in demonstrations. A secret deal between the Kennedy campaign and local Georgia Democrats secures his release.		
		(November) By rallying black support over King's arrest, Kennedy narrowly defeats Nixon in the presidential race.	

(continued)

Date	Personal events	National events	International events
1961		(January) Kennedy's inauguration.	Bay of Pigs fiasco raises fears that Kennedy is too inexperienced to manage US foreign policy effectively. Soviet Premier Khrushchev takes a hard line in early meetings.
	(March) King defends his father's moderate position against militants' charges of "Uncle Tom-ism."		
	(May) White mob besieges King at a mass meeting for the Freedom Rides in Montgomery. Bobby Kennedy uses federal marshals to protect the meeting. King refuses to join Riders on buses to Mississippi.	(May) CORE launches Freedom Rides. Riders attacked in Alabama.	
		(June–August) Kennedy officials encourage civil rights groups to focus on the Voter Education Project rather than desegregation protests.	
			(August) Construction of the Berlin Wall to end exodus of refugees from East Germany.

Date	Personal events	National events	International events
		(September) Interstate Commerce Commission orders bus companies to desegregate terminal facilities by December.	(December) Tanganyika secures independence from Great Britain.
	(December) King drawn into Albany campaign. (16th) Pledges to stay in jail through Christmas but bails out (18th) after local leaders reach "oral" agreement with the city authorities.	(December) Escalating protests produce over 500 arrests in Albany, Georgia.	
1962	(January) Albany settlement unravels.	Kennedy forces US steel producers to cut their prices. The launch of Telstar permits the first international TV satellite broadcasts, speeding up the circulation of world news.	Algeria wins independence from France and Uganda from Great Britain.
	(July) Renewed SCLC involvement in Albany deepens SNCC mistrust of King because he fails to stay in jail and refuses to defy a federal court order. (August) Under federal pressure King leaves Albany, supposedly to promote local negotiations, but his reputation suffers.		

Date	Personal events	National events	International events
	(September) SCLC convention in Birmingham prompts local stores to remove segregation signs to avoid protests. King attacked by neo-Nazi.		(October–November) Cuban missile crisis brings the world to the brink of nuclear war. The resolution of the crisis, however, greatly boosts Kennedy's credibility as a world leader.
	(October) FBI formally investigates whether SCLC is communist.	(October) James Meredith becomes the first African American to attend the University of Mississippi but only after federal marshals occupy the campus and local whites riot in protest.	(November) Chinese and Indian border clashes.
	(November) Bobby Kennedy authorizes wire-tapping.	(November) President Kennedy at last signs a desegregation of federal public housing order, an improvement that he had said could be done "with a stroke of a pen" during the 1960 campaign. Publication of Betty Friedan's *The Feminine Mystique* helps promote a women's rights movement.	
1963	(January) Dorchester meeting to plan the Birmingham campaign.		Organization for African Unity (OAU) formed by thirty of the thirty-two independent nations of Africa.
	(March) The need for a run-off election between Bull Connor and Albert Boutwell forces SCLC to postpone its campaign (5th).		

(continued)

Date	Personal events	National events	International events
	(April) Boutwell wins but Connor stays on to confront King (2nd). SCLC campaign begins with lunch-counter sit-ins (3rd). King goes to jail to boost flagging campaign (12th–20th). (May) Bevel's children's marches expose Connor's brutality in the media (2nd–7th). King suspends protests (8th). Accord signed (10th). Bombing of Gaston Motel sparks violent racial clashes (11th–12th). (June) King warned to break with Levison and O'Dell.	(June) Governor George Wallace symbolically blocks desegregation of the University of Alabama, forcing Kennedy to federalize Alabama's National Guard and address the nation on TV to promise a civil rights bill (11th). Head of the NAACP in Mississippi, Medgar Evers, shot dead outside his home (12th). Kennedy hosts civil rights leaders to discuss March on Washington (22nd).	

(continued)

Date	Personal events	National events	International events
	(August) March on Washington – King delivers his "I Have a Dream" speech (28th). (September) Sixteenth Street Baptist Church bombing kills four girls in Birmingham. (November) SCLC plans for Danville protests ended by JFK's death.	(November) Kennedy killed in Dallas, Texas (22nd). His alleged killer Oswald killed by Jack Ruby (24th). State funeral for JFK (25th). Lyndon B. Johnson tells Congress that speedy passage of the civil rights bill would be the best memorial to JFK.	(August) Partial nuclear test ban signed by US and USSR; ratified by the Senate in October. (November) With US encouragement, a coup topples South Vietnamese leader Ngo Dinh Diem (1st).
1964	(May 26–June 30) SCLC campaign in St. Augustine, Florida.	(January) President Johnson announces his "War on Poverty." (February) Violent racial clashes in Cambridge, Maryland, read as sign that black nonviolence is fading.	

(continued)

Date	Personal events	National events	International events
		(June) After the longest debate in US history, Civil Rights Act passes (20th). Three civil rights workers disappear in Mississippi (21st). (June–August) Mississippi Freedom Summer campaign.	(June) UN passes resolution condemning South African apartheid after Nelson Mandela and seven others are sentenced to life imprisonment by the white South African regime.
	(July) King sees Civil Rights Act signed (2nd), tours Mississippi under heavy guard (21st–24th), tries to calm racial tensions in New York (27th–28th), and joins NAACP and Urban League in suspending direct action campaigns until after election (29th).	(July) Racial disturbances in Harlem, Brooklyn, and other New York black districts. MFDP organized to challenge the regular Democratic delegation at the National Convention.	
	(August) King lobbies to seat MFDP delegation at the Democratic National Convention in Atlantic City.	(August) Huge federal search finds bodies of missing workers. MFDP rejects offer of two seats at large at Atlantic City Convention. Federal Office of Economic Opportunity set up to coordinate War on Poverty grants.	(August) Reported attacks on US destroyers in the Gulf of Tonkin prompt Congress to give President Johnson power to escalate US military involvement in Vietnam.
	(October) King urges blacks not to vote for Republican Barry Goldwater. Hospitalized with exhaustion, he learns he has won the Nobel Peace Prize (13th).		(October) Soviet Premier Khrushchev resigns. Communist China explodes its first nuclear weapon.

(continued)

Date	Personal events	National events	International events
	(November) King announces resumption of direct action (4th) and is denounced by J. Edgar Hoover as "the most notorious liar in America" (18th).	(November) Johnson defeats Goldwater by a landslide.	
	(December) King receives Nobel Prize in Oslo.		
1965	(January) After Coretta King opens anonymous FBI blackmail letter and tape, top SCLC staff meet with FBI to try to stop smear campaign (11th). King attacked in Selma (18th).	President Johnson launches his "War on Poverty" in his State of the Union address.	
	(January–March) Selma campaign.		
	(February) King in Selma Jail (1st–5th). State troopers fatally wound Jimmie Lee Jackson in Marion, Alabama (18th). SCLC announces Selma-to-Montgomery march (26th).	(February) Malcolm X assassinated in Harlem (21st).	(February) Vietcong attacks on US bases in South Vietnam prompt bombing raids on North Vietnam.

(continued)

Date	Personal events	National events	International events
	(March) "Bloody Sunday" – Alabama police are filmed attacking peaceful marchers, on the outskirts of Selma (7th). "Tuesday Turnaround" – a federal judge bans the march, and without consulting his followers, King leads them to a prearranged spot and then turns back to avoid breaking the ban. Later, white thugs fatally wounded James Reeb (9th). Selma-to-Montgomery march ends with King's address (21st–25th). Klansmen murder Northern white march volunteer, Mrs. Viola Liuzzo (25th).	(March) President Johnson addresses joint session of Congress to propose voting rights legislation. He concludes with the words: "And we shall overcome" (15th).	(March) South Africa tightens its apartheid laws.
		(April) Passage of federal aid to education bill gives the government greater leverage over school districts that resist desegregation. (May) Voting rights bill passes Senate.	(April) US invasion of the Dominican Republic intensifies international view of US as increasingly militaristic.
	(June–September) SCLC's disappointing voter registration drive (SCOPE).	(July) Johnson announces troop increases for Vietnam.	

(continued)

Date	Personal events	National events	International events
	(August) Despite board objections, King calls for negotiations in Vietnam.	(August) Voting Rights Act signed (6th). Racial disturbances in Watts, Los Angeles, leave thirty-five dead (11th–16th). White civil rights worker Jonathan Daniels murdered in Alabama (20th).	
	(September) King announces Chicago as site for next campaign.	(October–November) Wave of anti-Vietnam War protests internationally and on US campuses.	(December) Responding to critics, the US extends the Christmas ceasefire to create a de facto bombing halt but no talks follow.
1966	(January) King moves into North Lawndale apartment	(January) Senator Fulbright of the Foreign Relations Committee questions legality of powers granted to the President under the Gulf of Tonkin Resolution.	(January) Pope Paul VI calls for peace talks over Vietnam.
	(January–August) SCLC's Chicago campaign.	(February) National Council of Churches calls for a US ceasefire in Vietnam.	

(continued)

Date	Personal events	National events	International events
		(March) US Supreme Court upholds the Voting Rights Act in the face of legal challenges from Southern states.	(March) International day of protest against the war in Vietnam (26th).
		(May) Stokely Carmichael replaces John Lewis as head of SNCC.	
	(June 6–26) King involved in the Meredith march.	(June) James Meredith wounded on the second day of his "March against Fear" in Mississippi (6th). Stokely Carmichael launches his "Black Power" slogan (16th).	
	(July) Soldier's Field rally in Chicago (10th). King tries to calm racial clashes on Chicago's West Side.	(July) CORE's national convention endorses "Black Power" (4th). Roy Wilkins of the NAACP condemns it as "reverse racism" (5th).	(July) World Council of Churches condemns US policy in Vietnam.
	(August) Open housing marches in Chicago. Summit meeting (17th). Mayor Daley secures court order limiting marches. King endorses march into Cicero (19th). Summit Agreement signed (26th).		(August) India and Pakistan clash militarily over Kashmir.
	(September) Amid divisions, militants lead heavily police-protected march into Cicero.	(September) Civil rights bill to outlaw housing discrimination defeated in the Senate.	(September) Pope renews his plea for Vietnam peace talks.

(continued)

Date	Personal events	National events	International events
	(October) King refuses to join moderates in publicly condemning "Black Power."	(October) Black Panther Party founded in Oakland, California.	
	(November) King tells SCLC staff that the US needs a form of socialism.	(November) Elections suggest white conservative backlash. Ronald Reagan becomes Governor of California.	
	(December) King urges idea of a nationally guaranteed income before Senate committee.	(December) SNCC expels its white members.	(December) The number of US troops in Vietnam exceeds 400,000 for the first time.
1967	(January) SCLC's Chicago voter registration drive disrupted by heavy snow. King decides he must speak out publicly on Vietnam. (February) King struggles to finish *Where Do We Go From Here?*	(January) Johnson asks Congress for 6% tax hike to fund Vietnam War. Segregationist Lester Maddox elected Governor of Georgia.	
	(March) As one of several public actions, King and Dr. Benjamin Spock lead an anti-war march in Chicago.	(March) Draft reforms recommended to reduce bias in favor of the well-off. Federal appeals court orders school desegregation to begin in Alabama, Florida, Georgia, Louisiana, Mississippi, and Texas in September.	(March) North Vietnamese Premier Ho Chi Minh rejects US offer of talks.

1 Introduction

Historians still mistrust biography, although the reading public clearly prefers it. Biography can inflate the role of its subject and, with one person consistently placed in the foreground, it may overlook the contribution of less celebrated figures. It may also distort historical understanding by giving too little weight to structural forces that require less personal, even quantitative, analysis. This continues to be the mood among scholars of the American Civil Rights Movement, who honor Dr. King, but want us to appreciate a longer and more complex struggle (Dowd Hall 2005).

Martin And The Movement: A Concise View

In an early oral history interview, a critic of King, Ella Baker, complained that "the Movement made Martin, not Martin the Movement," and her view has been championed in several works that collectively insist that we need to pay attention to the numerous stories of ordinary people in the Movement rather than become fixated on the myth of a fallen hero (Grant 1998: 123). In this biography, when you read about the people behind the Montgomery Bus Boycott (Chapter 3), or about how others besides King set the pace for the Civil Rights Movement before 1963 (Chapter 4), or how the Birmingham campaign turned on the basis of tactics that King was unsure of (Chapter 5), or when you consider the criticisms leveled against King regarding the 1964 St. Augustine and the 1965 Selma campaigns (Chapters 6 and 7 respectively), you may detect that I have some sympathy with

Baker's view. Without the activities of the Movement, most of which he did not control, Martin Luther King might well have been no more than just another black Baptist preacher who spoke well.

This biography also tries to reclaim a Martin Luther King who risks being forgotten by giving due weight to the years after the Selma campaign and the passage of the Voting Rights Act of 1965. In the two and a half years of additional life that fate allowed him before he was gunned down in Memphis on April 4, 1968, King could point to no achievement to match the Voting Rights Act. His relationship with President Lyndon Johnson's administration deteriorated from mistrust to hostility. After his Riverside church sermon (April 4, 1967), condemning US policy in Vietnam in stark terms, he was vilified in the mainstream press, notably by important, moderate black leaders, as either a communist dupe or an ignorant publicity-seeker. At the same time, other African American voices, like those that had cheered in 1963 when Malcolm X had denounced King as a "chump" not a "champ," became more voluble after 1966, as they rallied behind the overt call for "Black Power." Such voices were not entirely new, but they were louder and the media heeded them in a cynical way since they fed a story-line that sold. They reported how African American militants jeered King at the "New Politics" convention of 1967 more readily than they explained why King was there. They noted how some ghetto youths even giggled during his speeches in Cleveland that fall, and seized upon the fact that Memphis gang members, stirred up by a militant youth group, the Invaders, broke up a nonviolent protest march that King was leading in their city in late March 1968 and looted stores. This was proof, it seemed, that King's nonviolence was at best a spent tactic and at worst a threadbare ruse. At the time of his death, the press saw King as a falling star more likely to damage America than to help it fulfil its creed.

We are already as far away in time from King's life as he was from World War I. His shocking death and the subsequent commemoration culminated in King becoming the first African American to be honored with a national public holiday in 1983. During this time distorted memory allowed conservative critics to cite King selectively in support of their resistance to affirmative action and renewal of key civil rights measures. King's humous image as a saint within America's civil religion mak harder to appreciate the hostility he generated because of ....c genuine radicalism he showed in 1968 when he threatened the functioning of the federal government in time of war by his Poor People's Campaign. FBI Director J. Edgar Hoover and other powerful figures regarded King, for all his advocacy of non-violence, as a dangerous demagogue. One can depict King's career as a classic case of rise and fall, and incorporate aspects of Ella Baker's charge. As the Civil Rights Movement expanded and intensified in the years prior to 1965, King's career prospered. But as the Movement fractured and the white backlash intensified, King's career correspondingly nose-dived. Martyrdom in Memphis rescued King's reputation in a way that his struggling efforts to mobilize a nonviolent army of the poor against the federal government seemed to have little chance of doing.

In practice, good polemic seldom corresponds to good history, and the line taken in this biography is more balanced. The pivotal Chicago campaign is extensively treated in Chapter 8, with particular attention being paid not simply to the arguments made that King, as leader of the Southern Christian Leadership Conference, should not have attempted to address racial inequality outside of the South, but also to the crucial distinction between "organizing" and "mobilizing." Under Ella Baker's mentorship, SNCC devoted most of its early energies to grassroots organizing in Mississippi and other Deep South states prior to 1966, as part of what Charles Payne has called "the organizing tradition." In this tradition, activists concentrated on developing the collective ability of ordinary local people to organize for the constant contest for power. As they did so, they laid the foundations for the success of various mobilizing campaigns, and had confirmed that what was needed was Black Power.

Although he was a shrewder, more experienced leader by 1966 than the man that Ella Baker had dismissed in 1960 as a hero with "feet of clay," King remained more suited to the task of mobilization. His charisma generated short-term enthusiasm and his public relations skills enabled him to present an issue as so pressing a moral wrong that it demanded action. In Chicago and subsequent campaigns, King struggled to reconcile his strategy to the fact that deep-seated problems of economic injustice required long-term organizing as well as short-term mobilization. He was unable to secure the kind of victories in his efforts to organize neighborhood unions against slums that could be first translated into federal law and then subsequently used to extract further concessions. Via the summer "Open Housing" marches in Chicago, he tried to dramatize the issue of housing segregation by a strategy of mobilization for nonviolent protest, but the practical effect of the Summit Accord, agreed in August 1966, depended on continuing organizational pressure, which King's campaign had failed to develop sufficiently as a self-sustaining force.

This biography argues that King's predicament in 1966 can be no more ascribed exclusively to his deficiencies than his earlier supposed successes can be attributed solely to his talents. King's failure to secure a significant improvement in the lives of Chicago ghetto dwellers crucially owed more to the opposition or lack of will of others, including many whites in churches and unions, than to his own failings. Accepting that King was more of a mobilizer than an organizer, one begins to see that some of the Movement setbacks of his later years sprang primarily from the failures of others. Some of the best recent scholarship provides a richer understanding of the Black Power thread that runs within the Freedom Struggle and argues that the post-1965 period saw vital successes rather than setbacks (Joseph 2006, 2010). This revisionist position requires the rejection of King's own judgment that, despite its emotional appeal and essential logic, Black Power was a slogan that was more effective in inducing solidarity among whites than among blacks. It also seeks to minimize the conservative counter-movement that used Black Power to mobilize against radical social change.

Black Power and King's relationship to it is central to understanding the growing racial crisis of the 1960s. Chapter 9 considers this topic and the concurrent challenge faced by King: how far should he publicly oppose US involvement in Vietnam? The two developments significantly reduced his room for maneuver as a strategist of the center by 1967. Black Power's resonance with African Americans whether in Mississippi, Alabama, California, Illinois, or New Jersey, made it a potent mobilizing strategy, but it seemed at times to generate a level of the black militancy that was hard to organize and sustain, especially in light of the white repression it fueled. Many Black Power leaders were forced into exile, imprisoned, or even killed before they could mature as organizers. In terms of mobilizing leadership, King's credentials had been best demonstrated by his ability to end rather than just lead demonstrations. In Birmingham, St. Augustine, and Selma, he had proved able to terminate campaigns that had served their purpose in key respects. Black Power advocates interpreted the ghetto disturbances after 1965 as uprisings expressive of their ideology of self-determination. To the chagrin of white conservatives, the Kerner Commission was unable to prove that the disturbances were sparked by black militants, but the latter's inability or reluctance to control the uprisings ultimately undercut demands for concessions to prevent renewed disorder.

A close examination of King's decision to speak out against the Vietnam War exposes both his initial reluctance (of which he remained disproportionately ashamed) and his limited options. By the time of his Riverside speech, remaining silent or even discreet about the war was earning African American leaders little of substance. The cutbacks to the War on Poverty were already severe, and the escalating costs and casualties offered no prospect of a reversal, until the Vietnam War was halted. The remaining argument for silence was one of fear and narrow self-interest, and King decided that if he was to continue in public life, he should do so for what he genuinely believed. As with the Chicago campaign, one can question not King's decision to speak out, but the political judgment of those, like Bayard Rustin, who counseled him not to. Nevertheless, while King took a vocal stand, he did not lead a nonviolent campaign against the war, as colleagues like James Bevel pleaded with him to do.

Already you may detect that my interpretation of King is paradoxical. I argue that Baker's charge that he was made by the Movement is most valid for the period up to the Voting Rights Act of 1965, the period of legislative achievements for which he is commonly accorded the greatest praise. Conversely, I contend that the Martin Luther King who emerges from the later struggles is the heroic figure, a radical leader striving to address injustice at the cost of unpopularity and isolation. In the process of highlighting this aspect of King's life, what follows is informed by a well-established scholarship on the conservative resurgence that reads the racial confrontations of the 1960s not simply in terms of immediate liberal, legislative victories, but also incipient, neo-conservative, political ones (Carter 1995). By 1968, the margin of victory for Republican Richard Nixon over veteran liberal Democrat Hubert Humphrey in the presidential race was narrow largely because Wallace siphoned away some of Nixon's conservative support. Four years later, the shooting of Wallace during the primary contests helped to ensure a Nixon landslide. The political tide had never been entirely on King's side, and at the time of his death it was clearly running against both him and his dreams.

King's career was not just made by the Movement, but shaped by the counter-movement. In many respects, this is a familiar argument that sees Southern outrages from Montgomery in 1956 to Selma in 1965 as generating national support for the civil rights cause. What is added here is a reminder of how potent Southern political influence remained and how shallow white sympathy proved. The Kennedy-assisted release of King from jail in 1960 actually entailed the cultivation of white Southern Democrats by the future president in a way that heralded his preferred, neutral stance on civil rights. By the summer of the Freedom Rides of 1961, King and Attorney-General Robert Kennedy regarded each other with more distrust, not less. Over the next twelve months, involvement in Albany, Georgia, demonstrated to King and other Movement activists that the Justice Department wanted order more than justice.

By 1963 when King published his "Letter from Birmingham Jail," much of his harshest criticism was leveled at white liberals and moderates, people who claimed to be sympathetic to African American calls for equality and yet found excuses as to why the dream should be deferred. The white contribution to the successful Selma campaign of 1965, however, seemed to lessen King's skepticism, albeit temporarily. Despite warnings from his white advisor Stanley Levison, he expected his Chicago campaign to enjoy support from white church congregations. But white, ethnic, working-class fears of black competition for jobs, housing, and schooling turned the union and parish halls of Chicago into recruiting grounds for George Wallace-style conservatism. The Alabama demagogue spoke about the federal government's threat to the little guy who had worked hard to buy his home and raise his kids. According to Wallace, "Big Government" was trying to increase his taxes to provide handouts to lazy blacks and to reduce the value of his home by allowing blacks to move next door. It threatened his children's education by busing in blacks from crime-infested schools, and would destroy not just his, but his son's, prospects by racially affirmative action in the workplace. With greater skill and geniality, Ronald Reagan would use these arguments to win the White House in 1980.

King fully appreciated the strength of white racism, and he was shrewd enough to realize that since 1966 the Black Power calls and summer ghetto disorders had boosted rather than drained it. Racism, materialism, and militarism were threatening to engulf the United States, and so he resolved to "go for broke." The Poor People's Campaign of 1968 was intended to show that nonviolent direct action was more effective politically than the previous summer's violent confrontations in Detroit and Newark. It was intended to force the needs of the American poor, the numerical majority of whom were white, onto the political agenda ahead of containing communism in Vietnam or landing a man on the moon before the Soviets did. King, of course, did not live to see the Poor People's Campaign, nor did he have to cope with its dispiriting defeat. Nevertheless, his plans confirm that he had developed a critique of American society that was revolutionary in its intentions, even though he remained ambivalent about the exact scale and intensity of the mass non-cooperation and civil disobedience campaigns that were the nonviolent concomitants of his vision. In early discussions of the Poor People's Campaign, the goal seemed to be nothing less than the complete disruption of government operations. Later, King seemed to retreat to more modest, symbolic actions, although in the eyes of the authorities, his plans remained deeply suspect and disturbing.

Given the 1999 court ruling that King was killed as a result of a conspiracy rather than solely at the hands of the now deceased James Earl Ray – the man convicted of his assassination – no new biography can properly ignore the fact that speculation persists about government involvement in King's murder. In the pages that follow, the hostility of J. Edgar Hoover's FBI to Martin Luther King is detailed, and the chapter on Memphis (Chapter 10) not only recounts the murder itself and Ray's capture, but briefly reviews the claims Ray made concerning the involvement of his mysterious accomplice Raoul, the accusations leveled against the Memphis Police Department, the suggestions of "Mob" or CIA involvement, as well as the more mundane but compelling fact of a bounty scheme for King's death funded by white supremacists.

The new edition gives greater treatment to King's commemoration and his paradoxical position in Obama's America. If the evidence for a conspiracy to kill King is still untrustworthy, the signs that his memory is being distorted are more abundant. Individuals like Jerry Falwell, founder of the conservative Moral Majority, once saw King as a dangerous subversive but now declare that they are following in his footsteps. The portion of his "I Have a Dream" speech in which he laments that America has given African Americans a "bad check" is hardly remembered, while the line that America will one day judge people "not by the color of their skin but by the content of the character" is wrenched out of context to support the idea that King opposed affirmative action and placed his faith in the free market. The King celebrated on King Day has become a gentle preacher who wants all Americans to think what they as individuals can do for others, and not the radical prophet who felt that the very architecture of American society had to be transformed so that it no longer sustained injustice and fetishized wealth but cherished the sanctity of every person by guaranteeing their human rights to food, shelter, health care, work and security. The elevation of King as an icon is most insidious when it forms part of the Civil Rights Movement as an episode in which good simply triumphed over an aberrant evil – symbolized by Bull Connor and his attacks on children or the murders in Mississippi and Alabama. What the Movement achieved was a partial and transient willingness on the part of ordinary people who did not see themselves as complicit in evil, to act so as to reduce its scale. The cause of justice is not yet won and King's radical and unfulfilled demands are a part of the story that needs to be remembered.

Barack Obama's presence in the Oval Office is evidence of the change that the Civil Rights Movement made, and King would have relished it. But King's call for justice would have continued no matter who was in power. Black Power radicals sometimes spoke of the ballot or the bullet. King mistrusted both, and saw nonviolent direct action (sustained protest) as the vital complement to the first and alternative to the second. Obama has spoken eloquently about King's example, even in his Nobel Peace Prize address, when he felt compelled to repudiate King's own pacifism. While Obama can endorse King's faith that the moral arc of the universe bends towards justice and urge Americans as individuals to accentuate the bend, he remains sufficiently the moderate and pragmatic politician to follow the polls as well as the Gospel. Ultimately, this biography seeks to remind readers that King and the Movement were co-dependent, and that their story still calls us to action rather than acceptance.

2 Junior

Becoming Martin Luther King, 1929-55

"Cast out the sinner!" That was the call in August 1848 when William Williams asked fellow members of the Shiloh Baptist Church in Greene County, Georgia (seventy miles north of Atlanta) to expel Willis, one of his slaves, for stealing. Slave owners commonly complained that their slaves stole, though some expected Christianity to deter theft. The slaves regarded taking from one's master differently than they did stealing from fellow slaves. It was not pilfering but an act of resistance. Masters regarded slaves as chattels, after all, and so the food they took was, in a sense, not even stolen – just stored differently. Preaching the Gospel to one's slaves may have reduced the incidence of theft but it also provided a powerful ideological framework for claiming equality and asserting human dignity. Despite efforts to limit their knowledge to scriptural passages that recommended submission, slaves readily embraced the idea that everyone was equal in the sight of God. They relished the prospect that their masters would face divine judgment, just like themselves. In October 1848, Willis presented himself to the Shiloh church elders. He confessed his offense, but added that the Lord had forgiven him. Preempted by the Lord Himself, the elders had little option but to receive Willis back into their communion. By skillfully obliging the church committeemen to be better Christians, Willis – a preacher among his fellow slaves – was a fitting ancestor for his great grandson, Martin Luther King, Jr. He sounded a drum for justice to which his famed descendant would march.

A Family Of Preachers And Race Leaders

Like many a son, Martin Luther King, Jr. tried to escape his father's shadow, yet followed his example. Born Michael King in Atlanta on January 15, 1929, the "Junior" in Martin Luther King, Jr. underlines the centrality of his relationship to his father, a powerful figure in his own right. A barely literate, Georgia country boy, Michael King, Sr. established himself as a minister and race leader in Atlanta through education, marriage, and shrewd management of the Ebenezer Baptist Church. With little childhood schooling, his adult education included classes at Morehouse College, which his sons would also attend. Rooted in genuine affection, King Sr.'s marriage in 1926 to Alberta, daughter of the Reverend Adam Daniel Williams, the slave preacher Willis's son, was socially advantageous. Williams was by then one of Atlanta's preeminent black clergymen, renowned for his ministry at Ebenezer on "Sweet Auburn" Avenue, the heart of the black business district and for his leadership of the local chapter of the National Association for the Advancement of Colored People (NAACP).

At the time of MLK's birth, Daddy King was preparing himself to succeed the elderly Williams at Ebenezer by ministering to two other Atlanta churches and studying for a bachelor's degree in Theology at Morehouse. After Williams's death in 1931, he met the challenge of sustaining Ebenezer financially and extending its community programs during the Great Depression. Such was his success that the church's initially skeptical deacons were willing to make their young Reverend King "the best-paid Negro minister in the city." King toured both Europe and the Holy Land in 1934, attending a world conference of Baptist ministers in Berlin. Around the same time he changed his own and his eldest son's name to Martin Luther King, possibly to fulfil the deathbed-wish of his own father. But within the family, King, Jr. was still generally called "Mike" or "ML" (Carson *et al.* 1992: 25-26, 30-31; Burrow 2014: 22; King Farris 2009: 21).

The new name seemed to signal the hope that "Junior" would one day have "Reverend" before his name, but young Martin harbored doubts. Despite his family's religious fervor, the youngster took pride in his own detachment. Aged 5, Martin joined the Baptist church during a spring revival at Ebenezer, but did so, he recalled, out of a childhood desire to keep up with his elder sister, Christine (King Farris 2009: 212). At the age of 13, he caused consternation among his fundamentalist-style Sunday school teachers by denying the bodily resurrection of Jesus. While King had reservations about evangelical Christianity's Biblical literalism, he was also attracted by its emotional power. He could feel how the church operated at the heart of community life and how, in the South's rapidly growing black urban communities, successful ministers were men of influence. They were not just expected to be able to tap into their congregation's emotions through word and song.

Ministers, King sensed, were the leaders to whom the people turned when crises erupted or personal problems threatened. By the 1930s, preaching, no matter how rapturous, was not enough to sustain the ministry of a large established church like Ebenezer. The Great Depression breadlines for the unemployed made a deep impression on the young Martin. He became committed to his father's Social Gospel that addressed their parishioners' everyday problems. Ultimately, King would also come to see how the liturgy, too, through communal singing and an emotive, interactive style of preaching, prepared ordinary people to do extraordinary things. As their charismatic leader, the minister could inspire his followers to overcome their fears, confront wrongdoers, and demand justice.

Both Daddy King and his father-in-law, A.D. Williams had entered a largely unprofessionalized ministry; the ability to preach was itself proof of a divine calling. Williams's powerful preaching helped Ebenezer's congregation to grow from just 14 to 400 members in its first decade. At the same time he completed a degree at Atlanta Baptist College (later renamed Morehouse College), and took a prominent role in racial politics. In 1906, shortly before Atlanta was shaken by a race riot, Williams joined the Georgia Equal Rights League to protest against lynching, the establishment of segregated public transportation, discriminatory treatment before the courts, and the exclusion of black men from juries, state militia, and electoral rolls.

Ratified in 1868 and 1870 respectively, the Fourteenth and Fifteenth Amendments to the US Constitution were supposed to guarantee equal treatment under the law and prohibit denial of the vote on grounds of race respectively. Under a federal system, the Constitution primarily defined the powers and jurisdictions of the national and state governments and so the Fourteenth Amendment prohibited discrimination by state governments rather than individuals and the Fifteenth Amendment directly defined the franchise for state and federal elections. Despite the Civil War's nationalizing tendency, legal orthodoxy still regarded federal power as intrusive rather than protective of individual rights and left many areas of life primarily under state law. By the turn of the century white Southerners had obtained constitutional sanction for segregation laws via the US Supreme Court's *Plessy* decision (1896), and had devised technically nonracial voting restrictions to eliminate African American electoral influence.

Nevertheless, such practices remained open to legal challenge, if black plaintiffs and lawyers were brave enough to persevere through a time-consuming appeals process. Southern state supreme courts were almost certain to confirm lower court decisions against blacks, but federal appellate courts would not accept jurisdiction until state remedies had been exhausted and the plaintiffs had shown a clear conflict between federal and state law. Organizations like the Georgia Equal Rights League helped to fund such protracted litigation. One of Williams's League colleagues was W.E.B. DuBois, who helped to found the NAACP three years later to coordinate the legal fight for racial justice nationally, while encouraging blacks to continue their local struggles. As president of Atlanta's NAACP chapter in 1918, Reverend Williams organized a voter registration drive to help blacks meet new registration requirements, and campaigned for equal, though legally segregated, educational facilities. Thus, Williams epitomized the preacher as race leader: an NAACP man, striving to uplift his people, amidst the active hostility of the surrounding white society.

White racism always threatened to blight black lives, despite their efforts to resist and escape it. Encouraged by his mother, Michael King had turned to the church "to ease the harsh tone of farm life," especially the unceasing toil, racial exploitation, and poverty that pushed his father, James King (ML's paternal grandfather), into alcoholism and violence (Carson *et al.* 1992: 14-17, 21). At the age of 15, after a confrontation with his drunken father, Michael left for Atlanta to seek his fortune. Like Williams before him, he initially did manual work to support his occasional preaching and evening classes. For both men, preaching was as much a matter of performance as of theological exposition. Daddy King felt that Reverend Williams had usefully corrected his over-emotional preaching style. Despite this moderating influence, Martin was still struck by the emotional abandon into which his father swept both his congregation and himself when the preacher "whooped" at Sunday services (Oates 1994: 4).

Martin Luther King would inherit and expand upon his family's oratorical gifts. As a toddler, he loved to listen to his grandmother – "Momma Williams" – tell vivid Bible stories. An amazing memory enabled him to recite Biblical passages verbatim and sing entire hymns by the age of 5. This remarkable aural memory meant that ideas became fixed in the cadence of particular phrases so that in his later career as a scholar and a preacher, he would commonly quote extensively words he had read or heard. While this inclined King the scholar towards plagiarism, it nudged King the orator toward poetry. It also contributed to his later leadership skills. After hours of listening to associates argue about policy, King had a gift for summarizing the debate and drawing it to a close. Relaxing among friends, he was a wonderful mimic, reducing colleagues to laughter by capturing the exact tone and mannerisms of others. King had a performer's voice as well as a performer's ear. His mother, Alberta, organist and choir director at Ebenezer, nurtured his musicality. With his mother as accompanist, young Martin belted out Gospel songs from the age of 6 and had church concert audiences rocking with joy. He performed his favorite, "I Want to Be More and More Like Jesus," with such "a blues fervor" that people wept (Carson *et al*. 1992: 30). Despite the rapturous reception, King, Jr. remained modest, even embarrassed, by the fuss around him.

A Member Of Atlanta's Black Elite

Eager for his son to have the education that he had been denied, Daddy King tried to sneak Martin into first grade a year early, a subterfuge that ended when a teacher overheard the child talking about his upcoming, fifth birthday. According to his sister Christine, Martin was not particularly studious at elementary school, although he enjoyed spelling bees. As members of Atlanta's black bourgeoisie, the Kings sent Christine and Martin to Atlanta University's experimental private school. By the mid-1930s, Daddy King was head of both the NAACP chapter and the Atlanta Civic and Political League. He organized mass voter registration drives and litigation to secure the equalization of teachers' salaries. His prominence attracted racist threats. A community role model, Daddy King also forbade his children from attending segregated theaters, and as far as possible refused to patronize segregated businesses.

Martin's schooling and secure family background nurtured self-confidence. While Daddy King was probably uneasy about his son's skepticism in scriptural matters, he took pride in the fact that the precocious Martin was able to skip ninth grade at Booker T. Washington High. Martin also showed early promise in public speaking. Having won the local heat of a national competition in April 1944, he traveled with a teacher to the small Georgia town of Dublin for the next round. Sponsored by a black fraternal organization, the Elks, the contest's theme, "The Negro and the Constitution," revealed the restiveness of African Americans during World War II as they rallied to the so-called "Double Victory" campaign against racism at home and fascism abroad (Carson *et al*. 1992: 35). The speech provides a glimpse of King's teenage views on race relations.

Martin's First Speech And His Experience Of Segregation

Like many of King's later writings, his speech as a 15-year-old was probably polished by others and has echoes of earlier, more famous addresses. After providing a conventional, potted history of slavery, the Civil War, and the constitutional promises of freedom, legal equality, and full citizenship for African Americans, King used the case of black opera singer Marion Anderson to illustrate his claim that in 1944 even "the winners of our highest honors face the class color bar" (Carson *et al*. 1992: 110). The Daughters of the American Revolution had refused to allow Anderson to sing at Constitution Hall in 1939. After an outcry, she had given a public concert from the steps of the Lincoln Memorial to a huge audience. Noting that even Anderson, one of Philadelphia's most distinguished residents, would not be served on racial grounds in many of its restaurants, King used Biblical language to underline his people's suffering. "America," he declared, "you have stripped me of my garments, you have robbed me of my precious endowment" (Carson *et al.* 1992: 110).

After this allusion to Christ's Passion and to the fact that segregation by custom, if not by law, prevailed in the North, King switched to pragmatic arguments against racial inequality in a nation at war. The ignorance, disease, crime, and poverty that racism fostered in the African American tenth of the population threatened the nation as a whole. Racial injustice contradicted America's claim to be a champion of Christianity and democracy. King declared that the best defense for "the federal ark of liberty from treason and destruction by her enemies" was ensuring African Americans the right to vote (Carson *et al.* 1992: 111). This may have referred to the case of *Smith* v. *Allwright*, the ultimately successful, constitutional challenge to the all-white party primary, which was currently before the US Supreme Court. If allowed to vote in these Democratic selection contests for candidates, African Americans could potentially transform the solidly white, and often conservative, Southern Congressional bloc.

King's concluding paragraphs celebrated "the example of Lincoln" and "the spirit of Christ" that would confound the demagogues and promote closer understanding between "Saxon and Freedman" (Carson *et al.* 1992: 111). Here, one suspects, Martin was very much articulating the views of his father, a long-time supporter of the party of Lincoln, the Republicans. He also used old-fashioned terminology that was losing its resonance as the freedmen, the generation of African Americans freed from slavery in 1865, passed away. The Great Depression had caused a significant realignment in US politics with Democratic President Franklin Roosevelt's New Deal attracting a broad coalition that, in Northern metropolitan areas especially, included African American voters. Even in the South, small, progressive Democratic factions were appealing to the relatively small number of registered black voters. Accordingly, young Martin ended his oration by looking forward positively to the day when, with his "brother of blackest hue possessing at last my rightful heritage and holding my head erect," he might "stand beside the Saxon – a Negro – and yet a man!" (Carson *et al*. 1992: 111).

The judges ranked King second among the young black orators they heard that day. But if Martin had not yet perfected his rhetorical skills, the gulf between his hopes of equal treatment and contemporary realities was wider still. On the crowded bus home, the white bus driver insisted that King and his teacher obey segregation law and give up their seats for some newly boarded, white passengers. When Martin refused, the driver called him "a black son-of-a-bitch." Such clashes were increasingly common in the wartime South where African American assertiveness could easily trigger white violence, and so King's wary teacher quietly cajoled him into compliance. They stood uncomfortably for the entire remaining journey. Years later, after the Montgomery Bus Boycott had swept him to fame and placed bus segregation on the road to ultimate extinction, King recalled that night as "the angriest I have ever been in my life" (Oates 1994: 16).

Although King's comfortable middle-class home insulated him from the worst of Southern racism, he felt its impact, nonetheless. White friends, whose parents had allowed interracial play among toddlers, were forbidden to associate with Martin once they started at the segregated grade schools. Once outside his black neighborhood, King confronted the demeaning etiquette of segregation. Although progressive by the standards of Georgia or other Deep South states, Atlanta remained a city bristling with "WHITES ONLY" signs. Where provided, the designated "COLORED" restroom – or waiting room or elevator or section of a movie theater – was commonly shabby and unkempt. Some stores refused African Americans service altogether, others offered it only at the rear or side of their premises. And when a black person spoke to a white person of whatever rank, their language had to signal a strict deference via "Yes, Sir" and "No, Sir," "Excuse me, Ma'am" and "Forgive me, Ma'am," and a litany of profuse thanks. In contrast, whites referred to African Americans of all ages as "boy" or "girl." A policeman once stopped Daddy King for a traffic violation and curtly demanded: "Boy, show me your license." "Do you see this child here?" the well-known preacher angrily retorted, pointing to Martin beside him. "That's a boy there. I'm a man. I'm Reverend King." Afterwards, he told his son: "I don't care how long I have to live with this system, I am never going to accept it. I'll fight it until I die" (Oates 1994: 10-12).

Many black Southerners chose to leave the South rather than spend their lives fighting its indignities. In 1900 roughly nine-tenths of the African American population lived in the South. By 1940, it was just over three-quarters and by 1950, it had fallen to barely two-thirds, with the trend still set downwards. Wartime mobilization increased the diaspora of Southerners, both black and white. African Americans who resettled in the North increasingly resented the discrimination they faced. In 1941 they supported A. Philip Randolph's March on Washington Movement to pressure the federal government to improve job opportunities. Along with many black Southerners, they also joined the NAACP in record numbers, funding a growing legal challenge to Northern as well as Southern discrimination. The war generated widespread mobility with millions experiencing for the first time life outside of the rural segregated South, either in the United States, or, in the case of members of the armed forces, overseas. For many black Southerners, this experience made their home region's segregation system still more abhorrent and unnatural. Taking a summer job in Connecticut in 1944, young Martin was struck by the fact that once he left Virginia, he could sit wherever he chose on buses and trains. On the way home, his recent experiences made him resent the Southern insistence on segregated dining facilities all the more.

Part Of A New Generation Of African Americans

The war accelerated Martin's educational progress. With so many college-age men in the armed forces, Morehouse College agreed to admit exceptional high school students. King, Jr. passed the entrance exam at 15 and prepared to follow in family footsteps and become a Morehouse man. The college had a controversial new president, Benjamin E. Mays, whose 1938 study, *The Negro's God* criticized ministers who failed to embrace a Social Gospel approach. After visiting India, Mays related how Mohandas K. Gandhi had developed "a new conception of courage" among the Indian masses. Once masses overcame their fears, Mays asserted, liberation had begun. King called Mays "one of the great influences in my life." An emphasis on the Social Gospel and on the development of a personalist "third way" between capitalism and communism became characteristic of King's philosophy, features that his later theological training reinforced (Carson *et al.* 1992: 37-38).

King's time at Morehouse coincided with an important period of social adjustment after World War II. Victory over the Axis powers brought not just great hopes, but fears compounded by Franklin Roosevelt's sudden death in 1945. The hopes were a by-product of a deepened national pride forged by the war itself, and the fears correspondingly were that, without war production, unemployment might return to the awful Depression levels. Since black workers had made significant inroads into industrial employment during the war, their fears were particularly sharp. Anxiety was further heightened by memories of the racial violence that black veterans had faced in 1919. Nevertheless, the mood was militant. In communities across the South, voter registration drives typically drew their impetus from returning soldiers.

The promise of the period was captured in a monumental report on US race relations by sociologist Gunnar Myrdal. Published in 1944, *An American Dilemma* stressed the contradiction between the American Creed of democracy and equality and the denial of rights and justice to African Americans. According to Myrdal, all Americans, even those in the Deep South, subscribed to the Creed. Now, Nazism had completely discredited the white supremacist ideology, which had previously resolved what the Swedish Social Democrat termed the cognitive dissonance between principle and practice. He also believed that the growing role of the federal government – evident in both the war and the preceding economic crisis – offered further opportunities for racial reform. Coming from a European tradition of centralized planning, Myrdal was over-sanguine that racial injustice could be eliminated by state social engineering. He did, however, foresee correctly that the enhanced international position of the United States would make its race question a vital postwar issue.

Despite the hopes of the many liberals who welcomed Myrdal's study, race relations in the immediate postwar period were volatile, continuing the tensions that had produced battles between black and white in the US armed forces, in Harlem, and in military production centers such as Detroit and Los Angeles. In the summer of 1946, the murder of black veteran Macio Snipes, the only registered black voter in Taylor County, and of two further Georgia black couples by another mob, prompted the 17-year-old King to write to the editor of the *Atlanta Constitution* (Carson *et al.* 1992: 121). Complaining that calls for decent treatment were perennially met by the ridiculous allegation that what blacks really desired was racial intermarriage, King declared:

> We want and are entitled to the basic rights and opportunities of American citizens: The right to earn a living at work for which we are fitted by training and ability; equal opportunities in education, health, recreation, and similar public services; the right to vote; equality before the law; some of the same courtesy and good manners that we ourselves bring to all human relations.

This was the first sign, according to Daddy King, that his eldest son would continue the family's activist tradition, but King was not yet a drum major for justice.

In most respects, the teenage Martin gave few indications that he was destined for the academy or the ministry, let alone world renown as a civil rights leader. His Morehouse transcript, indicating his major as sociology, and Benjamin Mays's reference for Crozer Theological Seminary both suggested a low "B" average student. Like his younger brother "A.D." (Alfred Daniel), Martin initially resisted his father's plans for them both to become ministers. Martin hoped to become a lawyer or perhaps a physician and expended more energy on college social life than on either his class-work or political activism. A.D. King could not recall a time when his older brother was not interested in girls. Women and food were his main weaknesses, Martin himself conceded. There was plenty of good Southern cooking at home and King's mellifluous baritone, his preppy clothes (which earned him the nickname "Tweed"), and his energy on the dance floor attracted the daughters of black Atlanta's social elite. Given that most black Baptist churches regarded public dancing as sinful, King's enthusiastic jitterbugging angered his father. On one occasion at the local YWCA, an enraged Daddy King dragged an embarrassed Martin from the dance floor. The elder King was known to "whup" his sons and in Martin's case the "whupping" lasted into his Morehouse years.

Learning A Social Gospel And A Personalist Faith

Young Martin's doubts about what he regarded as his father's outmoded religious outlook included matters of doctrine as well as prescribed social practices. In his final year at Morehouse, theologian George D. Kelsey's classes (in which King gained his only "A" grade) demonstrated that a more critical approach could ultimately lead to a stronger faith. Kelsey and Benjamin Mays provided Martin with models for a modern ministry that encouraged him to reconsider a religious vocation. In early summer 1947, he gave a well-received guest sermon at Ebenezer and its board of deacons licensed him to preach. Despite this step, Martin was keen to continue his education and applied to several Northern, theologically liberal seminaries. With his father's support, he chose Crozer, a small Baptist college southwest of Philadelphia. In his application, Martin attributed his call to the ministry to "an inescapable urge to serve society" that he dated from his summer in Connecticut in 1944 (Carson *et al.* 1992: 144).

Studying at Crozer proved to be an important phase in King's development, not least because it enabled him to escape black Atlanta, where he was essentially Daddy King's son and heir. It was also his first period of prolonged interracial contact as one of eleven black students out of a student population of less than a hundred. Although initially Martin's keenness to overturn negative racial stereotypes made him obsessively punctual, over-formal, and as he put it, "grimly serious," he relaxed gradually and eventually made several white friends (Oates 1994: 24). Regular contact with a family friend, J. Pius Barbour – Crozer's first black graduate – eased the transition. In an early letter home, Martin reported to his mother that since Reverend Barbour had told his congregation that the Kings were rich, "the girls are running me down." He then stressed how studious he had become. His final-year grades (with nothing lower than a single "A–") confirm his claim. In the spring of 1951, Crozer's Dean Charles Batten wrote that the 22-year-old King was "one of the most brilliant students we have had." The college awarded him its annual prize for scholarship and his contemporaries elected him their class president (Carson *et al.* 1992: 161, 406, 56).

King's studies reflected his interest in the liberal critique of fundamentalist theology. But his Crozer tutors also encouraged him to question the liberal theological position as well. Attracted to the Social Gospel, he discovered in the courses he took with George W. Davis in particular, a more sophisticated theological foundation for his sense of mission. King had already rejected fundamentalist claims of certainty in favor of a Christianity in which "the search for God is a process not an achievement," but he now also began to critique rationalists who discounted the nonintellectual sources of theological knowledge (Carson *et al.* 1992: 47-51). Historical studies might disprove the literal truth of Scripture but the metaphorical power of myth might yet be indicative of God's immanence. Religion, like music, needed to be understood holistically with room left for those intuitions found only in performance.

At Crozer, King was introduced to Edgar S. Brightman's work on personalism. As its name suggests, personalism took as its premise the inherent sanctity of each individual, a positive start-ing-point that contrasted with the 1940s' resurgent, neo-orthodox Protestantism. The violence and injustice of the twentieth century had led some prominent Protestant theologians to return to the concept of Man's inherent sinfulness to explain contemporary evils. In 1932 Reinhold Niebuhr argued in *Moral Man and Immoral Society* that while individuals might be capable of moral improve-ment, social groupings – such as classes and nations – were pow-erfully predisposed to act unjustly. In the aftermath of World War II, with a looming Cold War making fears of totalitarian control and mass destruction key leitmotifs of contemporary American cul-ture, Niebuhr's pessimism was intellectually dominant. Personalism provided a positive counterpoint.

Unlike Niebuhr, personalists insisted that human beings could and must overcome the social constraints of their situation to make ethical choices because their essence and origin was God, not sin. Ethically, personalists endorsed opposition to weapons of mass destruction that comprehensively ignored the sanctity of indivi-dual human life. They also insisted on individual will in a manner that paralleled the claims of secular existential philosophers. Ulti-mately, King would temper his personalism with Niebuhr's rea-listic appraisal of the structural constraints inhibiting group redemption. Even people of apparent goodwill might have to be coerced into changing deeply rooted, unjust practices.

King also continued to test the theological traditions he encountered against his African American background. In one essay, he reported that his growing respect for the harsh view of humanity in neo-orthodoxy "may root back to certain experiences that I had in the south with a vicious race problem." He added, however, that his attachment to liberal theology had been affirmed by "the gradual improvements of this same race problem" (Carson *et al.* 1992: 274). Here, King may have been referring to gains in Atlanta such as the equalization of teachers' salaries, better provision of public services, and more extensive black voting that his father had fought for, or to national measures such as President Truman's executive order desegregating US armed forces in 1948, and the succession of NAACP Supreme Court victories requiring desegregation in higher education. In another essay, King stressed how his secure and loving family background enabled him to believe in "a god of love" and a "basically friendly" universe. He attributed his strong belief in personal immortality to coping with the loss of his beloved grandmother "Momma Williams," who died when he was a child, and explained his fascination with the Christian admonition to love others as a reaction against the realities of white racism (Carson *et al.* 1992: 359-63).

King was well aware that his "basically friendly universe" contained many white racists. In the summer of 1950, he and three friends were refused service at a New Jersey tavern near Camden. The irate owner saw them off with pistol shots into the air. Even at the seminary, a gun-waving Southern white student once confronted King, accusing him of messing up his room. Although alarmed, Martin had calmly denied involvement and refused to press the college for action against the student, who subsequently apologized. King's election as class president partly reflected his peers' appreciation of his coolness during this episode. A more soul-searching experience was King's decision to end a six-month relationship with the white daughter of one of the college's ancillary staff, with whom he had fallen in love. Reverend Barbour and other close friends had warned Martin that a white wife, whatever her personal qualities, would ruin his ecclesiastical career and bring innumerable difficulties. King accepted their arguments and ended the affair.

Perhaps this triumph of group pressure over individual impulse reinforced King's respect for Reinhold Niebuhr's neo-orthodoxy.

Equally sobering was the outcome of his fieldwork placement at First Baptist Church in Queens, New York City. Pastor William Gardner, although a friend of the King family, pulled no punches. He warned that, despite superior mental ability, King exhibited "aloofness, disdain & possible snobbishness" in relations with "the rank and file of ordinary people." Worse, there were signs of "a smugness that refuses to adapt itself to the demands of ministering effectively to the average Negro congregation" (Carson *et al.* 1992: 381). Gardner probably knew that Daddy King was beginning to hint that seven years of higher education was ample for someone who must surely return eventually to Ebenezer. Gardner may even have heard that Martin was beginning to consider an academic career rather than a church pastorate. If Gardner's words alarmed Daddy King, they did not dampen his pride. With Crozer's graduation day prize of $1,200 to offset the cost of future studies and the still ringing plaudits of distinguished professors, Daddy King sent his heir proudly away to pursue doctoral study at Boston University in a brand new Chevrolet.

In 1951, King chose Boston in order to study with personalist theologian Edgar Brightman. In the event, he ended up taking most of his courses with Brightman's protégé, L. Harold DeWolf, who was less demanding than the elderly Brightman, particularly in terms of the technical demands of scholarship. In marking King's first essay, Brightman had urged King to consult the Manual for Students of Philosophy regarding citation practices and bibliographies, whereas DeWolf seemed oblivious to King's tendency to appropriate the insights of others without proper attribution. When Brightman died at the end of 1953, DeWolf became King's doctoral advisor in systematic theology.

Ironically by this stage, Martin's enthusiasm for a strictly academic career was waning as his skills as a pulpit orator matured. Daddy King's many contacts ensured that his son's preaching experience was not confined to summer Sundays at Ebenezer. In term time he would impress his fellow students with his ability to "mesmerize" the congregation at Roxbury's Twelfth Baptist Church and guest sermons along the eastern seaboard from Washington to Boston further boosted his reputation (Carson *et al.* 1994: 11, 15). Student friends also visited King's shared apartment to discuss philosophical questions, as members of the Dialectical

Society, a name that reflected King's interest in Hegelian thought. Although Martin struggled in a university seminar course on Hegel, he retained a fascination for dialectical reasoning. Whatever the subject, DeWolf recalled, "King never tired of moving from a one-sided thesis to a corrective, but also one-sided, antithesis and finally to a more coherent synthesis beyond both" (Garrow 1988: 46).

Courting Coretta And Returning South

Increasingly intellectually sophisticated, King remained both sociable and popular. One of the few graduate students with a car, he was remembered as "the one that got people together," and as someone who "loved to enjoy life." When Martin rang Coretta Scott for a first date in 1952, she recalled, he had "quite a line" in conversation. When they met, his "intellectual jive," as she terms it, more than compensated for his small stature (5 feet 7 inches). Indeed, he seemed to grow in size and presence as he spoke (Garrow 1988: 45-46). Although King enjoyed life as a bachelor, he was under increasing pressure to find a bride. Ministers were expected to be married. Aware of his parents' concern in this regard, King's friends would tease him, but it was no laughing matter for Martin, who feared that if he did not find his own soul mate, his parents would arrange a marriage. As his relationship with Coretta deepened, he confided that his father already had someone in mind, but added that he was determined to choose his own wife.

King had startled Coretta by announcing at the end of their first date that she had all the characteristics that he was looking for in a wife: character, intelligence, personality, and beauty. When she protested that he hardly knew her, Martin had neatly responded by asking for a second date. The more they dated, the more convinced he became that Miss Scott was the one. But Coretta was hesitant. Raised on a farm in rural Alabama, not far from Selma, she regarded successful black Atlantans as potential snobs. Her own religious background was Methodist and she harbored a certain denominational prejudice against stereotypically egocentric, black Baptist preachers. Her operatic singing ambitions had quickly pulled her away from the South. A graduate of Antioch College in

Ohio, she met Martin whilst studying voice and education at the New England Conservatory of Music. Listening to his plans for a committed pastorate in a Southern city, she realized that her own dreams of becoming an operatic diva would have to change (Scott King 1969: 66, 77-80).

Coretta did not instantly gel with the King clan. Her first stay with the family in August 1952 "was not an unqualified success," and tension remained evident when Martin's parents visited Boston in late November. "Let me ask you directly," Daddy King inquired, "do you take my son seriously, Coretta?" Assuming that the elder King was alluding to Martin's ready sense of humor, Coretta jested: "Why, no, Reverend King, not really." This ill-judged response prompted a tirade about the many fine Atlantan girls who were eager to marry Daddy King's son (Scott King 1969: 78, 81). Fortunately, Martin's mother knew the strength of Martin's feelings and reconciled her husband to the union. In April 1953, the local black newspaper, the *Atlanta Daily World*, carried the announcement of Martin and Coretta's engagement.

At the age of 24, the time had come for Martin Luther King, Jr. to complete the period of college study that had begun when he was just 15. He took a heavy course load for the 1952-53 year, supplementing his work at BU with two further philosophy courses at Harvard. By May he had completed the taught course elements of the doctoral program and planned to become a full-time academic or minister in 1954. His credentials, contacts, and genuine ability would ensure offers from both colleges and churches. Martin and Coretta were married by Daddy King on June 18, 1953 at the Scott family home in rural Alabama. Since no local hotel accepted African Americans, the couple spent their wedding night in the most lavish accommodation available – the home of a black undertaker. King would later joke about his honeymoon in a funeral parlor.

After summer in Atlanta, the newlyweds returned to Boston so that Martin could take his course exams, and Coretta could complete her own degree in music education via a punishing schedule of 13 courses, teaching practice in local schools, and proven mastery of four different instruments. She graduated in June 1954, but in the interval, the Kings' marriage was a remarkably progressive one for its time with Martin at home, cheerfully cleaning dishes and tending house, while his wife went off to her classes. It was an interlude never to be repeated. Martin's career would subsequently define the lives of his wife and family.

At first glance King had not strayed far from his father's footsteps. He had become a Baptist preacher, and the Sunday after their wedding, his Methodist-raised bride, Coretta, was baptized in Ebenezer's pool. Daddy King's achievements greatly facilitated Martin's ascent within the black Baptist fold. Atlanta's first black radio station, WERD, decided to broadcast the young pastor's summer sermons from Ebenezer, giving him far greater renown than that of other new ministers. Unlike most of the 15,000 delegates at the National Baptist Convention's (NBC) annual meeting in September 1953, Martin already knew most of the major players in the largest African American denomination in the country. Activist ministers like the Reverend Theodore J. Jemison, leader of the recent Baton Rouge bus boycott, took the opportunity of this Miami meeting to install the young, vigorous J.H. Jackson as NBC president. Daddy King's brother and fellow preacher, Joel, celebrated Jackson's victory by wildly sweeping the air with a broom "to demonstrate that the progressives had made a clean sweep" (Carson *et al.* 1994: 20-21). The new president then nominated Daddy King to the NBC Board of Directors and retained Martin's old mentor Reverend Barbour as editor of the *National Baptist Voice*. King, Jr. would later feud with Jackson, but at the time, his election seemed a positive sign.

Martin decided the time seemed ripe to return to the South. Passing his qualifying examinations in the fall of 1953, he started job hunting; confident that he could complete his dissertation while working full time. Daddy King persuaded Benjamin Mays to offer a Morehouse position. But Martin did not want to immediately co-pastor at Ebenezer, which would be likely with any Atlanta appointment, and his growing reputation and connections ensured other offers. Dexter Avenue Baptist Church in Montgomery, Alabama, had recently fired its well-known and outspoken preacher Vernon Johns. Dexter was known as a "big-shots' church" whose chair of deacons had acquired a discouraging nickname, the "preacher killer." However, its middle-class professional congregation suited King's scholarly background and it could afford to give the newly married pastor a comfortable parsonage and the highest black ministerial salary in the city (Carson *et al.* 1994: 29-30; Garrow 1988: 48).

Still weighing these considerations, King agreed to deliver a trial sermon at Dexter on January 24, 1954. He impressed them with a well-honed homily entitled "The Three Dimensions of a Complete Life," which he retitled "3-D in Religion" (an allusion to the then current craze for 3-D movies). The sermon didn't just suit the congregation's liberal intellectualism, it also had none of Vernon Johns's confrontational style. Despite worries that King would not stay long, the Dexter deacons unanimously invited him to be their pastor in early March. After considering other offers and negotiating renovations to the parsonage and other terms, King accepted with effect from September 1, 1954. The US Supreme Court's *Brown* decision declaring segregated schools unconstitutional was announced on May 17, 1954, overturning *Plessy*'s "separate but equal" judgment that had stood since 1896. The NAACP's litigation strategy seemed vindicated. Ignoring his wife's misgivings, King came South with confidence, urging his new congregation to join the NAACP and register to vote.

3 Loving Your Enemies

Montgomery, 1955-59

Martin Luther King arrived in Montgomery in September 1954, largely unknown outside of the network of black Baptist pastors, and his immediate circle of family and friends. By the time he submitted his resignation to Dexter Avenue Baptist Church on November 29, 1959, the Montgomery Bus Boycott had catapulted him to national and international renown. Over the same period, changes that would ultimately transform the South seemed, in the short term, to increase the rigidity of its race relations. In 1954 the city of Montgomery still relished its reputation as the Cradle of the Confederacy. By December 1956, however, national civil rights leader Roy Wilkins of the NAACP extravagantly described the city as "the peace capital of a new liberation movement" because of "the spontaneous protest of the city's Negro population against the humiliation of Jim Crow [segregation]" (Burns 1997: 315). At the time Wilkins spoke, the NAACP was unable to operate in Alabama due to injunctions secured by state Attorney-General and future Governor John Patterson, and outgoing Governor Jim Folsom declared that his moderate-to-liberal stance on racial matters had become so unpopular that he could not get elected to the post of city dogcatcher (Bartley 1995: 208).

During the Bus Boycott, white segregationist sentiment in Montgomery became so virulent that the entire City Commission publicly joined the White Citizens Council, and there was a succession of racially motivated attacks. When King left Montgomery to return to Atlanta in 1960, the Alabama state capital was generally regarded as a segregationist stronghold rather than a "peace capital." Later violent racial clashes there during the 1961

Freedom Rides sustained this reputation. King did not leave Montgomery racially transformed. When he departed, the Montgomery Improvement Association (MIA), which had marshaled the city's black population for 382 days of sustained protest, was a shadow of its former self. Troy Jackson concludes that while the boycott was a "stepping stone for a growing national civil rights movement, its sustained impact on the daily lives" of black Montgomerians "was minimal" (Jackson 2008: 3).

As an episode in King's life, the Montgomery years thus suggest how fluctuating forces beyond his control elevated King. Such a view does not deny his gifts, but simply indicates their limits. Able to unite the city's black factions in confrontation with the white authorities, he was unable to establish a movement that could sustain itself or meet the challenge of broadening its program, once bus desegregation had been ordered. Able to appeal to a national white liberal constituency through a potent rhetoric of Christian nonviolence, King enjoyed no great success in converting Southern white segregationist opinion. The Montgomery years taught King a great deal and gave him a media profile and a networked organizational base for the future. Time, however, would prove that much more was needed before he could exert the kind of reforming influence on public policy that he did in 1964 and 1965.

The Context: Montgomery In The 1950s

Numerically, whites held the balance of power in Montgomery in the 1950s. During the 1940s, the city's white population grew by nearly 50 percent whereas the pace of African American increase was only half that rate. By 1955, the roughly 50,000 African Americans constituted 37 percent of the city's total population, down from 45 percent in 1920 (Burns 1997: 1-2). Economically, the white population was much the more prosperous, with a far larger middle class enjoying the consumer pleasures of the decade. Unskilled manual jobs and domestic service were the main black employment sectors. Symbolizing postwar prosperity, the high levels of white car ownership ensured that local bus services increasingly relied on black patronage. Nearly $50 million a year of federal defense spending at the Maxwell and Gunter Air Force

Bases boosted Montgomery's economy, allowing it to mock rivals such as Selma, another old cotton town further down the Alabama River. To the restroom slogan "Flush the toilet," high school wits would add, "Selma needs the water." But the same federal largesse that boosted Montgomery exposed it to pressures for racial reform that operated most strongly at the presidential and international level in the early Cold War years (Branch 1988: 13).

On July 26, 1948, with a tricky election in prospect, and under the threat of mass black protests from A. Philip Randolph, President Truman ended segregation in the US armed forces by executive order. By the time King arrived, the desegregated local military bases, where many Montgomerians of both races worked, constituted anomalies within a still deeply segregated community. The need to attract Northern black voters in key electoral states, as well as concern over the communist bloc's use of racial incidents as propaganda, had forced Truman's hand. The Missourian had already upset his former Southern Congressional colleagues by establishing a liberal-packed President's Committee on Civil Rights in 1946. Its recommendations had formed the substance of Truman's historic civil rights message to Congress in February 1948. The President shrewdly recognized that Southern lawmakers would ensure that no legislation ensued. But he hoped that his public stance, plus extensive Redbaiting, would suffice to nullify former Vice-President Henry Wallace's challenge to his reelection.

When liberals, such as the young Hubert Humphrey of Minnesota, secured the inclusion of a progressive civil rights plank in the Democrats' 1948 platform, they complicated Truman's balancing act. Grover C. Hall, veteran editor of the Montgomery *Advertiser*, described the National Convention's attitude to the South as "cold, forbidding and contemptuous." Alabama's Governor Frank Dixon complained that nationally the Democrats had become an "unholy alliance of left-wingers, pseudo-liberals and radicals of as many hues as Joseph's coat" (Bartley 1995: 76, 78). Delegates from states such as Mississippi and Alabama left the convention appalled. They nominated their own "Dixiecrat" presidential ticket of governors, Strom Thurmond of South Carolina and Fielding Wright of Mississippi. In Alabama, Democrats had Thurmond, not Truman, as their ballot-listed presidential candidate.

What scholars refer to as the "long civil rights movement" was accompanied by a similarly long conservative backlash (Dowd Hall 2005: 1233-63).

Although Truman won a surprise victory in November 1948, political commentators agreed that liberal efforts to reconstruct the South had stalled. While King pursued his studies in the North, the postwar decade proved a time of frustrated hopes for Montgomery residents and radical New Dealers, Virginia and Clifford Durr. They crusaded against the discriminatory poll tax, joined the anti-segregationist Southern Conference for Human Welfare (SCHW), backed Henry Wallace, and endorsed the CIO's Operation Dixie (a union-organizing drive). But their efforts were dwarfed by a racist paranoia in Alabama that was an inextricable part of the national "Red Scare." In March 1947, President Truman established the Federal Employee Loyalty Program to purge communists and "fellow travelers" from government service. Concurrently, the FBI smeared left-wing unions and liberal reform groups by making interracial association a defining criterion for subversive organizations. Virginia Durr recalled that by 1948: "We were surrounded by the FBI." Unable to identify any communists in the SCHW's ranks, the House Un-American Activities Committee nonetheless branded it as "perhaps the most deviously camouflaged Communist-front organization" in the country (Bartley 1995: 55).

Despite the Durrs' efforts, the racially liberal Wallace campaign in Alabama disappeared beneath a Dixiecrat landslide in 1948. Shortly after this debacle, the SCHW folded, and within a year, Operation Dixie, launched with great hopes in 1946, had also collapsed. Unable to make serious inroads among the South's white textile workers, the CIO was further damaged by internal disputes. At its 1949 convention, the CIO expelled several left-wing unions – Food and Tobacco; Mine, Mill and Smelters; and the Packinghouse Workers – all of them at the forefront of interracial politics. If African Americans hoped to secure their rights in the postwar United States, they would have to rely chiefly on a movement rooted in their own black institutions, most notably their churches, and they would struggle valiantly to force the nation to confront economic inequalities (Korstad and Lichtenstein 1988: 786-811).

Black self-reliance had been equally essential a century earlier. In 1867, 700 communicants of the First Baptist Church in Montgomery had marched solemnly from its doors to an empty site on Ripley Street and declared themselves the First Baptist Church (Colored), the first "free Negro" institution in the city. On January 17, 1954 when King arrived to give his trial sermon at Dexter, his future partner in protest, Ralph David Abernathy, was First Baptist's pastor. According to Taylor Branch, King drove over to Montgomery with Vernon Johns, Dexter's most recent, controversial incumbent, who was scheduled to be Abernathy's guest preacher. Easily cajoled into sampling Juanita Abernathy's fine Southern cooking, King learned of the long-standing rivalry between the two churches (Branch 1988: 1-11, 104-7).

It had begun in 1877 when the self-declared "higher elements" left First Baptist to pursue their spiritual and status aspirations at a new church on Dexter Avenue, barely a stone's throw from the state capitol building where Jefferson Davis had become the Confederacy's first and last president. First Baptist had flourished thanks to flamboyant preachers who attracted a mass membership. Briefly, around 1900, it had been the largest single black congregation in the United States. Dexter Avenue, in contrast, had become a deacons' church whose lay members managed it like a country club. Dexter reputedly discouraged any new members who might dilute its elite status.

Both churches were said to favor a remarkably restrained liturgy by the black Baptist faith's emotional standards. But Dexter was much the more decorous. Abernathy told King that Dexter's elegantly dressed, middle-class communicants liked sermons littered with allusions to Socrates and Plato, whereas at First Baptist, he was still allowed to mention Jesus. Having enraged Dexter's deacons by selling fresh produce (notably catfish and watermelon) at the church entrance, Vernon Johns had shocked its music director by asking for traditional Negro Spirituals. Rebuffed, he had called upon the organist during one Sunday service to lead the congregation in an impromptu rendition of "Go Down, Moses," only to be met with passive resistance. Dexter's snobs considered these slave songs beneath them. They boycotted Spirituals before they boycotted buses. Against such a background, King's ability to bridge the class divide among black Montgomerians during the year-long protest was extraordinary.

On taking up his post, King told Dexter's deacons "leadership never ascends from the pew to the pulpit, but invariably descends from the pulpit to the pew" (Carson *et al.* 1994: 287). Yet the story of the Bus Boycott disputes his claim since the initiative for the campaign sprang from the pews of Dexter and other black churches. Head of the Alabama section of A. Philip Randolph's black trade union, the Brotherhood of Sleeping Car Porters, and a veteran NAACP activist, E.D. Nixon had led several hundred African Americans to the county courthouse in an unsuccessful attempt to register to vote in June 1941 and ran unsuccessfully for office himself in 1954. In 1954, the colored section of the *Montgomery Advertiser* named Nixon its "Man of the Year" (Jackson 2008: 62). His rivals included black undertaker and Dexter church member Rufus Lewis, famed locally for coaching a championship-winning football team at Alabama State. When returning black war veterans added momentum to voter registration efforts, Lewis formed the Citizens Club to supplement (critics said to supplant) the efforts of Nixon's Voters League. Tensions between Lewis the African American entrepreneur and Nixon the labor leader symbolized divisions that hampered the movement throughout King's career; King himself would side with labor.

A few outspoken preachers such as Vernon Johns and African Methodist Episcopal (AME) minister Solomon Seay, had protested previously against incidents of rape and police brutality in the late 1940s; episodes that also prompted the formation of the largest, best-organized, and most assertive black civic group in Montgomery, the Women's Political Council. Founded in 1949 by Mary Fair Burks, chair of Alabama State's English Department, the WPC aimed to foster civic involvement and voter registration as well as to aid the immediate victims of rape. Another Alabama State teacher, Jo Ann Robinson, made mistreatment on the buses a WPC concern. Not long after her arrival in Montgomery, she had been set upon by a bus driver for unwittingly sitting in the whites-only section. Succeeding Burks as president, Robinson concentrated on lobbying for better treatment on the buses and from police officers, and for improvements to black public facilities, such as parks and playgrounds. When King arrived at Dexter, he instituted a new committee structure. Remarking that "the gospel of Jesus is a social gospel as well as a personal gospel seeking to serve the whole man," he established a Social and Political Action Committee. Mrs. Burks was chair and Mrs. Robinson co-chair. Rufus Lewis was also a member, and the committee's goal was to see that every adult at Dexter was a registered voter and an NAACP member (Carson *et al.* 1994: 290).

Bus Segregation

Most African Americans, from the Alabama State lecturers who attended Dexter to the more numerous domestic servants who belonged to the larger First Baptist, Holt Street, or Bethel churches, hated bus segregation. During the war in particular, maintaining white supremacy on the South's congested public transportation system made the buses flashpoints for racial conflict, as King well remembered from his teenage ride back from a Georgia public speaking contest. The Montgomery City Lines reserved the last ten bus seats for blacks and the first ten for whites. The engine lay under the rear seats, a solace perhaps in winter, but a more frequent source of discomfort in Alabama's long summer months. The white section was sacrosanct. Even if all ten white seats were empty and every other seat was taken, blacks were not permitted in the white section. They were not even allowed to walk through it. Having purchased their tickets from the driver at the front, they had to get off the bus and re-enter at the rear. Heavily burdened shoppers or tired commuters resented this requirement, especially when the rain was pouring, or worse, when a malicious driver drove off before they reached the rear door. Between the designated white and black seating was a zone of sixteen seats assigned provisionally according to need. Since African Americans constituted 75 percent of bus passengers, they often took these seats, but once the white section was full, the driver could demand their surrender. So rigid was the requirement of racial segregation that no black person was allowed to sit alongside a white one. Once the white section filled, the next white passenger to board could require as many as four black riders to stand (Fairclough 1995a: 17-18).

Upholding segregation fell most immediately to the white bus drivers, some of whom relished the task. Nevertheless, with growing frequency in the postwar decade, black Montgomerians refused to obey. They learned that the municipal ordinance's wording implied that blacks should only be required to surrender a seat in the middle section, if another seat was available in the black section. This would approximate the *Plessy* doctrine of separate but equal provision for each race, requiring whites to stand in the white section once blacks had occupied the "neutral" zone, and vice versa. On May 24, 1954, a week after what segregationists called "Black Monday" when the US Supreme Court overturned the *Plessy* doctrine in the field of education, Jo Ann Robinson reminded Mayor W.A. Gayle that the WPC had raised grievances against the bus company at a hearing on a proposed fare rise. Unless more courteous treatment was assured, she warned, community plans for a bus boycott would gather pace.

As the number of registered black voters in the city had risen, such racial diplomacy had yielded slight improvements, but not after Black Monday. By the municipal elections in March 1955, defending segregation was proving the surest way to corral the larger white vote. During the election, E.D. Nixon organized a forum at which the various candidates (all white) stated their position on the bus situation and other issues. A noncommittal Gayle, a moderate segregationist Frank Parks, and an openly segregationist candidate Clyde Sellers subsequently romped home (Mills Thornton 1980: 163-235).

Around election time, a bus driver asked a 15-year-old black schoolgirl, Claudette Colvin, and other black passengers to stand so that white passengers could be seated. Colvin refused, insisting: "It's my constitutional right to sit here" (Burns 1997: 6). Three policemen dragged her from the bus, handcuffed her, charged her with a breach of the city code, and kept her in a cell until her parents bailed her out. In response, Mrs. Robinson led a delegation, which included King and the secretary of Montgomery's NAACP branch, Rosa Parks. The mayor, city commissioners, and bus company officials were unsympathetic and the disappointed black leaders again threatened a boycott (Robinson 1987: 41-42). But the white authorities were undeterred. Two weeks later, the juvenile court found Colvin guilty of violating the state bus segregation law and of assault and battery while resisting arrest. She was placed on indefinite probation. Montgomery's only African American attorneys, Fred Gray and Charles Langford, appealed the ruling, and Rosa Parks raised funds for the NAACP. On May 6, Circuit Court Judge Eugene Carter affirmed the assault conviction but dismissed the segregation violation. This ruled out further appeals to challenge the legality of bus segregation. In retrospect, however, King saw the Colvin case as the moment when "the long repressed feelings of resentment on the part of the Negroes had begun to stir" (King 1958: 42).

King was establishing himself as a community leader, despite a busy schedule. Every morning until its completion in April 1955, he rose at 5.30 to work for three hours on his doctoral dissertation. He also devoted considerable time to pastoring Dexter, preparing his sermons studiously, and ensuring that his committee system was running smoothly. He attended various church association meetings, which introduced him to the intrigue and personalities on the local ecclesiastical scene and strengthened his friendship with Ralph Abernathy. The two arrived so frequently together that other preachers came to regard Abernathy and King as a double-act: Mr. Rough and Mr. Smooth (Branch 1988: 125).

Having joined Montgomery's only significant, interracial reform group, the Alabama Council on Human Relations, and the local NAACP chapter, King, like Abernathy, was one of black Montgomery's activist clergymen. The Supreme Court's implementation decree, sometimes called *Brown II* (May 31, 1955), had devolved the process of school desegregation to local federal courts with vague, even contradictory, instructions to proceed with "all deliberate speed." On June 19, 1955, King warned his NAACP colleagues that while Jim Crow might be on its deathbed, "We must do everything to keep it down." This would require courageous leadership and continuing voter registration drives, litigation, and education. King also agreed to join the branch executive committee (Carson *et al.* 1994: 36).

Rosa Parks's Arrest

The aftermath of *Brown II* underlined the question of whether litigation alone could achieve racial justice. The summer of 1955

Back home, Nixon heard from Jo Ann Robinson. The time for a boycott had clearly arrived. In the Alabama State mimeograph room, Robinson and a colleague ran off thousands of leaflets asking people to stay off the buses on Monday, the day of Mrs. Parks's trial. There had been another arrest on the buses, the leaflet explained, and there would be more unless black Montgomerians did something to stop it. "The next time," it warned, "it may be you, or your daughter, or mother." Since most bus riders were black, a boycott should quickly force the company to recognize that "Negroes have rights too." Accordingly, the leaflet urged "every Negro to stay off the buses Monday in protest" even if it meant missing school or postponing a trip to town. "If you work," it added, "take a cab, or walk." Students and WPC members began house-to-house distribution the next day (Garrow 1988: 14-16).

An effective protest needed the backing of Montgomery's black clergy. Once the confrontation began, teachers like Robinson would have to work in the background and rely on Alabama State President H.C. Trenholm to mollify the institution's white paymasters. Like undertaker Rufus Lewis with his exclusively African American clientele, black ministers were shielded from white economic intimidation. Working for an all-black trade union with a national, Northern-based company had made E.D. Nixon's activism possible. But some blacks regarded him as reckless and ill mannered. Alone, he could not unite the community. Local preachers, on the other hand, had their congregations' confidence and offered the campaign respectability. Churches were meeting places, and in a city with neither a widely read black newspaper nor a black radio station, they offered an important means of communication. They would shortly prove able to support a viable alternate transportation system (Fairclough 1987: 17). Before leaving on his Pullman run to New York via Atlanta and back, Nixon phoned Ralph Abernathy to arrange an emergency meeting of ministers. Young "Mr. Rough" readily agreed and suggested that Nixon contact King since Dexter Avenue was the best venue. When Nixon phoned, however, King was wary. Certainly, Dexter's meeting room would be available, but "Mr. Smooth" wanted time to think about the proposed campaign (Garrow 1988: 17).

King – The Reluctant Leader

King had decided recently to try to limit his commitments. He had thrown himself into his first independent pastorate with gusto, a decision complicated by the fact that his wife had taken at least six months to come to terms with their return to the Deep South. Coretta's restlessness probably encouraged King to reconsider an academic appointment, notably the post of Dean of Religion at Dillard University in New Orleans, which he declined shortly after securing his doctorate. By the time his degree was conferred in June 1955, Coretta was pregnant and the arrival of their first child, Yolanda Denise, on November 17 was largely behind King's cool response to Nixon. But there were other factors.

The WPC's one-day boycott was primarily a cathartic gesture, expressing the outrage of black bus-riders at innumerable insults. It was intended to convince the white leadership that the status quo was untenable. Mass protest was not, however, integral to the NAACP's strategy of litigation whereby segregation itself was ruled unconstitutional and outlawed. Mrs. Parks's arrest provided a basis for such litigation but that would take months, even years, from her first court appearance on December 5. Aware of Nixon's fiery reputation, King was probably keen to ensure that the community did not attempt too much. Certainly, his fellow ministers shared his hesitancy. The one-day boycott was a *fait accompli* but whether it should be continued was uncertain.

Calls to support Monday's boycott rang from black pulpits that Sunday. Bolstering Robinson's leaflet campaign, Nixon had contacted a friendly reporter with the *Montgomery Advertiser*. Its Sunday front page warned of a bus boycott and local radio and television picked up the story. Word spread. When King checked a succession of Monday morning buses, he gleefully spotted "no more than eight Negro passengers" (King 1958: 54). He and other leaders had agreed to meet later to consider how to proceed in the light of both support for the boycott, and the immediate filing of an appeal against Rosa Parks's conviction, that morning, for violation of the segregation law. Their recommendations would go before an evening mass meeting at Holt Street Baptist Church, a large church in a working-class district.

Even before King arrived, the empty buses had convinced his colleagues to establish the Montgomery Improvement Association to continue the campaign. But ministers were worried. Police Commissioner Clyde Sellers had assigned squad cars to trail the buses in order to tackle what he called "Negro 'goon squads'." Perhaps, someone suggested, the MIA should operate in secret to minimize the threat of white retaliation? Back in town, E.D. Nixon was appalled. "You ministers," he declared angrily, "have lived off these wash-women for the last hundred years and ain't never done nothing for them." Now, while working women faced arrest and intimidation, the clergymen were looking to hide like "little boys." If they tried, he would expose them all as cowards. Arriving just at this moment, King felt obliged to respond. Calming the situation, he said good-naturedly: "Brother Nixon, I'm not a coward," and he backed Nixon's demand that the MIA operate through an openly named leadership. Seeing his chance, Rufus Lewis, who feared that Nixon might dominate the new group, proposed his pastor Reverend King as MIA president. The choice was unanimous (Branch 1988: 136-37).

King recalled that it all "happened so quickly I did not even have time to think it through." Had he had time to consider, he "would have declined the nomination" (King 1958: 56). Besides blocking a rival, Lewis's move served to strengthen the MIA's appeal to wealthier black Montgomerians: the private car owners who, like King himself, had rarely experienced the mistreatment endured by bus commuters. As a Baptist preacher, King was more acceptable to the conservative clergy and could appeal to the many regular black churchgoers. And if the confrontation with white Montgomery ultimately went badly wrong, the highly educated King with his powerful Atlanta family was better placed than other ministers to continue his career elsewhere. He was elected unopposed. The new MIA president had barely twenty minutes to prepare his first speech, but the fact that it took him fifteen minutes to push his way through the crowds inside and outside Holt Street Church signaled that here was a mass movement crying out for leadership.

After paying tribute to Rosa Parks's exemplary character and acknowledging that her arrest was simply the latest case of abuse, King thrilled his audience by rhapsodizing on their new insurgency. A recording captured the growing communion between the charismatic preacher and his responsive audience (Carson *et al.* 1996: 72). There "comes a time," King declaimed,

> when people get tired of being trampled over by the iron feet of oppression. [*thunderous applause*] There comes a time, my friends, when people get tired of being plunged across the abyss of humiliation, where they experience the bleakness of nagging despair. (*Keep talking*) There comes a time when people get tired of being pushed out of the glittering sunlight of life's July and left standing amid the piercing chill of an alpine November. (*That's right*) [*applause*] There comes a time. (*Yes sir, Teach*) [*applause continues*]

King was keen to distinguish the MIA's Christian protest from both Klan violence and the White Citizens Councils' economic intimidation. City Commissioner Sellers had already suggested that support for the boycott was coerced and local newspapers had likened it to the Councils' tactics. Accusations of communism or un-Americanism were bound to follow. Hence, King stressed that the protest was quintessentially American, something they could not do if they "were incarcerated behind the iron curtain of a Communistic nation." The "great glory of American democracy," he declared, "is the right to protest for right." Unlike their white opponents, African Americans would not burn crosses, or lynch people, or "stand up and defy the Constitution of this nation" (Carson *et al.* 1996: 72-73).

Having assured them that the Supreme Court, the Constitution, and God Almighty were all on their side, King urged his listeners to remain united and "Christian in all of our actions." By staying off the buses and remaining nonviolent, by pursuing justice through its twin tools of persuasion and coercion, they would advance a process of both "education" and "legislation," and achieve their destined place in history (Carson *et al.* 1996: 73-74). As historian Adam Fairclough concludes, King's Holt Street speech was "the kind of oratorical tour de force that would become his hallmark ... Striking a skillful balance between militancy and moderation, he aroused righteous anger on the one hand, while stressing discipline and responsibility on the other" (Fairclough 1995a: 20-21).

For all the emotion of this occasion, however, moderation was the dominant characteristic of the Montgomery movement initially. At the first fruitless negotiations between the city, bus company, and MIA on December 8, black demands were limited to three conditions that could be met within segregation. Outlined in a letter to the parent company, National City Lines (Carson *et al.* 1996: 81), they were:

1 Courteous treatment by bus drivers.
2 Seating of Negro passengers from rear to front of bus, and white passengers from front to rear on "first-come-first-serve (*sic*)" basis with no seats reserved for any race.
3 Employment of Negro bus operators in predominantly Negro residential districts.

The MIA expected its proposals to be accepted. The company could not afford to lose three-quarters of its riders, and the first-come-first-served system they suggested was already operating in Mobile in Alabama itself. In a press statement, the MIA pointed out that the 1947 state segregation law *authorized* and *empowered* bus companies to provide racially separate accommodations but did not *require* them to do so. It left the practicalities of segregation to local adjudication (Burns 1997: 100-101).

With no agreement after three weeks of the boycott, the MIA paid for a half-page advertisement in both the Christmas Day *Advertiser* and the smaller *Alabama Journal* to publicize the protest's origins, its reasonable demands, and its own willingness to resolve the situation. For the first time, the leaders identified nonviolence as a key feature of their campaign, which they described as "a movement of passive resistance, depending on moral and spiritual forces." Two days later, the NAACP's executive secretary, Roy Wilkins, informed his Alabama field director W.C. Patton that the Association would not help the Montgomery protesters since they were "asking merely for more polite segregation" (Burns 1997: 109-10).

The Counter-Movement Nurtures The Movement

The rejection of MIA's modest demands illustrates how the strident defense of white supremacy in the post-*Brown* era closed the door on old-style racial diplomacy. The aggressive white response ensured the Bus Boycott's eventual national significance and was a key factor in solidifying mass black community support. Veteran civil rights activist Ella Baker would famously remark that "Martin did not make the movement; the movement made him" (Grant 1998: 123) but one should add that the white counter-movement made him, too. Not only had white newspaper "scare headlines" publicized the planned boycott, but clumsy police efforts to abort the one-day boycott had kept wary African Americans off the buses.

Efforts to stop black taxi-drivers from offering cut-price fares encouraged the MIA to establish its own car pool, and wage a longer-term campaign. King contacted the Reverend T.J. Jemison who explained how his Baton Rouge activists had organized "Operation Free Lift" during their ten-day Bus Boycott in June 1953. Police harassment of all black motorists forced the black middle class to become actively involved, and more importantly, the bus company withdrew service on two heavily used, black commuter routes. According to MIA historian Norman Walton, the "decision to slash bus runs in Negro sections did more to crystallize the movement than any act thus far" (Garrow 1988: 26-28).

Demonstrating that the holiday season had fostered no goodwill among the white leadership, a White Citizens Council rally on January 6 heard Police Commissioner Sellers boast that he would never trade his "Southern birthright for a hundred Negro votes." He drew even louder cheers by publicly joining the Council (Branch 1988: 150). The *Advertiser* commented that Sellers's publicity stunt made the Montgomery police force, in effect, "an arm of the White Citizens Council" (Garrow 1988: 52). Meanwhile Rosa Parks was sacked by the department store where she worked. A week later, her husband Raymond lost his job as well. The couple also had to endure death-threatening phone calls (Theoharis 2013: 101-2).

White leaders next tried to isolate King as *the* troublemaker. Rumors began: why had this publicity-hungry newcomer (who no one had ever seen on a bus) displaced more established figures? King was alleged to have used MIA donations (nearly $7,000 so far) to buy himself a Cadillac. When these jibes seemed to increase King's preeminence, the city fathers tried to bypass him. Late on

Saturday January 21, King learned from reporter Carl Rowan of a wire story announcing a Bus Boycott settlement. The Sunday *Advertiser* was set to announce that, after meeting with "prominent Negro ministers," the city and company had agreed to provide some special "all-Negro" buses during the rush hour, to require courtesy from drivers, but to keep the existing seating arrangements on normal services. Rowan was able to get Commissioner Sellers to confirm the story, and more importantly, to reveal the unnamed ministers' denominations: Baptist, Presbyterian, and Holiness. No Holiness minister was in the MIA, and very few Presbyterians.

With these clues, King and his concerned associates identified the mayor's three stooges as minor "country preachers" and learned how they had been duped. But the hoax might still work. While most MIA ministers began phoning fellow preachers to ensure that the news was spread from every friendly pulpit, King set out with a smaller group to visit black nightspots. Stopping the Saturday night revels momentarily, he warned that whites were trying to trick them and that blacks should stay off the buses. At morning services, bleary-eyed preachers repeated this message to their congregations (Branch 1988: 155-57). Despite hardship, black Montgomerians remained loyal to the boycott, sharing lifts where possible, walking where necessary, and staying home, if they had to. African American solidarity increased white hostility and economic retaliation. The women of the MIA's Welfare Committee had to deal with more and more cases of eviction and job loss.

After the failure of his "false settlement" ruse, Mayor Gayle announced that until the boycott was suspended, there would be no further negotiations. He and fellow commissioner Frank Parks proclaimed that they too had joined the White Citizens Council, and Gayle called upon Montgomery's white housewives to stop chauffeuring their black maids. For his part, Police Commissioner Sellers warned that his officers would disperse groups waiting for the car pool rides and would pay even greater attention to its drivers. The latter were repeatedly pulled over while officers checked their headlights, taillights, and windshield wipers. Almost every day brought another fine. The voluntary pick-up system began to weaken and leaders sensed that "the protest movement seemed to be wavering" (Garrow 1988: 55).

Ironically, the arrest of King himself halted this decline. On January 26, he was stopped for driving at 5 miles over a 25 miles per hour limit. Taken to the dingy north Montgomery jail, he was kept in a filthy group cell, while the jailer stalled the bail process. Once angry black crowds gathered, however, King was released on his own recognizance. The MIA held seven hastily organized, overflowing, mass meetings to calm community anger. A Fisk University researcher captured far from nonviolent feelings. "I'm so mad I don't know what to do," one neatly dressed maid said:

> Do you know those bastards put Rev King in jail last night, and this morning they all parked on the corners and asking folks how come they didn't ride the bus. They think they bad 'cause they got guns but I sho hope they know how to use 'em, 'cause if they don't I'll eat them up wid my razor.

Another woman expressed similar defiance. "Dey trying to be smart," she declared, "but if they beat dat boy [King] dere is going to be hell to pay" (Burns 1997: 125). It was the walking feet of women like these that carried the boycott forward.

King Finds His Faith And Preaches Nonviolence

King himself was feeling the pressure. He later told how shortly after this arrest, late on January 27, he experienced what Christians call a dark night of the soul. Unable to sleep, he sat in the kitchen and wondered how he could leave Montgomery without appearing a coward. Life had been so easy under Daddy King's protection, but now he was alone at midnight with the words of the last threatening caller still ringing in his head. "Nigger, we are tired of you and your mess now," the voice had hissed, "And if you aren't out of this town in three days, we're going to blow your brains out, and blow up your house." The threat was not just to him but to his wife and baby daughter as well, and the horror of losing them became heart-stoppingly real. With an intensity he had not known before, he began to pray. And suddenly he heard an inner voice. He believed forever that it was "the voice of Jesus saying still to fight on." The voice "promised never to leave me," he wrote later, "never to leave me alone." And with that promise

came an extraordinary resurgence of confidence. His fears faded
and the uncertainty was gone. In the coming weeks, he would
refuse his father's pleas to leave the movement and return home.
He had been born again. The next morning he serenely attended
court, was convicted, and filed an appeal (Garrow 1988: 61, 56-58).

White intransigence persuaded the MIA to file a federal suit to
challenge bus segregation itself citing the *Brown* decision as precedent. Knowing the state would limit the constitutional implications of Mrs. Parks's case, the MIA's attorneys sought new
plaintiffs. The ultimately successful case of *Aurelia S. Browder et al.*
v. *William A. Gayle* was filed on February 1, 1956 on behalf of
five women including Claudette Colvin. The previous evening as
King was presiding at a mass meeting, the threatened bombing of
his house occurred. Coretta, baby Yolanda, and a family friend
luckily escaped injury. Racing home, King found the police
struggling to restrain an angry, armed crowd of his followers, as
detectives, the mayor and commissioners inspected the scene.
King urged the crowd to put away their guns since the movement
did not advocate violence (Burns 1997: 134-35). "I want you to
love our enemies," he declared, adding "if I am stopped, our work
will not stop. For what we are doing is right. What we are doing
is just. And God is with us" (Carson *et al.* 1996: 115).

The personal attack made King's calls for nonviolence all the
more impressive to observers. In 1994, Coretta King said that the
bombing incident had been very significant "in terms of injecting
the nonviolent philosophy into the struggle" (Burns 1997: 17).
Gradually, King developed the nonviolent philosophy for which
he was later famed. Initially, he complained to MIA colleagues
that by denying gun permits to his bodyguards, the sheriff was
essentially "saying 'you are at the disposal of the hoodlums'." In a
confidential interview on February 4, he even commented: "Maybe
its [*sic*] good to shed a little blood. What needs to be done is for a
couple of those white men to lose some blood; then the Federal
Government will step in" (Carson *et al.* 1996: 120, 125).

Beginning in late February 1956, the pacifist Fellowship of
Reconciliation's (FOR's) former field secretary, Bayard Rustin, and
its current field secretary, Glenn Smiley, separately tutored King
in Gandhian nonviolence. They pointed out that having guns
around his home was incompatible with nonviolent leadership.

The two men represented different approaches. Whereas Rustin, the flamboyant African American, believed in mass action, along the lines of the 1930s' labor movement, Smiley, the white Texan, embodied FOR's tradition of relying on symbolic, small-group demonstrations of nonviolence within a larger educational repertoire that sought both justice and reconciliation. King told Smiley that although he knew who Gandhi was, and had read some statements by him, he actually "knew very little about the man" (Garrow 1988: 68). Recalling his own initial meetings, Rustin declared that to assume that King was already prepared for his role gave him too little credit. "The glorious thing is that he came to a profoundly deep understanding of nonviolence through the struggle itself, and through reading and discussions which he had in the process" (Burns 1997: 169).

White violence continued. February 1956 began with a bomb exploding on E.D. Nixon's front lawn. On February 6, white rioters in Tuscaloosa induced the University of Alabama to exclude Autherine Lucy, a black student admitted by court order. This drew national media attention to the state. Four days later in Montgomery itself, Mississippi's Senator Eastland told 10,000 White Citizens Council supporters that the "one prescription for victory" was to "organize and be militant" (Branch 1988: 168). Montgomery's white leadership indicted the MIA leaders under a 1921 anti-boycott law on February 13. The Montgomery struggle now became a litigation race. The MIA, with NAACP backing, pressed to get the *Browder* case successfully through the appeals process before the city's attorneys could suppress the boycott as an illegal conspiracy.

Ironically, before the mass indictments, on January 30 and February 2 the MIA leadership seriously considered ending the boycott once the constitutionality of Alabama's bus segregation was securely before the courts. No one had envisaged such a long campaign, but stopping it was potentially as problematical as continuing it. The people – especially the working women – were aroused and would see any return to the buses without concessions as an affront to their worn-out walking shoes. On February 20, a mass meeting of several thousand firmly rejected a deal brokered by Montgomery's senior white businessmen. Mindful of the people who had walked – come rain or shine – rather than break the boycott, Jo Ann Robinson told a reporter: "The leaders couldn't stop it if they wanted to" (Garrow 1988: 68). MIA leaders also recognized that the boycott gave them more chance of preventing an embarrassing and escalating series of violent confrontations. Already the protest's nonviolent character and sustained unity was attracting external support, with King and others making fund-raising trips.

King And The Larger Stage

The indictment of 89 boycott leaders for violation of the 1921 statute on February 21 drew attention to Montgomery like the earlier bombings. The boycott made the front page of the *New York Times* for the first time and even the TV networks gave it coverage. King's plea not to "let anyone pull you so low as to hate them," his emphasis on "the weapon of love," and other echoes of Gandhi intrigued the nation's liberals. After meeting King for the first time on February 28, Glenn Smiley wrote: "why does God lay such a burden on one so young, so inexperienced, so good? King can be a Negro Gandhi, or he can be made into an unfortunate demagogue destined to swing from a lynch mob's tree" (Burns 1997: 164).

Like King, the MIA was learning by doing. With King away in Atlanta, the other leaders greeted the mass indictments with a public display of resolve. Noisily supported by the rank and file, the charged movement leaders cheerfully gathered at the courthouse on February 22 to present themselves and file bail bonds. Whites were flabbergasted. Having resisted Daddy King's best efforts to stop him from returning to Montgomery, King (with Daddy at his side) reported the next day and was released on bond. The indictments proved a tonic. As Virginia Durr wrote to a friend, it "was the very thing that was needed to make them more determined." With nearly $12,000 donated in two weeks, a flood of outside contributions further boosted morale (Garrow 1988: 64-65, 71, 69). King skillfully used this external support to encourage his followers. All over the nation, he told a February 27 mass meeting, men and women were telling them: "You've gone too far; you can't turn back now" (Carson *et al.* 1996: 144). At the same time, King and others realized that their opponents would dearly love to portray the movement as a Yankee as well as a communist plot.

The New York-based Bayard Rustin's recent involvement, unfortunately, gave substance to both charges. He had belonged to the Young Communist League in the 1930s. True, like his co-editors at *Liberation* magazine, he had concluded, long before Khrushchev's denunciation of Stalin on February 14, 1956, that the Popular Front's slogans had "become empty patter and jargon" (Burns 1997: 237). But his past still carried risks. The Red Scare in the South pre-dated Senator McCarthy's crusade, and continued well past his 1954 fall. It would dog King himself to his grave and beyond. With enemies out to discredit them, the presence of Rustin, a homosexual with a 1953 conviction for indecency, worried local leaders and some of Rustin's own Northern associates. Prudently, Rustin withdrew, but he continued to advise King in private meetings or by mail or phone.

King's focus remained maintaining the boycott, meeting the legal threat of the conspiracy indictments, and advancing the MIA's own court case for bus desegregation. Rustin, however, was already considering how to spread the Montgomery insurgency across the South. He saw King's charismatic public persona as instrumental to this process. King's reception at Northern fund-raising events confirmed his wide appeal. A less enthusiastic Virginia Durr reported how black Montgomerians loved King. "They adore him," she wrote, "and my wash lady tells me every week about how she hears angel's wings when he speaks, and God speaks directly through him and how he speaks directly to God" (Fairclough 1987: 26). While a skeptical Durr may have scorned this personality cult, she could not deny that it helped the campaign. It had been one thing to stay off the buses for a day, but now these ordinary men and women had done so for months because, with King's encouragement, they sensed that they could truly make a difference.

Rustin and his white New York associate, attorney Stanley Levison, a seasoned supporter of left-wing causes, prized King's star qualities. The age of television had begun and hints of its power had been evident in the way popular support for Senator McCarthy had faded with the televised army hearings in 1954. But another New York associate, Ella Baker, took a different view.

A former Director of Branches for the NAACP, she had always resented the pretentiousness of preachers, and taken equal offense at the egotism of so-called race leaders. Only Randolph among national civil rights figures met her exacting standards by his devotion to practical organizing. Under Randolph's name, the three New Yorkers had formed a support group, In Friendship, to help "victims of racial terror" in the South. In May 1956, they organized a benefit at Madison Square Gardens, which raised $7,000, half of which went to the MIA. Such fund-raising enabled the MIA to buy stationwagons and pay drivers instead of relying on volunteers using their own vehicles.

Spring had seen the two sides dig in. The Alabama state legislature on March 6 had introduced a Massive Resistance program, including a bill strengthening bus segregation. The Southern Manifesto, denouncing the *Brown* decision, had been issued on March 12 with the unanimous support of Alabama's Congressional delegation. And after four days of testimony, King was found guilty of conspiracy on March 22. The sentence of a year in jail and a $500 fine, along with the legal proceedings against other indicted leaders, were suspended, pending appeal. Outside the courthouse, King urged his supporters to continue "in the same spirit of nonviolence and passive resistance" (Garrow 1988: 74). Well coached by his lawyers, King had been studiously evasive under cross-examination, a sign that he did not wish to practice the idealistic nonviolence of his FOR tutors. Nonetheless, he spoke increasingly about the similarities between the movement he headed and Gandhian nonviolence. Speaking in Brooklyn, he said that using passive resistance, the "little brown man in India – Mohandas Gandhi" had "brought the British Empire to its knees," adding, "Let's now use this method in the United States" (Carson *et al.* 1996: 210).

King had always emboldened local supporters by stressing the historic significance of their actions. He now began to link the boycott even more strongly to national and international trends. In "The Death of Evil upon the Seashore," a sermon delivered before 12,000 people in New York's Cathedral of St. John the Divine on May 17, 1956, he dwelt expressly on the decolonization struggles in Africa and Asia as part of the "great struggle of the Twentieth Century" for freedom (Carson *et al.* 1996: 260-61). King knew that these new nations had excited concern in US diplomatic circles by their proclamation of a nonaligned stance in the Cold War at the Bandung conference just over a year earlier. Understandably, these postcolonial nations took a keen interest in US race relations. At the NAACP's annual convention in San Francisco on June 27, King warned: "if America doesn't wake up, she will discover that the uncommitted peoples of the world are in the hands of a communist ideology" (Carson *et al*. 1996: 308). Speaking on December 3, 1956, he transferred the imagery of trampling iron feet and seasonal contrasts that he had employed in his first MIA address to the global uprising against white rule. By protest, he declared, the colonized had acquired "their own governments, their own economic systems, their own educational system" (Carson *et al*. 1996: 454).

Occasionally, these global parallels revealed a similarity of tactics as well as grievances. On April 17, 1956, Africans commenced a boycott of buses in Cape Town, South Africa, to protest the imposition of segregated seating. But more usually, the pattern was one of divergence. Coincidentally, on the first anniversary of the start of the Montgomery Bus Boycott, South African police arrested for high treason the man who would eventually join King as an icon of the global freedom struggle, namely, Nelson Mandela (Meredith 1997: 139).

Other Boycotts, Legal Battles, And Scandal

Despite his international references, King's main concern in 1956 was nurturing a new militancy in the American South. Students at South Carolina State College in Orangeburg began a boycott of classes on April 16 after state police broke up a campus civil rights protest. In Tallahassee, two students from Florida Agricultural and Mechanical College disobeyed the local bus segregation law on May 26 and were arrested. Under the leadership of C.K. Steele, Pastor of Bethel Baptist Church, the Inter-Civic Council (ICC) launched a bus boycott. Black Tallahasseans were aware of the Montgomery protest, especially since Steele had previously pastored there. But theirs was no mere imitation, not least because the ICC faced a smarter adversary. The Tallahassee authorities quickly conceded ICC demands for greater courtesy and the employment of black drivers. They also agreed to the "first-come-first-served" principle as long as "members of the different races" did not "occupy the same seat." Defending segregation beneath a veneer of friendliness and professionalism, City Police Commissioner Frank Stoutamire avoided Clyde Sellers's mistakes (Fairclough 1987: 19-20).

When the US Supreme Court dismissed the white defendants' appeal in *Flemming* v. *South Carolina Electric and Gas Company* on April 23, 1956, many newspapers erroneously reported this as equivalent to declaring all intrastate bus segregation unconstitutional. Bus companies in 13 Southern cities desegregated immediately, and City Lines indicated that it intended to do so in Montgomery. In reaction, Police Commissioner Sellers warned that he would arrest bus drivers who failed to enforce segregation and on May 9 the circuit court required the bus company to retain segregation. Thus, by the time the Tallahassee protests began, genuinely moderate communities had already desegregated their buses and white Tallahassee's position only seemed liberal by comparison with Montgomery's. On June 5, in *Browder* v. *Gayle*, a federal appeals court voted two to one to rule Alabama's bus segregation laws unconstitutional on the basis of the precedent set by the *Brown* decision. Its injunction against bus segregation was suspended, however, pending appeal to the Supreme Court.

The positive legal rulings heartened the MIA leadership but there could be no complacency, and no relief for ordinary black Montgomerians, who were walking now in the heat of a Southern summer. The appeals court ruling had included a dissenting opinion which upheld the principle of *Plessy* v. *Ferguson*. This bolstered Alabama's case before the Supreme Court. Whites would also exploit technical pitfalls as they demonstrated on July 20 when the Alabama Court of Appeals rejected an appeal against King's conspiracy conviction on the grounds that it was filed too late. With white authorities so evasive, the MIA needed the most specific and authoritative ruling it could secure for desegregation, and so it opted for the slower route of a full Supreme Court hearing. Nonetheless, things seemed to be moving in the MIA's favor, especially since the movement had overcome another test.

Trouble erupted while King and Abernathy were vacationing and fund-raising in California. On June 11, the MIA's recording secretary Reverend U.J. Fields, who had recently been replaced in a board reshuffle, publicly charged his fellow officers with "misusing money sent from all over the nation" (Burns 1997: 274). These were damaging allegations for a movement that increasingly relied on external donors and the trust of its local mass following. King flew back immediately to quell the controversy. He persuaded Fields to withdraw his accusations publicly, and then urged the community to forgive the young pastor. The MIA had lax accounting procedures and some individuals took from monies raised in the national fund-raising drive. The accusations, reiterated in Fields's later autobiographical account, set a pattern for later smear campaigns and official harassment of King (Fields 1959; Burns 1997: 277, note 8; Jackson 2008: 138-39).

The Boycott's Uncertain End And SCLC's Shaky Beginning

While waiting for the Supreme Court to uphold the lower court's outlawing of bus segregation, the MIA decided to use nonviolent training "to prepare the people to go back to integrated buses with a sense of dignity and discipline" (Carson *et al.* 1996: 377). On October 1, at Hutchinson Street Baptist Church, King directed the MIA's first training session. Two women explained how they would react if white women began name-calling, or even shoving, when they sat next to them. The first felt she could ignore the name-calling, but admitted that, "If she were to start pushin' me, maybe I would give her a little shove." King, and various congregation members, pointed out that retaliation would achieve nothing. The second volunteer took up the point. "It isn't going to do us any good to get mad and strike back," she declared, "'cause that's just what some of them *want* us to do." King commended the second speaker and said the exchanges revealed the challenge posed by desegregation (Burns 1997: 293-94). The session provides a glimpse of the suppressed anger lurking at the movement's grass-roots, and also shows that boycott supporters had only a limited understanding of nonviolence, even at this late stage.

The litigation race was reaching a nail-biting finish. On November 13, 1956, King attended the circuit court as the city sought a temporary injunction against the car pool. While there, a reporter relayed to him news that the Supreme Court had affirmed

Gayle v. *Browder*. This ruling overshadowed the circuit court's injunction, which effectively ended the MIA car pool. King assumed that the Supreme Court's formal order would be issued within days, but further legal maneuvers delayed the order until December 17. In the interim, weary black Montgomerians still had to walk or rely on private lifts. Finally, at two mass meetings on the evening of December 20, the MIA repeated its guidelines on how to behave on the desegregated buses, and King proclaimed that the time had come to "move from protest to reconciliation." At 5.45 the next morning, when the first bus of the day pulled up near King's home on South Jackson, news photographers snapped as the MIA president paid his fare, took a seat at the front of the bus, and was joined by the FOR's white field secretary, Glenn Smiley. After 382 days of hard struggle by hundreds of ordinary African Americans, the boycott was over (Garrow 1988: 82).

Despite King's hopes for reconciliation, white violence continued. A gunshot hit the King home on December 23 and five white men assaulted a black teenage girl at a bus stop on Christmas Eve. After further sniper fire, including one incident in which a pregnant black woman was hit in both legs, the City Commission suspended evening bus services on December 29, 1956. The Alabama Christian Movement for Human Rights (ACMHR) in Birmingham similarly faced increasing violence as it tried to implement *Gayle* v. *Browder*. On Christmas night itself, 15 sticks of dynamite exploded beneath the parsonage of its leader, the Reverend Fred Shuttlesworth. Amazingly unharmed, he emerged from the wreckage to lead 200 followers onto the buses to test desegregation and face arrest.

King wrote to urge Shuttlesworth to continue his direct action rather than rely exclusively on litigation to enforce desegregation. In a moment of unwitting prophecy, that would take over six years to fulfill, King exhorted: "If necessary, fill up the jails of Birmingham" (Carson *et al.* 1996: 496). King expected fellow activist preachers like Shuttlesworth and C.K. Steele of Tallahassee to play a key part in a "Southern Leadership Conference on Transportation" to be held in Atlanta over January 10-11. His Northern advisors, Rustin, Levison, and Baker, saw this meeting as crucial to the development of a coordinated, regional protest strategy.

In the early hours of January 10, however, agitated phone calls from Montgomery informed the King household and their guests of an unfolding bombing campaign. A shaky, but uninjured Juanita Abernathy told her husband Ralph that the front of their home had been gutted. Hutchinson Street Baptist Church was in ruins. The home of MIA member Robert Graetz, the white pastor of a black congregation, had also been hit. The terrorists attacked three other black churches, including First Baptist, which city authorities subsequently condemned for demolition. Leaving Shuttlesworth and Coretta King to preside over the meeting, King and Abernathy sped back to Montgomery. By the time King returned, the first incarnation of what would eventually be called the Southern Christian Leadership Conference (SCLC) had approved a statement extolling the merits of nonviolence, drafted telegrams to the President, Vice-President, and Attorney-General calling on them to intervene against the terror campaign in the South, and named King as its temporary chairman. It had also agreed to meet again in New Orleans.

Rustin's position papers for the conference had urged both mass protest and voting power. But precisely what kind of protest would be effective became less clear as 1957 proceeded. Escalating violence gave the Montgomery City Commission grounds to suspend all bus services, thus threatening to rob black Montgomerians of the victory they had just won. The Tallahassee Bus Boycott had ended on December 23, 1956 with the city authorities still committed to segregation, and the attempted Birmingham Bus Boycott had fizzled out after a few weeks. A six-month boycott in Rock Hill, South Carolina, simply bankrupted the bus company. Perhaps the Montgomery model was, in Glenn Smiley's words, "not exportable" (Fairclough 1987: 43).

A deflated SCLC moved away from bus boycotts to voter registration. The belief that African Americans should hold white politicians accountable and press for equal treatment through formal electoral channels had received a boost with the Supreme Court's 1944 ruling that the crucial Democratic Party primary elections, which selected candidates, could not exclude voters on racial grounds. A further fillip had been the courtship of the black vote in electoral contests since 1948, not just in non-Southern states like California, Illinois, Michigan, Ohio, Pennsylvania, and rk (prime destination points for black migrants since 1910), an increasing number of Southern cities, such as Atlanta, his, and New Orleans. King had told Dexter's Social and Po... ical Action Committee that voter registration and NAACP membership went hand in hand, but now his changed priorities disturbed NAACP leaders, who saw his SCLC as an opportunistic competitor for members, media attention, and money.

King himself seems to have had no clear idea what to do next. He had risen to prominence as head of the MIA, now an SCLC affiliate, and a floundering one at that, by early 1957. The renewed factionalism, the bombs, and the absence of racial reconciliation depressed him. The constant travel exhausted him. Shortly after the bombing wave, at a mass meeting held on his 28th birthday (January 15), he broke down. From the pulpit in a state of unusual emotion, he prayed: "Lord, I hope no one will have to die as a result of our struggle for freedom in Montgomery. Certainly, I don't want to die. But if anyone has to die, let it be me!" As the sobbing congregation shouted "No! No!" a suddenly silent King seemed transfixed, his hands locked to the lectern for support, before colleagues ushered him to his seat (Branch 1988: 200-201). Quizzed the next day, King played down the incident and certainly, by January 27, when twelve sticks of dynamite failed to explode outside his home, the young pastor was sufficiently recovered to tell his Dexter congregation about his experience of divine reassurance the previous year, declaring: "If I have to die tomorrow morning I would die happy, because I've seen the promised land and it's going to be here in Montgomery" (Garrow 1988: 89). His own death remained a recurrent theme in King's speeches.

As Richard Lentz points out, "the first major promotion" of King in the national media was *Time* magazine's February 1957 front cover, which tailored him to the house style and audience of the magazine. Like *Time*'s founder Henry Luce, King "had risen from nowhere to become one of the nation's most remarkable leaders of men." He was depicted as such "an expert organizer" that "the hastily assembled Negro car pool under his direction achieved even judicial recognition as a full fledged transit system." The cover story shrewdly excluded the suspect Karl Marx from its list of philosophers King had studied, and described the preacher as "no radical." Instead of stressing the confrontational, even anarchistic aspects of Gandhian nonviolence, *Time* equated it with Christian meekness, made more palatable for its readers by a manly bravery in the face of potential death (Lentz 1990: 34-37).

Such media recognition was double-edged. It enabled King to act as a key ambassador and lobbyist for the freedom struggle and ultimately helped to create the political coalition that would pass the crucial civil rights measures of 1964 and 1965. But the media spotlight simultaneously aggravated King's relations with others. Colleagues from E.D. Nixon in the MIA to Ralph Abernathy at the SCLC, and rivals from Roy Wilkins of the NAACP to black Congressman Adam Clayton Powell, would envy King's media prominence and resent how it eclipsed their own efforts. Others, like Ella Baker, were irritated by King's "Great Leader" image and his apparent readiness to accept plaudits for the work of others. In an August 1957 sermon, King spoke of the burdens of his celebrity status, about not being able to walk down the street without being stopped, adding that the boycott would have happened even if he had never been born (Jackson 2008: 156-57).

By the summer of 1957, Martin Luther King was already a star, more famous for being famous and for his words than for his current actions. On March 5, he and Coretta joined other dignitaries in Accra for Ghana's independence ceremonies, mingling with the country's first President, Kwame Nkrumah, and US Vice-President Richard Nixon. On May 17, from the steps of the Lincoln Memorial, King spoke to a disappointingly small crowd at the so-called Prayer Pilgrimage. Scheduled for the third anniversary of the *Brown* decision, the rally was originally intended to press President Eisenhower for stronger support for school desegregation, but once Congress began consideration of what would become the Civil Rights Act of 1957, the focus switched to guaranteeing voting rights. Accordingly, King's closing speech gave the reporters their headline with its repetitive, yet inspiring peroration: "Give us the ballot!" But the high-profile SCLC leader also faced criticism. When he emerged from a lengthy meeting with Vice-President Nixon on June 13 with no tangible federal action to report, one black newspaper lamented that he was simply "not ready for the political big-time" (Reddick 1970: 77).

As Congressional discussion of black voting rights continued in August 1957, King announced that the SCLC would launch an ambitious "Crusade for Citizenship." Besides boosting the African American electorate ahead of the mid-term Congressional elections, the Crusade would gather evidence of discrimination to present to the Justice Department. Passed in September, the 1957 Civil Rights Act established the Civil Rights Commission and allowed the Justice Department to file suit against discriminatory voting registrars. But SCLC's new program seemed to duplicate the NAACP's established strategy of litigation and voter registration, and predictably, it announced its own registration initiative.

King wondered what else the SCLC could do. Judging by the poor attendance at the MIA's second annual institute on nonviolence, local enthusiasm for direct action had dissipated. One encouraging sign for the Movement in general was that white segregationist attempts to block the court-ordered admission of black students to Little Rock's Central High School that autumn had finally forced Eisenhower to act. In the face of Arkansas Governor Orval Faubus's courtship of the segregationist vote, Eisenhower reluctantly sent in federal troops. The Little Rock students' stoicism in the face of white harassment and the sympathetic reaction of national public opinion prefigured what would happen during later, explicitly nonviolent, demonstrations. But overall, the Little Rock crisis showed both how far the movement remained wedded to the NAACP's legalistic approach and how slow progress would be under that strategy. For King personally, a rare bright spot in a depressing year was the birth of his second child, Martin Luther King III, on October 23, 1957.

By the end of 1957, both the SCLC and its Crusade were floundering. No executive director had been found to provide administrative oversight, and the Crusade remained little more than a letter of invitation to black leaders and white sympathizers asking for financial and moral support. Despite considerable organizational abilities, Bayard Rustin was simply too controversial to work prominently in the South itself. Instead, Ella Baker was drafted in as the SCLC's temporary director – she was certainly not adequately consulted. Arriving in Atlanta in January 1958, she found an organization with no office, and had to use the pay-phone at her hotel for business calls. Ebenezer Baptist Church's mimeograph machine was available to her only after 5.00 p.m. With these resources, she had six weeks to prepare the Crusade for Citizenship for launch on Lincoln's birthday, February 12. The results were understandably limited. Baker reported that Jacksonville, Florida, Houston, Texas, and Memphis, Tennessee had their largest and most enthusiastic meetings for many years. With far greater satisfaction, however, white officials in Montgomery claimed a decline in the number of black applicants to the registrar's office during the SCLC's supposed drive.

Caught in a double bind, the SCLC could only launch programs if it had sufficient funds and would only receive ample funds if it were seen to have effective programs. Nine months after the Crusade's launch, it had neither registered thousands of new voters as promised nor provided the new Civil Rights Commission with evidence of discrimination. John Tilley, a Baltimore pastor appointed SCLC executive director in May 1958, was sacked in April 1959 for failing to improve this situation. Baker was obliged to fill the breech once more. A debilitating round of fund-raising speeches and traveling entrapped King himself. Fund-raising needs also dictated that he complete his account of the Bus Boycott, *Stride Toward Freedom*, rapidly. In his hurry, he exactly reproduced or closely paraphrased without attribution passages from two books he had studied at Crozer.

No one found fault with this plagiarism at the time, but his failure to keep Ella Baker informed of his whereabouts and his tendency to take too long (in Baker's view) over routine decisions grated on the more experienced activist. To her dismay, King the celebrity remained the SCLC's sole asset. In June 1958, an inconclusive meeting with President Eisenhower alongside A. Philip Randolph, Roy Wilkins, and Lester Granger of the National Urban League earned King more press coverage. In early September, he secured further headlines when overzealous police officers in Montgomery arrested him as he tried to attend a lurid assault case involving an allegedly cuckolded husband and Ralph Abernathy. Belatedly realizing the dangers of giving King mass publicity, Police Commissioner Clyde Sellers paid King's fine rather than allow him to garner further attention by staying in jail. King's adversaries were getting smart.

Assassination Attempt: King Retreats And Regroups

About two weeks later, on September 20, 1958, King was in Blumstein's department store in Harlem, promoting *Stride Toward*

Freedom. An odd-looking, middle-aged black woman in sequined spectacles and a blue raincoat approached. "Is this Martin Luther King?" she asked. Assuming her to be just another fan, King replied, "Yes, it is." With that, the woman slammed a seven-inch Japanese letter opener into his chest. Mrs. Izola Ware Curry made no attempt to escape and was quickly arrested. Her deranged comments indicated that this was a psychotic attack rather than a politically motivated assassination attempt. With the hilt of the blade sticking out of his chest, King calmly waited for the ambulance. He was perilously close to death. A team of surgeons had to remove two ribs and portions of his breastbone before they could safely extract the blade, which had grazed the aorta. The preacher was left with a scar in the shape of a cross directly above his heart (Branch 1988: 243-45).

This near fatal attack did nothing to energize the SCLC, although the incident did bring in valuable additional donations. In early December, the third MIA Institute on Nonviolence consisted largely of tributes to the wounded leader. To Ella Baker, SCLC's parlous performance and finances scarcely justified self-congratulation. There was nothing at the meeting, she complained, "that dealt with people or involving people." Nothing, in other words, that would reestablish the mass enthusiasm that had previously made hundreds walk rather than ride a segregated bus. Confronted by Baker, King rather lamely responded, "Well, I can't help what people do" (Grant 1998: 107-8). Six months later in mid-May 1959, Fred Shuttlesworth essentially echoed Baker's complaint. "When the flowery speeches have been made," he declared, "we still have the hard job of getting down and helping people" (Garrow 1988: 116). But with a still frail King caught up in a round of public appearances, the SCLC remained too understaffed and unfocused to mount a significant campaign.

It was easy to see how the time passed. Leaving Baker and Tilley to organize voter registration work, King – now hailed as the American Gandhi – visited India in February and March 1959. Observers there felt that King and his party behaved more like tourists than pilgrims intent on learning about Gandhi's work (Jackson 2008: 170). In April, as a national race leader, he spoke at the second Youth March for Integrated Schools in Washington, addressed a conference on employment discrimination organized by Vice-President Nixon, and then hosted a dinner for Kenyan leader Tom Mboya. Although indicative of King's status and his deepening understanding of national and global problems, such treading of the world stage produced little of immediate consequence. Certainly, it did not advance what Ella Baker identified in September 1959 as the SCLC's aims: namely, to facilitate coordinated action by local groups and to nurture potential leaders (Garrow 1988: 120).

King realized the gulf between the SCLC's aims and its achievements. Determined to do better, on Sunday November 29, 1959, he announced that he was leaving Dexter Avenue to serve as his father's co-pastor in Atlanta. Since the Bus Boycott, he had been trying to do the work of "five or six people" and had wilted under the pressure of almost daily travel and "the general strain of being known." He risked becoming, he declared, a "physical and psychological wreck" (Branch 1988: 267). He was haunted by the feeling that in the plethora of things to do, he did nothing well. As a pastor, his attention to Dexter was a pale shadow of what it had been in 1955. As MIA president, his ability to bring rival factions together had evaporated under the spotlight of a fame so intense that figures like E.D. Nixon could not help but feel neglected. Voter registration efforts in Montgomery had renewed the Nixon-Lewis rivalry and the additional goal of school desegregation excited more concern than conviction amongst the MIA's black schoolteachers. Trying to spotlight fresh MIA achievements in 1959, King stressed increased African American self-reliance: a new YMCA building and a cooperative grocery store that symbolized the potential of pooled economic resources. But he also noted the limits of such black power and lamented the stalled integration agenda (Jackson 2008: 174-75).

Montgomery was not a good base for King's national agenda, however ill-defined. Atlanta had advantages. Assuming his travel itinerary remained hectic, the ambitious Georgia city was already emerging as an airline hub. Still temporarily run by Ella Baker, the SCLC offices would hopefully find King more accessible, and the demands of Ebenezer, with his father still in post, would be less than those of Dexter. Although Georgia's racial politics had been soured by the white backlash to *Brown*, Atlanta was pushing its credentials as "the city too busy to hate." Its bi-racial regime would seek to accommodate the process of racial adjustment, allowing, even encouraging, the SCLC leader to concentrate on struggles further afield.

On February 1, 1960, King was feted in an extravagant evening, "Testimonial of Love and Loyalty." A succession of speakers and choirs paid black Montgomery's tribute to the departing King. Having announced that the generous cash collection would be divided between the MIA and SCLC, King added that he could not "claim to be worthy of such a tribute" (Branch 1988: 270). The movement and its adversaries in Montgomery had made him famous. Ironically, on that very day, another movement – this time of students protesting against segregated lunch counters – had begun in Greensboro, North Carolina. A new wave of nonviolence would follow and, as long as his enemies blundered, it would carry King on to greater achievements and even more enduring fame.

4 Finding His Way, 1960-62

By moving to Atlanta in 1960, Martin Luther King admitted that he could not be both a local and a national leader. With the support of his family, he intended to be a national figure. It was a brave decision. He had already sensed how difficult it would be to meet growing African American expectations or to induce white Americans to make racial justice a national priority. Despite a radical reputation in the South, King had thus far tacked his course toward moderation. With older, acknowledged black leaders, he had lobbied the federal government, completed an exhausting round of speaking engagements, and urged African Americans to register and vote. But as the new decade began, he had not yet organized a single successful protest campaign at the SCLC. It would be 1963 before he would. In the interim, critics charged that King's reputation rested on other people's efforts.

Through the sit-ins of 1960 and the Freedom Rides of 1961, students established a repertoire of nonviolent direct action that changed the political agenda, and they did so without King's active leadership. Instead, they drew King into campaigns that he had not planned. These protests stimulated a general acknowledgment of a growing racial crisis that bolstered and defined King's leadership position. In particular, they strengthened the significance of his advocacy of nonviolence, which the press defined in ways that bred misunderstanding. Yet even when King became directly involved in the Civil Rights Movement's first, sustained, mass direct action campaign in Albany, Georgia, in 1961-62, his efforts were widely judged a failure. Six years after the start of the Montgomery Bus Boycott, King had still not found his way.

Throughout his public career, Martin Luther King was as frequently reviled as he was revered. He had to deal with adversaries, rivals, and critics of both races. When asked about the civil rights leader's return to Georgia in early 1960, Governor Ernest Vandiver was emphatically unwelcoming. "Wherever M.L. King, Jr. has been," he declared, "there has followed in his wake a wave of crimes including stabbing, bombings, and inciting of riots" (Kuhn 1997: 590). Of course, Daddy King was proud to have his famous son home once more and he reinforced the impression of Martin's, at least temporary, retreat from activism by saying "he's not coming to cause trouble" (Garrow 1988: 128). As part of Atlanta's established black leadership, the elder King believed that he had an understanding with white city leaders that desegregation would occur at a gradual pace that avoided controversy. By 1960, Atlanta's buses were desegregated, and a federal court had set September 1961 as the start date for school desegregation (no more than ten African American pupils admitted initially to all-white schools). Mayor William Hartsfield, Police Chief Herbert Jenkins, and Ivan Allen of the local Chamber of Commerce had promised compliance. Racial diplomacy, and black votes for relatively progressive white politicians, had brought some gains, evident in the presence of black police officers on the street, and even an African American member on the city school board. But progress was slow and extremely partial. Most public places – restaurants, lunch counters, and theaters – operated a color bar. Despite Hartsfield's progressive rhetoric, there were still separate drinking fountains and restrooms for whites and blacks at city hall. As an acclaimed champion of racial justice, King, Jr. found the backwardness of his hometown shameful, but student militants would soon be dismayed by King's own reluctance to intrude on his father's turf.

The Sit-Ins And Internal Movement Rivalries

Getting along with Daddy was just one of many challenges that King faced in 1960. The February student sit-in protests articulated the view that the accepted timetable for change was too slow. Sit-ins had the merit of simplicity. When refused service at a segregated lunch counter, protesters remained seated, thus reducing the facility's trade. As Ezell Blair, Franklin McCain, Joseph McNeil, and David Richmond showed by their demonstration in Greensboro, North Carolina, on February 1, the tactic initially required courage, but no great planning (Ling 2000: 36-38). The needs of a successful campaign, however, grew as it progressed. Participants had to display what became their hallmark – a stoical nonviolence – in the face of verbal abuse, physical assault, and arrest. Prosecutions also brought legal costs and required a willingness to endure jail. Frequently, such repression inspired older segments of the African American community to march in sympathy and to boycott downtown stores. During the Montgomery Bus Boycott, the young Dr. King had seemed to pioneer new tactics. Over the course of 1960, action became the key criterion for race leadership. A sense that older leaders were too hesitant permeated the student protest movement, and it appeared that the 31-year-old King shared the flaw.

Black student militancy was unexpected and it was not until the sit-in movement drew both escalating violence and national media coverage that the majority of black students paid much attention. Since a college education was a relatively uncommon, and frequently hard-earned, opportunity for African Americans, most black students in 1960 were actually quite conservative. When protest leader Diane Nash went to study at Fisk University, a distinguished black college in Nashville, Tennessee, she found her classmates were mainly interested in fraternity and sorority pledges, and entering a profession or finding a spouse. They wanted to be respectable and strove to keep out of trouble. Nash joined only a handful of Fisk students who attended the Reverend James Lawson's workshops on nonviolence.

When King addressed a gathering of student sit-in protesters from different North Carolina cities on February 16, 1960, he noted the novelty of a movement "initiated, fed, and sustained by students" (Garrow 1988: 129). By the end of 1960 about 70,000 African American students had "sat in" at a lunch counter, or otherwise demonstrated. Over half of them had been arrested as a consequence, and particularly in the Deep South states of Louisiana, Mississippi, Alabama, Georgia, and South Carolina, hard-pressed college presidents had been induced to expel these "trouble-makers." But this unexpected student revolt occurred, for the most part, independently of King. SCLC affiliates struggled to keep up. The MIA, under King's successor, Ralph Abernathy, for instance, failed to generate support for the sit-in students from Alabama State on anything like the scale of the famed Bus Boycott (Fairclough 1987: 59-61).

Despite community elders' scolding, the student activists relished their independence. Just as importantly, they savored success. In upper South states like Tennessee, North Carolina, and Virginia and fringe areas like Texas and southern Florida, lunch-counter segregation crumbled under their assault. Consequently, the students who attended the Southwide Youth Leadership Conference, held at Shaw University on the weekend of April 15-17, 1960, were self-confident and wary of adult advice. Knowing that her time at the SCLC would end soon, Ella Baker had organized the conference to allow the students to discuss common concerns and future plans. She was equally determined that it should not provide an opportunity for an SCLC takeover. Encouraged by Baker, the students organized their own "Temporary Student Nonviolent Coordinating Committee" to sustain the momentum of the protest campaign. As the SNCC (an acronym pronounced "Snick" in Movement circles), this organization became the Movement's avant-garde, an SCLC competitor, and for King personally, a frequent source of criticism.

A more immediately salient division inside the Civil Rights Movement of 1960 lay between the NAACP and other groups. A wave of hostile legislation and investigations in the South had engulfed the senior African American protest organization since its legal victory in the *Brown* school desegregation cases of 1954. Under pressure, the NAACP found that its legalistic strategy had seemingly little to show by 1960. Despite President Eisenhower's belated dispatch of federal troops to ensure desegregation at Little Rock's Central High School in 1957, the reality was that, due to school closures to evade desegregation, half of the Arkansas capital's black high school students did not go to school during the 1958-59 academic session. Only the prospect of losing entire school systems rallied Southern white moderates to achieve token desegregation in cities like Little Rock in 1959-60. But in rural areas, like Prince Edward County, Virginia, all public schools were shut down by 1960, leaving poor African American families without access to education.

Although the NAACP remained the only established civil rights organization in many black communities across the South, its harassed state explains why Roy Wilkins regarded the SCLC with suspicion and irritation. Just in terms of fund-raising, King's competing appeal aggravated the NAACP's predicament. When King announced in 1958 that the SCLC was moving away from bus boycotts to voter registration, the sniping began in earnest. King's disappointing and overambitious Crusade for Citizenship angered NAACP officials, who resented any other group intruding on *their* field of work. They continued to stress political lobbying and test case litigation, but due to concerted Southern white resistance, both federal legislation and court orders seemed ineffectual. Some local NAACP leaders grew frustrated at the denial of justice and legal protection. Most notoriously, Robert Williams organized an armed self-defense team to deter Klan activities in Monroe, North Carolina. Alarmed that such militancy would damage its respectable image, the NAACP suspended Williams, and the episode aggravated the national leadership's fears for the future (Tyson 1999).

During the 1950s, the NAACP had also tried to develop its youth councils, some of which, in border-states like Oklahoma, experimented with sit-ins. Consequently, while the NAACP certainly did not instigate the sit-in wave of 1960, it readily saw this development, like all other initiatives, as properly subordinate to its overarching strategy. The sit-ins produced a growing docket of legal cases to be defended, often at considerable cost to the NAACP. As Atlanta student leader Julian Bond recalled, "for years afterward the NAACP is complaining about, 'You get the headlines – we do the work. You get the headlines – we get the bills'" (Greene 1997: 387). When sympathy for the sit-ins generated donations, both the NAACP and the student protest leaders resented the fact that King's high public profile attracted some of that money to the SCLC. Outside of the South, anger at segregationist outrages fed ghetto frustration at NAACP limitations. This added to the bickering inside the emerging Movement.

Segregationist harassment added to the pressure upon the SCLC leader from these internal Movement disputes. On February 17, Atlanta deputies arrested King under a warrant for his extradition to Alabama to face criminal charges of perjury. State authorities alleged that he had falsely sworn to the accuracy of his 1956 and 1957 Alabama state tax returns. King had wrongly assumed that the tax question had been settled when, after an audit, he had reluctantly taken his lawyers' advice and paid $1,600 in alleged back taxes. The new prosecution threatened not just imprisonment in Alabama, but the shredding of King's public reputation. Ever since the Bus Boycott, there had been rumors that King was making money from his activism; that he had secret bank accounts, a lavish home, and a flashy car. If proven, the tax charges would give substance to these lies. While his family and inner circle of colleagues saw King's private distress at these false charges, in public he appeared unperturbed. After the formal indictment on February 29, Stanley Levison, Bayard Rustin, and Harry Belafonte formed a New York-based committee to raise $200,000 to hire a first-class legal defense team and fund the SCLC's continuing voter registration efforts. Claims about the latter in appeal letters angered the then NAACP Program Director, James Farmer. The letter was misleading, Farmer told Wilkins, and oral claims being made were even more deceptive and King should desist (Garrow 1988: 129-31).

The looming tax case helped to ensure that King was in no mood in April 1960 to fight Ella Baker for the "soul" of the student movement at the Shaw University conference. The conference's star was not King, but the Reverend James Lawson of Nashville, a militant Gandhian. Julian Bond remembers his fellow students warming especially to Lawson's call for a "nonviolent army" to secure a moral "revolution." "This Movement is not only against segregation," Lawson told them, "It's against Uncle Tom Negroes, against the NAACP's over-reliance on the courts, and against the futile middle-class technique of sending letters to the centers of power." He poured scorn on such "half-way efforts to deal with radical social evil" (Fairclough 1987: 63).

Predictably, such words infuriated the NAACP, and a tactful King did not offer Lawson an SCLC job as previously planned. Of course, King remained far more sympathetic to the students' direct action campaigns than was the NAACP. Leading NAACP attorney, Thurgood Marshall, derided tactics such as "Jail, Not Bail" as simply ridiculous. His job was to get people out of jail, he declared, not prolong their stay. With a presidential election approaching and a bill to strengthen federal protection of voting rights nearing passage in Congress, King's current emphasis, too, was on the potential of black ballots rather than direct action. In contrast, his white advisor, Stanley Levison, a veteran of the Old Left, wrote in March that the sit-in movement demonstrated the futility of trusting in Congress and the courts. These nonviolent protesters represented "the true forces of struggle," which, as the standing of the NAACP dwindled, Levison averred, "will move into effective leadership" (Fairclough 1987: 65).

In April 1960, the overall Civil Rights Movement needed leadership but King seemed still overwhelmed. Moving back to Atlanta had not reduced the pressures, as his tax trial before an all-white Alabama jury loomed. Given their prejudice, the expert legal team seemed a waste of money. Worse still, a fund-raising ad in the *New York Times*, highlighting King's case against the backdrop of Alabama's suppression of student protests, had prompted state officials to sue for libel not just the newspaper, but the four resident Alabama ministers, whose names had been listed. Ralph Abernathy and Solomon Seay of Montgomery, Joseph Lowery of Mobile, and Fred Shuttlesworth of Birmingham would now need financial assistance; and each new demand made King's exhausting itinerary of fund-raising speeches all the more essential. When he traveled to rallies, there were bomb threats, and when he came home to Atlanta, the Klan set a fiery cross upon his front lawn. Martin knew he could not stop, but he already wondered for how long he could continue.

The Alabama tax case began at last on May 25. After three days, it was clear that the discrepancy between King's reported income for 1956 ($9,150) and his total bank deposits ($16,162) could be readily explained by payments made to reimburse expenses, incurred whilst traveling to speak about the Montgomery Bus Boycott in many distant cities. Nevertheless, King did not expect the twelve white male jurors to acquit him. To general astonishment, however, they did. Some white Alabamans, it seemed, hated the taxman more than they did Martin Luther King. King's treasured reputation for financial probity was vindicated and an immense burden of worry evaporated. The news that the ebullient Reverend Wyatt Tee Walker of Petersburg, Virginia, had agreed to become SCLC executive as of August 1, 1960 reinforced King's buoyant mood. Other staff joined that summer as more systematic postal fund-raising efforts, and the national publicity from both King's trial and the student protests, boosted donations. Once again, King had ultimately benefited from his enemies' attacks.

King And The 1960 Election

With Walker poised to bring order to SCLC's operations, King could resume his search for an effective strategy. The forthcoming national party conventions were logical targets for demonstrations, and on June 9 King and black labor leader A. Philip Randolph announced their "March on the Conventions" of both the Democrats in Los Angeles and the Republicans in Chicago. The emphasis on mass action seemed to underline the split with the NAACP. An unnamed King "lieutenant" was quoted complaining about the NAACP's reluctance to engage in direct action, and angry NAACP officials immediately demanded a retraction. Ten days later, another feud erupted, this time with the flamboyant, black New York Congressman, the Reverend Adam Clayton Powell Jr. Keen to maintain his status as a "power-broker," Powell urged King to drop the convention protests. He alleged that King and Randolph were being used as a front by socialists Bayard Rustin and Stanley Levison, New York radicals with whom the Harlem minister had previously clashed. Privately, he threatened to tell the press that King and Rustin were homosexual lovers. Martin knew this was a lie, quipped Rustin, because "you can't sleep with a guy without his knowing it." Still shaken by the tax case, however, King was not ready to call Powell's bluff. He learned through intermediaries that only Rustin's removal would appease Powell, and when Rustin offered his resignation, King accepted it. The convention picketing went ahead in July, but drew little notice (Garrow 1988: 138-40).

Still new to the hard-boiled world of politics, King emerged from the Powell–Rustin debacle with little credit. In the midst of it, on June 23, he had met Democratic presidential front-runner John F. Kennedy. The election was shaping up to be a close one with the likely Republican nominee, Vice-President Richard Nixon, expected to profit from Eisenhower's widespread popularity.

The African American vote had been overwhelmingly Democratic since it swung behind Franklin Roosevelt in 1936, and its concentration in pivotal, Electoral College states outside of the South had helped to secure Harry Truman's surprise victory in 1948. Nevertheless, under Eisenhower, there had been signs of renewed Republican support among black voters. King told a shocked Virginia Durr, a liberal who had suffered during the Red Scare, that Nixon would occasionally phone him long distance for advice. While he retained doubts about the Californian anti-communist, King remarked, Nixon was "the ONLY candidate that does these things" (Fairclough 1987: 72). Like most Southern blacks of his generation, Daddy King was a Republican partisan, so Kennedy could not take King Junior's endorsement for granted.

At their meeting, the millionaire senator from Massachusetts listened as King called for strong presidential leadership, particularly in terms of action against states that denied the right to vote and against racial discrimination in federally funded housing schemes. Strong executive leadership was vital, Kennedy agreed, and voting rights enforcement should be a priority. Since Kennedy had voted with Southern senators to weaken the 1957 Civil Rights Act, King was wary, but the face-to-face meeting, and the presence of active civil rights supporters, like Harris Wofford, on Kennedy's team reassured him that on civil rights, Kennedy "would do the right thing." In July, Nixon and Kennedy won their respective party nominations and with very similar civil rights plans. Kennedy's choice of a white Southern running mate, Lyndon Johnson of Texas, seemed designed to court white Southern support, so King remained noncommittal when he met the Democratic nominee again in mid-September. When Kennedy mentioned that he felt that blacks still held his 1957 vote against him, King agreed bluntly, saying "something dramatic must be done to convince the Negroes that you are committed on civil rights" (Garrow 1988: 139, 142).

The chance for Kennedy to convince black voters emerged when King was obliged to do something dramatic by Atlanta's student protest leaders. At a large SNCC conference in mid-October, King nodded approval as James Lawson presented the case for a "Jail, Not Bail" strategy. By this stage, local students had lost patience with the procrastination of Atlanta's supposedly progressive leadership and had decided to resume lunch-counter sit-ins on October 19. They told King pointedly that if he intended to remain one of the Movement's leaders, he was going to have to join them in jail. Reluctantly, King agreed and, after demanding service at the restaurant in Atlanta's largest department store, Rich's, the demonstrators were arrested for trespass. King informed the press that, like his companions, he would neither seek bail nor pay a fine.

King's arrest brought Atlanta the sort of negative media attention that Mayor Hartsfield strove hard to avoid. Following the newswire, Kennedy campaign staffer Harris Wofford decided to check on King's predicament, and in an ill-judged attempt to win favor with Kennedy, his party's nominee, Hartsfield mentioned the call when he announced that he had struck a deal with the traditional black leadership. All the detained protesters would be freed without charge in return for a thirty-day suspension of the protests. Alarmed that his apparent "Yankee" interference might alienate Southern white voters, Kennedy promptly insisted that he had done no more than ask for clarification (Fairclough 1987: 74).

At this point, a fateful complication arose. In early September, a neighboring DeKalb County court had found King guilty of driving without a Georgia state permit. Paying a $25 fine, King overlooked the fact that Judge J.O. Mitchell had also imposed a parole period of twelve months, which King had now breached. Instead of being released with the others on October 25, King was transferred to DeKalb Jail, and the next day Judge Mitchell sentenced him to four months' hard labor. In the final stages of her third pregnancy, with Martin III (just turned 3) and Yolanda (nearly 5) to take care of, Coretta King cried openly in court at the thought of her husband on a Southern chain gang. As if to fulfill his wife's fears, in handcuffs and leg-irons, King was bundled into a police car early the next morning. "Where are you taking me?" he repeatedly asked. As they drove the dark country roads in silence, King expected the car to stop, at any moment, and like so many African Americans before him, to be summarily killed (Oates 1994: 164).

However, 300 miles later, King arrived at Reidsville State Penitentiary where he was issued with his convict's uniform and placed in a narrow, cockroach-infested cell. By now, his attorney had learned of his transfer and a distraught Mrs. King had phoned Harris Wofford, begging for help. Unsure of his standing with the candidate after Hartsfield's impolitic announcement, Wofford contacted Kennedy's brother-in-law Sargent Shriver and asked him to suggest that Kennedy call Mrs. King. Once Shriver had explained the situation, Jack Kennedy immediately phoned the King residence to convey his sympathy. Meanwhile, Martin was finding his virtually solitary confinement hard to bear. He later told Coretta that at one point, he simply broke down in tears. To keep his spirits up, he wrote to urge his wife to be strong during this ordeal. It "is extremely difficult for me to think of being away from you and my Yoki and Marty for four months," he declared,

> but I am asking God hourly to give me the power of endurance. I have the faith to believe that this excessive suffering that is now coming to our family will in some way serve to make Atlanta a better city, Georgia a better state, and America a better country. Just how I do not yet know, but I have faith to believe that it will.
>
> (Fairclough 1987: 75)

An odd combination of political forces quickly ended King's ordeal. When Jack Kennedy phoned Ernest Vandiver about King's imprisonment, the Georgia Governor tried to identify someone who might persuade Judge Mitchell, an arch-segregationist, to soften his stance. He eventually tapped George Stewart, secretary of the state Democratic Party and a friend of former Governor Herman Talmadge. On Stewart's recommendation, Talmadge had appointed Mitchell to the bench, and now, to secure King's release, Stewart tempted Mitchell with the possibility of a federal judgeship from a grateful Kennedy administration. Intrigued, Mitchell agreed to release King, provided he could have the Kennedys' interest confirmed. At that point, Bobby Kennedy phoned the judge, at Vandiver's urging. On October 27, Mitchell accepted a bail application and released King on a $2,000 bond. Wyatt Walker chartered a private plane to fly King back to Atlanta, where, before the waiting press, he was reunited with Coretta and the children. On the final Sunday of the presidential campaign, the Kennedy team circulated a flyer, "'No Comment'

Nixon versus a Candidate with a Heart, Senator Kennedy: The Case of Martin Luther King" in black churches. Despite pleas from African American advisors, like baseball legend Jackie Robinson, Nixon did not intervene and he rued the decision (Kuhn 1997: 583-95). The margin of Kennedy's victory – just 112,881 votes out of over 68 million cast – could be attributed to the three-to-one preference for the "candidate with a heart" among African American voters. Several weeks after the election, President Eisenhower complained that Nixon had lost because of a "couple of phone calls" (Garrow 1988: 149).

The episode confirmed the press perception of King as African Americans' chief spokesman. Although King did not endorse JFK's candidacy, Kennedy enjoyed significant African American support by being associated with him. However, the full account of King's release and imprisonment underlines a more poignant reality of his life at this stage. Despite his lofty public status, he remained more commonly the object of other people's plans than the instigator of events. As each development occurred – from the threatened tax suit in March to his imprisonment in October – King was carried along by the actions of others. White Georgia Democratic Party hacks, like Mitchell and Stewart, as well as the Kennedy campaign, milked the King arrest to the improbable satisfaction of antithetical interests. To their segregationist supporters, men like Mitchell, although not rewarded with a federal judgeship, had given the hated King a rough time – a period of imprisonment and release on a $2,000 bail bond for a traffic offense surely could be interpreted as a tough line? Meanwhile, for a different constituency of largely non-Southern black voters, King's release became a story of Kennedy courage and compassion. Behind the hype, it had been a familiar case of behind-the-scene fixes, with Governor Vandiver allegedly securing an understanding that Kennedy would not send federal troops into Georgia the way Eisenhower had sent them into Arkansas. Trumpeted by some as a sign of King's importance, the episode was actually evidence of a deeply entrenched, white political establishment with whom the Kennedys knew they would have to strike deals in the future. During the transition, King had no contact with the President-elect or members of his team, nor was he invited to the inauguration for fear of offending Southern white politicians (Branch 1988: 381).

The truncated, overwhelmingly white electorate of the South tended to return the same Congressmen and Senators time and time again. Reelection ensured seniority and seniority was the key principle in assigning committee positions in Congress. For any President, the success of their legislative program depended heavily on the influence they had with the chairmen (and they were men at this time) of the House and Senate Committees, which considered all bills. Consequently, when Kennedy took office on January 20, 1961, he already knew that his key policies of tax breaks to boost the economy, of increased defense spending, and a more assertive stance against international communism had to negotiate a committee structure dominated by Southern politicians. As an issue, the civil rights of African Americans jeopardized the rest of Kennedy's legislative program and the administration's priority was to contain that threat. No new legislation would be sought, positive executive measures would be taken discreetly and opportunely, and racial confrontations would be avoided or diffused as quickly as possible. Already politicians were sensing the deepening resentment of working-class whites in the North at the threat the Movement seemed to pose to their hard-won "rights" to union-protected jobs and private home ownership in de facto segregated neighborhoods. In this light, King was a potential nuisance rather than an ally, jeopardizing Kennedy hopes for racial calm. King himself, urged the new President to use his executive powers to the full (Jackson 2007: 124-25).

The Freedom Rides Of 1961

Fortunately for the Civil Rights Movement, King's SCLC was not the only civil rights organization striving to galvanize the new administration into action. The Congress of Racial Equality, a pioneer of nonviolent direct action in the 1940s, had been largely on the margins of the developing Movement because, with chapters chiefly in Northern and Western cities, it lacked a strong Southern base. When King declined an offer to be its national director, CORE turned to one of its founders, James Farmer, who had grown weary of NAACP bureaucracy (Branch 1988: 390). Having seen how the sit-ins had increased public interest in the civil rights issue, Farmer made plans for CORE to test a recent US

Supreme Court ruling (*Boynton* v. *Virginia*) that prohibited segregation in all terminal facilities serving interstate bus passengers. Such a Freedom Ride involving highly trained and motivated nonviolent activists would move the struggle from the local to the national level, and importantly, would publicize CORE as an exponent of nonviolence. Farmer scheduled the Freedom Rides for May 1961.

SNCC, too, was keen to make 1961 a year of action. On the first anniversary of the Greensboro sit-in, student activists staged protests across the South, including the South Carolinian town of Rock Hill. There, ten students, sentenced to a $100 fine or thirty days' hard labor, solemnly refused to pay their fines and launched the Movement's first jail-in. Hearing of their stand, four leading SNCC members, Diane Nash, Ruby Doris Smith, Charles Sherrod, and Charles Jones pledged to join their comrades in Rock Hill's jail, setting a new standard of commitment to the struggle. Simultaneously, a student of James Lawson's, Jim Bevel, escalated protests to end Nashville's movie theater segregation to such a pitch that community elders feared a race riot. Their pleas for caution did not deflect Bevel or his colleague, John Lewis, from direct action. Committed to nonviolence, Lewis also answered CORE's call for volunteers for its Freedom Ride (Branch 1988: 392-95).

By comparison with Lawson's disciples, King seemed a cautious bystander. The monthly cost of running the SCLC had risen to $7,000 and King toured the country to cover these costs. Five years after the Bus Boycott, he knew that segregationist pressure was close to forcing Ralph Abernathy and Fred Shuttlesworth to leave Alabama. Meanwhile, King's hometown of Atlanta had still not desegregated its lunch counters and student protests were producing more and more arrests. On February 15, King endorsed the students' stance that the protests must continue until white merchants agreed to desegregate. Disturbed by the negative publicity, the city's business elite cut another deal with the older black leadership. However, on March 10 when the Old Guard presented this settlement, which promised store desegregation within thirty days of the start of the school desegregation scheduled for that September, the students were hostile. The agreement required the protests to end immediately, they complained, yet tied progress on the lunch counters to school desegregation, which was already six years behind schedule.

When Daddy King urged the crowd to trust elders like him because they knew what they were doing, he was roundly jeered as an "Uncle Tom." Stung by the accusations against his father, Martin King unexpectedly took the podium. Skillfully, he defended the negotiators and made an impassioned plea for generational unity. If this "first written contract" between black and white Atlanta is to be broken, he declared, "let it be by the white man." His intervention transformed the meeting, which dispersed shortly thereafter having tacitly accepted a deal that moments earlier seemed destined for rejection. Some observers felt King's was one of the most powerful orations they had ever heard (Garrow 1988: 152). Significantly, for his future role in the Movement, it was an appeal for unity in support of a negotiated settlement rather than a call to arms.

That spring, the militant cry came first from CORE. It expected the Freedom Rides to receive the SCLC's practical support. Both Fred Shuttlesworth in Birmingham and Ralph Abernathy in Montgomery knew that they might receive an emergency call in mid-May once the Riders had begun their circuitous journey south from Washington on May 4. James Farmer had explained the schedule and purpose of the Freedom Rides in letters to both the White House and the FBI in late April. He did so in the hope that the alerted authorities would be prepared to respond quickly to any violent confrontations en route. But unlike Alabama's Klansmen, neither Kennedy's staff nor J. Edgar Hoover's agents paid much heed to the CORE announcement. Apart from a scuffle in Rock Hill, South Carolina, the Freedom Riders had faced little trouble by the time King greeted them in Atlanta on May 13. Publicly, he praised their courage and celebrated the fact that they had tested the desegregation of terminal facilities over nearly 700 miles of the South without mishap. Privately, he warned black reporter Simeon Booker that the party would "never make it through Alabama," where segregationist feeling was running especially high (Branch 1988: 417). Within forty-eight hours, he was proved right.

Even before the Freedom Riders reached Birmingham, the Alabama Klansmen attacked. Their first bus was pursued along Highway

78 by a convoy of some fifty cars after a mob had tried to slash its tires at Anniston station. Forced to stop, its passengers had to flee when a firebomb was thrown through a broken window. They were only saved from fatal injury by the presence of two under-cover detectives who belatedly kept the mob at bay. By the evening of May 15, newspaper editors around the world had picked up the photograph of the burning bus, with smoke billowing from its sides and flames pouring from its front window. James Farmer's calculation that Southern bigots would produce a confrontation that Kennedy could not ignore was proving all too sound. As the first casualties were ferried to hospital, white thugs boarded the second bus in Anniston. They beat up two white CORE members and ensured no "Negroes" occupied any front seats before the bus sped off. Another mob awaited these already battered freedom fighters in Birmingham. Details of a police-Klan agreement that would allow the mob fifteen minutes' "beating" time had been forwarded to FBI headquarters in Washington several times since May 5. Knowing its futility, the FBI nevertheless did no more than relay this information back to the Klan's allies inside the Birmingham City Police Department. Alighting at the terminal, the Riders were attacked a second time. As blows rained down on the Riders, bystanders, and reporters, Simeon Booker fortuitously slipped outside and frantically hailed a cab to take him to Fred Shuttlesworth's home (Branch 1988: 417-22).

Shuttlesworth's followers collected the CORE protesters from both the terminal and Anniston Hospital. Despite threats of arrest from Birmingham's Police Commissioner Eugene "Bull" Connor, Shuttlesworth sheltered the interracial group and presented the battered survivors to his congregation that evening. "When white men and black men are beaten up together," he declared, "the day is coming when they will walk together as brothers." Hostile criticism of Connor in Birmingham's morning newspapers and concerned phone calls from Attorney-General Robert Kennedy boosted Shuttlesworth's optimism. However, Governor John Patterson refused to guarantee protection for what he termed "this bunch of rabble rousers," and local drivers refused to drive any bus carrying the Freedom Riders. With a final rally scheduled for New Orleans on May 17, CORE decided that its purpose of drawing national publicity to Southern noncompliance with desegregation orders had been achieved. Accordingly, after spending May 16 waiting at Birmingham's besieged bus terminal, they agreed to complete their journey by air. Despite two bomb scares, they escaped on the 10.30 p.m. plane (Manis 1999: 267, 269-70). During these events, King remained a sympathetic spectator, involved only indirectly. Like Bobby Kennedy, he probably breathed a sigh of relief when he learned that CORE had suspended its efforts. Certainly, unlike the student veterans of the Nashville sit-ins, he made no move to ensure that the Rides continued.

On the evening of May 16, Diane Nash, spokeswoman for the Nashville students, informed Shuttlesworth that a new group of ten Riders would set out from Nashville the next day in order to prove that the Civil Rights Movement could not be stopped by violence. Alerted by wiretaps, Birmingham city police arrested the Riders and took them back to Tennessee, but they returned undeterred and the Freedom Ride left Birmingham on May 19. What followed illustrated both the steadfastness of the student activists and the undiminished fervor of Alabama's segregationists. Despite federally obtained assurances from Alabama that steps would be taken to protect the Riders, the new group was set upon as soon as it alighted in Montgomery. The local police chief followed Bull Connor's example and absented his men so that the mob could attack. In the ensuing fracas, Justice Department representative John Seigenthaler was knocked unconscious and three of the Riders were seriously injured. An angry Bobby Kennedy secured a federal court order against interference with interstate bus travelers and assembled 400 federal marshals at Maxwell Air Force Base outside Montgomery as a precaution. Against this backdrop of an escalating federal/state confrontation, King agreed to fly from Chicago to Montgomery to preside over a rally for the Freedom Riders on Sunday May 21. Previously an onlooker, he descended into the heart of a seething confrontation (Garrow 1988: 157).

By early evening, the First Baptist Church in downtown Montgomery was full to capacity. Already, shouts from massing white segregationists encircling the building interrupted the sermons and singing inside. A thin line of federal marshals kept the mob from entering the church and when rocks began to shatter the stained-glass windows, they fired tear gas to try to disperse the crowds. Urging calm, King explained to the congregation the seriousness of their situation: they were under siege. He then went to a basement office to call Bobby Kennedy. According to Kennedy's special assistant for civil rights, Burke Marshall, King sounded "panicky." Kennedy tried to reassure him that help was on the way. But when he added that since King was in church, he might as well say a prayer, the jest was not appreciated. Unless extra marshals arrived soon, a desperate King warned, he and 1,500 others might burn to death (Garrow 1988: 158). The arrival of Kennedy's last available detachment of marshals did momentarily stop the mob, but the tear gas they fired so close to the church soon wafted back inside the building, increasing the distress of those trapped inside. Just as Bobby Kennedy stood poised to deploy federal troops, however, he learned that Governor Patterson had proclaimed martial law. Minutes later, the church was surrounded by Alabama National Guardsmen and Montgomery police officers.

Believing their rescuers to be federal troops, King and his fellow ministers stressed to the congregation the enormous significance of federal forces being dispatched to stop a lynch mob. Their mistake became apparent, however, when the prolonged service ended after midnight. Governor Patterson had sent orders that no one should leave the church. Keen to minimize the state-federal confrontation, Bobby Kennedy had withdrawn the federal marshals. The congregation remained trapped. Phoning the Attorney-General, King asked angrily what kind of justice could there be in a land that allowed churchgoers to be first terrorized, and then forced to huddle all night in a building with broken glass on the floor from its shattered windows? This was a betrayal. Beset with his own worries, and weary from a night of crisis management, Kennedy forcefully reminded King that US marshals had just saved his life. Recognizing the futility of further recriminations, King resigned himself to the task of organizing the congregation's sleeping arrangements. Nevertheless, his words lingered with Kennedy. When an equally irate Governor Patterson phoned to blame Kennedy for the day's violence, the Attorney-General demanded guarantees of protection. The National Guard could ensure the safety of everyone, except Martin King, Patterson declared, because any suggestion that he had protected the most despised man in Alabama would be politically suicidal. At 4.30 a.m. the first groups left the church in National Guard trucks. Afterwards, Fred Shuttlesworth spoke jokingly of enjoying Patterson's special protection (Branch 1988: 462-65).

The question of how to complete the Freedom Ride remained. The Nashville contingent not only insisted on continuing into Mississippi, they expected King to join them. Wyatt Walker argued that as a fund raiser and racial statesman King was too important to risk but, when the students consulted Ella Baker, she dismissed this as Walker just worrying "about his little group." King somewhat lamely pointed out that he was still on probation, to which several students retorted that they were as well. Needled by their persistence, King declared: "I think I should choose the time and place of my Golgotha." Some of the students found King's comparison of himself to Christ pompous and tasteless and they nicknamed him "de Lawd" (Branch 1988: 466-68).

When King told a press conference that the "Freedom Riders must develop the quiet courage of dying for a cause," and then waved them off on a bus bound for Jackson, Mississippi, he compounded SNCC's growing ambivalence towards him (Garrow 1988: 159). Always ready to contest King's insistence on non-violence, Robert Williams sent King a bitter telegram from Monroe. It read:

> The cause of human decency and black liberation demands that you physically ride the buses with our gallant Freedom Riders. No sincere leader asks his followers to make sacrifices that he himself will not make. You are a phony. Gandhi was always in the forefront, suffering with his people. If you are the leader of this nonviolent Movement lead the way by example.
>
> (Tyson 1999: 246)

Abandoned by the Mahatma of Montgomery, the students prepared to ride, unaware that Justice Department negotiations with the Alabama and Mississippi state authorities had produced an unsavory agreement. It minimized the likelihood of further mob violence, but also ensured that all Riders were summarily arrested and unconstitutionally imprisoned. With a heavily armed escort and extensive roadside and aerial reconnaissance, the bus sped to Jackson. Leading the group, James Lawson complained that such protection contradicted the essence of nonviolence, which required the Riders to "accept the violence and the hate, [to] absorb it without returning it." A final personal appeal from one of the new Riders induced James Farmer – perhaps in deliberate contrast to King – to set aside his responsibilities as head of CORE and leap aboard a second bus from Montgomery even before the first bus had completed its journey. News of this second contingent shook Bobby Kennedy, who had assumed that extraordinary, protective measures would be needed only once. Fresh reports of a third group of Riders gathering in Montgomery – this time including William Sloane Coffin, Yale University's chaplain – confirmed that the headline-grabbing controversy would continue. Kennedy urged a "cooling-off period" and warned the public that future Rides would probably attract self-serving publicity-seekers (Branch 1988: 469-75).

The "Jail, Not Bail" policy adopted by the Freedom Riders in Jackson added to the Attorney-General's problems. In frustration, he phoned King to recommend the campaign's suspension. He could not understand why the Riders refused bail. Reiterating Lawson's point that the armed convoy contradicted the Rides' purpose, King explained that the protesters felt that they "must use their lives and bodies to right a wrong. Our conscience tells us that the law is wrong and we must resist, but we have a moral obligation to accept the penalty." A dismayed Kennedy insisted that the government would not be swayed by what looked to him like blackmail. "The fact that they stay in jail," he snapped, "is not going to have the slightest effect on me." Exasperated, King became sarcastic: "Perhaps it would help if students came down here by the hundreds – by the hundreds of thousands." To which Kennedy replied: "The country belongs to you as much as me. You can determine what's best just as well as I can, but don't make statements that sound like a threat. That's not the way to deal with us" (Branch 1988: 475).

Pausing to allow both of them to regain their composure, King tried to convey his own difficulties as an African American spokesman. "It's difficult to understand the position of oppressed people," he said. They needed an outlet, and Kennedy should appreciate that the nonviolent Movement offered a creative and moral way out, one that was "not tied to black supremacy or Communism, but to the plight of the oppressed." He should acknowledge that African Americans had "made no gains without pressure" and help King to keep that pressure "moral, legal, and peaceful." Returning to the immediate issue of the imprisoned Riders, Kennedy pointed out that the problem would not be resolved in Jackson, but at a federal level, adding that he could get them out of jail, if they wanted to get out. Keen to encourage federal action, King responded diplomatically that the administration's recent actions were appreciated, but that the Riders would stay in jail. Thus, a potentially instructive exchange concluded (Garrow 1988: 159-60).

Moral advocates of nonviolence at this stage stressed its educational role, suggesting in a Gandhian fashion that, when confronted with the true nature of their evil actions, oppressors would begin a process of repentance and reform. In Alabama and Mississippi, there was little sign of penitence in the summer of 1961. More evident within the Movement was the fact that nonviolent direct action instilled a new self-respect, as well as a growing belief that, by its forceful and dramatic demonstration of injustice, it moved spectators away from a morally neutral stance. But the latter shift seemed slow and partial. On May 25, as Jackson city police hurried a second wave of Freedom Riders into custody, John F. Kennedy told Congress about the unfolding battle for freedom across the globe without once referring to the civil rights struggle within the American union itself. Briefed by Bobby Kennedy, that day's *Washington Post* reported that the Freedom Riders' decision to stay in jail was just "good propaganda for America's enemies." An equally unsympathetic *New York Times* greeted King's announcement on May 26 that the Freedom Rides would shortly resume with full force by declaring: "Non-violence that deliberately provokes violence is a logical contradiction." As Taylor Branch notes, this was the last time the Freedom Rides made the *Times*'s front page. By June, a Gallup poll reported that 63 percent of Americans disapproved of them (Branch 1988: 477-78). The soul of America, to use SCLC's motto, was proving slow to redeem.

At the same time, King remained aware that African American grievances were far from confined to the South. CORE activists, mobilized in support of the Freedom Rides, also embraced direct action to protest against job and housing discrimination in the North. South Chicago's Woodlawn Organization conducted their own "freedom ride" to city hall, demanding "better housing," "jobs," and as a sign of restiveness against Mayor Daley's machine politics, the "vote." King also realized that a renewed hard-line in the Cold War threatened domestic priorities. After Kennedy's botched Bay of Pigs invasion of Cuba, he wrote privately that Americans did not understand the global revolution that was taking place against colonialism, dictatorship, and exploitation. Even Kennedy's seemingly progressive impulses, like the Peace Corps, would only succeed, he wrote elsewhere, if it strove to work with the underprivileged and not simply *for* them in a paternalistic neo-colonialist way (Jackson 2007: 136-37; 130).

Voting Rights And The Growth Of Civil Rights Field Work

King's remark that gains never come without pressure was vindicated. Keen to resolve the embarrassing situation in Jackson, Robert Kennedy petitioned the Interstate Commerce Commission to issue a ruling requiring all licensed carriers to provide desegregated terminal facilities. Hounded by Justice Department officials almost daily from May 29 onwards, the ICC issued a desegregation order on September 22 requiring compliance by November 1. Since the ICC normally took years to formulate its regulations, Branch views this as "a bureaucratic miracle." King himself applauded the ICC ruling as "a remarkable victory and one which would not have come without the national media coverage sparked by the Freedom Rides" (Branch 1988: 478; Oates 1994: 178).

The tendency of nonviolent campaigns to escalate into headline-grabbing national crises prompted the administration to encourage civil rights organizations to switch their focus back to voter registration, a line advocated at an earlier March 6 meeting with civil rights leaders to which King was not invited. Sensitive to the hostility the SCLC leader aroused, Bobby Kennedy and Burke Marshall had instead met King and Stanley Levison for an off-the-record discussion in a private dining room at the Mayflower Hotel in early

April. Marshall stressed that *in law* the Justice Department was best placed to move on the issue of voting rights. King welcomed such initiatives and promised to step up SCLC's efforts.

By the summer of 1961, the SCLC was better placed for a campaign to increase the Southern black vote. Organizationally, a major development was its acquisition of the Citizenship Education Program from the Highlander Folk School. The Tennessee-based Folk School had been a thorn in the side of the Southern establishment since its formation in 1933. Its focus had been the union drives that had produced the Congress of Industrial Organizations, but organized labor had severed its ties in the late 1940s when Highlander refused to follow the CIO's policy of excluding communists. As one of the few places in the South that would host interracial meetings, Highlander was soon at the forefront of efforts to achieve school desegregation – a stance that confirmed its pariah status for white supremacists. When King attended Highlander's 25th anniversary celebrations in 1958, he was photographed seated next to a deliberately planted Communist Party member and the photograph was placed on billboards across the South with the caption: "King at Communist training school." Highlander was predictably targeted during the white South's "Massive Resistance" campaign. State authorities raided the school, closing it on spurious charges in 1960.

While vainly seeking to reverse this outcome through the courts, Highlander's director Myles Horton arranged the Citizenship Education Program's transfer. Developed to enable black South Carolinians to pass the literacy test required of potential voters, the CEP had recently been tried in coastal Georgia and northern Alabama as well (Ling 1995: 399-422). Impressed with this work, a Northern charitable foundation, the Marshall Field Foundation, had awarded the project a grant of $26,000 to train individuals to return home to run Citizenship Schools of their own.

As well as training and teacher expenses, the grant paid the salary of a program director. Highlander had already hired a black Congregationalist minister, Andrew Young, to take this role. Already in her sixties, Septima P. Clark, Highlander's director of workshops and a veteran black activist from Charleston, South Carolina, also joined the SCLC under this separately funded scheme. Less experienced in the field than Mrs. Clark, Wyatt

Walker's protégé, Dorothy Cotton was hired to scour the South for potential teachers. Teacher training would take place at a Congregationalist facility, the Dorchester Center, near Savannah, Georgia. Once program graduates had established their classes, both Walker and Young were convinced that their Citizenship Schools would give the SCLC a vastly expanded "trained local leadership" (Garrow 1988: 161, 164; Fairclough 1987: 68-70; Cotton 2012).

The SCLC's new program meshed nicely with the Kennedy administration's push for the Movement to concentrate on voter registration work. The administration induced liberal foundations to fund what became the Voter Education Project via the Atlanta-based Southern Regional Council. Quite apart from the considerable appeal of money for the cash-strapped civil rights organizations, the Justice Department in the summer of 1961 gave Movement representatives the impression that they would enjoy a greater degree of federal protection if they engaged in voter registration work rather than demonstrations. To members of the Nashville students' movement, who remained wedded to James Lawson's dream of a nonviolent army, and who had learned as Freedom Riders that the Kennedy priority was to maintain order rather than secure justice, the project seemed designed to produce the "cooling-off" period, which they had refused to grant in May. As an observer, King attended a heated SNCC meeting at Highlander in mid-August 1961. Asked his opinion, the apostle of non-violence spoke in favor of voter registration work. SNCC's more trusted mentor, Ella Baker, brokered a compromise by suggesting the creation of two wings: one for direct action, headed by Diane Nash, and another for voter registration, under Charles Jones (Fairclough 1987: 83).

Baker suspected that, in terms of the white reaction that they would elicit in the Deep South, the distinction between registration work and demonstrations was academic, and SNCC's first field worker, Robert Moses, soon corroborated this view. Under joint SCLC-SNCC sponsorship, his efforts to register local African Americans to vote in McComb, Mississippi, met intense, and frequently violent, opposition. Wherever young SNCC activists went, local people were apt to call them Freedom Riders; and, true to their reputation, they sparked confrontations. Such drama convinced community elders that the newcomers were dangerous, but simultaneously made them glamorous heroes to the young. Whether demonstrations began because SNCC activists remained committed to direct action or because local youngsters yearned to emulate their new idols, they complicated the task of voter registration. Consequently, older local leaders complained about SNCC's lack of discipline. Joined in McComb by some genuine Freedom Riders after their release from Parchman Penitentiary, Moses found his slow efforts to secure communal trust overturned by a sit-in that resulted in the arrest of several local teenagers and their subsequent exclusion from high school (Branch 1988: 512-14).

Another SNCC group went to Robert Williams's hometown of Monroe, North Carolina, to see if they could use nonviolence to end its escalating racial crisis. Williams's followers did not welcome this intrusion, but Williams himself "saw it as an opportunity to show that what King and them were preaching was bullshit" (Tyson 1999: 266). Within days, the situation in Monroe had deteriorated to the verge of open race warfare as the sight of interracial protesters prompted whites to threaten a pogrom, and Williams to organize armed black resistance. Accused of kidnapping a white couple who had driven provocatively into the black district, Williams was forced to flee to Canada. From there, Cuban agents spirited him to Havana. Most of the SNCC group were in jail, from where they appealed to the SCLC. Wyatt Walker agreed that SCLC would cover SNCC legal costs but only if SNCC followed his orders. He then went to Monroe personally, where he was beaten almost senseless while waiting to see the sheriff. Despite this, Walker's high-handed manner drew more resentment than gratitude from the SNCC group. Neither organization had yet mastered the skills needed to enter a community and conduct an effective mass campaign. Their difficulties suggested the need for caution but, as Williams's flight from Monroe indicated, tensions in the South were extremely high.

The Albany Campaign

Albany, Georgia, was the setting for the first mass protest campaign of the classic Civil Rights Movement, surpassing the Bus Boycott, sit-ins, and Freedom Rides in the range and scale of participation; and highlighting the development of the Movement since 1956. Then, a black community had united to stay off the segregated buses, but now the challenge was greater: to persuade virtually an entire community to march to jail, while simultaneously preventing the crisis escalating into a Monroe-style shootout. Fresh from the brutalities of McComb, two SNCC field workers, Charles Sherrod and Cordell Reagon, arrived in Albany to launch a voter registration drive. The old cotton town, with its population of 56,000 people, roughly half of them African American, seemed to epitomize the old Southern politics of courthouse cliques, sustained by deference, patronage, and, if local whites deemed it necessary, unpunished violence. Not to provoke trouble had become the unspoken aim of many black residents. Even before demonstrations erupted, local black leaders viewed the SNCC pair with suspicion, and administrators at Albany State College tried to keep them off campus. A few members of the black elite, such as osteopath William Anderson, property developer Slater King, and his attorney brother C.B. King, were sympathetic, but most recommended running them out of town. Tom Chatmon feared that these Freedom Riders would drag his Youth Council members into suicidal demonstrations. He and Marion Page represented the dominant NAACP faith that negotiation and the legal process would gradually change their city, and the fear that protest would only make matters worse (Branch 1988: 525-26).

As a compromise, a joint SNCC-NAACP Youth Council test of Albany's compliance with the ICC ruling requiring desegregation of interstate transport facilities was scheduled for November 1. Forewarned, Albany's police ordered nine local students to leave the bus station before they had even entered the white waiting room. Tame by Movement standards, the incident nonetheless encouraged more youths to attend SNCC meetings at Shiloh Baptist Church. With the pressure for action building, seven Albany organizations plus SNCC formed the Albany Movement on November 17. In addition to desegregation of the bus and train stations and all municipal facilities, the meeting called for fair employment and, prompted by a recent shooting in neighboring Baker County, an end to police brutality. It was an ambitious program that the group hoped to achieve by negotiation rather than protest. In both scope and method this proved naive (Fairclough 1987: 87).

The divisions within the Albany Movement, its failure to identify a clear target for its campaign, and its misgivings about protests were weaknesses that Albany's Police Chief Laurie Pritchett exploited. Initially, youth action crystallized community support. Five young blacks were arrested testing desegregation at the bus station on November 22 and their trial prompted a prayer pilgrimage of nearly 600 people to City Hall. Seeking to maintain the momentum, the SNCC agreed to send an interracial group of Freedom Riders from Atlanta, provided the better-off SCLC bought the tickets. On December 10, Chief Pritchett arrested the Riders on charges of disorderly conduct, obstruction, and failure to obey an officer – all offenses ostensibly unrelated to segregation. Pritchett knew that the City Commissioners expected firmness. On the day of the trial, December 12, he arrested 265 members of a protest march to City Hall. When a further 200 arrests followed the next day, Charles Sherrod enthused that they would soon fill the jails. But older Albany Movement leaders already fretted that cash bail bond requirements had consumed almost all of black Albany's spare cash. Meanwhile, Pritchett quietly arranged to ship prisoners to other jails within a thirty-mile radius.

The head of the Albany Movement, William Anderson, believed they needed outside help. State and regional NAACP officials told him their financial support depended on the Movement becoming an NAACP operation. When Anderson then rang his old college friend Ralph Abernathy to see if King would visit Albany, local NAACP stalwarts feared that their organization would be simultaneously marginalized and burdened with litigation costs. In town as one of the Freedom Riders, SNCC executive secretary James Forman also opposed calling in Dr. King like some kind of messiah, since this would undermine what he regarded as a potentially strong "people's movement." But since Forman and SNCC itself were newcomers, his argument that the Movement needed to rely on local resources proved unpersuasive. Anderson invited King to address a mass meeting on Friday December 15. Even the threat of King's visit seemed to soften white Albany's position. Mayor Kelley told a Thursday press conference that he was always ready to discuss "problems with responsible *local* [emphasis added] Negro leadership." That afternoon, an informally sanctioned, bi-racial negotiating committee met clandestinely and made progress on train and bus station desegregation. White officials were even prepared to release local demonstrators without bail, but they remained determined to make an example of the outside troublemakers. When King's visit was not cancelled, the City Commission quickly withdrew all concessions (Garrow 1988: 181-82).

The nearly 33-year-old King who came to Albany was more worldly-wise than the novice leader who had accepted the MIA presidency just six years earlier. A growing awareness of his leadership role had made him a more formal, public figure, who sometimes appeared "remote" on first meeting. Interviewed in London for the BBC's *"Face to Face"* series at the end of October 1961, he spoke of the "inner sense of security" that enabled him to endure the daily constraints of being a symbol of African American aspirations in general and the Southern freedom struggle in particular (Garrow 1988: 164-65, 171). The relentless travel required of a national figure meant that he was rarely at home. When there, he would throw himself into his children's play, as if to compensate, rolling on the floor and chasing them, until the house was turned upside down. It was left to his wife Coretta to say "Enough!" During his frequent absences, she had to raise the children, maintain the home, and live her own, profoundly constrained, symbolic role as the preacher-leader's wife. Sometimes she would tell close friends about the pressures: the knowledge of constant danger, the regular death threats, and her nervousness at every news bulletin (Oates 1994: 181-82). The coming years brought little respite.

By the time of Albany, King had some grounds for confidence. The Freedom Rides had shown that dramatic press coverage could spur an outcry large enough to compel positive action, even from a Kennedy administration that wished to remain noncommittal. Over the summer of 1961, King had tried to persuade the Kennedys that their own interests were best served by backing the Civil Rights Movement, building on the positive steps of the ICC ruling and the planned Voter Education Project. Rebuffed, he ended the year seeking labor allies. On December 10, in a major address to the AFL-CIO convention in Florida, he argued that self-interest made organized labor the Movement's natural ally. Alabama's continuing libel action against the SCLC and the *New York Times* could set a fresh precedent for harassing labor organizers in the largely un-unionized South, King warned. He also explained how the sit-ins drew on the CIO's sit-down strikes of the 1930s and, most contentiously, he urged the unions to tackle their own segregationist practices. A. Philip Randolph's public complaints about such continuing discrimination had recently earned him a formal censure from the AFL-CIO's Executive Council, but King's speech brought the convention to its feet. The ovation enhanced King's prestige in the eyes of professional politicians and he entered Albany on a high (Branch 1988: 538-39).

On December 15, black Albany gave the young minister a still more enthusiastic reception. Over 1,500 people had crammed themselves into the two churches of Shiloh and Mount Zion on either side of Whitney Avenue. As King arrived, the two congregations were singing the song "Freedom," adapted from the spiritual "Amen," and the avenue echoed to the amplified sound:

FREE-DOM
FREE-DOM
FREE-DOM, FREE-DOM, FREE-DOM!

As King made his way to Shiloh's pulpit, the congregations dramatically invoked his name:

Martin King says FREE-DOM
Martin King says FREE-DOM
Martin King says FREE-DOM
FREE-DOM FREE-DOM!

A young soloist, Rutha Harris, then began a new song, "Woke Up This Morning With My Mind Set On Freedom." As the audience took up her call, the fervor of the all-enveloping sound mesmerized Pat Watters, a white reporter, and even King felt the rapture of the occasion, comparable to the best Montgomery boycott meetings. Experienced in such matters, he perceived that the people needed first to be calmed rather than exhorted. And so he began by explaining how Albany was linked to the decolonization struggles in Africa, and how nonviolence applied Christian ethics to global politics.

Having soberly established the grand historical tableau to which these ordinary people now belonged, King quickened his pace to ready them for battle. "They can put you in a dungeon," he enthused, "and transform you to glory." To loud calls from the audience, he invited the upturned faces to say to the white man: "We will win you with the power of our capacity to endure." Using his customary rhetorical litany of questions – "How long will we have to suffer injustices?" – and sonorous answers – "Not long" – he made faith so real that the two congregations spontaneously sang his final phrase: "We Shall Overcome." On cue, the anthem of the Civil Rights Movement began *sotto voce*. King gently nurtured the unity of his people in this afterglow. "Walk together, children," he said fondly, "Don't ya weary. There's a great camp meeting coming." As he stepped from the podium, the sound of "We Shall Overcome" increased in volume. A trembling William Anderson pledged that the Albany Movement would keep moving, and to crown the evening, with tears in his eyes, he invited Dr. King to lead the next morning's protest march (Branch 1988: 545-47).

This was more than Martin had bargained for, but there was no dignified way of refusing. As he later wrote: "I didn't come to be arrested. I had planned to stay a day or so and return home after giving counsel" (Carson 1998: 154). The next day's march went ahead with King, Ralph Abernathy, and Anderson to the fore. Through the drizzle, Chief Pritchett challenged the approaching marchers. "Do you have a written permit to parade or demonstrate?" he shouted, well aware that they did not. Surely, responded King, going to City Hall to pray did not require a permit? When the marchers did not disperse, Pritchett ordered their arrest (Branch 1988: 548-49). Deploying men on either side, he shepherded the demonstrators into an alley near the jail and began processing them for shipment to outlying jails. With an armed escort for extra security, he dispatched King, Abernathy, and Anderson to the Sumter County Jail in Americus in his own car.

Over a year earlier, in great trepidation, King had been driven through the dark to Reidsville. With Abernathy beside him, he now faced imprisonment calmly, but, according to historian Taylor Branch, William Anderson did not. The intense emotions of the last twenty-four hours were too much. Looking at King in their dingy cell, an overwrought Anderson saw his Lord. "You are Jesus," he proclaimed, and gazing round at the prison's other occupants, he added: "And we are the saints. The hosts that no man can number." Although Abernathy and King tried to calm him, Anderson's hallucinations continued through the night. Close colleagues had long suspected that Abernathy's snores could stir the dead, and each time they awoke Anderson, he saw fresh visions. An understandably groggy King told reporters the next day that he expected to spend Christmas in jail, and hoped that thousands would join him. Abernathy posted bail at first light, hurrying to Atlanta to rally the campaign nationally. King urged the still deranged Anderson to go, too. Horrified at this request to repudiate his Lord, Anderson declared: "I am no Simon Peter" (Branch 1988: 550-51).

Wyatt Walker announced that the SCLC would commit all its resources to Albany. There must be further protests now that King's arrest had drawn greater media attention. Nationally, he urged supporters to send their donations to the SCLC in Atlanta rather than to the Albany Movement and, imperiously, he took charge of the next mass meeting. Appearing on television from Atlanta, Abernathy reinforced the impression of an SCLC takeover, deepening suspicions that it intended to fill its own coffers via headlines generated by black Albany's predicament. Newly arrived in town, Ella Baker joined her SNCC protégés in encouraging local people to reassert themselves (Fairclough 1987: 89). The press quoted one Albany Movement leader as saying: "Why can't these national organizations understand that this is a local Movement? It is only for and by Albany Negroes. We do not want to make a national Movement out of it" (Garrow 1988: 185).

Anderson's deputy, Marion Page, met independently with Police Chief Pritchett and effectively agreed a truce. Page's priority was the release of the imprisoned, some of whom were adults with pressing family commitments. Pritchett's priority was King's departure. The verbal agreement they concluded suggested that a suspension of protests would secure desegregation of the bus and train terminals and the mass release of prisoners. Albany's City Commission would then consider other African American grievances at its January meeting. The Albany Movement's attorney, C.B. King, wanted written undertakings and, when informed of the negotiations, Dr. King, too, urged this course. Others, however, felt that the white leadership would honor its word. Still skeptical, Dr. King recommended that the local movement should swiftly issue a public statement detailing the agreement. After filing bail, King and a still shaky Anderson arrived to hear Page announce the agreement. Reminded by reporters that only forty-eight hours earlier, he had spoken of staying in jail through Christmas, King explained that he did not want to "stand in the way of meaningful negotiations" (Branch 1988: 556). Walker ensured that Anderson, whom reporters described as "haggard," escaped close questioning and went home to recuperate. Only Branch mentions his breakdown.

Disguising his misgivings, King boasted that the deal "thoroughly integrated" the bus and train stations, swept away bail requirements for hundreds of protesters, and set the stage for a bi-racial committee to tackle the whole segregation issue. But even as he spoke, Chief Pritchett was denying his every claim. Pritchett insisted that Albany had already complied with the November ICC ruling on interstate travel facilities, with police stationed only to deter clashes. The released prisoners would be brought to trial in due course; no charges had been dropped. As for the bi-racial committee, the council at its next meeting would consider a proposal for such a body (like any other proposal). The "outside agitators" had won nothing. On December 19, 1961, the *New York Times* called Albany "one of the most stunning defeats" of King's career (Branch 1988: 556-57).

Who was responsible for this rout? David Lewis says SNCC, since it encouraged local leaders to settle in order to be rid of the SCLC (Lewis 1978: 154). Taylor Branch also points the finger. Press coverage of these internal squabbles, especially a *Time* article of January 12, 1962, he declares, created SNCC's "public identity more than all its previous campaigns" (Branch 1988: 557). Adam Fairclough, on the other hand, contends that the local leaders' blunders were more important than SNCC's sniping. Having nearly secured a deal with Mayor Kelley before King arrived, they mistakenly assumed that city authorities would make further concessions when faced with the prospect of a campaign involving Dr. King himself. Instead, fresh demands and national publicity stiffened the Commissioners' resolve, and then local black leaders panicked, becoming particularly anxious over reports of dreadful, overcrowded jail conditions (Fairclough 1987: 89-90). Wyatt Walker's imperious manner did not help, of course, nor did SNCC's desire to escape from SCLC's shadows, and nor did the media's tendency to accept Pritchett's version of events. The scholarly consensus, then, is that King was less responsible for the Albany defeat than most. He deserved his family Christmas at home in Atlanta.

Although Albany's disappointing outcome was primarily the fault of others, it still indicated the immaturity of King's leadership. Ironically, the chief flaw was that, despite Walker's posturing, neither King nor the SCLC had the capacity to take over. King was poorly briefed before coming to Albany and failed to foresee the need to prepare for a sustained involvement. Even the negative press coverage of the setback did not immediately prompt a review of the SCLC's strategy. When its board met in early January, the main initiatives were to hire a new public relations director and to approach some SNCC members about the possibility of joining the SCLC's field staff. The latter move was due more to the prospect of VEP funding than any recognition that the SCLC had failed in Albany because it had no real roots there.

Albany's racial situation deteriorated in the New Year. The "honorable" truce unraveled. Cash bail bonds were not refunded and the Albany Movement retaliated by boycotting downtown stores. The arrest of a black student for refusing to move to the back of a city bus triggered a bus boycott, and the City Commission greeted formal petitions of racial grievances with prevarication; in part, because it was divided over how to respond. On February 27, King and Abernathy returned to face trial for their part in the December 16 march, but Judge A.N. Durden postponed his verdict. This meant that others similarly charged remained free only on bond, and so were reluctant to jeopardize their money by engaging in further protests. Only the boycotts attracted mass support and, in the face of white intransigence, demands for a bi-racial committee were dropped. When King, at last, returned for sentencing in July, the Albany Movement looked to him more desperately than it had in December. Unfortunately, black hopes were matched by Police Chief Pritchett's preparations.

From reading about nonviolence, Pritchett knew that, when Durden sentenced King and Abernathy to a $178 fine or forty-five days in jail on July 10, they would choose jail in order to draw public attention. He also recognized that Albany's authorities would face considerable external pressure as long as King remained. Pritchett maintained cordial relations with various local black leaders, notably Marion Page with whom he had negotiated the failed December agreement. Anxious to avoid a racial con-flagration, Page spoke almost nightly with Pritchett; and additional informants enabled the police chief to boast that he could learn details of any Movement meeting within hours (Ricks 1984: 13). But he needed no intelligence network to see how King's return rejuvenated the Albany Movement. "As much as we may disagree with MLK about the way he and SCLC do things," SNCC's Bill Hansen reported, "one has to admit that he can cause more hell to be raised by being in jail one night than anyone else could if they bombed city hall" (Fairclough 1987: 101-2).

In Washington, the press asked: what would President Kennedy do on King's behalf? Surely a President could do more than a mere nominee had done in 1960? The official line was that the President had asked his brother for a full report. Privately, he instructed Burke Marshall to speak to Mrs. King and to Albany's commissioners. On this occasion, he chose not to phone Mrs. King himself. Instead, he took a call from Albany's most prominent white citizen, James Gray, an old family friend and chairman of Georgia's Democratic Party. During the December crisis, Gray had used his local television channel to rant that King's activism was "a highly productive practice for the acquisition of a buck." As the July sentencing hearing approached, he denounced the Movement afresh in the *Albany Herald*, the newspaper he owned, and turned to his friend Jack Kennedy for help. The President explained that he could not intervene formally, but advised Gray to consult the Attorney-General. Bobby Kennedy, in turn, endorsed Gray's wish that King's stay in Albany be transitory (Branch 1988: 553-54, 600, 603-5).

Unaware of these consultations, King and Abernathy learned only that an "unknown well-dressed Negro man" had paid their fines, just two days into their sentences. Vainly King protested, while Pritchett smugly instructed two deputies to drive the SCLC leader to Shiloh Church. There, King lamely complained about "subtle and conniving tactics." His anticlimactic release weakened an already fragile movement. "The people are confused," Hansen reported: "Now that MLK is out of jail they don't have anything to rally around" (Fairclough 1987: 102). To SNCC's dismay, King did not immediately seek a fresh arrest. Bobby Kennedy publicly welcomed King's release, saying that it "should make it possible for the citizens of Albany to resolve their differences ... in a less tense atmosphere" (Branch 1988: 607). Having lied about who paid the fines, Pritchett raised black hopes again by implying that the city might concede bus and railroad station desegregation, and drop charges against bailed protesters. When this promise proved as empty as Pritchett's previous ones, the Albany Movement belatedly insisted on face-to-face talks with the City Commissioners.

Branded inept by the press, King had to find a way to prove himself yet still maintain his fund-raising for SCLC. City authorities consistently portrayed his involvement as the obstacle to negotiations and the Justice Department chimed in that only local negotiations would solve Albany's problems. By July 17, even SCLC members like Andrew Young admitted that rumors were circulating that King "was going 'chicken'" (Fairclough 1987: 102). His release contrasted starkly with a pregnant Diane Nash's decision to serve a lengthy prison term in Mississippi. "It is time for us to mean what we say," she had announced pointedly (Garrow 1988: 202). In the circumstances, King seemed set to go to jail again in Albany. But, on July 20, the first scheduled day for renewed demonstrations, US District Court Judge J. Robert Elliott issued an order banning protest marches. A strident segregationist and recent Kennedy appointee, Elliott symbolized the administration's use of traditional patronage to court Southern Congressional support.

King spent most of the day discussing how to respond to this grave blow. SNCC members argued that the march must proceed. It would take far too long to secure a judicial reversal and, if King allowed Elliott's order to stall the Movement, other racist judges would employ the same tactic. By reinstating the ponderous tempo of the courts, they would, in effect, rob the Movement of its principal resource: the right to protest. Others urged compliance. Robert Kennedy phoned to remind King that by disobeying a federal court order, he would place himself on the same footing as the countless segregationists who sought any excuse to disobey federal desegregation rulings. Burke Marshall added that if King marched, he would be jailed for contempt of court rather than any breach of segregation law, and worse still, he stressed, King would undercut the Movement's ability to appeal to federal authority. Reluctantly, King decided to comply until the order was overturned (Branch 1988: 610-11).

From a back room at Shiloh Church, King watched as a local preacher, not named in Elliott's order, rallied well over a hundred people to follow him in procession to City Hall. There were 160 arrests that night, but little pandemonium to report. Pritchett had drilled his officers to use the minimum of force in public, preventing the movement from exposing the full brutality of the racist social order before the watching press. His shipment of demonstrators to neighboring county facilities not only ensured that Albany's jail did not fill, it also meant that ill-treatment occurred off camera. Marion King, the pregnant wife of Albany leader Slater King, was beaten while visiting prisoners at the Mitchell County Jail; she later miscarried. By the time Judge Elbert Tuttle, an Eisenhower appointee to the federal appeals court in Atlanta, vacated Elliott's temporary restraining order on July 24, black anger at this outrage jeopardized King's nonviolent plans.

Around forty marchers left Mount Zion Baptist Church for City Hall that evening, but a far larger group of black onlookers followed and threw rocks and bottles when the arrests began. To the national press, this disorder seemed momentarily to justify Judge Elliot's order. "Did you see them 'nonviolent' rocks?" Chief Pritchett quipped. Aware that further black violence would provide a pretext for repression and anxious to protect his reputation, King suspended demonstrations and announced a "day of penance." Although this drew directly on Gandhian precedents, it nonetheless infuriated SNCC. The violence against Marion King that lay behind the evening clashes was further obscured, and the Movement's momentum was halted again in what was already a spasmodic campaign. As SNCC members excoriated King for his tactical retreat, the *Atlanta Daily World*, the South's only black daily, carried an editorial urging him to withdraw from Albany entirely (Branch 1988: 618-20).

Albany's black citizens were weary. When King, Abernathy, Anderson, and seven others were jailed on July 27, the evening mass meeting generated just fifteen volunteers (Garrow 1988: 211). Two days later, despite further police brutality, the number of people willing to protest had fallen to five, and Pritchett shrewdly did not even bother to arrest them. After all, he told reporters, they were too few to disturb anyone. Outfoxed, King and other Movement leaders railed against the federal government's moral equivocation. At his August 1 press conference, President Kennedy called on Albany's city council to negotiate, pointing out that currently he was preparing to negotiate with the Soviets in Geneva. Despite this supportive comment, Attorney-General Bobby Kennedy privately told civil rights groups the next day that a locally negotiated solution was needed and, before talks began, King would have to depart (Fairclough 1987: 105).

With protest fervor visibly diminishing, the campaign sputtered to an end. On August 8, a sick and exhausted King testified at hearings to determine whether Judge Elliott should issue a more permanent federal injunction against the Albany Movement's activities. The Justice Department's active opposition to such a move persuaded Elliott to announce an indefinite recess. Two days later, King and Abernathy faced State Judge Durden over their July 27 arrests. From the stand, King announced that he would leave Albany if this would ensure good faith negotiations, and, by suspending King's sixty-day sentence and $200 fine, Durden opened the way for his departure. That evening, King left for Atlanta, promising to return if no progress was made (Garrow 1988: 214-15).

Warned that federal courts would ultimately require the desegregation of all publicly owned amenities, hardliners on the City Commission closed Albany's parks, swimming pools, and library. To obfuscate the issue, municipal ordinances requiring segregation in private facilities, such as hotels and restaurants, were repealed. But everyone knew that local police would arrest blacks for trespass or breach of the peace, if they sought service. Lacking local volunteers, the SCLC resumed protests on August 28 with a "prayer pilgrimage" by Northern ministers and rabbis. Despite giving Chief Pritchett what he termed "some of my most tiring times," this clerical influx could not shift the City Commission.

William Anderson announced that the Albany Movement would now concentrate on voter registration and run a black candidate in the next municipal elections. They were re-grouping for the long haul. King and the SCLC supported this move through its Citizenship Schools and SNCC staff also remained. But the mass protest campaign was over. Visiting the city two years later, shortly after the 1964 Civil Rights Act had made the desegregation of public accommodations a legal requirement, journalist Reese Cleghorn described Albany as "a monument to white supremacy" (Fairclough 1987: 106).

Explaining The Albany Defeat

On August 18, 1962, the *New York Times* identified four factors behind the failure of SCLC's most extensive campaign to date. Chief Pritchett's skillful opposition headed the list. He had recognized that the nonviolent Movement would try to "fill the jails" and so he negotiated extra capacity. The Movement ran out of protesters before he ran out of jails. Looking back, one of King's lieutenants, C.T. Vivian, conceded: "Pritchett was a pretty smart boy. He wasn't just a dumb policeman." Having King in jail drew hostile attention to Albany and Pritchett twice precipitated King's release. But these successful tactics rested on two elements that the *Times* did not mention. Consistent with its earlier willingness to allow Mississippi authorities to arrest Freedom Riders as long as they maintained public order, the federal government was content to stand aside in Albany, as long as violence was kept in check. Federal inaction was partly a reflection of public concern, as shaped by press coverage. Wyatt Walker complained that Pritchett was "the darling of the press," and his success had included a public relations victory (Fairclough 1987: 108-9).

Pritchett was also aided, the *Times* believed, by the growing unity of hostile whites. The newspaper went on to stress the Movement's "internal rivalries," which Pritchett shrewdly exploited. There had been divisions in black Albany before the protests began. First, SNCC, and then SCLC, discovered that the town had "too many Uncle Toms," anxious to preserve their own status and connections with the white establishment (Oates 1994: 199). SNCC fueled recriminations by its contempt for some local

NAACP leaders and, once the Albany Movement was underway, the state and national NAACP deepened divisions by pursuing organizational preeminence. The SCLC's Wyatt Walker's imperious manner made this bad situation worse, but was regarded all the more sourly thanks to promptings from Ella Baker and SNCC leaders.

Such factionalism was compounded by what the *Times* called "tactical errors," the chief of which came in December 1961. According to historian Adam Fairclough, with King's arrival imminent, Albany Movement leaders mistakenly escalated their demands and made the City Commission more obdurate. Thereafter, tactical mistakes proliferated. With no agreed chain of command established before King and other senior figures went to jail, whites could exploit divisions and induce the fateful acceptance of an "unwritten" settlement. With hindsight, King felt that December was when victory eluded him. Renewed involvement in July 1962 spawned further dilemmas. SNCC leaders believed that King should have ensured his own rapid re-arrest after Pritchett's sneaky bail-out and that he should not have obeyed Judge Elliott's flagrantly unconstitutional injunction. In retrospect, SCLC conceded that the latter had broken their backs.

Disobeying federal court orders was destined to remain a major operational dilemma for SCLC, since cultivating a positive relationship with the federal government was integral to its strategy. Similarly, other tactical problems reflected larger strategic challenges. The SCLC eventually concluded that a basic failing of the Albany campaign was too broad a list of demands. A more targeted approach was needed to ensure morale-boosting victories. King also accepted that his spontaneous involvement had been a mistake. His national credibility was at stake wherever he became personally involved and so, strategically, he needed to select his own battlegrounds.

The South was full of communities in racial crisis by the summer of 1962. After Albany, King told his staff that he would undertake no more "rescue" missions. "I don't want to be a fireman anymore," he declared (Branch 1988: 632). It was an interesting choice of metaphor. In the coming months, King would come to realize that sadly the fires of racial discontent had to burn brightly, if the Jim Crow order was to be destroyed. What was already an emergency for African Americans had to be made into an equally compelling crisis for all Americans, most of whom remained blindly indifferent to racial injustice. King would have to ensure that he was as incendiary as his enemies alleged. Where he chose to go, "trouble" should follow. He needed what he came to call "creative tension," and in the next two years he found a way to create it.

5   Let The Children Come To Me

Birmingham, 1963

By choosing Birmingham, Alabama, as the site of SCLC's next major campaign, King deliberately confronted segregation in its heartland. Fiery preacher Fred Shuttlesworth, who led the Southern steel town's SCLC affiliate, the Alabama Christian Movement for Human Rights (ACMHR), said bluntly that Birmingham was "very close to hell itself," and he was well placed to judge (Carter 1995: 116). On Christmas night 1956, a bomb blast that literally blew the mattress out from under him, in his words, "blew him into history." Bombers attacked his church, Bethel Baptist, in a working-class district of Birmingham, three times between 1956 and 1963. When he attempted to enroll his daughters Pat and Ricky at the all-white Phillips High School in September 1957, a mob attacked him and his family with baseball bats and bicycle chains. Earlier that month, Klansmen castrated a local black man as a warning of what they would do to African American children if school desegregation proceeded. They also abducted Shuttlesworth's ACMHR associate, Reverend Charles Billups, tied him to a tree, and whipped and branded him, and all while he prayed for his persecutors (McWhorter 2001: 114-15, 124-28, 153-54). Like the Mississippi of murdered teenager Emmett Till, Birmingham's dreadful reputation gave it a special significance.

Why Birmingham?

King chose Birmingham because of Fred Shuttlesworth. Convinced that God had chosen him to fight racial injustice, the fearless preacher had targeted segregation with a mixture of boycotts, litigation, and direct action for seven years by 1963. Named among the signatories to a *New York Times* advertisement that condemned Alabama authorities for their brutal suppression of sit-in demonstrations, Shuttlesworth was convicted of libel in November 1960. Keen to show that they would collect the $500,000 damages awarded against Shuttlesworth and others, police confiscated his car. Although mounting intimidation prompted him to accept a larger pastorate in Cincinnati, Shuttlesworth visited his followers so regularly that he remained "the man most feared by southern racists." Despite this long-distance leadership, his bravery evoked extraordinary devotion. "I would follow Shuttlesworth quicker than I would Martin Luther King," declared ACMHR stalwart James Armstrong decades later, "because, to me, he was a much stronger man. Now, Martin knew how to say it; Fred know how to do it ... I've had good preachers to preach to me, but Fred has preached to me in action" (Manis 1999: 4, 255).

King also chose Birmingham because of Police Commissioner Eugene Theophilus Connor. By inflaming white opinion, Shuttlesworth's militancy in 1956-57 unintentionally resurrected this veteran segregationist's political career. Born in 1897, "Bull" Connor used his popularity as a radio announcer to win the post of Commissioner of Public Safety for the first time in 1937. Prominent in the so-called "Dixiecrat" revolt against President Truman in 1948, he had shown a natural flair for Red-baiting. However, in 1952, scandal over his affair with his young secretary interrupted the Bull's defense of segregation from the "communist conspiracy." Narrowly reelected to his former position by agitated white citizens in November 1957, Connor was determined to yield nothing to black protests. According to his wife, he saw his job as being "to keep the nigger in his place for his own good as well as the good of the city" (Manis 1999: 138). To Birmingham's lasting shame, Shuttlesworth had to lock horns with the Bull for seven years in his quest for racial justice.

When a *Baltimore Afro-American* reporter questioned the legality of Connor's systematic surveillance of the ACMHR, he retorted: "Damn the law. Down here we make our own law" (Manis 1999: 190). Ready to defend segregation at all costs, Connor and his fellow Commissioners closed the municipal parks in January 1962, after Shuttlesworth secured a court desegregation order. While using his official powers to harass blacks, Connor was equally happy to abet white vigilantes. However, when he allowed a mob to beat the Freedom Riders at Birmingham's bus station in May 1961, the negative publicity threatened future investment in the city. White business and professional leaders thereafter ceased to tolerate Connor's excesses. In late 1962, a reform faction, headed by David Vann and Charles Morgan of the Young Men's Business Club, and backed by real estate executive Sidney Smyer of the Chamber of Commerce, secured a referendum vote in favor of replacing the City Commission with a mayor and council. Connor faced political extinction unless he could secure election to the new post of mayor in March 1963 (Fairclough 1987: 113-14).

Alabama's frenzied political climate meant that removing seg-regationists like Connor would be difficult. To the acclaim of white voters, George Wallace had pledged during his successful 1962 gubernatorial campaign to block integration by personally "standing in the schoolhouse door." To cheering inaugural crowds on January 14, 1963, he shouted his defiance of any attempt to repeat in Alabama the university desegregation that the Kennedy administration had secured so dramatically in Mississippi the previous October. "I draw a line in the dust and toss the gauntlet before the feet of tyranny," Wallace proclaimed. "And I say, 'Seg-regation now! Segregation tomorrow! Segregation forever!'" (Manis 1999: 315, 333).

In counter-pursuit of his "Freedom Now," King had called upon President Kennedy to issue a "Second Emancipation Procla-mation" in May 1962, adding that he believed that "segregation will end in my lifetime." Dismayed at having to use federal mar-shals to ensure James Meredith's safe admission to the University of Mississippi that fall, Kennedy feared that the ensuing riot had alienated crucial, Southern Congressional support. It had other unintended consequences. The media spectacle of occupied Oxford helped to pass business-sponsored municipal reform in Birming-ham as insurance against precisely this kind of public relations disaster. At the same time, Kennedy's actions in Mississippi, alongside his ignoring of King's appeals, made the SCLC leader seek a battle to secure federal action. At SCLC board meetings, Fred Shuttlesworth pressed his case: "I assure you, if you come to

Birmingham, we will not only gain prestige but really shake the country." As head of SCLC's most active Alabama affiliate, he had sustained King's hopes when the Albany campaign had failed to induce Kennedy's intervention. Now, he boasted about the boycott of downtown stores, which was continuing, despite Bull Connor's spiteful suspension of a surplus food distribution program that was essential for many poor black citizens (Garrow 1988: 199). After empty courtroom victories for the last seven years, Shuttlesworth had concluded that the situation "needed something more than what we were doing" (Manis 1999: 320-21).

King responded by scheduling the SCLC's 1962 convention in Birmingham out of respect for Shuttlesworth and to spotlight the boycott of downtown stores. After Albany, he may have needed to restore his reputation, but he was still a magnet for the national media, which white Birmingham had begun to fear. The threat of King's drawing the cameras to Birmingham was enough to prompt Sidney Smyer to establish a bi-racial Senior Citizens Committee, composed of leading downtown businessmen and the more "respectable" black leaders, like millionaire A.G. Gaston and Miles College President Lucius Pitts. The white moderates feared that Connor would use any demonstrations to defend the commission system of government against their reforms (Garrow 1988: 220). The black elite sympathized with these white city fathers, but confessed that only Fred Shuttlesworth could ensure that King's visit passed uneventfully. With the convention less than a week away, downtown store owners agreed that the hated segregation signs would be removed from restrooms and water fountains. In return, Shuttlesworth agreed neither to stage demonstrations nor inflame the situation by publicizing the merchants' concessions (Manis 1999: 323-25).

The SCLC convention proceeded without drama until its closing day, September 28, 1962. Late that morning, as King was speaking, a young Nazi Party member, Roy James, left his seat in the sixth row and approached the dais. As the incredulous audience watched in stunned silence, he punched King in the face. Addressing his attacker calmly in the moments before onlookers wrestled James away, the SCLC leader stood his ground without retaliation, despite several blows. The episode demonstrated how completely King now accepted the discipline of nonviolence to which he had been introduced in 1956, and most witnesses were deeply impressed by his courage and self-control (Garrow 1988: 221).

The desegregation in place for the SCLC convention proved temporary. Using the threat of closure for minor building and fire code violations, Bull Connor pressured the store owners to revert to segregation. By canceling their charge accounts on news of integration, white customers also drained the proprietors' anemic enthusiasm for change. The downtown boycott recommenced, and Shuttlesworth warned that King and SCLC were "still on call if Birmingham needs them" (Manis 1999: 328). King was increasingly convinced that economic leverage was a major weapon in the fight for racial justice. In the autumn of 1962, while he spoke of recruiting a "nonviolent army" to promote voter registration and the desegregation of public facilities in Alabama's major cities, he also approved "Operation Breadbasket," a selective buying campaign in Atlanta to induce companies to hire more African Americans (Garrow 1988: 222-23).

Simultaneously, Shuttlesworth urged King to launch a Birmingham protest campaign during the downtown stores' crucial Christmas shopping period. However, King listened to men such as insurance executive John Drew, a friend from his Morehouse College days, and John T. Porter, pastor of the Sixth Avenue Baptist Church, who had been King's assistant minister in Montgomery. They persuaded him to wait since a postponement would help the white moderate Albert Boutwell in the mayoral contest with Bull Connor. As a poignant reminder of the virulence of Birmingham's racism, Shuttlesworth's former church, Bethel Baptist, was bombed five days later. Several children were in the church rehearsing a Christmas play and two were hospitalized with facial injuries. By telegram and in person, King vainly urged President Kennedy to take federal action in the city sometimes referred to as "Bombingham" (Manis 1999: 329).

By the New Year, King had decided to move on Birmingham. On January 3, 1963, he called a special retreat at the Dorchester Center, outside Savannah, Georgia, solely to discuss plans for the campaign. There, an inner circle of around a dozen began their deliberations by analyzing the recent Albany debacle. In Albany, "we took on all segregation," Wyatt Walker declared ruefully, "We bit off more than we could chew" (Fairclough 1987: 116).

The first lesson to be applied in Birmingham was for SCLC to choose quite deliberately to focus narrowly on those aspects of segregation where it could win. Recent events had shown both that the downtown store owners were susceptible to pressure and that African American economic influence could be mobilized. The assault on Birmingham would initially target the downtown lunch counters. But Walker insisted that it must build to a crescendo with a generalized boycott, and then mass marches to fill the jails.

The last resort would be to recruit outside sympathizers from across the country to come to Birmingham, like Freedom Riders. By publicizing Birmingham's moral bankruptcy, they would break its economic capacity to resist. In Birmingham, King argued, SCLC must not repeat the Albany mistake of attacking the political structure directly. "In Birmingham we knew in the beginning," he explained,

> that Negroes did not have enough votes to move the political power structure, but we knew that Negroes had enough money, enough buying power to make the difference between profit and loss in almost any business. So we decided to center it on the economic power structure.
>
> (Garrow 1988: 226-27)

Even the anticipated mass arrests were calculated in economic terms with Walker setting bail costs for SCLC against jail costs for the city (Branch 1988: 690).

Shuttlesworth's ACMHR and Bull Connor were fundamental to King's decision to make Birmingham his next battleground. King declared that Shuttlesworth "had proved to his people that he would not ask anyone to go where he was not willing to lead." The fanatical loyalty previously demonstrated by Shuttlesworth's ACMHR followers contrasted with the disunity and indecisiveness SCLC had encountered within Albany (Manis 1999: 331). Bull Connor, whose policing style differed sharply from the subtle ruses of Albany's Chief Pritchett, was another SCLC asset. Connor's infamous short fuse meant that he would, in Walker's words, "do something to benefit our movement. We didn't want to march after Bull was gone." A characteristically strong reaction from

Connor would grab headlines, creating just the kind of crisis to compel a reluctant Kennedy administration to intervene. As King put it: "The key to everything is federal commitment" (Garrow 1988: 228). Thus, alongside his emphasis on local economic pressure tactics, King had a national, media-orientated, political strategy.

The Campaign's Timing And Targets

King's insistence that his next campaign had to induce federal intervention reveals how his priorities and Shuttlesworth's differed. Both men wanted a national and a local victory so it was a matter of emphasis. King craved a victory with national ramifications, while his national appeal might give Shuttlesworth the local victory in Birmingham that had eluded him. Shuttlesworth told King, "If segregation is going to fall, we've got to crack Birmingham. In fact, if you can break the back of segregation in Birmingham, Alabama, then you can break the back of segregation all over the nation" (Manis 1999: 332).

The two goals were interrelated. However, in the major case study of the Birmingham campaign, Glenn Eskew argues that, over the course of the campaign, local and national goals diverged. He, in effect, indicts King for his betrayal of Shuttlesworth's hopes (Eskew 1997). Interviewed in 1990, Shuttlesworth said:

> We would not have gone through with it … had I felt in the least bit that Martin was using Birmingham to just stage something in his own interest, rather than progress in Birmingham *as well as* a victory [for the SCLC].

He stressed the synonymous nature of their goals: "Martin never gave me any indication that he was any less concerned about total and complete victory in Birmingham, Alabama, *itself*. Because victory in Birmingham, Alabama, *itself* meant victory to the nation" (Manis 1999: 335, emphasis added).

As will become clear, Shuttlesworth was not as sure of King's commitment at the climax of the Birmingham campaign as he was in later years. However, to promote unity, King and Shuttlesworth agreed terms for SCLC/ACMHR cooperation. Decision making during the campaign was to be based on prior consultation. The two organizations would communicate jointly with the media, and Shuttlesworth insisted that SCLC "could not stop in Birmingham unless we got some definite commitment" from the city fathers (Manis 1999: 336). The agreed goals began with the desegregation of department store facilities and the hiring of African American sales staff, both concessions within the power of the store owners themselves. Learning from Albany, the Birmingham Movement planned also to insist on the dismissal of all charges from previous protests and the establishment of a bi-racial committee authorized to pursue further desegregation. Shuttlesworth insisted that the recently closed municipal recreation facilities should be required to reopen on a desegregated basis, and, as a clear breach of the color bar, there should be equal employment opportunities for blacks in city government. Modest though these demands appear in hindsight, they would prove difficult to achieve in Bull Connor's Birmingham.

The active mass involvement of local African Americans was vital. This justifiably worried SCLC staff. The ACMHR alone was insufficient. Older, conservative black figures in Birmingham, like A.G. Gaston, seemed likely to oppose the campaign, and even the backing of most black preachers was doubtful. When Wyatt Walker warned the Dorchester conclave that he had heard that the Ministerial Alliance might actively oppose them, Shuttlesworth interrupted. "Don't worry, Martin," he said, "I can handle the preachers." Smiling ruefully, King responded, "You'd better be right" (Branch 1988: 691). King knew through his contacts with black businessman John Drew that conservative black and moderate white opinion set great store by the change of governmental system that seemed likely to replace Connor with the more respectable Albert Boutwell. To moderates, it seemed fair to give the new regime a chance to prove itself before launching a protest campaign that might spill blood on the streets.

To placate such sentiments, and perhaps to ensure *New York Times* coverage, which had been interrupted by a strike, King and Shuttlesworth postponed the campaign until after the mayoral race on March 5, and delayed it again when the election result necessitated a run-off between Connor and Boutwell on April 2. Unwilling to relinquish control, even after his defeat, Connor joined his fellow Commissioners in a legal challenge, claiming that they should be allowed to serve out their full terms as stipulated under the previous city charter. On the one hand, this ensured that the delayed protests did occur before the "Bull" was gone. On the other, it meant that in April 1963 Birmingham had two competing city governments, and so could make no substantive progress on any issue. Like Birmingham's moderates, the Kennedy administration suggested that this justified a further postponement. King responded that the election outcome would make little difference since Albert Boutwell (who had drafted a pupil placement law to evade school desegregation, while in the state legislature) was very unlikely to desegregate voluntarily. Nevertheless, when Walker's "Project X" (as the Birmingham project was initially called) was launched on April 3, it was viewed as ill-judged and untimely in many influential quarters (Garrow 1988: 238-39).

With his 34th birthday approaching, King had ended the January retreat by reminding everyone of Birmingham's reputation for violence. "Some of the people sitting here today," he had said solemnly, "will not come back alive from this campaign." A warning to his youthful colleagues, the sobering thought also articulated King's own fears. Underlining the threat he faced, after a speech at Chicago's Orchestra Hall later that month, he saw Roy James, the young Nazi, approaching again, but this time with five comrades. "You're the one who attacked me," King called out, and the alerted police ensured that the six men left without incident (Garrow 1988: 232).

Other pressures compounded the stress from such hazards. Fund-raising for SCLC kept King away from home for nearly half the year and when there, he was usually besieged by incoming calls. Unable to finish his long overdue book of sermons, he had taken to spending nights "across town" rather than returning home. The King children remember their mother Coretta functioning as a virtual lone parent. Aware of the many demands upon Martin, she tended not to bother him with domestic matters but, understandably, his separation from family life and her confinement to that realm bred resentment. Rumors of sexual liaisons had circulated about King almost from his first emergence as a national figure (Garrow 1988: 96, 223, 236). By 1963, his friends knew that they were true. The mayhem of his public life seemed to deepen his need for sexual encounters to such an extent that he was prepared to jeopardize everything he loved for the pleasure and solace they offered.

Additional organizational problems also surfaced as the Birmingham campaign loomed. SCLC staff had failed to document adequately the registration work they claimed to have done under the terms of their Voter Education Project grant. The VEP's Jack Minnis reported that in several areas "SCLC either has not tried to or has failed to stimulate local leadership." On February 28, King admitted to VEP officials that SCLC had underperformed, but new staff in the main inactive areas should change that. A contrite Andrew Young promised to improve SCLC's reporting procedures, and on this basis, VEP funding was restored (Garrow 1988: 233-34). Another problem sprang from federal demands that King no longer associate with the "known" communists Stanley Levison and Jack O'Dell. King had become reliant on both. Levison had been a shrewd advisor and friend since 1956, and O'Dell had recently set up a direct mail fund-raising system that was making SCLC solvent for the first time. Their presence at the Dorchester retreat signaled their importance to King, whom they had assured that their Communist Party connections were in the past. But the Kennedys were not convinced.

Known communist ties provided grounds for the FBI to begin wiretapping Levison from March 1962, and the bugging campaign, which soon extended to King himself, meant that King's plans, views, and ultimately his private life, were exposed to J. Edgar Hoover. Since the days of Marcus Garvey in the 1920s, the FBI chief had viewed African American militancy as a species of subversion, and he plainly hated Martin. As early as February 1962, he described King as "no good in any way" (Branch 1988: 565, 568). His animus eventually became public knowledge in November 1964 when he told reporters that King was "one of the lowest characters in the country" (Garrow 1988: 360).

Wyatt Walker was determined that the new campaign's military precision would boost his leader's reputation. ACMHR members showed him the target stores, and together, they organized committees to handle the campaign's logistics. From the Gaston Motel, Walker measured how long it would take a person walking to reach downtown – whether they were a youngster, an old person, or in their early thirties like Walker himself. He not only found out exactly where the eating facility was in each store, but even counted "how many stools there were, [and] where the places of ingress and egress were." As a precaution, he selected secondary targets – federal buildings and City Hall, and even some outlying shopping malls – just in case Connor effectively sealed off downtown. King may have stressed economic leverage, but Walker wanted public clashes to press the case for federal intervention. Whatever happened, he recalled, "we were going to have a confrontation somewhere" (Fairclough 1987: 116).

The run-off election ensured that King was home for the birth of his fourth child, Bernice Albertine, on March 27, an event celebrated in "happy family" photographs for the black celebrity magazine *Jet*. But King quickly returned to the task of raising money. At Harry Belafonte's New York apartment on March 31, he told an invited band of well-heeled, Northern supporters what SCLC was planning, and asked Shuttlesworth to explain why their aid was desperately needed. King recalled that Shuttlesworth's graphic summary of racial injustice in Birmingham "brought a sense of the danger as well as the earnestness of our crusade into that peaceful New York living room." In response, the glitterati promised $475,000 to underwrite the campaign. Afterwards, relaxing with a glass of Harvey's Bristol Cream, King looked at his friend Abernathy fondly and prayed: "Let me be sure to be arrested with people who don't snore" (Branch 1988: 705-6; Manis: 1999: 342).

A Faltering Start

Abernathy's nasal trumpet, King well knew, would be the least of his worries in Birmingham. At first, few things went to plan. Having phoned the 350 names on his "willing to go to jail" list, Walker discovered that only sixty-five volunteers actually materialized. Where was the mass support that Shuttlesworth had promised? Equally unexpected, any dramatic reaction from Bull Connor was slow to come. "B-Day" – Wednesday April 3 – saw just twenty-one arrests. On the campaign's second day, a lunchtime mass demonstration had to be cancelled, and at four of the five lunch counters targeted, well-rehearsed staff simply advised their white customers that the counters were closing. Turning out the lights, they left the protesters wondering what to do next. Instead of following the projected upward curve, the arrest chart plummeted to four. King tried to stick to his economic tactics by stressing the total boycott of downtown stores, including phone orders, at Thursday's mass meeting. But as early as the first Friday of the campaign, Movement leaders had decided to redirect the marches to City Hall in order to goad Connor's police force. Visible, violent arrests, they believed, would generate active support, as community outrage overcame the understandable fear of arrest and loss of employment, and set the press cameras clicking (Manis 1999: 345-48).

Predictably, the newly elected Mayor Albert Boutwell complained of publicity-seeking "outside elements and agitators." Unlike his defeated adversary Bull Connor (who promised, given half a chance, to "fill that jail full"), Boutwell urged "everyone, white and Negro, calmly to ignore what is now being attempted in Birmingham" (Branch 1988: 709, 711). Less expected was a public rebuke from a prominent white liberal, Father Albert S. Foley. Having labeled the protests "poorly timed and misdirected," the Jesuit priest declared that local African American leaders were "suspicious of the motives of Shuttlesworth and King coming into the city to stir people up, hold mass meetings, raise money, then move elsewhere." Foley, the chairman of the Alabama Advisory Committee to the US Civil Rights Commission, derided King as a leader who stumbled through "one failure after another." Doubts inside black Birmingham persisted. A relative newcomer, Reverend Porter of Sixth Avenue Baptist Church, viewed Shuttlesworth as an "unstable dictator." Reverend J.L. Ware of the Baptist Ministers Conference and businessmen John Drew and A.G. Gaston had hoped that Shuttlesworth's move to Cincinnati would allow respectable racial diplomats like themselves to set the community's agenda. To them, street protests still seemed a bizarre way to mark Bull Connor's removal from office (Manis 1999: 338, 349).

King had intended to go to jail himself on Day 3 but the flagging demonstrations made him reconsider. Instead, Shuttlesworth and forty-two followers were arrested for parading without a permit. King next asked his brother, A.D. King, pastor of First

Baptist in nearby Ensley, along with Reverend Porter and ACMHR minister Nelson Smith, to lead a march the following day, Palm Sunday. To Wyatt Walker's delight, the police and press mistook the black spectators that followed this march as part of the march itself, exaggerating the movement's support. Even better from Walker's standpoint, bystander Leroy Allen provoked a police dog. A melee of spectators, police dogs, and their handlers ensued, and drew press attention. Sunday's arrests brought the total number of jailed protesters to 102, well below the four figures needed to fill the jails. But the snarling dogs generated the press coverage that the faltering campaign craved, and Walker and Dorothy Cotton of the SCLC danced gleefully. Observing their reaction, SNCC's James Forman was appalled. To him, "it seemed very cold, cruel and calculating to be happy about police brutality coming down on innocent people, bystanders, no matter what purpose it served" (Garrow 1988: 239-40).

Sunday's clashes did not silence King's black critics, who reiterated their call to give Boutwell a chance. With Shuttlesworth in jail, the more emollient King explained the need for action to local black ministers and professionals. He tried to appeal to their pride by declaring: "The Man cannot ride your back if you can stand up." Meanwhile at a mass meeting, the coarser Abernathy urged the common folk to "get rid of the Uncle Toms" (McWhorter 2001: 332). Caught between extremes, black ministers rejected Reverend Ware's resolution condemning the protests and, when asked by lame-duck Mayor Arthur Hanes to intervene, A.G. Gaston replied simply that blacks would no longer "accept the status quo" (Manis 1999: 349-52).

King's segregationist opponents had their own debates over strategy. In Montgomery, they introduced legislation to raise the maximum appeal bond in misdemeanor cases from $300 to $2,500, a move designed to drain SCLC's bail fund. Albany Police Chief Laurie Pritchett acted as a consultant to Birmingham's police. When Bull Connor boasted his readiness to use dogs and water cannons, Pritchett urged him to deactivate them immediately (McWhorter 2001: 340). The Boutwell administration and leading Birmingham businessmen shrewdly refused Governor Wallace's offer to send a hundred of his toughest-looking state troopers to help contain the demonstrations. Any step that pushed the situation toward violent confrontation would backfire, they argued. Instead, Birmingham would seek an Albany-style court order.

In the early hours of April 11, King and other Movement leaders were served with a blanket injunction signed by state judge William Jenkins, supposedly in the interests of public order and safety. At a press conference, King distinguished between obedience to the federal courts, which had ruled against segregation, and compliance with state courts that were blatant tools of racial injustice. He could not in good conscience obey Judge Jenkins's order, he declared, and so the next day, Good Friday, he would defy it. Despite his public statements, King was uncertain. The number of jailed protesters in Birmingham was lower than in Albany, but SCLC's bail fund was shrinking fast. King would soon have to raise more money, or assume that the prospect of an indeterminate stay in jail would not decimate the already inadequate supply of demonstrators. His dilemma boiled down to leaving Birmingham temporarily for a fund-raising blitz, or going to jail as an act of faith. The boycott and recent violence had unsettled Birmingham's economic elite, but Sidney Smyer's opening inquiry to Shuttlesworth on April 9, "What is it you niggers want?" captured the gulf of understanding to be spanned (Manis 1999: 353, 355).

King In Birmingham Jail

Even on Good Friday morning, a nervous King still listened to those who urged him to concentrate on fund-raising. He recalled how "a sense of doom began to pervade the room." After retiring to a side room to pray, however, King returned, dressed in the jeans and work shirt that were his jail clothes. "I have to make a faith act," he said quietly. "I don't know what will happen or what the outcome will be. I don't know where the money will come from." He then asked a reluctant Abernathy to accompany him (Carson 1998: 182-83). Daddy King, who had come to dissuade his son, made one final plea. But Martin was firm. "If we obey this injunction," he replied, "we are out of business." "Well, you didn't get this nonviolence from me," his father shrugged. "You must have got it from your Mama" (Branch 1988: 730).

When King set out that Good Friday afternoon, a devout follower called: "There he goes, just like Jesus" (Manis 1999: 356). As proof of the campaign's fragile state, only fifty supporters and no major Birmingham preachers stood ready to march with him. King's procession was soon stopped. Police led an apprehensive-looking King away, and on arrival at the city jail, they added to his unease by placing him in solitary confinement. King remembered that long night, without contact, as some of "the longest, most frustrating and bewildering hours I have ever lived" (Garrow 1988: 242-43). When eventually Walker was allowed to see him, he was tetchy. "You must resume demonstrations immediately," he snapped, "Don't let the local support committee stop you. We have got to keep the pressure on Birmingham." Walker tried to run through his list of ongoing activities, but King cut him off with a dismissive "But we still don't see anything." According to Andrew Young, King always reacted badly to imprisonment, "it made him very moody and difficult to handle." His irritability transmitted itself to Walker who "came from these meetings with Martin pumped up and giving orders" (Young 1996: 220-21).

Walker's tendency to bark commands had grated on office colleagues in Atlanta, and proved equally unwelcome in the field. James Bevel in particular resented it. A Nashville student activist, who, with his wife, Diane Nash, had been among SNCC's most committed practitioners of nonviolence, Bevel had recently joined SCLC. King believed him to be an astute tactician who would attract younger protesters. An eccentric, Bevel wore a Jewish yarmulke on his shaven young head as a tribute to the Old Testament prophets. He described himself as a "chicken-eating, liquor-drinking, woman-chasing Baptist preacher," and his habits had not changed upon marriage to the poised and beautiful Diane Nash (Branch 1988: 559, 734, 753). Walker did not complain about Bevel's extravagant diet or libido since they were SCLC standard issue, but he would not stomach insubordination. "You cannot order me to give my life," yelled Bevel in one shouting match between the two, "This is a movement, not a military operation" (Young 1996: 221). After the Birmingham campaign ended, King refused Walker's demand that he sack Bevel, and Walker began to look for fresh challenges beyond SCLC.

Such clashes partly reflected the pressures as Walker clutched at straws over that Easter weekend. Already, he had begun to schedule all demonstrations for noon to draw watching lunchtime crowds, and obscure the campaign's lack of support. He had contacted Harry Belafonte about the desperate financial situation and, using the issue of King's treatment in jail, he had telegrammed both the Justice Department and the White House. At his insistence, Coretta King phoned as well to register her fears. On Easter Sunday, Robert Kennedy returned her call and said that he would make inquiries about King's treatment.

Offsetting fleeting signs of federal interest, the *Birmingham News* featured a letter from a group of liberal clergymen in the city who praised the press and the police and condemned the protests. Many of these same ministers, priests, and rabbis had recently risked their reputations by criticizing Governor Wallace's intemperate inauguration speech. However, they now wrote: actions that "incite hatred and violence, however technically peaceful those actions may be, have not contributed to the resolution of our local problems. We do not believe these days of new hope are days when extreme measures are justified in Birmingham." They also praised the local police for restraint (Branch 1988: 738).

Walker's efforts bore small fruit on Monday April 15. National newspapers carried pictures of police violently dispersing black crowds. King's attorney Clarence Jones arrived to announce that Belafonte and others had raised enough money to reactivate the bail fund. And finally, on Monday afternoon, President Kennedy phoned Mrs. King to reassure her that the FBI had confirmed that her husband was safe and that he had arranged for her husband to call shortly. Thirty minutes later, a puzzled King came on the line. He was elated to learn that his jailers' uncharacteristically compassionate invitation to phone his wife was the product of Presidential intervention. Barely bothering to ask about his newborn daughter, he pressed Coretta to notify Walker of this development (Garrow 1988: 243-45).

But Walker's obedient efforts to portray Kennedy's call as heralding intervention in Birmingham cut little ice. The national press seemed hostile. The *Washington Post* was particularly so, seeing the whole campaign as "prompted more by leadership rivalry than by the real need of the situation." Welcoming Mayor

Boutwell's swearing-in on April 15 as a hopeful sign for the future, the *New York Times* editorialized that it did not expect enlightened racial views to sweep Birmingham "overnight," but that King "ought not to expect it either." The President's call was in response to Mrs. King's hysteria, a product of her emotionally overwrought, post-natal state (Branch 1988: 736-37).

That Easter, evangelist Billy Graham asked "his personal friend" Martin Luther King to "put the brakes on;" an odd exhortation to campaign insiders struggling to recruit volunteers. Sensing defeat, A.G. Gaston evicted some civil rights activists from one of his offices, accusing them of using dope and whiskey (McWhorter 2001: 354, 356). Even more dishearteningly, Burke Marshall of the Justice Department told Movement leaders that there was no legal basis for federal action in Birmingham, a position he underlined for the *Birmingham News* on April 14. Unless some federal law was broken, there would be no federal intervention (Manis 1999: 361). In a private meeting with Shuttlesworth, after King had been in prison a week, however, Marshall said the administration would try to help behind the scenes. Afterwards, he warned Bobby Kennedy that the Birmingham situation "continues to be dangerous." Many African Americans were armed and most had "no confidence at all in the local police" (Fairclough 1987: 123).

While Shuttlesworth lobbied and Walker scurried, King wrote a reply to the Birmingham clergymen, explaining the reasoning behind his current campaign and the rationale for nonviolence in general. Available first as a press release in mid-May and later included in King's book *Why We Can't Wait* (1964), the "Letter from Birmingham Jail" has become the most widely read of King's writings, a celebrated model of expository prose. However, it attracted public attention largely as a result of later events, and was read in the context of violent scenes that had not yet occurred at the time of its creation (Bass 2001: 135). Its relevance to the Birmingham campaign itself lies in what it reveals about King's understanding of how nonviolence works and what obstacles it confronts. While it mentioned certain necessary preliminaries for nonviolence – investigation of the problem, efforts to negotiate, and self-purification – King's presentation of his nonviolent creed strongly stressed its cathartic, psychological functions. It provided a "creative outlet" for the pent-up resentments of African Americans and brought to the surface the repressed race problem of a mal-adjusted nation. "We bring it out into the open where it can be seen and dealt with," he wrote. Nonviolent direct action worked "to create such a crisis and foster such a tension that a community which has constantly refused to negotiate is forced to confront the issue. It seeks to so dramatize the issue that it can no longer be ignored" (Carson 1998: 188-204, quotations, 190, 195).

Since the letter responded ostensibly to moderate clerical critics and was subsequently published in an effort to sway liberal Christians, it was particularly revealing in terms of how Movement setbacks sharpened King's view of whites of goodwill. He had almost concluded, he wrote, "that the Negro's greatest stumbling block is not the White Citizen Council-er [sic] or the Ku Klux Klanner, but the white moderate who is more devoted to 'order' than to justice" (Carson 1998: 195). Lamenting especially the failure of white clergy to join the crusade for racial justice, King sighed that maybe he had been too optimistic. In Birmingham, he would ultimately be pragmatic, ruthlessly escalating the tension until no one could deny the issue or the need for change. He expected further voices of disapproval. However, when King and Abernathy filed bail on April 20 and prepared to fly home to preside over their respective Sunday services, it was unclear how such a hard-nosed intensification of the campaign would occur.

The prospects remained bleak during the following week's trial. On Friday April 26, Judge Jenkins found King and ten others guilty of criminal contempt for disobeying his restraining order. The sentences of five days in jail and $50 fines would be suspended, pending appeal. A week of nightly movement mass meetings attracted small crowds and recruited few nonviolent foot soldiers. In mid-week, the murder of a white civil rights protester, postman William Moore, on a protest walk through Alabama drew fleeting attention from the press. King feared that unless the Birmingham campaign caught fire soon, the media would leave town to pursue this or some other story. A remedy, however, was taking shape in James Bevel's afternoon workshops for student volunteers. Invited to stay on for Wednesday night's mass meeting, these high school, and even elementary school, students shared in the tributes to Moore's bravery and then embarrassed King by forming the majority of the mere score of volunteers who came forward. Their readiness to suffer was appreciated, he said, and their example should inspire their parents, but Birmingham Jail was no place for children (Branch 1988: 748-51).

The Children's Crusade

By Monday April 29, King was not so sure that the children should not participate. James Bevel had explained to him that if the scheduled May 2 protest march was to be the massive demonstration needed, it would have to include the student volunteers who were flocking to his workshops. King knew that the city would deny them a parade permit and so all march participants would face jail. Every Birmingham leader, except Shuttlesworth, strongly opposed the idea of involving students younger than college age. King's middle-class hosts in Birmingham, John and Deenie Drew, asked King to remember that even the early Christians had discouraged their children from facing the lions in the Coliseum. A.G. Gaston and Reverend Porter agreed. Children are not cannon fodder, they told King (Branch 1988: 752-53).

To Porter's astonishment, the SCLC leader stressed the exigencies, not the ethics, of the campaign. "We've got to pick up everything," he observed bluntly, "because the press is leaving." Other SCLC men agreed that rekindling media's interest was imperative. Walker regarded the use of high school students sanguinely. "We had run out of troops," he recalled, "We had scraped the bottom of the barrel of adults who could go." Moreover, he added, "We needed something new" (Garrow 1988: 247). High school students' interest in the campaign had been boosted by the recruitment of James Orange, a recently graduated football star from Parker High, one of the city's biggest black schools. Using his contacts, he persuaded the current football captains, and then the student presidents and homecoming queens, to join the movement. Soon the protest campaign was "the thing to do," and parental misgivings only added to its popularity among the teenagers (Young 1996: 236-37).

A permanent staff member from Birmingham onwards, James Orange understood, like Bevel, the practical advantages of juvenile recruits. "The parents were working," he explained. "They couldn't go march ... [because] if they marched, they'd lose their jobs. But there was nothing for the kids to lose" (Fairclough 1987: 125). For Bevel, church membership was the key determinant of the age of responsibility. If schoolchildren as young as 6 could decide their eternal destiny by a conscious acceptance of Christ in the Baptist faith, he reasoned that they were old enough to choose to march against segregation, whatever their parents said. "Against your Mama," he told King, "you have a right to make this witness." Had he said "Daddy," King would have smiled appreciatively (Branch 1988: 755).

Making no firm decision, King agreed only to the children being invited to gather at Sixteenth Street Church at noon on May 2. King, Abernathy, Shuttlesworth, and Walker flew out Monday for an SCLC board meeting in Memphis, leaving Bevel and Young to organize Thursday's march, and they concentrated unashamedly on the schools. Local FBI agents warned city police that leaflets found in the black high schools invited students to quit school at noon Thursday. A local DJ, "Tall Paul," began broadcasting that there would be a "big party" that day at Kelly Ingram Park, just across from the Sixteenth Street Church (Branch 1988: 755). But even on Thursday morning (May 2), which Walker had christened "D-Day," King was still wrestling with his conscience at the Gaston Motel and listening to the complaints of those who felt that using children was simply unthinkable; he was still there when the first wave of fifty teenagers emerged, singing and clapping, through the church's front doors (Garrow 1988: 248).

As police filed the first group into waiting vehicles, another fifty students emerged, and then another, and then another. Wyatt Walker directed them to test different routes toward City Hall. Outnumbered, a local police officer called across to Reverend Shuttlesworth: "Hey, Fred. How many more have you got?" "At least a thousand!" responded Shuttlesworth happily. "God Almighty," said the policeman (Branch 1988: 756-57). As officers relayed the scale of the demonstration to headquarters, Bull Connor tried to mass all available police officers and fire engines between the protesters and downtown. Accordingly, Walker determined to disperse his adversary's forces. He dispatched "eight to ten guys to different quarters of the town to turn in false alarms." He followed the practice of plausible deniability and did not tell King about these tactics (Garrow 1988: 248-49).

Ironically, the Birmingham campaign – the campaign that rescued and restored King's faltering fortunes as a civil rights leader – swung in his favor largely because of tactics that he had not approved.

With the May 2 children's march, Bull Connor's ability to contain the Movement without resorting to extensive street violence began to falter. By 4.00 p.m. he had arrested 600 children and shipped them in commandeered school buses to the city jail. This left the jail so full that, from his standpoint, he could soon see no alternative but to respond in the violent way that SCLC had calculated. On Friday May 3, over a thousand youngsters listened to final instructions inside Sixteenth Street Church. Blocking the eastbound cross-streets that led downtown, Connor had massed school buses, police cruisers, K-9 units, and to the fore, fire engines. Initially, after warning the first wave of protesters at the corner of Kelly Ingram Park to disperse, the firemen simply drenched them "with spray through fogging nozzles." But when one group refused to retreat, special water cannons were trained upon the singing children. Strong enough to strip the bark off the park trees, the water bounced people like litter in a gale. High above, in his office in the Gaston Building, the black millionaire A.G. Gaston had been confiding his wish that King would leave town, to David Vann of the city's white reform group. But as he spoke, he saw the fire hoses hit a little black girl and roll her "right down the middle of the street." In anguish, he told Vann he just couldn't speak any more (Branch 1988: 758-59).

When marchers probed alternate routes, police arrested 250 and sent them to the already overcrowded jails. Remembering his jail crisis, Connor ordered K-9 units to press both marchers and spectators back into either the Sixteenth Street Church or the African American neighborhood to the west. The bared teeth and snarled lips of these attack dogs proved an effective deterrent and most people fled at their approach. But three black teenagers were bitten badly enough to require hospital treatment and the sight of one dog sinking its teeth into the stomach of a 15-year-old boy was captured by an Associated Press photographer. The image made newspaper front pages around the world that weekend (Branch 1988: 760-61).

The images of white aggression belied the relative lack of lethal severity. In March 1960 South African police had opened fire on demonstrators, killing 69 Africans and wounding at least 180, including women and children. Most had been shot in the back. From the standpoint of his own stupid obsession that no protest should reach City Hall, Connor had won the battle. After half an hour of dog bites and water bombardment, the park was empty, the onlookers had fled, and saturated protesters were dripping onto the pews of Sixteenth Street Church. But King sensed correctly that Connor was losing the war. King could keep the remaining 500 protesters in reserve and turn his attention to building on the public revulsion at the day's events.

Federal Intervention

That evening's mass meeting was packed and King sensed a new mood of insurgency in the crowded church. He felt able to joke about the water cannon. Black Baptists had relished this total immersion. Their people pressure had matched the water pressure, and so, despite Robert Kennedy's calls, there would be no suspension of demonstrations: "Yesterday was D-Day," he declared, "and tomorrow will be Double-D Day!" King's confidence indicated how the campaign had been transformed (Branch 1988: 764). Only days earlier, Wyatt Walker had planned protests on the basis of a shortage of volunteers; now he enjoyed a superabundance. King's own spell in jail had barely dented the neutrality of the White House, but when Saturday's newspapers carried photographs of Connor's use of dogs and water cannon, President Kennedy described them as "sickening." Burke Marshall sped to Birmingham to mediate (Garrow 1988: 250). The youth marches had solidified black support, swamped local jail facilities, and ensured that the nation's media and President remained focused on the King-Connor duel.

The advantage held by King that Saturday of May 4 was precarious, however. From the outset, black spectators had watched Bull Connor's mistreatment of their African American compatriots with understandable anger that always threatened retaliatory violence. On Saturday afternoon, Connor's men trapped the bulk of the demonstrators inside Sixteenth Street and other churches. They then used water cannon to expel the few protesters left in Kelly Ingram Park. Watching these unarmed youngsters being bowled over by the water, black onlookers launched a salvo of rocks. Realizing that a riot would undermine the movement's efforts to win public sympathy, James Bevel managed to persuade a police officer to loan him a megaphone. Darting around the square, he successfully urged the "troublemakers" to leave. Then, without consulting his superiors, he unilaterally announced that there would be no marches on Sunday as the Movement paused to purify itself in readiness for nonviolent protests on Monday. Leaving Walker fuming over this insubordinate grandstanding, King escaped to preach in Atlanta (Branch 1988: 765). Off the record, Walker was prepared to concede that the "Battle of Ingram Park" was more spectacle than substance, with youths frolicking in the hose spray and sucker-punching the police dogs (McWhorter 2001: 378). Preventing "further retaliatory violence was one of the finest achievements of our campaign," recalled Andrew Young, recognizing how quickly public opinion could turn against the Movement (Jackson 2007: 165).

Meanwhile, Burke Marshall delicately and slowly edged Birmingham's white business and black protest leadership closer together in a series of separate meetings. Despite his Justice Department role, he tried to limit the negotiations to store accommodations and jobs rather than tackle politicized issues like school desegregation and voting rights. On the evening of May 4, he told white representatives that concessions on private sector issues might be enough to end the protests. At the same time, he warned them that King's and Shuttlesworth's ability to contain mounting black anger at Connor was faltering. Several prominent store owners were Jewish and very aware of their precarious and suspect status within the Southern city's business elite. The idea of negotiating with the protest leaders was so offensive that Marshall sensed that only the threat of mass bloodshed would force them to consider it. As he later noted, there "were many whites that wouldn't talk to any blacks, and there were many more whites that wouldn't talk to certain blacks, and there were no whites, I think, except for David Vann, who would talk to Martin King." A mistrustful Shuttlesworth warned King that face-to-face negotiations were essential because only then would they "all know what everybody said." King was equally wary but the fact of federal involvement outweighed his doubts (Manis 1999: 374-75).

Marshall interpreted King's wariness as confusion, and Bobby Kennedy relayed his view at a Cabinet meeting, declaring: "the Negro leadership didn't know ... whether they were demonstrating to get rid of Bull Connor or whether they were demonstrating about the stores ... and none of the white community knew what they were demonstrating about." King's muddle-headedness became an abiding memory for Marshall. Interviewed two decades later, he said that it was "hard to negotiate with King because he had no specifics. What he wanted was something" (Branch 1988: 769). The Movement's demand for the merchants to pressure the city both to drop charges against demonstrators and to establish a bi-racial committee to develop future desegregation and racial hiring policies was unacceptable to white moderates. They "absolutely refused to deal in any way with matters before the courts or the prerogatives of city government." Even the desegregation of store facilities and the hiring and promoting of black staff would be hard to settle, they argued, until the legal wrangle between the Boutwell and Connor regimes ended (Garrow 1988: 252). Previously quiet, Shuttlesworth warned that such intransigence meant continuing demonstrations and that was bad for business. "This is your city," he chided Sidney Smyer and the others. "Bull Connor is not the whole city" (Manis 1999: 375).

Marshall summarized the whites' position for King on Monday May 6, but failed to convince him to cancel that afternoon's demonstrations. Instead another thousand people, including a significant number of adults, willingly submitted to arrest. Civic leaders had asked Connor to minimize his use of force but, with no permanent detention facilities available for his prisoners, he had to hold hundreds in an uncovered outdoor pen. As rain swept in, SNCC's James Forman pressed King to insist that some shelter was provided and eventually King asked Marshall to intercede (Branch 1988: 769-72). After five weeks of campaigning, a total of 2,425 arrests testified to the success of Bevel's more confrontational approach, but more in terms of triggering federal involvement by generating a crisis than in terms of using direct black economic leverage to extract concessions. But economics mattered. Since the demonstrations threatened serious disorder, they had economic effects and in the absence of clear-cut legal authority, federal intervention also largely took the form of quiet, boardroom pressure on national businesses with Birmingham interests.

With the stores offering only to promote a handful of their existing black employees, the ACMHR-SCLC forces realized that they had not yet broken white resistance. Nevertheless, King was now confident that they would do so. Downtown Birmingham was increasingly deserted, as white housewives as well as black shoppers decided not to risk a trip to the stores. Just as importantly, the dismayed industrialists, lawyers, and bankers behind Birmingham's traditional coal, iron, and steel interests saw the city likened across the world to a Gestapo camp. To maintain the pressure, the protest leaders decided to flood the business district with hundreds of demonstrators converging from many different directions the next day. At 10.00 a.m. on May 7, King and Shuttlesworth warned that the protests would continue until the city met their demands, and within hours what was termed "Operation Confusion" had begun (Manis 1999: 376).

As groups of black youths successfully evaded police and noisily aired their grievances on downtown streets, the so-called Senior Citizens Committee, composed of leading white businessmen, met to consider whether to seek a settlement on the basis of the four black demands of desegregated store facilities, new hirings and promotions, an amnesty for protesters, and a bi-racial committee to oversee future desegregation. Marshall warned them that continuing disorder would soon compel Governor Wallace or President Kennedy to impose martial law. Although some older figures urged a martial solution, the clashes outside and official confirmation that the jails were full spurred the majority to appoint a subcommittee to develop an agreement with "responsible Negro leadership" (Manis 1999: 379-80).

Impressed by the success of the lunchtime demonstrations, King and Walker ordered a second downtown *sortie* in late afternoon. By then, Connor had readied his police and firemen with orders to repel the protesters with dogs and water cannon. Racing to the Gaston Motel to plead with King to call off the demonstrators, James Forman found the SCLC leader, like a general behind the front line, relaxing in silk pajamas, enjoying a steak, and chatting on the phone. He turned away in disgust (Garrow 1988: 254). Earlier, Shuttlesworth had dragged a reluctant King and Abernathy around Birmingham to see how the campaign prospered. King had then returned to the motel, but Shuttlesworth headed to Kelly Ingram Park to help James Bevel in his efforts to stop violent black retaliation. A firefighter saw Shuttlesworth heading toward Sixteenth Street Church, and released a carefully aimed water-blast that slammed the preacher against the wall. Informed that Shuttlesworth had left in an ambulance, Bull Connor muttered that he wished it had been a hearse (Manis 1999: 377-79).

King Decides To Settle

Sedated for his injuries, Shuttlesworth could not attend the evening negotiations with the white delegation nor consult with King over Burke Marshall's renewed demands for compromise. A.G. Gaston, Lucius Pitts, and leading black attorney Arthur Shores were white Birmingham's idea of "responsible Negro leadership," and King sent the urbane Andrew Young to join them as SCLC representative in negotiations with Smyer and Vann. A major stumbling block threatened to be the fate of hundreds of arrested demonstrators, but more generally the two sides wrangled over the timing, extent, and verification of desegregation measures. Young suggested what he termed "a stair-step approach." As a sign of good faith, immediately a settlement was announced, the downtown merchants would remove the WHITES ONLY and COLORED notices from restrooms, water fountains, and waiting areas, and begin interviewing existing black staff suitable for promotion. Ten days later, lunch-counter desegregation would be tested along with verification of the above changes. After thirty days, the movement required complete desegregation of downtown stores and after forty-five days the first phase of a fair employment policy would see the hiring of at least one black clerk by each store. By year's end, 10 percent of store staff should be African American. The business leaders insisted that they could not guarantee an amnesty for arrested demonstrators and thus $160,000 remained tied up in bail bonds, and cases would have to be contested in court. Eventually, to prevent the Birmingham settlement foundering on this one detail, Burke Marshall persuaded four unions, most notably the United Auto Workers, to underwrite the bail bonds on his assurance that federal courts would overturn the charges (Young 1996: 245-46; Garrow 1988: 258).

As with most agreements, the danger lay in the detail. The white representatives wanted delay and vague phrases to reduce the likelihood of reprisals against them, and the African American negotiators wanted swift compliance and precise terms to minimize the chances of evasion or betrayal. This contradiction was evident in the settlement's discussion of employment where there was ambiguity over whether hiring was on the basis of each store or the stores as a group. In general, desegregation was promised in stages and subject to the resolution of Birmingham's continuing governmental crisis in favor of Mayor Boutwell. In King's judgment, however, the negotiations had reached a vital threshold by the morning of Wednesday May 8; and the public announcement of a temporary suspension of protests would bolster the position of those whites backing a settlement. King also favored a suspension because it had become increasingly difficult to maintain nonviolent discipline. A truce might ensure that if further protests were needed, they would continue to convey the clear message that men and women of goodwill should side with the black demonstrators. Accordingly, he scheduled a press conference.

While sound in his tactical thinking, King neglected his relations with the ACMHR at this point. Local movement people felt the truth in reporter Claude Sitton's observation that King had been rarely seen during the recent demonstrations and they resented it. Shuttlesworth's "battle wound," by contrast, confirmed his trustworthiness (McWhorter 2001: 411). The hospitalized Shuttlesworth had spent a restless Tuesday night. Neither King nor Abernathy had visited or called the hospital about his condition, nor had they ensured that he was consulted about the unfolding negotiations. No sooner was he discharged on Wednesday morning than they summoned him to the Drews' suburban home for an emergency meeting. Given his condition, Shuttlesworth thought, surely King could have come to him? On the way over, he began to worry that King might have yielded to pressure from Marshall and black moderates, like the Drews, and called off the protests before they had secured their agreed demands. When he entered, King stood silent and aloof, even seeming to avoid eye contact, and Shuttlesworth's suspicions increased. He eventually asked what was so important that he had to leave his sickbed? At last, turning to address his wounded colleague, King said, "Fred, we got to call off the demonstrations" (Manis 1999: 381).

King's unfortunate choice of words suggested a far more permanent curtailment than a one-day truce, and he compounded his error by adding that the store owners were saying that they could not negotiate while demonstrations continued. Was King ending the campaign just to get negotiations rather than definite concessions? Angrily, Shuttlesworth told King that the people who had accused him of stirring things up in Albany and then backing down before he achieved anything had been right. Calling off the demonstrations went against all King's pre-campaign promises that decisions would be made jointly and that the protests would continue until they had secured the agreed demands. If you want to go against that, Shuttlesworth raged, "go ahead and do it. But I will *not* call it off and I don't think you can call it off without me" (Manis 1999: 382).

SCLC colleagues tried ineffectually to mollify the livid Shuttlesworth who had tried to storm from the room but had fallen back dizzily into his chair. When members of King's entourage mentioned the upcoming press conference, they fanned his fury. "I thought we were going to make joint statements," Shuttlesworth barked. "Go ahead, Mr. Big, and call it off," he said derisively to King,

> I'm gon' wait until I see on TV that you've called it off, and then with the little strength I have left, I gon' get up and lead those three or four thousand kids back in the streets, and you'll be dead.

A visibly shaken King turned to Marshall, saying, "Burke, we got to have unity. We just got to have unity." This vain appeal to white authority snapped the last vestiges of Shuttlesworth's self-control. "I'll be damned if you'll have it like this," he declared menacingly. "You may be Mr. Big now, but if you call it off, you'll be 'Mister Shit.' You're way up here, but you'll fall way down low, and you'll be Mr. Nothing. I'm sorry," Shuttlesworth added as he headed for the door, "but I will not compromise my principles and the principles we established" (Manis 1999: 382-83).

For several hours afterwards, Shuttlesworth railed against King's betrayal to ACMHR members who came to check on their injured leader. Many of the young protesters were particularly keen to continue the demonstrations and SNCC's James Forman readily painted King as a leader who had sold them out, even though they had rescued his reputation. A local court ruling, however, restored King's standing a little by afternoon. It demanded that he and Abernathy either immediately furnish $2,500 in appeal bonds against their Good Friday convictions or go to jail. They chose jail. Considering this a typical white Birmingham betrayal, Shuttlesworth prepared to organize street protests. Desperate to save the settlement, Andrew Young physically restrained Shuttlesworth until he could be persuaded to take a phone call from Bobby Kennedy, who assured him that if he held his fire, an agreement was imminent. King had hoped that his imprisonment might act as a ratchet, pressing the claims of the over 2,000 other prisoners still held. But Kennedy had also phoned A.G. Gaston to bail out King and Abernathy. Bailed again without his consent, King held a joint press conference with Shuttlesworth to announce a truce: demonstrations would resume if a settlement was not reached by 11.00 a.m. the next day (Branch 1988: 784-86).

This May 9 deadline passed, but King did not renew the protests. Instead his comments suggested a further dilution of the movement's original demands. As long as negotiations were progressing positively, he implied, in a way that promised store desegregation and improved employment opportunities in the future, the protests would be deferred. The timetable for implementation had become dangerously vague, and the charges against arrested demonstrators had not been dropped, although King hoped that the merchants would "recommend" this action strongly. By late Thursday evening, David Vann, Andrew Young, and others had finalized the "Birmingham Truce Agreement," which tied the timetable of desegregation largely to the court's confirmation of the Boutwell administration as Birmingham's government. Even with this proviso, the white signatories were so frightened of the potentially violent white backlash against them that they insisted that the text should not be made public. King would be allowed to announce only its general terms the next day (Manis 1999: 386-87).

According to Taylor Branch, King delayed his press conference until it was confirmed that the bail money to release the jailed protesters had been funneled from several Northern sources to Birmingham's bond clerks. To demonstrate the movement's restored unity, he asked Shuttlesworth to announce the terms. Before collapsing from exhaustion and being hurried back to hospital, Shuttlesworth ran through the details: store desegregation would be complete within ninety days; nondiscriminatory hiring and upgrading would commence within sixty days; and a bi-racial committee would be established within fifteen days of the cessation of protests. That evening, King warned a jubilant congregation that the world would try to belittle their achievement. They must not be fooled into underestimating the power of the movement. "These things would *not* have been granted without your presenting your bodies and your very lives before the dogs and the tanks and the water hoses of this city!" he declared. He then explained how their local actions were part of a larger geopolitical process rooted in the Cold War. President Kennedy, he observed,

> is battling for the minds and hearts of men in Asia and Africa
> – some billion men in the neutralist sector of the world – and
> they aren't gonna respect the United States of America if she
> deprives men and women of the basic rights of life because of
> the color of their skin. Mr. Kennedy *knows* that,

King added emphatically, pointing out that this was why their actions had forced the administration to reassess its ineffectual civil rights policy (Branch 1988: 790-91).

King was keen to maintain the pressure on the Kennedy administration, whose main priority remained the containment of racial confrontations and of the internationally embarrassing images they generated. Just before midnight on Saturday May 11, a powerful bomb destroyed the Ensley home of King's brother A.D., whose family fortunately escaped injury. A second explosion rapidly followed, this time targeting King's Gaston Motel suite, which he had vacated to return for Sunday services in Atlanta. A detachment of Alabama state troopers, who had earlier been aggressively patrolling the area around the motel, had mysteriously withdrawn before the bomb detonated. Along with a mounted posse of around a hundred white deputies from Selma headed by Dallas County Sheriff Jim Clark, they now returned, to confront growing crowds of angry African Americans.

Vainly, city leaders begged Governor Wallace's director of public safety, Colonel Al Lingo, not to add to the night's violence. "Get your cowardly ass back to your office," spat Lingo, "I'm in charge now and my orders are to put those black bastards to bed" (McWhorter 2001: 433). With night-sticks and rifle butts, troopers lashed out against anyone within range, including Wyatt Walker's wife. Throwing bricks and rocks and overturning and setting alight a car, blacks stormed the streets, providing some of the earliest images of urban race riots of the 1960s. Bobby Kennedy warned his brother that this could trigger disturbances around the country, and the President asked aides to plan for possible military intervention and for a civil rights bill if the Birmingham agreement faltered. Consulted by phone, King assured Burke Marshall that provided there were no more racist attacks, he could "control his people" (Garrow 1988: 260-61).

King's promise was a rash one, since most who followed him were only provisionally and temporarily committed to nonviolence. As one local activist put it: "We kept 'em nonviolent while marching, but we knew in our heart that they were violent" (McWhorter 2001: 438). In hostile comments on King's leadership in the summer of 1963, Malcolm X seized upon the concurrence of the retaliatory violence of Birmingham's black citizens and the increased activity of the Kennedy administration. As long as whites were beating black people, who remained nonviolent at King's behest, he complained, Kennedy had insisted that he could not intervene, but as soon as blacks started to fight back and break some "crackers'" heads, Kennedy decided that he did have power to act. Typically, Minister Malcolm's comments contained some truth and even greater emotional appeal. Members of the administration did fear that black anger might spread into widespread violence. Nevertheless, Malcolm distorted the realities of the Birmingham campaign when he tried to present it as ultimately a victory for his philosophy of black militant retaliation rather than King's coercive nonviolence. Without the preceding weeks of nonviolent demonstrations and escalating white attacks, the White House response to the May 12 race riot would have been different. Although it was not acknowledged, the decision to ready federal troops sprang more from fears over the rising level of officially condoned white violence than from alarm that blacks had begun to fight back (Garrow 1988: 262).

The White House announced on the Sunday evening of May 12 that army units had been moved to Fort McClellan, some eighty miles from Birmingham, for rapid deployment, if necessary. President Kennedy endorsed the Birmingham agreement and declared that he would "not permit it to be sabotaged by a few extremists on either side" (Branch 1988: 800). King had returned from Atlanta earlier in the day to quell the understandable anger of black Birmingham. Instead of demanding more of the administration in the wake of what were essentially failed assassination attempts against both himself and his brother, King urged restraint on his own followers. "We must work passionately and unrelentingly for first-class citizenship," he declared, "but we must not use second-class methods to gain it" (McWhorter 2001: 440). Complicating his task but inspired in part by a desire to calm feelings in their own community, white leaders were trying to minimize the terms of the Birmingham accord. Sidney Smyer pointedly insisted that no white representatives had ever dealt with King or other outsiders and that the commitment on employment amounted to one black sales clerk in a downtown store. Fred Shuttlesworth countered that the agreement had spoken of "clerks," which obviously implied more than one.

After a week of uneasy calm, movement leaders faced further provocation on May 20 when school authorities expelled 1,100 black students for truancy during the demonstrations. As angry local leaders called for a total boycott of schools and white businesses, King hurried back and urged them to reconsider. This was just another attempt to undermine the agreement, he warned. At his recommendation, the movement cancelled the protests and sought instead to secure a federal court order reinstating the students. Chief Judge Elbert Tuttle of the Fifth Circuit Court of Appeals granted their petition the next day (Garrow 1988: 262-63). King displayed considerable leadership during this period, when successive crises threatened to destroy the local agreement. However, it was a responsible style of leadership more readily appreciated in Washington and among whites in the nation at large than in Birmingham itself. Among African Americans, Malcolm X's charge – "Real men don't put their children on the firing line" - triggered a reflex nod of assent (McWhorter 2001: 442).

Birmingham's Significance

When King committed the SCLC to Birmingham in January 1963, he had been ambiguous about both his aims and his methods. He had joined Fred Shuttlesworth in the goal of breaking the back of segregation in one of its most infamous citadels and had believed at the outset that economic pressure on the city's commercial elite could secure a breakthrough. At the same time, having noted how the Kennedy administration intervened in the Freedom Rides after widely reported violent confrontations but stayed aloof in Albany so long as Chief Pritchett maintained both order and good public relations, King went to Birmingham eager to secure federal action on civil rights, and expectant that confronting Bull Connor would produce embarrassing headlines for the Kennedys around the nation and the world.

In both respects, King's assessment of the power of white elites was more optimistic than their own. White businessmen, particularly the city's Jewish store owners, were deeply unsure that they could lead Birmingham away from entrenched patterns of discrimination in the face of ever more vociferous, political calls for the defense of "Southern" customs. Threatened with black boycotts and protests on one side and segregationist intimidation and counter-boycotts on the other, their calculation of economic self-interest was not as simple as King implied. Similarly, the Kennedy administration viewed King's calls for federal intervention in Birmingham as unrealistic in law, and as politically fanciful as King's earlier suggestion that the President outlaw the whole of segregation by executive order. Allusions to Lincoln's Emancipation Proclamation merely deepened JFK's fears. The last thing Kennedy sought was a second civil war or a second reconstruction. Like the businessmen, the Kennedys were agitated by the white South's threat of massive resistance. They would sooner do less for the Movement than more.

Birmingham suggested to King that a community's history of white resistance might prove an opportunity to be exploited, a chance to generate creative tension. In contrast, Birmingham's lesson for the administration was that it must maneuver to avoid any repetition, to redirect grievances to the courts and to legislative debate, and so deprive white demagogues like George Wallace of the oxygen of public confrontation. Critics of King could point in May 1963 to the fact that neither his tactics of economic leverage nor his dramatic use of children to bait the police had changed much of substance in Birmingham itself. Thanks to the strife of the previous two months, Connor's departure did not improve race relations. The white businessmen continued to interpret the accord narrowly and Mayor Boutwell publicly refused to be bound by it. On the other side, local black leaders were so exhausted and battle-weary by the summer that they dreaded the idea of resuming protest to expedite the accord's implementation. In short, Birmingham could not easily be counted a victory in terms of its immediate, direct, local effects.

Yet Birmingham gave the Movement unprecedented momentum. In this sense, Martin had found his way. Far more than on earlier occasions, more than after Montgomery in 1956, or the Atlanta sit-ins of 1960, or the Freedom Ride siege of 1961, or Albany in 1962, King knew what he had to do. When President Kennedy refused his request for a conference on May 30, King outlined his next step in a wire-tapped conversation with Stanley Levison. There must be more Birminghams. "We are on the threshold of a significant breakthrough," he enthused, "and the greatest weapon is the mass demonstration." Even the threat of a mass "March on Washington," he told Levison, "may so frighten the President that he would have to do something." By June 10, King was complaining to the *New York Times* that Kennedy had "not kept his campaign promises." If he did not publicly call for desegregation very soon, the Movement might sponsor an interracial march on Washington, complete with sit-ins on Capitol Hill (Garrow 1988: 265, 267).

White Maneuvers

While King threatened another embarrassing crisis, the Justice Department was striving to avoid a dramatic clash with Governor Wallace over the court-ordered desegregation of the University of

Alabama, scheduled for June 11. Robert Kennedy had visited Montgomery on April 29 to try to reach an understanding with Wallace. Driving past hostile picketers with placards that denounced him as part of the "Kosher Team – Kennedy/Kastro/ Kruschev [*sic*]" and as the "Mississippi Murderer," the astonished Attorney-General had murmured: "It's like a foreign country." After a deeply unproductive meeting, he recognized that talking to Wallace had been a waste of time. On May 19, with the mayhem of the Birmingham campaign fresh in the memory, Wallace met President Kennedy briefly. Asked about the recent turmoil, the Governor told Kennedy that the real problems came from outside agitators like King and Fred Shuttlesworth. They were not seeking to solve Birmingham's problems, he complained, they were too busy competing to see "who could go to bed with the most nigger women and white and red women too." Not only that, he added venomously, they "ride around town in big Cadillacs smoking expensive cigars." Kennedy enjoyed a good cigar, owned a Cadillac, and pursued recreational sex, so Wallace's attempt at character defamation was singularly ill judged. According to Press Secretary Pierre Salinger, Kennedy found the Governor's comments "outrageous." They confirmed his suspicion that the turbulent field of race relations was an irrational political terrain within which his fabled "cool" cut little ice (Carter 1995: 120, 123, 128, 134).

So, Kennedy asked his advisors on June 1, how far did he need to go to stabilize the civil rights situation? A bill seemed unavoidable but should it concentrate on voting rights, like its predecessors of 1957 and 1960? Or should it require desegregation in public accommodations, a proposal likely to arouse hostility in the Upper as well as the Deep South? Vice-President Johnson responded that he did not feel the administration could secure the votes necessary in the Senate for the latter to pass. But an impassioned Bobby Kennedy urged the strongest possible bill as the only likely way to dampen black militancy. At the same time, he complained that he could no longer find "a reasonable black leadership" (Carter 1995: 134).

The competition between King, Wilkins, and others was a problem, another colleague agreed, quoting black Congressman Adam Clayton Powell as saying: "I'm not going to watch the parade pass me by. I'm gonna lead it." Protest was popular. Almost every day in May had seen another black community rise up and begin to fill the jails. In Cold War terms, this was humiliating. Intelligence reports indicated that the Birmingham crisis had been the subject of 1,420 anti-US news items on Soviet broadcasts in the two weeks since the supposed Birmingham settlement of May 10. By the end of the meeting, the President had agreed that a bill must include at least some attempt to address the public accommodations issue. Interested parties should be invited for off-the-record soundings. But King should be among the last called, insisted Kennedy; he "is so hot these days that it's like [Karl] Marx coming to the White House." Priority should go to Southern governors, mayors, or businessmen and the bill should be introduced before he met King. "Otherwise," the President concluded, "it will look like he got me to do it" (Branch 1988: 806-9).

The pending desegregation of the University of Alabama at Tuscaloosa also shaped the administration's plans. Governor Wallace obviously wanted to make political capital out of a dramatic confrontation in which he, as a symbol of States' Rights, would play the martyr. Bobby Kennedy feared that, as at the University of Mississippi, events might spiral out of control with the President obliged to send in the troops and even arrest Wallace. He did not want to reproduce the grimly ironic spectacle of October 1, 1962, when his brother had praised white Mississippians on national television for their compliance with the law, even as they rioted in defiance of it. No plans for civil rights legislation would be mentioned publicly until the events of June 11 had unfolded. King may have found in Birmingham a way of reshaping the political agenda, but others still influenced its schedule.

6 Along A Tightrope, 1963-64

The period from June 1963 to August 1965 was one of extraordinary influence for Martin Luther King, Jr. By utopian standards, he fell short, but by any reasonable gauge of human attainment, he advanced the cause of freedom against the odds. The American political elite remained apprehensive on civil rights, and this impelled King to stage dramatic nonviolent demonstrations to stiffen their resolve. At the same time, prominent politicians feared that further protests might send the already tense state of race relations into a freefall of violence, which would jeopardize President Johnson's newly announced War on Poverty. The racial disturbances in Birmingham, Harlem, and then Los Angeles in successive summers, even while they exposed the need for this war, frightened the white majority. Against this backdrop, the introduction of a civil rights bill by President Kennedy in June 1963, and the passage of both a strong Civil Rights Act in July 1964 and a Voting Rights Act in August 1965 under President Johnson, cannot be fully explained without reference to King's leadership. However misrepresentative of his overall philosophy, King's nationally broadcast "I Have a Dream" speech at the March on Washington in late August 1963 fixed him in public memory more than any other event. But it did so in a selectively idealistic way at odds with his necessarily calculated protest style (Dyson 2000: 15). While he continued to be deeply detested by segregationists, fiercely resented by powerful federal officials, and vehemently criticized by African American rivals, his status as America's preeminent racial diplomat was most assured during this twenty-six-month period. International recognition came with the award of the Nobel Peace Prize in December 1964, just short of King's 36th birthday. If any period warrants Taylor Branch's label of a King era, this short interval was it (Branch 1988, 1998).

King possessed the ability to dramatize his cause in word and deed, and this transported him from star to superstar status. Leaders like Roy Wilkins of the NAACP resented the adulation that King inspired and, as part of a well-established SNCC critique of SCLC's reliance on charismatic leadership, Julian Bond complained that King had "sold the concept that one man will come to your town and save you" (Lewis 1978: 231). SNCC's mentor, Ella Baker, had warned the students not to trust leaders with "feet of clay" in April 1960 and the guiding spirit of its Mississippi campaigns, Bob Moses, had famously responded to a hyperbolic celebration of King as the all-saving leader of his race with the words: "Don't you think we need a lot of leaders?" (Cook 1998: 155). According to Andrew Young, it was only during the Birmingham campaign that King "came to accept, finally, that he could never walk away from the awesome responsibility of the civil rights leadership that had fallen upon his shoulders" (Young 1996: 186). From starkly different directions, people and processes took over his life. They carried him forward and held him back. He was pursued relentlessly and felt compelled to race to force the pace of change. Asked by reporters what King wanted most desperately, James Bevel half-jokingly replied: "Sleep" (Garrow 1988: 289). He normally rose at 6.00 a.m. and retired – usually to a hotel room, and too often, jet-lagged – at around 2.00 a.m. He had little time to dream, but he was expected to devise ways of making the country anew. Along a tightrope of pressures and expectations, he moved precariously.

Before The March: An Ambiguous Summer

By late 1962, black labor leader A. Philip Randolph and his associates, most notably Bayard Rustin, were so concerned about the disproportionately high unemployment among African Americans (twice the white level) that they proposed a two-day "mass descent" on Washington by around 100,000 people. Their initial idea was for demonstrators to block legislative business on Capitol Hill but, by March 23, 1963, this had been toned down to simply lobbying Congress on the first day and inviting President Kennedy to speak on the second. National Urban League executive Whitney Young and the NAACP's Roy Wilkins had remained unenthusiastic. Randolph's march threatened their good relations with Congress, they said. At the time, King had been too preoccupied with the faltering Birmingham campaign to make any commitments. But by June, with money and support pouring in from across the country, he was ready to resurrect Randolph's expiring plans by merging a march for jobs with a march for freedom (Garrow 1988: 266-67).

The Kennedy administration's immediate civil rights problem was Governor George Wallace. On June 11, at a largely staged event on the University of Alabama campus, Assistant Attorney-General Nicholas Katzenbach approached Wallace to require that he submit to the court-ordered admission of two black students. Addressing the cameras, the Governor stated defiantly: "There can be no submission to the theory that the central government is anything but a servant of the people." Alabamans, he boasted, were defending "the free heritage bequested (*sic*) to us by the Founding Fathers." Invoking the Founders as models of resistance to central government had been a rhetorical trick of the Southern secessionists in 1861, but Wallace's appeal against the faceless liberal bureaucrats of "Big Government" in Washington ultimately proved more pioneering than old-fashioned, foreshadowing successful allure of the New Right from Reagan to the Tea Party (Branch 1988: 821-22). Opposing historical trends bore both King and Wallace forward in the mid-1960s, and ultimately destroyed their respective creeds. Legal segregation was swept away before Wallace was crippled by a gunman's bullet in 1972, while the hopes of racial liberalism were crumbling in 1968, the time of King's murder.

Thirteen years after the Supreme Court outlawed segregation in higher education, Wallace's so-called "stand in the schoolhouse door" underlined for King the need for more vigorous federal action. However, on a day when he had federalized the Alabama National Guard to ensure two black students' safety, President Kennedy ordered a fifteen-minute slot on network television not to explain why he was doing so little, but why he was doing so much. In a hastily drafted speech that required him to extemporize, he committed himself to civil rights reform as a "moral issue." "The time has come for this nation to fulfill its promise," he declared. "The events in Birmingham and elsewhere have so increased the cries for equality that no city or state or legislative body can prudently choose to ignore them." Accordingly, he would ask Congress "to make a commitment it has not fully made this century to the proposition that race has no place in American life or law." In states like Alabama and Mississippi, such a proposition was heretical for those whites who regarded themselves as increasingly besieged defenders of the American way. Even in Jackson, Mississippi's state capital, the supposedly cautious NAACP was backing a store boycott and sit-ins to press for concessions along Birmingham lines. On June 1, the national NAACP leader, Roy Wilkins, had submitted to arrest on a Jackson picket line alongside the battle-hardened head of the NAACP's state conference, Medgar Evers. Within hours of Kennedy's speech, Evers lay dying on his own doorstep, killed by Byron de la Beckwith, a white supremacist, who believed that he was defending the true heart of American life. After two hung juries, he was eventually convicted of Evers's assassination in 1994 (Branch 1988: 823-25).

The signs for King that summer therefore were profoundly contradictory. The national media coverage of widespread black protest, the President's public commitment, and a massive increase in contributions to SCLC suggested that Birmingham had marked a breakthrough. The murder of Medgar Evers, the arrest and torture by Mississippi police of a party of Citizenship School teacher trainees, and a succession of brutal attacks on demonstrators in Gadsden, Alabama, and Danville, Virginia, illustrated equally emphatically that the counter-movement was more virulent as well. King might have a new belief in Kennedy's willingness to propose legislation, but he had to find a way through the Congress. The Southern Congressional caucus was a formidable opponent, especially in the Senate, where Senator Richard Russell had used his mastery of parliamentary procedures to prevent the undiluted passage of all previous civil rights measures since World War II.

Russell was renowned for his mastery of the "filibuster," a tactic of prolonging debate by a relay of hostile speeches, amendments, procedural motions, and points of order. Crucial to the success of this technique was cloture, the requirement that a motion to close debate must secure a two-thirds majority of all members present and voting in the Senate: at least 67 of the maximum 100 votes available. On civil rights, this would require an extraordinary degree of liberal consensus at a time when conservative Republicans, like Barry Goldwater, were beginning to sense their affinity for the anti-federal domination stance of Southern Democrats, like Wallace. More pragmatically, all participants knew that support for civil rights would be sapped not just by a filibuster, but by the conduct of vital Congressional committees where Southern influence was disproportionately strong. The morning after Evers's murder and his own television address, President Kennedy learned from House majority leader Carl Albert that a $450 million provision within the administration's public works bill had been voted down, and this was before debate on a civil rights bill had even begun. On any close issue, whether domestic or foreign, defeat loomed because of Southern defections. Wearily, Kennedy agreed that the civil rights issue was "just in everything" (Branch 1988: 827-28).

King had to counter the pressure on Kennedy to compromise. Speaking to a Birmingham mass meeting on June 20, he revealed his plans. "As soon as they start to filibuster," he declared, "I think we should march on Washington with a quarter of a million people." The next day, two black labor allies of Randolph announced plans for the march, which would focus on the need for jobs rather than lobby for civil rights legislation. Whatever its purpose, the President did not want the march. Summoning the civil rights leadership to the White House on June 22, he voiced his concern. With his bill not even in committee yet, their announcement had been a blunder, he declared. "The only effect is to create an atmosphere of intimidation," he went on, "and this may give some members of Congress an out." Lecturing the assembled black leaders on the practicalities of "the legislative phase," Kennedy concluded that to secure vital votes, they would have to first "oppose demonstrations which will lead to violence, and second, give Congress a fair chance to work its will." Vice-President Johnson underlined the same point. Success would hinge on twenty-five publicly uncommitted Senators. To get their votes, he warned: "we have to be careful not to do anything which would give those who are privately opposed a public excuse to appear as martyrs." With others, King defended the march. It would channel legitimate discontent into disciplined nonviolent demonstrations and dramatize the issue so as to mobilize "support in parts of the country which don't know the problems at first hand" (Garrow 1988: 271-72).

Hearing the familiar official line that "now" was not the time for demonstrations, King added: "Frankly, I have never engaged in a direct-action movement that did not seem ill-timed. Some people thought Birmingham was ill-timed." Like the Attorney-General, said the President wryly, glancing at his brother. It had been Bull Connor who had changed things, and to underline the perils of unintended consequences, Jack Kennedy observed that Connor had "done a good deal for civil rights legislation this year" (Oates 1994: 247). His ironic comment implied that liberal indiscretions might damage the civil rights cause just as Connor's impolitic opposition had inadvertently advanced it.

In private conversations that Saturday morning, first Burke Marshall, then Robert Kennedy, and finally the President himself, stressed to King that his association with Stanley Levison and Jack O'Dell threatened the cause. Marshall claimed to have hard intelligence that Levison was "a paid agent of the Soviet Communist apparatus," but declined to show King the proof. Bobby Kennedy warned that Levison's apparent sincerity should not fool King, and in the ironically "bug-free" Rose Garden, the President asserted that O'Dell ranked fifth in importance among American communists with Levison as his link to the Comintern. Alluding to a contemporaneous British scandal, he argued that just as Prime Minister Harold Macmillan might "lose his government because he has been loyal to a friend [John Profumo, a defense minister]," so King could grievously damage the Civil Rights Movement and, with it, the Kennedy administration, out of friendship for Levison and O'Dell. To his credit, King still demanded proof (Branch 1988: 835-38).

When Randolph had threatened a march in 1941, he had insisted that it should be all black, thereby excluding white communist sympathizers from the Popular Front. This was not possible in 1963. All the major civil rights organizations were committed at this stage to the ideals of interracialism and integration. Even Randolph's Negro American Labor Council was keen to involve major white unions, like the United Auto Workers (UAW). The march's politics were conspicuously coalitionist, with a deliberate attempt to cultivate Kennedy's idea that this was a "moral issue" by appealing to people of goodwill via church groups. During the long ensuing struggle to pass the civil rights bill, such groups proved particularly influential with Congressmen from the Midwestern and Rocky Mountain states. The march thus fulfilled King's hope of mobilizing support in parts of the country with little direct appreciation of black grievances.

Conscious that segregationists would launch a "Red" smear campaign, march organizers announced their rejection of "the aid or participation of totalitarian or subversive groups of all persuasions" (Garrow 1988: 280). After the *Birmingham News* reported that a known communist, Jack O'Dell, was working at SCLC's New York office, King reluctantly decided to sever ties. With a copy to Burke Marshall in the Justice Department, King formally ended O'Dell's employment. The "situation in our country is such," he wrote, "that any allusion to the Left brings forth an emotional response which would seem to indicate the SCLC and the Southern Freedom Movement are Communist-inspired. In these critical times we cannot afford to risk any such impression" (Oates 1994: 248). The naming of O'Dell convinced Levison that a smear campaign had begun, and he insisted that King end direct contact. Instead, they used black New York attorney Clarence Jones as a go-between. With noticeably less reluctance after their sometimes uneasy partnership during the Birmingham campaign, King downplayed Fred Shuttlesworth's SCLC role after the Cincinnati preacher became head of the already Red-smeared Southern Conference Educational Fund (McWhorter 2001: 469-70). Despite George Wallace's trumpeting of Shuttlesworth's move before a Congressional committee, Robert Kennedy felt able to tell suspicious Senators on July 17 that there was no evidence of communist influence on King or other civil rights leaders (Fairclough 1987: 152).

The interracial character of the march was cultivated both to quell growing white fears of black militancy and to check the separatist sentiments that were growing in the African American community. Observing the escalating May violence in Birmingham, the *Wall Street Journal* had warned that demonstrations would inevitably breed a hostile reaction that would injure "the Negro's own cause." By unleashing such mayhem, leaders like King, it suggested, gave "ammunition to those who say the Negro is socially and politically immature" (Fairclough 1987: 154). King himself was also concerned about the Movement's ability to keep the new African American militancy "from rising to violent proportions." After Birmingham, King had concluded that: "The Negro in the South can now be nonviolent as a stratagem, but he can't include loving the white man ... Nonviolence has become a military tactical approach." His preoccupation with nonviolence as a method of converting the oppressor by moral suasion had been superseded in his quest for coercive force (Garrow 1988: 273).

The competing appeal of Malcolm X made maintaining nonviolent discipline in the face of both white brutality and social inertia more difficult. Already pursued by white reporters for his quotable remarks, Malcolm, as the charismatic spokesman for a separatist sect, the Nation of Islam, had consistently condemned King's approach in Birmingham. While allegations flew that King was a rabble-rousing, communist-backed revolutionary, Malcolm insisted that the nonviolent preacher was "just a twentieth century Uncle Tom." The white man "subsidizes Reverend Martin Luther King," Malcolm sneered, "so that Reverend Martin Luther King can continue to teach the Negroes to be defenseless. That's what you mean by nonviolent, be defenseless" (Oates 1994: 251-52).

The acclaim that eventually greeted King's March on Washington speech should not obscure the resentment he aroused in nationalist circles. Traveling around the nation in late June 1963, King usually enjoyed a hero's welcome. However, in Harlem, some Malcolm X sympathizers threw eggs at King as he arrived at a church rally. The episode's immediate impact was to leave King "feeling sorry for himself and rejected," but it also highlighted King's perennial difficulty in appeasing increasingly frustrated African Americans, particularly those living outside of the South, where institutional discrimination perpetuated racial injustice without recourse to blatantly racist legislation (Garrow 1988: 276). Back in Birmingham, the city council actually repealed the segregation ordinances for public accommodations and testing of the lunch counters proceeded without incident from July 29 onwards. Blacks could now get a hamburger at the same counter with whites downtown, provided they had the money, a point that made the white business leaders' reluctance to meet the accord's employment requirements all the more telling. Increasingly, King's thoughts turned to the predicament of the poor in a rich land.

Neither the Civil Rights Movement nor the Kennedy administration was sure that it wanted the alliance that King seemed to be promoting that summer. Within the Movement, his apparent faith in Kennedy was criticized. Keen to convey the impression of unity, Rustin had secured CORE and SNCC involvement by initially hinting that the march would be a militant occasion with opportunities for direct action against both Congress and dilatory federal agencies. As planning proceeded, it became clear that this would not be the case. SNCC was particularly unhappy with the idea of uncritically backing Kennedy's proposed bill. Rustin had simultaneously courted NAACP involvement in the march with promises of a well-organized rally that would do nothing to embarrass lobbying efforts on Capitol Hill. Roy Wilkins eventually agreed to participate, but not before stating tartly that the NAACP had no wish to spend its funds to stage a benefit concert for King's SCLC (Garrow 1988: 266, 274).

"I Have A Dream"

As the date of the March, August 28, neared, the Kennedys fueled SNCC anger by announcing that the Justice Department would seek criminal indictments against nine civil rights activists in Albany, Georgia, on charges including intimidation of a federal juror. The intimidation took the form of a boycott of white juror Carl Smith's store shortly after a local sheriff was acquitted despite shooting a black prisoner. Much of SNCC's bitterness at the indictments stemmed not just from the conviction that Smith had helped a vicious man escape justice, but from the Justice Department's refusal to pursue other police brutality cases. On August 13, the Attorney-General declined to investigate complaints of police brutality in Americus, Georgia, where the local sheriff had repeatedly used an electric cattle prod on an SNCC field worker, Don Harris. The Congress of Racial Equality, as it strove to sustain voter registration efforts in Plaquemines Parish, Louisiana, similarly saw little sign of a federal protection. There, violent white reactionaries forced CORE's national leader, James Farmer, to escape hidden in the back of a hearse.

Aware of Movement frustrations but equally alert to the panicky state of white public opinion, King joined Roy Wilkins on NBC's "Meet the Press" on August 25. The pair faced largely hostile questioning. How could they promise that there would be no trouble, a panelist asked, when Mayor Richard Daley and National Baptist Convention President the Reverend J.H. Jackson had been abused and heckled at a recent NAACP gathering in Chicago? King had little sympathy for the conservative and autocratic Jackson, who had condemned the March on Washington, or for Daley's stupid declaration to a black audience that there were no ghettos in Chicago, but he replied circumspectly. No, he couldn't condone every recent action, but commentators should remember that the United States "is in the midst of a social revolution, and no social revolution can be neat and tidy at every point." Just in case that untidiness spilled over next Wednesday, 4,000 federal troops were stationed in Washington's suburbs with a further 15,000 paratroopers on standby in North Carolina. Local hospitals postponed elective surgery, and stores transferred "lootable" items to warehouses and accepted a citywide ban on liquor sales. The city courts readied themselves for round-the-clock sessions to process offenders (Branch 1988: 865, 869, 872).

The March was to consist of a parade down the Mall to the Lincoln Memorial with a program of seven-minute speeches interspersed with music. Bayard Rustin oversaw each detail, allowing only authorized placards and badges, and providing a battery of parking and restroom facilities. Speakers were required to submit prepared texts by Tuesday August 27, a requirement which King failed to meet; he arrived late that evening with no finished text. However, this was overlooked as a storm erupted over the draft speech submitted by SNCC. The Kennedy bill was too little and too late, the speech declared, not least because it would do nothing to extend protection to those seeking the right to vote or the numerous people who had already "been arrested on trumped-up charges." Celebrating the bill misrepresented not just an administration that had appointed "racist judges," but the whole of American politics, since both Republicans and Democrats contained prominent enemies of the Movement. The established political order was composed of "cheap political leaders," the speech continued, "who build their careers on immoral compromises and ally themselves with open forms of political, economic and social exploitation." SNCC was already being drawn to the idea of independent third-party politics. But this was just the sort of radical rhetoric that the President felt sure would win no votes on Capitol Hill (Garrow 1988: 281-82).

The SNCC speech ended by explicitly comparing Movement hopes of eradicating segregation and transforming the South to General William T. Sherman's famously destructive "March to the Sea" toward the end of the Civil War. "We shall pursue our own 'scorched earth' policy and burn Jim Crow to the ground – nonviolently," it vowed. Despite the qualifying adverb, this provocative analogy shocked moderates. Cardinal Patrick O'Boyle announced that he would not attend, unless the SNCC speech was toned down. Labor leader Walter Reuther of the UAW also registered concern. With the matter still unresolved only minutes before the program began, SNCC chairman John Lewis found himself in a huddle behind Lincoln's statue. He remembers that Martin made a personal appeal to him to accept revisions. "I think I know you well," King said, "I don't think this sounds like you." According to Ralph Abernathy, King's plea sprang from his grave fears that fiery words might trigger violence that day. "If that happens, Ralph," he confided, "everything we have done in Birmingham will be wiped out in a single day" (Abernathy 1989: 275). Pressed from all sides, particularly by an emotional A. Philip Randolph, SNCC agreed that Lewis would give a more temperate speech.

Disappointing attendances at civil rights rallies in the late 1950s had threatened to discredit Randolph's grand tactic of a march on Washington. However, this time, police estimated the noon crowd along the Mall at over 200,000. Equally pleasing to the leaders, the audience was nearly 25 percent white, and network television relayed images of interracial fellowship around the nation. By the time King emerged to deliver the final speech of the afternoon, ABC, CBS, and NBC had switched from their usual afternoon soap operas to live coverage of the march. This gave

King an unprecedented opportunity to use the relatively new medium of television to touch the nation. Ironically, if Rustin had stuck by his threat to remove any speaker who overran his allotted time, the formal speech, which is rarely remembered, rather than the "I Have a Dream" peroration, would have been all that people heard. However, in the event, the program was ahead of schedule, and so King was allowed to extemporize. He did so by drawing on his extensive back catalog, and in particular, on the climax of his recent speech to 125,000 supporters in Detroit. There, he had spoken of his dream.

The prepared text invoked the centennial example of Lincoln's Emancipation Proclamation as King urged the country to make good its promise of freedom. He reiterated his frustration with those who insisted that "now" was not the best time for African Americans to demand equality. In a characteristic litany of rhythmic predicates and paired oppositions, King almost sang his insistence that:

> *Now* is the time to make real the promise of Democracy. *Now* is the time to rise from the dark and desolate valley of segregation to the sunlit path of racial justice. *Now* is the time to lift our nation from the quicksand of racial injustice to the solid rock of brotherhood.

Less frequently cited than the "I Have a Dream" extemporization, the earlier prepared text captured King's precarious position. He alluded to the fact that nonviolence had proved difficult to sustain and implored his fellow blacks not to "allow our creative protest to degenerate into physical violence." Prompted partly by his New York advisors, his presentation of Southern evils also acknowledged national grievances. It was not just Southern segregation, he declared: "We cannot be satisfied as long as the Negro's basic mobility is from a smaller ghetto to a larger one." On the issue of voting rights, he observed: "We cannot be satisfied as long as a Negro in Mississippi cannot vote and a Negro in New York believes he has nothing for which to vote." There was much to be done, and he tried to warn his fellow Americans that it had best be done quickly, or he would be unable to contain "the whirlwinds of revolt."

But in the closing portion of what was to be the day's finale, King rightly sought to rekindle the faith of the Movement's supporters by offering a positive vision. Explicitly setting aside "the difficulties of today and tomorrow," he spoke instead of the better country that they should seek, of "a dream deeply rooted in the American dream." It was rooted in the words of the Declaration of Independence, which Americans learned by rote in school: "We hold these truths to be self-evident – that all men are created equal." But having alluded to a text that his audience knew well, King then presented a set of images that were shockingly beyond their experience. At a time when school desegregation was ferociously resisted, and when many of the civil rights protests continued to focus on segregated eating places, King spoke of the children of both races sitting "down together at the table of brotherhood" and joining hands "as sisters and brothers." The utopian character of King's dream can only be grasped by acknowledging that in the "red hills of Georgia," the feverishly racist state of Mississippi, and the racially rabid state of Alabama, to which King alluded in turn, such images of black and white children were simply appalling. The image was so filled with tangled fears of sex and family shame, that it was still used to whip up defenders of segregation by Wallace supporters in 1970.

It was in this context that King declared that he dreamed that one day his four little children would "live in a nation where they will not be judged by the color of their skin but by the content of their character." The nicely balanced rhythm and alliteration of this line in King's most frequently cited address, and his posthumous reconstruction as a national hero, have ensured that for conservative opponents of affirmative action, this constitutes the true essence of King's philosophy. Arguing against racial preferences in education and employment, black conservatives such as Shelby Steele and Glenn Loury present King as a fellow advocate of a "color-blind" society (Dyson 2000: 24-29). This not only ignores King's many statements in favor of compensatory mechanisms to redress centuries of white exploitation, it also ignores the fact that the sentence is part of a larger utopian vision. The time to judge solely on the basis of character will be, King implies, the day foretold by the prophet Isaiah, when

> every valley shall be exalted, every hill and mountain shall
> be made low, the rough places will be made plain, and the
> crooked places will be made straight, and the glory of the
> Lord shall be revealed, and all flesh shall see it together.

Whereas his New Right appropriators see King's statement as
justifying a meritocratic hierarchy, King himself placed the judging process within an apocalyptic leveling of all creation before
God. Once all flesh sees the same glory, without low or high, then
there is a chance for color-blind justice.

To interpret King's speech only from the text would be
incomplete since this was undeniably a performance. For the
African Americans present, it was a virtuoso rendition in a familiar
style. As he preached, even some of King's platform colleagues
began interjecting cries of "Preach it" and "Dream some more!"
But to many whites, particularly those watching on television, this
was a kind of speech they had not heard before. The closest analogy was the style of white evangelists, like Billy Graham, but this
was preaching shaped not just by Jesus but by jazz. Familiar
Biblical phrases, and even the words of the national anthem, were
re-sounded to resounding effect. Party convention tricks, as when
speakers appealed to state delegations by name as they looked out
across the crowd, were re-inflected by King to build a crescendo
on a line that King had taken from the 1939 Lincoln Memorial
recital of the heroine of his teenage oration, contralto Marion
Anderson: "Let Freedom Ring." Like a presidential candidate, he
rang first in New Hampshire, and did not overlook the Electoral
College votes of New York, Pennsylvania, and California. But this
was a Southern crowd (by birth and ancestry, if not residence) and
King knew they would cheer the irony of having freedom ring
from Stone Mountain of Georgia (home base of the Ku Klux Klan)
and Lookout Mountain of Tennessee (a former Confederate
stronghold). They would even relish the bluesy self-mockery
of ringing freedom not just from the hills, but the molehills,
of Mississippi, and they would applaud how neatly he segued
back into the national anthem: "From every mountainside, let
freedom ring."

Standing firmly behind the podium and with his baritone soaring through the PA system to a clearly exultant crowd, King

brought the speech back to his prepared text via an appeal to the unity of apparent binaries to reach one of his trademark musical conclusions. He gloried in the day

> when *all* of God's children – black men and white men, Jews and Gentiles, Protestants and Catholics – will be able to join hands and sing in the words of the old Negro spiritual, "Free at last! Free at last! Thank God Almighty, we are free at last!"

A stupendous ovation followed and the still elated crowd roared approval to each of Bayard Rustin's demands of the march: not just passage of the Kennedy civil rights bill, but desegregation of schools, a federal public works program, a $2 minimum hourly wage, and a federal bar on employment discrimination. Morehouse College President Benjamin Mays gave the benediction and the march was over. While Rustin prepared his team for a huge tidying up operation, King left with other leaders to meet a relieved President Kennedy.

It had been a spectacular success. Once Kennedy had congratulated King on his performance, others seized the opportunity to urge the President to strengthen his proposed bill. Randolph warned that in an age of increasing automation, job discrimination was producing a dangerous sense of hopelessness among black teenagers who were dropping out of school in record numbers. The bill must ensure equal opportunities. Now that the march had forged "the broadest working legislative coalition" that liberals had ever mustered, argued Walter Reuther, Kennedy should use the proposed bill to extend the litigation responsibilities of the Attorney-General from school desegregation to other manifest denials of civil rights. This would silence those, like SNCC, who asked: which side was the federal government on?

But Kennedy was not to be bounced into ambitious new proposals. The existing bill faced obstacles enough, he reminded them. It would only pass if the civil rights forces concentrated their fire on the Republicans to support a bi-partisan consensus rather than pressing him for a counter-productive, liberal Democratic crusade. King remained relatively silent, suggesting only that a private moral appeal be made to former President Eisenhower in the hope that he, in turn, might influence House

Minority leader Charles Halleck. Kennedy was unconvinced (Branch 1988: 883-85). Despite the euphoria of the occasion and the plaudits of the press, the politicians remained skeptical about the march's practical effects. "All this probably hasn't changed any votes on the civil rights bill," observed prominent liberal Democratic Senator Hubert Humphrey, adding "but it's a good thing for Washington and the nation and the world" (Lewis 1978: 229-30). The FBI was not so sure. Assistant Director William Sullivan saw King's "powerful demagogic speech" as proof that he was "the most dangerous and effective Negro leader in the country" (Fairclough 1987: 155).

After The March: An Autumn Of Horrors

Even at this moment of widespread acclamation, King faced powerful enemies, including segregationist opponents who would kill to preserve their way of life. He knew well that the momentum for positive change could easily be lost. From September 5 to 7, SCLC members returned to the Dorchester Center to consider the lessons of Birmingham and draft future plans for discussion at the annual convention in Richmond later that month. Taken together, Albany and Birmingham underlined the importance of planning and preparation, of being alert to the danger of internal divisions, and of selecting limited goals to sharpen the focus and maximize the likelihood of, at least some, tangible gains. Tactically, the two campaigns confirmed the utility of economic boycotts, and more especially the value of mass participation by those with "nothing to lose." To maintain the pressure, new campaigns in other target communities – Savannah, Georgia, Danville, Virginia, and Williamston, North Carolina – were taken under consideration (Garrow 1988: 290).

Even before SCLC's September retreat, the approach of a new academic year had reignited the question of school desegregation. Just five African American students were scheduled to register at three previously all-white schools in Birmingham on September 4. Some local leaders appealed for calm, but the night before schools reopened, a National States Rights Party rally heard J.B. Stoner urge white Birmingham to "use any and every method to stop" integration. Predictably, outside the three schools, angry white mobs gathered the next morning, and out of fear or prejudice, 50 percent of parents refused to send their children to school. That night, the home of black attorney Arthur Shores was bombed for the second time in a month. After the blast, African American residents angrily took to the streets, and in the ensuing gunfire from white police and vigilantes, a 21-year-old black man, John Coley, was fatally wounded. Witnesses claimed that he had been mistaken for Fred Shuttlesworth (Manis 1999: 401-2).

King condemned the violence in a telegram to John Kennedy, and attributed the white hysteria to Governor Wallace. In the interest of safety, supposedly, Wallace quickly closed the schools in Birmingham, Tuskegee, Huntsville, and Mobile, thus stopping desegregation temporarily. The schools reopened a week later but Birmingham remained on a knife-edge and Wallace was whetting the blade. On September 5, he told the *New York Times* that what the country needed was "a few first-class funerals, and some political funerals, too" (McWhorter 2001: 503). There was a succession of segregationist rallies, one of which on Saturday September 14 saw white students, waving Confederate flags, storm Mayor Boutwell's office. The next day was the first ever Youth Sunday at Sixteenth Street Baptist Church, a traditionally staid and conservative church, despite its role in the May demonstrations. In new white robes, Denise McNair, aged 11, and Cynthia Wesley, Carol Robertson, and Addie Mae Collins, all 14, attended Sunday school. After studying the topic "The Love That Forgives," they went to what was decorously called the Women's Lounge to check their hair, just as a bomb exploded. Blowing a hole in the side of the church, it killed the four girls and sent survivors screaming into the street. "My God," wept one woman, "we're not even safe in church!" Holding the white dress shoe of his slain granddaughter, Denise McNair's grandfather gave a grief-stricken roar: "I'd like to blow the whole town up!" he yelled (Branch 1988: 889-90).

As rage engulfed the black community, white psychosis continued its deadly work. Two white teenagers, returning from a segregationist rally, fired a pistol at two African American boys riding double on a bicycle, killing the 13-year-old who was perched on the handlebars. As racial clashes sparked along Birmingham's color line, Governor Wallace sent in 300 state troopers under arch-segregationist Colonel Al Lingo and 500 National

Guardsmen. A further 500 city police and 150 deputies, heavily armed, cruised black neighborhoods to stamp out disorder. With grim, sickening predictability, state troopers shot one fleeing African American dead and seriously wounded another (Branch 1988: 890-91).

King was stepping into his home pulpit in Atlanta when word came of the Birmingham church bombing. Warning of the "worst racial holocaust this nation has ever seen," he implored the President to intervene, while in his telegram to Wallace, he was blunt in condemnation: "The blood of our little children is on your hands" (McWhorter 2001: 530). By the next available plane, he arrived in a city ready to erupt. Burke Marshall landed too, with presidential orders to help restore calm without the intervention of federal troops. Despite circumstances that required him, a US Assistant Attorney-General, to reach his destination lying prone in the back of a car with a helmet on, Marshall argued that troops were unnecessary. On behalf of local black leaders, King renewed his plea at a Monday morning press conference for federal forces to take over Birmingham "because Negroes are tired now, tireder than ever before" (Garrow 1988: 292).

The administration's response was typically limited. The requested meeting between the President and Birmingham's black leaders was scheduled. FBI agents, including bomb experts, were sent to investigate and, on television, President Kennedy damned the bombers and praised "the Negro leaders of Birmingham who are counseling restraint instead of violence" (Lewis 1978: 205). He also implicitly condemned Wallace by stating that the "disparagement of law and order has encouraged violence which has fallen on the innocent" (Garrow 1988: 292). To focus attention on this massacre of the innocents, King tried to ensure a mass funeral, even going so far as to intercede personally with the grieving parents of Carole Robertson, who stubbornly insisted on their right to privacy (Branch 1988: 892). None of the four had been among the children who marched in May and Carole's mother told King bitterly that her daughter died "because of the movement" he had brought to Birmingham. Other African Americans had always regarded King's advocacy of nonviolence with disgust. In New York, James Baldwin overheard his sister saying: "Negroes are thinking seriously of assassinating Martin Luther King," and

Jet magazine ran a picture of armed black Birminghamites who were ready to meet the next white attack (McWhorter 2001: 533, 539). Far from being nonviolence's proving ground, Birmingham seemed to be its cemetery. Yet, on Wednesday September 18, just three weeks after the March on Washington, King spoke over three child-size caskets on the theme of redemptive suffering. "They did not die in vain," he declared, "God still has a way of wringing good out of evil" (Oates 1994: 269).

Faith in the purposeful nature of life was fundamental to King's Christianity, but in that autumn the providential hand was hard to discern. Some Southern whites were truly ashamed. The editor of the *Atlanta Constitution* asked fellow Southerners metaphorically to take the slain Denise McNair's shoe in their hands, to "see it straight and look at the blood on it," and progressive white Birmingham attorney Chuck Morgan excoriated his hometown as a morally dead community of cowards. Judge Clarence Allgood, who had previously approved the school expulsions of May's youthful demonstrators, now convened a federal grand jury to investigate the orchestrated obstruction of court-ordered school desegregation. Although incensed by King's unfair portrayal of them as Bull Connor's clerical cheerleaders, Rabbi Grafman and Episcopalian George Murray, two of the ministers addressed in King's "Letter from Birmingham Jail," established a fund to pay for the victims' funeral expenses (McWhorter 2001: 535-37).

But shame was a slow solvent of the white Southerner's fear of breaking ranks. Not one white city official attended Wednesday's funeral services, and when Bull Connor told a Citizens Council meeting in Mobile that he hoped the bombers would be caught, he also floated the possibility that someone in "King's crowd" had bombed the church (Manis 1999: 406-7). The Birmingham settlement seemed to have been whittled down to the store desegregation achieved by the end of July. Downtown stores had not hired African American clerks and the bi-racial committee had not met by October. Token gestures, such as the hiring of a black police officer, a reasonably common feature in other Southern cities by 1963, were resisted by a fearful Boutwell administration. The September bombings, the ensuing disorder, and the accompanying social tensions, kept white leaders fixated on the white violence that any further concessions might trigger (Fairclough 1987: 132).

The Kennedy administration was similarly mesmerized by the panicky, white public opinion. When the President met King and black Birmingham leaders on September 19, he stressed that there was little he could do, and that his bill's fate before Congress depended on the containment of black retaliatory violence. "I can't do much, Congress can't do much, unless we keep the support of the white community throughout the country," Kennedy told the dismayed delegation (Garrow 1988: 295). Apart from words of sympathy, the best he could offer was to send two personal emissaries to mediate Birmingham's racial crisis. Press Secretary Pierre Salinger had announced the appointment of former Army Secretary Kenneth Royall and former West Point football coach Earl Blaik just minutes before King led his delegation into the White House. The two white military retirees were better suited to calming white Birmingham than to empathizing with its black community. Royall was a corporate lawyer from North Carolina and "Red" Blaik's prowess as a coach might win him friends in football-mad Alabama. But the caliber of the panel hardly seemed proportionate to the crime that prompted its appointment (Branch 1988: 893-95).

With Kennedy seemingly keen to minimize his civil rights commitments and with black anger rising, King faced pressure for renewed protests. James and Diane Bevel had initially reacted to the church bombing by seriously considering tracking down the bombers and summarily executing them. But their commitment to nonviolence endured and, by the time of the funerals, they had drawn up a plan for a nonviolent army to lay siege to Governor Wallace's administration in Montgomery. The core of this army, they argued, was already available among the young demonstrators of Birmingham, who had conscientiously undertaken voter registration work that summer. Under their proposal, massed trained protesters would physically surround the state capitol building and sever transportation links while, simultaneously, other volunteers would phone ceaselessly to tie up the state government's switchboard. Following Gandhian precedents, Movement supporters would be urged to withhold their state taxes and pressure would be placed on the Kennedy administration to withhold federal funds until protection of the right to vote in Alabama ensured Wallace's downfall (Garrow 1988: 294).

When King listened to the Bevels' plans on the evening of September 18, the emotional stresses of the last three days made him almost laugh out loud at their extravagance. The Birmingham teenagers had been chafing at the bit of nonviolent discipline after less than a week in May, yet here was a scheme to place thousands of them deliberately in harm's way as they lay across roads and rails and even runways around the Alabama capital. His tactful response was to insist that the scheme's practicalities must receive further consideration. However, by the time of the SCLC annual convention on September 24, rumors of the Bevels' suggestion of an all-out Alabama campaign had found a sympathetic response among CORE and SNCC activists. King knew that many within SCLC itself also believed that the Movement must respond conspicuously to the Birmingham atrocities (Garrow 1988: 294-95).

Banal realities limited King's ability to fulfill his followers' wishes. Despite a surge in donations that enabled SCLC to report an income of $750,000 in the year ending August 31, 1963, King's organization could barely afford more than one major campaign a year. Based on the Birmingham experience, any war chest had to contain hundreds of thousands of dollars for bail bonds and legal costs. As SCLC strove to organize voter registration efforts at the local level, its staff mushroomed to sixty-one members, all of whom had to be paid. A refusal by King's immediate lieutenants to accept tight financial controls meant that unauthorized motel and car hire bills wasted part of the budget. Never slow to assert his own importance, Wyatt Walker demanded a tripling of his salary and the sacking of several insubordinates, especially James Bevel, at the September board meeting. When these requests were not granted, he threatened resignation. Meanwhile, a sulky Ralph Abernathy complained that his convention hotel room was not on a par with King's (Branch 1988: 898-99).

To these petty issues of money and personality were added tactical debates. When the SCLC convention began, the local Virginia trouble spot of Danville seemed the most likely site for the next campaign. But the failure of Kennedy's emissaries to make immediate meaningful contact with Birmingham's black leadership on their arrival increased the pressure on King not to be seen to abandon that troubled community. Birmingham dominated the convention's award ceremonies with the ACMHR predictably receiving Affiliate of the Year, and Fred Shuttlesworth, the Rosa Parks Freedom Award. However, King was unenthusiastic when the board called for renewed protests. Quite apart from the fact that SCLC already had $300,000 locked up in bail bonds in Birmingham, any successful new campaign would have to be even larger than the May demonstrations. It would face opposition from many black residents and would have to sustain itself in an even more volatile climate. The next bomb might touch off a race war that would confirm black novelist John Killens's dire prediction that the church killings marked the end of nonviolence (Oates 1994: 268). At the same time, as news of further explosions arrived, King knew he could not stand aloof.

Closing the convention, King therefore concealed his own misgivings. Bewailing the lack of progress, he declared himself ready to return to Birmingham. Shuttlesworth himself announced a boycott of downtown stores from October 1, and when King returned to the city on October 7, it seemed as if "Birmingham II" was about to begin. However, King was bluffing. Privately, he told colleagues, protests "must be an absolute last resort on our part." The real challenge over the coming weeks, he explained, would be "to keep the threat of demonstrations alive" in the eyes of both a local and national audience, while "constantly find[ing] face-saving retreats in order to avoid demonstrations if possible." By frequent visits to Birmingham that October, King tried to convince the city he was in earnest. But, the bluff failed. Mayor Boutwell ignored King's deadlines for action. The most prominent white signatory to the accord, Sidney Smyer, not only told the press that King and Shuttlesworth should keep out of the city, but added that the four church bomb victims and "others would be living today," were it not for King's demonstrations. The Kennedy administration chimed in that King's threat of renewed demonstrations was simply keeping "whites in Birmingham mad." After a traumatic year, Lucius Pitts said, black Birmingham was "sick, frightened, angry, disappointed, [and] disillusioned," and A.G. Gaston and Arthur Shores responded to fresh segregationist attacks on their homes with a plea for "outsiders" (i.e., King and Shuttlesworth) to stay away. What had seemed a victory felt like a defeat. Over the coming months, as the federal government permitted local authorities to botch the bombing investigation and to give two white teenagers a suspended sentence for willful murder, King's dejection over Birmingham increased (Fairclough 1987: 158-59; McWhorter 2001: 551).

Bayard Rustin began to see even the March on Washington as an ephemeral triumph. Progress, he wrote on November 5, "if measured against the goal to be reached, has been minimal." Opposition was growing and the Kennedys' commitment was commensurately wavering. In Rustin's view, a new phase of direct action was needed to ensure that Congress voted right, and that the Kennedys finally surrendered all hope of party unity via compromise with the hardline Dixiecrats. Pressure was needed, King agreed, but Birmingham, despite its media notoriety, was no place to apply it. It was too riddled with disaffection, he reasoned. Danville, Virginia, was the better prospect. Reports indicated that whites there were split, with local businessmen keen to ease racial tensions. Black tobacco growers had boycotted local warehouses and processing plants, and the city's largest industry, Dan River Mills, feared a nationwide boycott of its textile products. Once again, King believed that economic leverage was the key. By November 12, there were signs that white Danville might concede demands for nondiscriminatory hiring, and six days later Andrew Young reported that, despite local NAACP's hostility, "things seemed to be picking up" (Fairclough 1987: 161; Garrow 1988: 304, 306).

The assassination of John F. Kennedy in Dallas, Texas, on November 22, 1963 threw King's plans for action, like the nation as a whole, into disarray. Among the reasons offered for the President's murder in a Southern town, anger at his recent support for civil rights competed as a motive with the specter of retaliatory violence from international enemies, aroused either by Kennedy's repeated attempts to assassinate Fidel Castro of Cuba, or by American endorsement of the recent South Vietnamese coup against President Diem. More tangled conspiracy theories involving gangsters, such as Sam Giancana, and even Vice-President Lyndon Johnson would emerge subsequently. However, in the immediate aftermath, King publicly ascribed the President's death to what he delicately called a "morally inclement climate" that had been previously signaled by the murder of "Medgar Evers in Mississippi and six innocent children in Birmingham, Alabama."

Privately, he warned his wife Coretta that the assassination reinforced his own fears. "I keep telling you that this is a sick society," he said (Lewis 1978: 236).

With none of King's tact, Malcolm X fatefully responded to a reporter's invitation to explain the President's death by saying bluntly that it was a case of "the chickens comin' home to roost." More controversially, he added that "as an old farm boy himself, 'chickens coming home to roost' never did make me sad, they've always made me glad" (Branch 1998: 184). For this indiscretion, the Right Honorable Elijah Muhammad suspended Malcolm as the Nation of Islam's main spokesman. Increasingly ostracized within the Nation, Malcolm began to redefine himself and his politics, but the process was incomplete at the time of his own murder on February 21, 1965. In November 1963, the internal politics of a black separatist cult aroused less concern than did the implications of Lyndon Johnson's becoming President. To be fair, the Texan's presidential ambitions had ensured that he had been one of the few Southern senators not to sign the Southern Manifesto of 1956 denouncing the Supreme Court's school desegregation decision. He had also been among a similar Southern minority who voted for the Civil Rights Acts of 1957 and 1960, and had spoken forcefully on the moral case for equal rights as Vice-President. But his Texan political base meant that he had never championed civil rights in his rise to Senate majority leader and in the shocked political aftermath of Kennedy's assassination, his reputation as a Senate insider dominated assessments of the new President. King wondered what would happen to the hard-won civil rights bill, especially when he learned that his recent clandestine consultations with Stanley Levison had been observed and might form part of a fresh "Red Scare" campaign during the forthcoming Congressional debates on the bill (Garrow 1988: 308).

Helping The Johnson Civil Rights Bill

Vying for public opinion would be a vital part of passing this contentious legislation. On November 26, as the nation still reeled from the televised shooting of Kennedy's assassin, Lee Harvey Oswald, while under police escort, King joined fellow members of the Council on United Civil Rights Leadership in calling for the civil rights bill's immediate passage as a tribute to JFK. Gratify-ingly, the next day President Johnson, in his first address to Con-gress, declared: "No memorial oration or eulogy could more eloquently honor President Kennedy's memory than the earliest possible passage of the civil rights bill for which he fought so long" (Oates 1994: 274). This exaggeration of Kennedy's com-mitment to civil rights was astute. The new President also decided to see Roy Wilkins of the NAACP on November 29, and Whitney Young of the Urban League two days later, before conferring with King on December 3. Johnson, like Kennedy, saw King as con-stituting as much a public relations problem to be managed as an ally to be cultivated. King emerged from their meeting, never-theless, encouraged by the Texan's hardheaded promise to achieve civil rights reform for the good of their common, native region.

Despite Johnson's private assurances, King remained convinced that, after a respite due to national mourning, the Civil Rights Movement must resume its protest activities. In December 1963 the most active campaign center disconcertingly threatened to be King's hometown of Atlanta, where SNCC was busy highlighting the lack of genuine desegregation in the city reputedly "too busy to hate." Although King spoke at an early rally on December 15 and allowed his colleague Wyatt Walker to draft a battle plan for total desegregation, in the new year he largely watched the inconclusive campaign unfold from the sidelines. Making his hometown into another Birmingham would have meant directly confronting his father and other older black leaders, and this was unpalatable (Fairclough 1987: 175-77).

To help decide SCLC's course, King organized a retreat (January 20-23, 1964) at Black Mountain, near Asheville, North Carolina. There, he reviewed his options for putting pressure on Congress when the Southern filibuster began. Walker suggested that King should undertake a Gandhi-like public fast. The proposal may have been mischievously inspired by the fact that *Time* magazine, while making King its "Man of the Year," had alluded to the fact that a regime of sedentary travel and endless dinner engagements had ensured that, on the eve of his 35th birthday, the short-statured SCLC leader was "a heavy-chested 173 lbs" (Oates 1994: 281). However, King ostensibly gave the proposal consideration, informing the SCLC board in April 1964 that they should leave it to him to decide whether the hunger strike should continue to the point of death. James Bevel's proposed massive assault on George Wallace's Alabama remained the main alternative. The focus should not be desegregation, Bevel argued, but voting rights, a shift already made by many of his former SNCC colleagues, both in Alabama and, more especially, Mississippi (Fairclough 1987: 177-79).

Characteristically deferring his final decision on Bevel's Alabama plan, King came to the retreat encouraged by a recent meeting with Johnson. Unlike Kennedy, the new President exuded a confidence that he would soon have the entire civil rights bill through the House of Representatives "without a word or a comma changed." Johnson's boast was proved false, however, on February 8 when Virginia Representative Howard Smith mischievously proposed adding the term "sex" to the list of forbidden grounds for discrimination in employment in Title VII of the bill. His amendment carried: 168 to 133. While intended to derail the bill, Smith's espousal of rights for women could not prevent the bill's otherwise unmodified passage by the House on February 10 by a comfortably 160 votes' margin. However, the fact that previous civil rights legislation had been blocked or significantly diluted in the Senate dispelled any euphoria among supporters (Branch 1998: 210, 231-34).

King still believed that a protest campaign would secure legislation. With his blessing, Bevel pursued his Alabama plan, using a base in Montgomery to recruit students for his "Freedom Army." By May, he claimed to have active training programs in twelve separate communities. He told an SCLC executive meeting that the campaign would pivot on Governor Wallace's refusal to accept a "decent voting law" thereby justifying a demand for the President to "protect all citizens' right to vote in November's election." He anticipated an escalating eight-month campaign that would require "large numbers of people staying in jail for at least 4 or 5 months," and warned King that the leaders would have to remain in jail also (Fairclough 1987: 179). If King embraced his plan, Bevel pointed out, a Freedom Army would move against Alabama at the same time as the predominantly white, Northern, "Freedom Summer" volunteers invaded Mississippi. The Council of Federated Organizations (COFO), which coordinated civil rights efforts in the latter state, was SNCC dominated and Bob

Moses attended SCLC's May meeting to explain COFO's summer project. The Northern volunteers would help to launch a new Mississippi Freedom Democratic Party and duly elected MFDP delegates would challenge the seating of the regular all-white Mississippi Democratic delegation at the national party convention in Atlantic City in late August. Skeptical of grand battle plans, King asked Bevel to find a more "concrete goal in Montgomery" for his scheme that might nonetheless "lead to [the] larger voter registration goal" (Garrow 1988: 324).

By the May executive meeting, Bevel had largely lost his battle to site SCLC's next major campaign in Alabama. The unpunished church bombing and the failure to implement the 1963 accord had left Birmingham polarized and embittered. Despite his continuing public threats, King was wary of resuming the struggle there. The state capital of Montgomery was another rejected target, despite the appeal of confronting Wallace, who had drawn sizable support from white blue-collar Democrats in the 1964 Democratic presidential primary contests in Wisconsin and Indiana. Since the Bus Boycott, the MIA had declined in energy and effectiveness. Without effective local leadership, it was judged unwise for King to try to resuscitate the spirit of 1956. The presence of rival organizations ruled out Mobile and Selma. Veteran activist John LeFlore held Mobile for the NAACP and Bernard LaFayette had established SNCC's presence in Selma. LeFlore was certain to oppose King's coming to town, while SNCC still held a grudge over King's conduct in Albany. By a process of elimination, St. Augustine, Florida, a tourist resort known as the "Nation's Oldest City," and scheduled to celebrate its quadricentennial in 1965, became SCLC's next target. A quaint town of around 25,000, with a relatively small resident black population (not more than 25 percent of the total), St. Augustine attracted thousands of tourists, many of them Northerners. Perhaps clumsily, but in determined fashion, King would apply there the lessons of the Birmingham campaign.

Exploiting St. Augustine

White reporter Pat Watters notes that, if a case could be made that SCLC had "exploited the local Birmingham situation," the same argument "was stronger in St. Augustine" (Watters 1993: 279). The east Florida resort had an ultra-segregationist city government with Klan ties, and the over 1,000 registered Klansmen in the larger nearby city of Jacksonville were eager to join their St. Augustine brethren in the defense of white supremacy. For all its historic charm, St. Augustine was a racial powder keg. Ignoring the recent desegregation clashes that had rocked other Southern communities and damaged their public image, city fathers had applied for numerous federal grants to renovate historic buildings for quadricentennial celebrations, and were banking on a significant increase in tourism. This direct reliance on federal subsidies and economic vulnerability attracted King. On the downside, the city had little proven black leadership, especially in terms of nonviolence. Local militancy dated only from 1963 when dentist Robert B. Hayling assumed control of the NAACP Youth Council. Older black residents regarded Hayling as a troublemaker after he publicly threatened to disrupt Vice-President Johnson's visit to the city in March 1963 unless African Americans were included in the city's welcoming party. To force concessions, Hayling had also pressed national NAACP leaders to lobby against the city's $350,000 federal grant proposal. By June 1963, black moderates feared "an ugly Birmingham situation" that would "mean TOTAL COLLAPSE [emphasis in original] for our economy and tourist business" (Colburn 1991: 35).

A Korean War veteran, Hayling sounded more like his fellow NAACP militant Robert Williams, or Malcolm X, than Martin Luther King. After several death threats, he told reporters on June 19 that he would not practice "passive resistance." To avoid the fate of the recently murdered Medgar Evers, he intended to "shoot first and ask questions later" (Colburn 1991: 35). On September 18, while King preached endurance at the Birmingham funerals, Hayling decided to eavesdrop on a Klan rally. He and three NAACP colleagues were captured and severely beaten before sheriff's deputies arrived in time to prevent their lynching. County authorities prosecuted the four black men as well as four members of the Klan. As a sign of St. Augustine's racism, at the November 4 trial, the charges against the Klansmen were dismissed but the battered Hayling was found guilty of criminal assault (Branch 1998: 141-43).

The national NAACP regarded Hayling as needlessly provocative. Rejected, he turned to SCLC in March 1964, and King responded positively, with one eye on the task of securing increased national leverage on Congress. While Fred Shuttlesworth has insisted that the Birmingham campaign had simultaneously local and national objectives, he is on record as seeing the St. Augustine campaign as explicitly a means of pressuring Congress to adopt the civil rights bill. SCLC's director of branches, the Reverend C.T. Vivian, who recommended SCLC involvement in the city, has also stated that: "passage of the civil rights bill was a primary goal of the SCLC in St. Augustine." King wanted a setting for a nationally broadcast drama, and newspaper headlines over Easter 1964 illustrated St Augustine's suitability. As head of a new SCLC affiliate, Hayling invited Northern supporters to visit the resort to protest against segregation. The subsequent imprisonment of Mary Peabody, wife of Episcopalian Bishop Malcolm Peabody and mother of Governor Endicott Peabody of Massachusetts, catapulted St. Augustine's racial conditions onto the nation's front pages on March 31 (Colburn 1991: 56-63, quotation 63, 67).

In choosing St. Augustine, King seemed to retrace his Birmingham reasoning. He stressed the city's reliance on tourism, including a high proportion of Northern visitors. By deterring visitors, protests against the resort's segregated hotels, lunch counters, and restaurants would constitute an economic boycott. At the same time, the spectacle of nonviolent demonstrators being arrested or mistreated for requesting services that most white Americans took for granted would excite popular sympathy. Wyatt Walker wanted the St. Augustine movement to "visually pull the nonviolent thrust of the Negro back on center." He complained that the media now termed every form of African American dissent, nonviolent or not, a "demonstration." SCLC needed to "re-capture the moral offensive" by reminding the nation of the Southern movement's special dignity and discipline (Fairclough 1987: 181-82). White Southern violence was the vital foil for that dignity.

King had now recognized how essential "creative tension" was to his influence. During late May demonstrations, Klan violence, directed by local bootlegger Holstead "Hoss" Manucy with the active cooperation of Sheriff L.O. Davis, graphically illustrated that St. Augustine's defense of segregation could be as headline-grabbing as Birmingham's. Historian Adam Fairclough dismisses the claim that SCLC leaders willfully chose St. Augustine because it was a Klan stronghold where they were guaranteed a violent white response that would unwittingly serve their national purposes (Fairclough 1987: 184). However, once violence erupted on May 28, they seemed intent on provoking it further. SCLC campaign coordinator Hosea Williams quickly matched Jim Bevel as a creator of dramatic racial confrontations. His preferred tactic was the night march, which he had developed a year earlier in his home resort community of Savannah, Georgia. Williams claimed the tactic was unavoidable since most African Americans were at work during the daylight hours. But he and King knew that a black protest march through St. Augustine's poorly lit, narrow streets offered a highly inviting target for the Klan, which was similarly more able to rally support after, rather than during, the working day. The media seemed to attract particular antagonism during night marches. On May 28, NBC cameraman Irving Gans was slashed with a bicycle chain and photographer James Kerlin was beaten to the ground. While King himself remained keen to minimize his followers' injuries, he recognized that white violence intensified press sympathy for the civil rights demonstrators (Branch 1998: 324).

Escalating violence caught on camera seemed the most likely trigger for federal intervention. Drive-by shootings into the rented houses used by King and his aides illustrated the potential for lethal violence and King relayed details of Sheriff Davis's visible collusion with Hoss Manucy's Klansmen to the Justice Department. At the same time, however, Florida Senator George Smathers told President Johnson on June 1 that he reckoned that the shooting episodes were a publicity stunt by King's people. "It would be very bad if the federal government did anything more than confer with [Governor] Bryant," he added (Branch 1998: 326). A Justice Department report saw immediate mediation efforts as pointless, especially since the issue of desegregation of public accommodations would shortly be addressed by the civil rights bill, which was being filibustered in the Senate. The best hope of federal action lay with US District Court Judge Bryan Simpson to whom Movement attorneys had complained over both Mayor Shelley's denial of the right to protest and local police conduct. Simpson was visibly moved by accounts of Davis's crowding of protesters into the so-called "chicken coop," a shade-less cage outside the sun-baked county jail. He was also appalled that Hoss Manucy, whom he had sentenced for bootlegging, was one of Davis's special deputies (Garrow 1988: 328-29).

With the civil rights bill nearing a vital vote to end debate in the Senate, the black leadership agreed on June 3 to suspend night marches until Judge Simpson ruled on their complaints. The following day, King flew in to rally his "heroes of St. Augustine," and a day later announced that further demonstrations would be unnecessary, if city officials agreed to a Birmingham-style list of demands (Branch 1998: 326). They must desegregate hotels and restaurants within thirty days; hire twelve new black city employees within ninety days; promise that all city businesses would accept job applications from blacks; drop all charges; and establish a bi-racial committee on which two-thirds of the African American representatives must be SCLC nominees. King then left for two pre-scheduled appearances in Connecticut and New York, illustrating both the intermittent nature of his involvement in local campaigns, which his SNCC critics found so offensive, and his itinerant lifestyle, which was eroding his marriage.

FBI agents had taped an angry phone call from Coretta the previous weekend, which they now offered to share with Florida state officials in order to embarrass King. They rescinded the offer, however, when it threatened to expose their now extensive bugging operations. Late in the afternoon of June 9, Judge Simpson upheld the movement's complaints and required police authorities to protect the constitutionally guaranteed right to peaceful protest and end their mistreatment of prisoners. At 7.38 p.m. that evening Senator Robert Byrd of West Virginia began a speech, which at fourteen hours and thirteen minutes proved to be one of the longest in Senate history. But when at last he yielded shortly before 10.00 a.m. on June 10, the vote of cloture ending the filibuster was passed: 71 to 29. Whilst Byrd was speaking, Andrew Young was being beaten as he led a double column of around 300 marchers to St. Augustine's Old Slave Market. Police ignored the incident (Branch 1998: 333-36).

Even with judicial backing and the great hurdle of Southern resistance in the Senate overcome, King decided that the protest campaign in St. Augustine had to continue. After urging federal intervention again on June 10, he approved another night march. Thanks to the efforts of reassigned Florida state highway patrolmen, who used tear gas against the much larger crowds of whites, the 400 demonstrators escaped serious injury. Privately, King was preparing an eventual retreat from St. Augustine, signaling through intermediaries that just a clear willingness to address racial problems would induce him to withdraw. But publicly, he needed to appear militant both to provide a channel for black anger and to sustain the pressure for reform. On June 11 he submitted to a well-publicized arrest at the Monson Motor Lodge, the preferred motel for visiting journalists. Reluctant to protect their hated prisoner, local police swiftly arranged for King to be transferred to Jacksonville's Duval County Jail. Restless in solitary confinement, King learned that Senator Smathers had offered to raise his bail if he would leave the Sunshine State, and that J.B. Stoner and other white supremacists had led a heavily protected night march of around 200 segregationists through Lincolnsville, St. Augustine's black residential district (Branch 1998: 338-45).

From custody, King secretly testified to a Florida grand jury – set up to investigate the city's crisis – that the establishment of a bi-racial committee would end his campaign. He filed bail on June 13 to keep engagements in New England and to consider who should replace Wyatt Walker as SCLC executive director. Andrew Young seemed the obvious choice. Noting a lull in demonstrations, a Miami reporter induced Young to confess that SCLC was "just over-programmed and everybody's tired" (Fairclough 1987: 186). St. Augustine had largely served its purpose and was becoming a drain on SCLC. Ultimately, the campaign would reinforce for King the lesson of how important it was to prepare a path for disengagement.

However, SCLC's immediate actions seemed designed to prolong rather than terminate the campaign. On June 15 Governor Bryant announced that he was creating a Special Police Force to restore order in St. Augustine. This promised much more vigorous policing of the hostile white crowds who had attacked the night marchers. Sensing that these marches no longer excited the press, Hosea Williams developed tactics with greater potential for photogenic violence. A large press corps covered a "wade-in" off previously segregated beaches on June 17, photographing state police as they struggled to keep whites and blacks apart in the rolling surf. SCLC also rerouted its marches so that they passed through upper-class, white residential neighborhoods, where limited street lighting and lush vegetation made policing counter-demonstrators more difficult. Visits by celebrities like baseball star Jackie Robinson and by groups of Northern white sympathizers added further photo opportunities.

Another publicity bonanza occurred on June 18, when a party of rabbis tried to register at the Monson Motor Lodge and an integrated group jumped into the hotel's swimming pool. This stunt so incensed the Monson's owner James Brock that he tried to scare the demonstrators by pouring what he claimed to be acid into the water. When they refused to move, a local police officer leaped into the pool and began pummeling the protesters. Observing the mayhem, King was alleged to have said: "We are going to put Monson out of business," although whether this was a statement of malicious intent, or a sanguine assessment of how the negative publicity would hurt the hotel, is unclear. The bizarre swimming pool battle appeared on evening news broadcasts and photos made the front page of both the *New York Times* and the Soviet Union's *Izvestia* (Colburn 1991: 96-100).

The Monson pool incident seemed deliberately to divert attention from the grand jury report issued the same day. SCLC knew in advance that a key recommendation would be the formation of a bi-racial committee after a thirty-day cooling-off period. Although King wanted a committee, he balked at the report's stated precondition of a lengthy suspension of protest. He sensed that he needed to bolster his claims as a militant leader among a national black audience. Repeating a point from his "Letter from Birmingham Jail," he complained that the grand jury wrongly claimed that racial harmony had existed before his arrival. St. Augustine "may have had a negative peace which was the absence of tension," he declared, "but certainly not a positive peace which is the presence of justice." The first concession should come from local whites. They should appoint a bi-racial committee immediately and, once it convened, protests would be suspended for one week (Colburn 1991: 100-102).

King was also unwilling to end the St. Augustine campaign before the civil rights bill passed. The cloture vote in the Senate guaranteed passage, but the need to reconcile House and Senate versions provided a last opportunity for conservatives to dilute the statutory powers granted. King believed that incidents like those at the Monson Motor Lodge demonstrated the need for federal law to regulate discriminatory practices, even in quite small businesses. Unlike the situation with Fred Shuttlesworth in Birmingham in May 1963, King's eagerness to continue the protests for national reasons complemented Robert Hayling's desire to continue for local gains. Active protest and national publicity provided the only leverage local African Americans had in a community that relied on neither their purchasing power nor their political support. At the same time, however, St. Augustine resembled Birmingham in that active local support for demonstrations was falling and the prolonged campaign was aggravating SCLC's already overstretched financial condition. Ultimately, King would have to leave St. Augustine, and probably before tangible local gains were made. However, he needed to maneuver carefully both to retain the respect of black militants, who might compare his stance unfavorably to SNCC persistence in Mississippi, and to keep the sympathy of white liberals, whose commitment he always had reason to doubt.

Leaving St. Augustine

King's national objective, the Civil Rights Act, was passed on June 20, without significant dilution of its provisions. That same day, Judge Simpson refused to allow Governor Bryant to ban further nighttime demonstrations. Segregationist outrage ensured that even daytime confrontations became more vicious over the following week; and the authorities doubted their own ability to forestall a descent into inter-communal warfare. Having brought the problems of St. Augustine dramatically to the surface, King sought now to defuse the crisis sufficiently to allow the task of renegotiating race relations in the city to begin. Through white intermediaries, discussions resumed. At a secret meeting over the weekend of June 26, King spoke to State Attorney Dan Warren. "I want out of St Augustine," he allegedly said, "but I can't go out of here a loser and will not go out of here a loser" (Colburn 1991: 110). The earlier grand jury proposal had offered a bi-racial committee in a negative way that suggested that King had misled his followers. The formation of the committee now, if accompanied by vigorous action against the local Klan, would boost the movement and King's credibility among black militants and white moderates.

On June 30, as divisions and fears among local whites threatened to block a settlement, Governor Bryant simply announced the establishment of a four-man "emergency bi-racial committee." It was what King needed. He quickly suspended the protest and announced to the press that SCLC resources would be redirected to Alabama. As with the Birmingham campaign, the gains in St. Augustine seemed meager in terms of the effort. The governor's bi-racial committee never met and, after the grand jury appointed its own committee on August 5, this too failed to materialize. The campaign left local race relations in shambles, with such widespread intimidation that few people were willing to serve on any committee dealing with racial matters. By staging protests that invited Klan attacks, SCLC left white St. Augustine ill-prepared for desegregation, and it failed to develop a tier of grassroots black leaders to continue the fight. The scenes of disorder may have spurred other Southern communities to desegregate voluntarily to avoid St. Augustine's traumas but, as David Colburn concludes, the Florida resort itself, "especially its black community, paid a heavy price for inviting King into their community" (Colburn 1991: 209-10).

The campaign's justification lay in Washington with the passage of the Civil Rights Act. King believed he had ensured its passage. He told colleagues at SCLC's October convention that "when we are idle, the white majority very quickly forgets the injustices which started our movement." St. Augustine, he explained, reminded everyone why the civil rights bill was proposed in the first place (Garrow 1988: 353). King's senior colleagues concurred; their campaign had secured the bill. However, if their role was so pivotal, how come the 63,000 pages of the *Congressional Record* occupied by the civil rights bill debate contain no direct references to the St. Augustine protests? For their own reasons, neither the NAACP's Roy Wilkins nor CORE's James Farmer refers to the St. Augustine demonstrations when they discuss the battle to secure the 1964 Act in their memoirs (Wilkins 1984: 295-302; Farmer 1985: 293-96). John F. Kennedy's assassination and Lyndon Johnson's political skills were more directly important than King's campaign (Mann 1996). But St. Augustine did make headlines in both March and June, pricking the consciences of white church leaders and religious groups outside of the South to whom King had appealed increasingly since Birmingham. Their letters of concern to Republican Congressmen and Senators bolstered a bi-partisan consensus that civil rights had become, in the words of Senate Minority Leader Everett Dirksen of Illinois, "an idea whose time had come" (Oates 1994: 298). St. Augustine also showed King's African American constituency that he was still actively and militantly engaged in the struggle at a time when rival direct action organizations – SNCC and CORE – were launching their most ambitious project yet: Freedom Summer. King's conduct in St. Augustine should be seen as part of an exhausting balancing act that enabled him to remain the one civil rights leader who commanded strong support on both sides of the racial divide and across the spectrum from moderate to militant.

Staying In The Middle: King, Johnson, And The MFDP

King flew to Washington for the formal signing of the Civil Rights Act on July 2. He listened after the ceremony as President Johnson lobbied black leaders for a curtailment of demonstrations, now that there was a basis for redress in law. Further protests, the President warned, threatened to fuel the white backlash, already evident in George Wallace's primary votes and Senator Barry Goldwater's likely selection as the Republican presidential candidate. It might even jeopardize Johnson's own cherished nomination at the Democratic convention (Garrow 1988: 338). King was weary. He had encouraged dozens of ordinary people to remain nonviolent in the face of white brutality during the St. Augustine campaign, and seen little sign of white contrition. His SNCC and CORE colleagues had the ongoing search for three missing civil rights workers foremost in their minds. Two white New Yorkers, CORE worker Michael Schwerner and summer volunteer Andrew Goodman, and Schwerner's black colleague, native Mississippian

James Chaney, had never returned from a visit to a burned-out church in Neshoba County on June 21 (Cagin and Dray 1988). If events in St. Augustine and Mississippi expressed the mood of the white South, King's proposed testing of compliance with the new law in Alabama and SNCC's and CORE's organizing of the Mississippi Freedom Democratic Party (MFDP) seemed set to produce a summer of unabated unrest. Advising Mississippi businessmen to ignore the new law, Governor Paul Johnson was already threatening "a very bad reaction against Lyndon Johnson" (Branch 1998: 389).

As the 1964 presidential contest intensified, King told an unsympathetic Republican platform committee that there would be no "cessation of demonstrations" until racial injustice was completely eliminated. He then saw the conservative-controlled convention nominate Goldwater, one of only six Republican Senators to vote against the Civil Rights Act. Since he "articulates a philosophy which gives aid and comfort to the racist," King urged supporters not to vote for Goldwater. Although never endorsing Lyndon Johnson, and with a deepening skepticism about the promised War on Poverty, King thereafter continued to tell audiences who not to vote for, which created the false impression amongst SNCC and CORE workers that he was becoming Johnson's lackey. A whistle-stop tour of Mississippi (July 21-24), intended to symbolize SCLC's support for the MFDP, wooed few SNCC activists back to "De Lawd," as they had nicknamed King. Colleagues, like Ralph Abernathy, aggravated the situation by using messianic terms when they introduced King at rallies. After years of complaining of inadequate protection, SNCC workers found the sight of King traveling from town to town with a police escort, and FBI protection, galling in the extreme, especially as he excited greater popular awe, and drew many more reporters than they ever did (Lewis 1978: 249).

King's lavish protection came only after direct presidential orders, reflecting the increase in number, ferocity, and specificity of death threats against him. Aware of the risks, he came close to canceling the tour until staff reminded him he had no choice. After sulking for an hour, King conceded that they had been right to remind him that he could not lead an ordinary life because he was not an ordinary man. In Mississippi, he discussed the MFDP's planned challenge to the credentials of the all-white regular delegation at the Democratic National Convention in Atlantic City. Committed to supporting this challenge, he listened attentively as Bayard Rustin warned of the risks of disrupting the Convention in the wake of Goldwater's nomination. Only days later, he consulted Rustin again when New York Mayor Robert Wagner requested his help in calming Harlem street disturbances that erupted after police shot a black teenager. Rustin advised him to talk to Harlem Unity Council President Livingston Wingate, who believed that King might boost demands for a civilian review board for police brutality cases. However, when King secured no concessions, Wingate quickly branded him an interloping Uncle Tom (Garrow 1988: 341-42; Branch 1998: 423).

Allegations that King was becoming the white man's cat's-paw sharpened after July 29 when he backed Roy Wilkins (NAACP) and Whitney Young (National Urban League) against James Farmer (CORE) and John Lewis (SNCC) in a debate over "a broad curtailment, if not total moratorium of all mass marches, picketing and demonstrations" until after the November election. Had he maintained his previous stance on the need for protest, the resolution would never have been released to the press (Garrow 1988: 343). The suspicion that King was becoming a moderate intensified further after the Atlantic City convention, where President Johnson feared any civil rights-related controversy might lead to a walk-out by Deep South delegations. On August 22, despite a sprained ankle that required him to use a cane, King appeared before the convention's credentials committee to endorse the MFDP's claim to represent Mississippi. This was "no mean issue" in world affairs, he declared, since recognition of the MFDP would say to disenfranchised millions "behind the Iron Curtain, [or] floundering in the mire of South African apartheid", or in election-less Cuba "that somewhere in the world there is a nation that cares about justice" (Branch 1998: 460).

Despite this appeal, and Mrs. Fannie Lou Hamer's even more compelling testimony about Mississippi's totalitarian-style brutality, the credentials committee succumbed to Johnson pressure and refused to seat the MFDP. Instead, it offered a compromise. It required the white regulars to take a loyalty oath to support the party's nominee and platform (i.e., Lyndon Johnson and the Civil Rights Act), a move that prompted most of them to head for home. It promised a commission to enforce nondiscrimination at the 1968 Convention and, as a token, it proposed seating the MFDP as honored guests, with the party's black chair Aaron Henry and white co-chair Ed King seated as voting delegates-at-large. Compared to men like Roy Wilkins, who treated the mainly lower-class MFDP delegates with contempt, King did not press hard for the compromise's acceptance. He could see good arguments both for and against it. Ed King recalled Martin's conclusion: "He said 'So, being a Negro leader, I want you to take this, but if I were a Mississippi Negro, I would vote against it.'" It was an adept straddling of the fence, but one quickly brushed aside by Bob Moses's denunciation of political expediency. "We're not here to bring politics to our morality," he said, "but to bring morality to our politics." The majority of MFDP delegates rejected the deal. "We didn't come all this way for no two seats," declared Mrs. Hamer (Branch 1998: 473-74).

Tired and troubled, King did not even stay to hear President Johnson's acceptance speech. He knew that the MFDP challenge had deepened divisions and his uneasy relationship with SNCC had deteriorated further. The last twelve months had exhausted him and alienated several colleagues. Relations with Fred Shuttlesworth had soured, Ralph Abernathy was keeping score on how often he was overlooked, and Wyatt Walker had left. A drained Andrew Young was now executive director and, with the St. Augustine campaign under his belt, Hosea Williams was ready to jostle James Bevel for his Birmingham-earned title of SCLC "hothead." The organization's current deficit was $50,000 on a budget nearing two-thirds of a million. In mid-September, King, Coretta, and the attention-craving Abernathy went on a short European tour that included Berlin, Rome, Madrid, and London. The SCLC preachers had an audience with Pope Paul VI but, there were too many speeches and press conferences for this to be a vacation. When King returned to the United States, his speaking schedule continued relentlessly. On October 13, he checked into an Atlanta hospital where doctors found him to be twenty pounds overweight, with high blood pressure and a viral infection. He desperately needed rest. After a night of sedated sleep, he awoke to a phone call. It was Coretta, telling him he had been awarded the Nobel Peace Prize. The tightrope of leadership had been raised to another level.

7   Across A Bridge Of Mistrust

Selma To Montgomery, 1964-65

Success for Martin Luther King was never complete, enduring, or unambiguous. As 1964 neared its end, he could take satisfaction in the newly passed Civil Rights Act. It had outlawed segregation of public accommodations, greatly strengthened the federal government's ability to secure school desegregation by threatening the suspension of vital grants-in-aid to noncompliant school districts, and provided a legal basis for affirmative action to remedy employment discrimination. The November elections had also been encouraging. President Johnson had won a landslide victory on November 3 over Republican Barry Goldwater, with 61 percent of the national vote. This included a remarkable 96 percent of the black vote, some of it swayed by King's anti-Goldwater speeches. The elections had also returned a Congress more supportive of civil rights. Fully half the Northern members who had opposed the 1964 Act were defeated to ensure that the forty-eight Democratic gains in the House temporarily accentuated its liberal outlook on racial matters (Branch 1998: 522).

With racial progress a product of so many factors, the media's attribution of black gains to the man nicknamed "De Lawd" intensely irritated SNCC activists. This made King defensive in public, and privately concerned not to appear self-serving. But his expressions of modesty and dedication on the award of the Nobel Peace Prize still struck some as sanctimonious. "History has thrust me into this position," he told reporters. "It would be both immoral and a sign of ingratitude if I did not face my moral responsibility to do what I can in this struggle" (Garrow 1988: 354-55). To preempt the resentment of rivals and the demands of

Coretta and other family members, King announced that he accepted the Prize on behalf of the whole Civil Rights Movement rather than himself. Accordingly, Movement organizations would share the entire $54,600 prize money.

To rebuff claims that he was now a presidential lackey, King told the *New York Times* on November 4 that civil rights protests must resume. The fact that only 21 percent of eligible black Alabamans and 6 percent of eligible black Mississippians could vote in the election, he remarked, highlighted why voting rights must be the next priority. Rumblings of violent discontent in the Northern ghettos, however, simultaneously forewarned King that securing the Southern black vote would not end his task. He warned his SCLC colleagues that they must develop nonviolent methods to address ghetto injustices, but their immediate focus must be ending Southern disenfranchisement. Despite recent gains, King reminded his staff that the struggle had to continue and broaden.

Securing The Right To Vote

Securing the vote had always been integral to the civil rights struggle. Both King's grandfather and father had used Ebenezer's pulpit to encourage voter registration, and a growing black vote had helped to liberalize Atlanta's politics relative to those of Georgia's rural districts. In Montgomery, King had encouraged Dexter Avenue Church members to be registered voters, knowing that the act of registration was a sign of racial self-assertion. By 1965, the political exclusion of African Americans had already been dented. A half-century of migration from the rural South, which created the Northern black communities to whom King turned on his frequent fund-raising tours, had established important black voting blocs in New York, Ohio, Pennsylvania, Michigan, Illinois, and California. Particularly after Harry Truman's surprise reelection in 1948, both parties' presidential candidates kept an eye on this black vote.

After the US Supreme Court's 1944 outlawing of all-white primary elections to choose party candidates in the solidly Democratic South, African American influence on regional politics seemed destined to grow in proportion to the number of registered black voters. Since 1962, the VEP, despite violent intimidation in the rural Deep South, had secured sizable increases in the Southern urban black vote. In Black Belt areas of Alabama, Arkansas, the Carolinas, Georgia, Louisiana, Mississippi, Tennessee, and Virginia, where African Americans were potentially in the majority, this potential electoral revolution, in combination with white supremacist fears of school desegregation, sparked a determined and, in some cases, murderous reaction from 1955 onwards. When King returned to Montgomery at the head of a mass march from Selma in the spring of 1965, he no longer simply threatened federal intervention to overturn segregationist practices but the entire local political establishment. The so-called courthouse cliques of the plantation districts would have to fight for their political lives.

Like most civil rights leaders, King saw African American disenfranchisement, and its corollary, the unaccountability of elected officials, notably the sheriff and the school board, as basic to the maintenance of racial inequality. Its consequences were visible in the way the paving and street lighting often stopped as one entered the black districts of a Southern town. Civil rights legislation, even the 1964 Act, did not ensure that blacks could freely register to vote. The burden of proving discrimination fell on Movement and Justice Department lawyers. Each case wound tortuously through the judicial process to produce, at best, a judgment applying to just one registration district. Moreover, the courts would permit complicated application procedures, inconvenient registration office hours, and literacy and "constitutional understanding" tests as long as the evidence suggested that they had been applied equally to all applicants (Hampton and Fayer 1994: 212).

Despite its urban successes, evident in the more economically diversified Upper South, the VEP mainly demonstrated how slowly the electoral balance of power in the rural Deep South would change without radical measures to overcome vehement white supremacist resistance. After two years of intensive work and several violent, unpunished deaths, activists had raised African American voter registration in Mississippi from below 5 to less than 7 percent in what was potentially a black-majority state. At a time when rapid social and economic change was fueling black out-migration, the electoral power that might demand political action to reduce the suffering of displaced black tenants and laborers was in danger of evaporating before it could be used. Within a year of the Selma campaign, liberal legislation, be it civil rights or anti-poverty measures, seemed inadequate for the revolution that King sensed was needed. Poverty, institutional racism, and disempowerment required the sustained mobilization of an army of the disadvantaged. The middle classes could never be as radical as "legions of the deprived" (Jackson 2007: 195, 203)

For much of 1964, James Bevel had lobbied King to launch an Alabama campaign focused on the right to vote. The prospect of teaming up with his former SNCC colleague, Bernard LaFayette, attracted Bevel to Selma, and the notoriety of Dallas County Sheriff Jim Clark, which matched that of Birmingham's Bull Connor, attracted SCLC more generally. So, too, did the fact that local registrars routinely rejected would-be African American voters, while enrolling whites of equal or less educational competence. Despite SNCC's efforts since 1963, whites comprised 99 percent of Selma's voters, although they constituted less than half the adult population of the city's 29,000 residents.

Local efforts to implement desegregation under the new Civil Rights Act in July 1964 prompted State Judge James Hare to ban all gatherings of three or more under the auspices of SNCC, SCLC, the Dallas County Voters League (DCVL), or any one of more than forty named persons and organizations. But neither Hare's blatant disregard for the First Amendment nor his open belief in white supremacy prevented this legal repression from staying in force for the rest of the year. According to an SCLC advance party, the only disadvantage to Selma as a site from which to dramatize the issue of voting rights was likely SNCC hostility. Two middle-class DCVL stalwarts, insurance agent Amelia Boynton and teacher Frederick Reese, reported that SNCC's effort had "just about run its course" by late 1964. They appealed to SCLC to come and rejuvenate an enfeebled movement. But King knew that SNCC would not readily surrender its turf. It would demand consultation vociferously both before and during any protest campaign (Garrow 1988: 359-60).

The Threat Of Scandal

When the new Nobel Laureate arrived in Selma on January 2 to extol the powers of the ballot to a mass meeting, however, it was not SNCC's critical presence that depressed him. Ever since November 18 when FBI Director J. Edgar Hoover had described King as the "most notorious liar in America," the enmity of this powerful figure had disturbed the SCLC leader. At the time, King was unaware of the intensity of the FBI's surveillance, although he suspected that Hoover knew that he had remained in contact with Stanley Levison, despite official warnings that he must ostracize anyone with known communist connections. Certainly, after meeting surreptitiously with CORE's James Farmer on November 30, King knew that Hoover's smear campaign included rumors of sexual impropriety. A hastily arranged meeting with the FBI Director on December 1 had produced no genuine rapprochement. Even while the two men conferred, one waiting newsman was offered "the dirt" on King in an adjoining room (Garrow 1988: 360-63).

Scandal had also threatened to erupt during King's trip to receive the Nobel Prize due to the unseemly conduct of his entourage. A tipsy Bayard Rustin created a scene at a US Embassy dinner in Oslo by loudly decrying the vices of King's traveling companions. Ralph and Juanita Abernathy nearly caused a diplomatic incident by trying to force their way into the limousine that Norwegian officials had assigned to carry the Laureate and his wife to the presentation ceremony. Finally, after Martin's high-toned Nobel lecture, commending the use of nonviolence in every field of human conflict, his brother A.D. King and other young men in the party came the closest to sparking a major scandal. Police were called in the early hours to arrest several prostitutes who had made off with money and belongings after promises that sexual favors would secure access to the "great man" himself proved false. His quick wits fortunately restored, Rustin persuaded the police not to press charges by warning that the incident would reflect badly on their security arrangements. He also secured a discreet silence from the "ladies" by allowing them to keep their loot (Branch 1988: 540-43; Garrow 1988: 366-67).

King rightly feared a smear campaign in 1965, and felt himself unworthy of the adulation he excited. The FBI's electronic surveillance had already caught the SCLC leader in some compromising situations, notably at the Willard Hotel in Washington in early 1964. Having determined as early as February 1962 that

King was "no good in any way," Hoover had become obsessed with King's private life (Branch 1988: 207, 565). In an internal report written after hearing the Willard Hotel tapes, he referred to King as "a 'tom cat' with obsessive degenerate sexual urges" (Garrow 1988: 312). Hoover's animus against King seems to have drawn strength from the Director's tangled feelings about his own sexuality. Andrew Young has insightfully commented, "The campaign against Martin and the movement was less about sex than about fear of sexuality," and of black male sexuality especially (Young 1996: 471; Dyson 2000: 159).

Shortly after Hoover's November remarks against King, Assistant FBI Director William Sullivan had a tape of "highlights" prepared. He composed a threatening cover note, seemingly from an anonymous black correspondent, and had the tape mailed to King from Miami to conceal its Washington origins. "You are done," the letter warned. "There is but one way out for you. You better take it before your filthy abnormal fraudulent self is bared to the nation." Intended to reach King before he accepted the Nobel Prize ("a grim farce," the poison pen letter called it), the letter gave King the thirty-four days until Christmas to withdraw from public life, or better yet, commit suicide. Buried in the office mail, the package was not opened until January 5. Realizing immediately that this tape was certainly not another recording to add to King's speech collection, nor part of the usual hate mail, Coretta King called her husband. With several confidants, King listened intently and repeatedly to the tape himself (Garrow 1988: 373-74).

The taped noises of sexual activity, lewd comments, and bawdy remarks came from at least three different locations, King estimated, which meant a concerted bugging campaign, almost certainly by the FBI. Deeply distressing to King personally, this vicious tactic of the "suicide package" nonetheless failed as a device to end his public career. At the time, Coretta publicly concealed any animosity she may have felt, and till her death in 2006, she remained dismissive of this "dirty tricks" campaign. Remarkably, newspaper editors of the day showed no great interest in publishing extracts from the FBI's King file and President Johnson, renowned for his coarse sense of humor, reportedly found the tape simply amusing. Thus, the campaign's effect was largely to increase the psychological pressure on King personally. Two days after hearing the embarrassing tape, King preached at Atlanta University about the need to fight the three basic evils of war, racism, and poverty. "When you stand up against entrenched evil," he warned, "you must be prepared to suffer a little more" and to "have some dark and agonizing moments" (Garrow 1988: 374-76).

Spending the weekend of January 8 discussing the FBI threat with his advisors at New York's Park Sheraton, King experienced such moments. In a bugged room and over wire-tapped lines, he kept listening agents alert as he raged against Hoover and his own frailties. "They are out to break me," he said plaintively. Andrew Young and Ralph Abernathy were dispatched on Monday to ask the FBI to halt its campaign. Well briefed as to their mission, Assistant Director "Deke" DeLoach stonewalled. He denied any FBI interest in King's private life or finances and said that, since Hoover ran a "tight ship," no leaks could be traced to the FBI (Branch 1998: 558). Young recalls how DeLoach pointedly inquired whether, as a minister, Young disapproved of "abnormal sexual behavior." Young countered that sexual conduct was "something each person has to work out between themselves, their families, and their God" (Young 1996: 331). With no peace offer from the FBI, King had to live with the fear of public disclosure and the knowledge of malicious surveillance.

White Selma's Tactical Divisions

Besides the threat of scandal, King had other difficulties to confront. By 1965, Southern white leaders had realized that dramatic confrontations, which attracted national press coverage, were basic to SCLC's style. Selma had recently elected a young, moderate segregationist mayor, Joseph Smitherman. As part of his program to modernize the city, Smitherman had appointed an experienced professional, Wilson Baker, as Director of Public Safety, controlling both fire and police services. Baker was aware that by using moderate rather than strong-arm tactics, Albany's Laurie Pritchett had outmaneuvered King in a way that Birmingham's Bull Connor had not. If Baker could only contain the volatile Dallas County Sheriff Jim Clark, whose law enforcement responsibilities in Selma itself were confined to the county courthouse and its immediate environs, then SCLC's hopes of a spectacular clash would be frustrated. Bolstering local efforts to avoid a crisis, the newly created federal Community Relations Service (CRS) had assigned two representatives to Selma. They immediately realized that their objective of reducing racial tensions ran "counter to Dr. King's objective of creating a kind of confrontation that will lead him to Montgomery and Governor Wallace." Alert to this possibility, King and his associates had already discussed the option of moving to the smaller, neighboring county seats of Marion and Camden (Garrow 1988: 369, 378-79).

Fortunately for King, voter registration for local residents was only available on the first and third Monday of each month at the registrar's office in the Dallas County Courthouse; in other words, in Clark's domain. On January 18 King and SNCC's John Lewis led 400 applicants to the courthouse, where they had to wait in an alley until being individually called to take Alabama's complicated literacy test. Simultaneously, demonstrators selectively tested compliance with the Civil Rights Act's required desegregation of public accommodations. The city police, under Baker's orders, did not interfere. "If we can only get the bastards out of town without getting them arrested," declared local newspaper editor Arthur Capell, "we'll have them whipped" (Fairclough 1987: 231). But King's presence attracted white supremacist groups. As he and his aides checked in as the Albert Hotel's first black guests, a thug gave the national press their storyline by landing two blows on the SCLC leader before Baker could arrest the Nazi newcomer. Anxious to avoid further headlines, Baker refused to allow American Nazi Party leader George Lincoln Rockwell or his followers to take up King's disingenuous invitation to attend that evening's mass meeting at Brown Chapel (Garrow 1988: 378-79).

King's adversaries continued to help him publicize Selma's racial situation. Sheriff Clark arrested 226 demonstrators outside the courthouse over the next two days. On January 19 he lost his limited composure when protesters were slow to obey his orders that they queue in an alleyway and enter the courthouse only by a side door. With well-established links to the Alabama Klan, Clark was swayed by his racist followers' visceral demands that he crush African American defiance. In front of television cameras and a watching press corps, he roughly manhandled local black leader Amelia Boynton. To ensure that journalists got the message, King described this as "one of the most brutal and unlawful acts I have ever seen an officer commit." The next day, despite Baker's efforts to dissuade him, Clark arrested three further waves of marchers, and Selma remained on the front pages (Garrow 1988: 379-80).

Fund-raising commitments made King an irregular presence in Selma, but the mass arrests and press attention boosted black community support. Symbolic of this increased solidarity, over a hundred black teachers marched to the courthouse on January 22 to highlight how racism rather than genuine educational attainment shaped the registration rules that denied them the vote. As respected members of the middle class, who owed their livelihood to white-dominated school boards, black teachers rarely participated in public protests. Rebuffed by Clark at the courthouse, the educators returned to a standing ovation from the mass meeting. It was not their courageous stand, however, that kept Selma in the news. On January 26, despite a federal court order enjoining Dallas County officials from hindering voter registration, Clark was involved in a second violent altercation. Mrs. Annie Lee Cooper reacted to Clark's hectoring tone and his deputies' pushes by slugging him in the face. Officers eventually wrestled Cooper to the ground, and press cameras caught the moment when an incensed Jim Clark brought his club "down on her head with a whack that was heard throughout the crowd" (Garrow 1988: 381). To ensure that an unambiguous image of white brutality was publicized, King allegedly prevented several black men from rushing to Mrs. Cooper's aid. However understandable, any recourse to violence by African Americans would, James Bevel reminded them, play into the hands of these racists. "Then they can call you a mob," he warned, "and beat you to death" (Oates 1994: 336-37).

King's Adept Leadership

Encouraged by Clark's intemperateness and need to placate his core segregationist constituents, King escalated the campaign. On February 1, he and Ralph Abernathy led a demonstration. Along with 260 others, they were arrested in what King admitted was "a deliberate attempt to dramatize the conditions in this city, state, and community" (Garrow 1988: 382). That afternoon, in an echo of the Birmingham campaign, 500 schoolchildren were arrested. Ostensibly written that day, a "Letter from Martin Luther King, Jr., from Selma, Alabama Jail" appeared in the *New York Times* on February 5. By this stage, King's "Letter from Birmingham Jail" had been widely reprinted so an articulate, liberal, national constituency was already primed. The new letter reminded readers that racial injustice remained a source of international embarrassment. It alluded to the way in which nonviolence evoked a reaction that "revealed the persisting [*sic*] ugliness of segregation to the nation and the world." Summarizing black Selma's political exclusion, King stated that there were "more Negroes in jail with me than there are on the voting rolls." He called for "the help of all decent Americans" and directed donations to SCLC (Oates 1994: 342).

King's past experiences made him a shrewder campaigner in Selma. From jail, he issued detailed instructions on how "to keep national attention focused on Selma." SCLC board member Joseph Lowery's task was to persuade the head of the CRS, Leroy Collins, to visit Selma to discuss speedier registration and more registration days with city and county authorities. Lowery was also to call presidential aide Lee White to induce LBJ to make "a plea to Dallas [County] and Selma officials in a press conference," or send a personal envoy, or announce Justice Department involvement. SCLC's Washington lobbyist, Walter Fauntroy, was asked to line up a sympathetic Congressional delegation to investigate conditions in Selma, allowing time for them to attend a mass meeting so their visit would boost local morale. Abernathy was to call black entertainer Sammy Davis Jr., and urge him to do a Sunday benefit concert for the Alabama project because, King explained, "I find these fellows respond better when I am in jail or in a crisis." The legal team was to prepare appeals to carry cases beyond local federal Judge Thomas, and bail out any staff member vital to the campaign. Just in case other staffers were "put out of circulation," King added, C.T. Vivian had better be recalled from California. In cooperation with SNCC and local leaders, Bernard LaFayette was asked to keep "some activity alive every day this week." SCLC director Andrew Young was to organize a night march to protest King's arrest as this would "let Clark show [his] true colors" and Young must "stretch every point to get [the] teachers to march" again (Carson 1998: 274).

After a public career of nearly a decade, the 36-year-old King had learned to use positively what we would now call "spin," but he remained at the mercy of events. As he planned to leave jail on February 5, he briefed Young the evening before on the timing and manner of his release. Ideally, it should be at 1.00 p.m., so he could meet the Congressional delegation before his 2.30 p.m. press conference for which Young should prepare a statement, with copies for the reporters. The press was bound to ask about Judge Thomas's latest court order so Young was directed to brief King thoroughly on its significance. Only after consulting King should Young publicly outline the movement's next step.

Subordinating The Local To The National

Thomas's injunction proved encouraging. It required Dallas County's registrars to increase their processing of applicants to 100 a day, to relax the literacy test, and to approve registration, even when there were minor mistakes on the application form. Rejected applicants were to have the right to appeal directly to Thomas himself and, unless all applications were duly processed by June, Thomas would appoint a federal referee to oversee the board's actions. Sheriff Clark was expressly enjoined from arresting activists who were peacefully encouraging would-be voters, and he was ordered to allow applicants to line up in front of the courthouse. President Johnson publicly endorsed black actions in Selma by asking all Americans to share his indignation "over the loss of any American's right to vote." Given these positive developments, Young disobeyed King's explicit instructions that he must be consulted and announced a suspension of demonstrations (Fairclough 1987: 234). King swiftly reversed Young's order. Thomas's ruling "was a partial victory," he conceded, "but we must not stop." A chastened Young was assigned to discuss several unresolved legal issues with the Legal Defense Fund coordinator, Jack Greenberg. Maintaining the pressure, a further 500 protesters induced Sheriff Clark to arrest them (Garrow 1988: 386).

While King maneuvered for maximum national advantage, however, the people of Selma began to ponder the cost of having him in town. More and more children had been arrested, and Selma's adults, like Birmingham's, were uneasy with this tactic, especially now that Judge Thomas's order seemed to promise a genuine breakthrough for black voter registration. Local leader Frederick Reese accepted a board of registrars' proposal for an "appearance book," that would allow the board to pre-book the required 100 applicants per day specified by Judge Thomas. SCLC's Jim Bevel opposed Reese's decision because it turned a suggested minimum into a maximum quota. More importantly, it threatened to end the media-drawing confrontations with Sheriff Clark. To illustrate the value of these, on February 8, Bevel and a few supporters, with reporters in tow, marched to the courthouse in defiance of the new booking arrangements, and a livid Clark hit Bevel repeatedly and arrested the entire group (Garrow 1988: 387-88).

While young black Selmans delighted in this goading of their irascible sheriff, to their elders it seemed reckless. Clark's wrath fell more frequently on local people than on SCLC staff. Two days after his confrontation with Bevel, Clark and his posse drove 165 young protesters out into the countryside using nightsticks and electric cattle prods. On this forced march of over three miles, one girl, who fell by the wayside, was "burned with prods until she staggered to her feet. Boys carried her along the rest of the way" (Watters 1993: 325-26). At the start of the Selma campaign, King had amused colleagues with his repertoire of mock funeral orations. The luck that allowed all of them to get out of Birmingham alive, he had declared, would not hold. If Ralph Abernathy were taken, Martin would naturally preach his eulogy. He would extol the merits of the tragically slain president of the National Association for the Advancement of Eating Chicken. Ralph had no rivals for his crown, King intoned – no one could challenge his preeminence in this field. When it came to eating chicken, he was a man among men (Hampton and Fayer 1994: 214; Young 1996: 328-29). A month into the Selma campaign, mounting segregationist fury suggested that soon the funerals would be all too real.

King's Search For "Creative Tension"

Clark's torture of young prisoners prompted King to hold a late-night meeting with SNCC staff and his own lieutenants on

February 10. He had just returned from Washington where what was ostensibly a meeting with Attorney-General Nicholas Katzenbach and Vice-President Hubert Humphrey had camouflaged (at LBJ's insistence) a meeting with Johnson himself. King revealed that the President had promised him a voting rights bill. Their objective in Selma – to force the administration to prioritize voting rights legislation – was nearly realized. But local people were growing weary and for King that raised tricky questions: "how do we wrap up Selma and what are we pushing for from now on?" To nods of agreement from Fred Reese, King proposed identifying some attainable concessions so locals "feel that they have some kind of victory." Andrew Young argued that the next phase should be in nearby Lowndes County, a notorious, white supremacist stronghold, but vulnerable because it fell under the jurisdiction of federal Judge Frank Johnson, who had a positive civil rights record. King felt that Lowndes' key advantage was it offered a strong prospect of a dramatic engagement with the forces of Massive Resistance. Backing Young's proposal to leave Selma, he reminded SNCC staff: "You should not only know how to start a good Movement, [you] should also know when to stop." The Selma campaign had put voting rights on the legislative agenda, but "to get the bill passed, we need to make a dramatic appeal through Lowndes and other counties because the people of Selma are tired" (Garrow 1988: 389).

In King's opinion, the Birmingham campaign had induced President Kennedy to introduce the civil rights bill, and the St. Augustine campaign had helped to ensure its passage in 1964, so SCLC should not expect Selma to maintain the pressure for voting rights legislation alone. Other communities must share the burden. After a weekend of bed-rest, spent in an Atlanta hospital on medical advice, a still fragile King returned to Alabama. There, he not only observed prospective registrants in Selma sign the "appearance book," but witnessed a similar procession to the Perry County Courthouse in neighboring Marion, where he and Coretta had married eleven years before. He remained determined to generate pressure for legislation via a public sense of crisis, and sadly nothing seemed to boost prospects as effectively as scenes of white brutality. In this respect, Sheriff Clark remained a godsend. Valentine's Day in Selma saw steady rain, but when C.T. Vivian entreated Clark to allow his followers to wait inside the court-house, the sheriff and his grim-faced deputies blocked the entrance. While cameras rolled, Vivian explained to the lawmen that, like Hitler and those who followed his orders, they, too, would eventually face justice. The analogy struck a nerve, and Clark lashed out at Vivian, bloodying his nose and sending him reeling down the steps. Belated police attempts to stop the film-ing only reinforced the impression of totalitarianism (Hampton and Fayer 1994: 222).

Still dogged by illness, King pursued dramatic confrontations outside of Selma to maintain and increase public sympathy. The SCLC used the dangerous tactic of the night march in Marion on February 18. Earlier in the week, local police had arrested SCLC's James Orange, and the march was a gesture of support for the prisoner. After Marion's Mayor Pegues claimed that local African Americans were planning a jailbreak, not a symbolic protest, Governor Wallace sent in state troopers under Colonel Al Lingo. Local whites also gathered, and Sheriff Clark was spotted (out of uniform, club in hand). Before angry segregationists cracked his skull with an ax handle, NBC reporter Richard Valeriani recalls seeing them "spraying the cameras with paint." Confirming municipal complicity, the streetlights cut out to provide protec-tion for the assailants. Having encircled the protesters, the troop-ers and local whites began, in the words of black leader Albert Turner, to "beat black people wherever they found them" (Hampton and Fayer 1994: 223). You "did not have to be marching," Turner recounts. "All you had to do was be black" (Fairclough 1987: 239). Down the hill from the march's starting-point, Viola Jackson and her son, Jimmie Lee, took refuge in a small café. When troopers stormed in, Jimmie Lee tried to protect his mother and was shot at close range. Fatally wounded, he died eight days later.

The brutality in Marion helped King to raise the campaign above the local level. Targeting Governor Wallace had always figured in SCLC plans since the Bevels proposed a concentrated nonviolent assault on Alabama after the murderous Birmingham bombings. Wallace's state troopers had permitted and participated in the latest wanton violence and the national press, some of whose members were victims, demanded prosecution of the assailants. Understandably, African Americans in Marion and Selma responded to the shooting with particular outrage. SNCC and SCLC disagreed over how best to channel this anger. Drawing on their experiences in Mississippi, SNCC workers stressed intensifying local efforts to prove that the Movement could not be intimidated, but would stand with local people. SCLC, on the other hand, felt that it was more important to focus the national spotlight remorselessly on the political unaccountability of Governor Wallace to African Americans, who were denied the right to vote.

At the same time, memories of black retaliation after the Gaston Motel bombing in May 1963 warned King that maintaining nonviolent discipline indefinitely in the face of escalating brutality was virtually impossible. This was why James Bevel backed the idea of a mass march from Selma to Montgomery. Like Gandhi, Bevel recognized that

> when you have a great violation of the people and there's a great sense of injury, you have to give people an honorable means and context in which to express and eliminate the grief and speak decisively and succinctly back to the issue.

He also realized that the five or six days of a fifty-mile mass march "would give you the time to discuss in the nation, through papers, radio, and television and going around speaking, what the real issues were" (Hampton and Fayer 1994: 226). Except for John Lewis, the most forceful figures in SNCC by early 1965 were no longer the Gandhians at the heart of its staff in 1960-61. Consequently, in the week after Jackson's death on February 26, SNCC's staff condemned SCLC's proposed march to Montgomery as a dangerous and wasteful distraction, intended to camouflage King's abandonment of Selma in his search for further publicity.

SNCC's ambivalence to nonviolence, its deep mistrust of federal authorities, and growing alienation from liberalism meant that the vibrant, angry rhetoric of Malcolm X had become especially resonant for some of its members by the end of 1964. Several key figures had met Malcolm in Africa that autumn, and shared his belief that the black freedom struggle was international. Summer disturbances in New York and other northern cities made the former Nation of Islam spokesman a potentially vital force. While King was in prison in early February, SNCC had invited Malcolm to speak in Selma. Reports suggest that local residents warmed more readily to King's rolling, Southern cadences than to Malcolm's New York accent and staccato style. But the brief visit confirmed that in his final manifestation as Malik al-Shabazz, Malcolm the fighter for human rights was far closer to King than the press suspected. On February 21, while SNCC workers still waited to hear whether Jimmie Lee Jackson would survive his wounds, news of Malcolm's murder flashed from Harlem.

"Bloody Sunday"

SNCC's decision on Saturday March 6 not to participate as an organization in the next day's Selma-to-Montgomery march marked a wider pattern of autonomous action which King acknowledged but could only limit. SNCC members who wished to march could do so as individuals. Consequently, when the march headed out of Selma towards the Edmund Pettus Bridge on Sunday, native Alabaman John Lewis was in the front rank. Beside Lewis walked not King, but Hosea Williams, because SCLC had concluded that the risk of King's assassination was too great. The day after Malcolm's murder, Attorney-General Katzenbach had phoned King personally to stress the need for heightened security. Anxious about their leader's safety, SCLC colleagues stressed to King that, by leading the march, he would imperil other participants. His absence in Atlanta on March 7 was evidence of this concern, however much hostile critics read it as symptomatic of how "De Lawd" sent others into the front line.

Anticipating the march's swift interruption and mass arrests, SCLC decided that King was better placed in Atlanta to rally national support for renewed protest. This was nearly a grave miscalculation. The segregationist authorities' own spies had suggested that the march organizers simply would not have the back-up resources in place by March 7 for its proposed mass trek. King and other leaders, Wallace's aides told him, were counting on being stopped. If the march were allowed to proceed down Highway 80, King would soon be "the laughing stock of the nation" as ill-prepared participants were forced to withdraw. King escaped this trap because a Lowndes County politician convinced Wallace that if the marchers ever reached his constituency (which straddled the route to Montgomery), shootings and explosions would follow. Ironically, in the light of what ensued, Wallace determined to stop the march on the outskirts of Selma to avoid vigilante violence. He denounced the proposed demonstration in a Saturday newscast as "not conducive to the orderly flow of traffic and commerce" in the state and, seeking to appease his supporters, added fatefully that state troopers would be instructed to "use whatever measures are necessary to prevent a march" (Raines 1983: 201).

Despite their conduct in Marion, Wallace believed that the same highway patrolmen would stop Sunday's marchers without bloodshed shortly after they crossed the Edmund Pettus Bridge, which marked Selma's city limits. That morning, he dispatched Colonel Lingo to meet Jim Clark's plane in Montgomery as the segregationist celebrity returned from a national TV appearance. Lingo's instructions were to detain Clark until the morning's confrontation was over, but the march set off hours late. By the time Williams and Lewis, with more than 500 followers, crested the bridge and saw the state troopers blocking the four-lane highway, Lingo and Clark's car was pulling up, and mounted members of Clark's Klan-ridden posse were gathered by the roadside. A small cluster of newsmen, including a television camera crew, had set up their observation post on an adjoining car-dealer's lot. They had a clear view of what followed.

Highway patrol commander Major John Cloud ordered the double-file column of protesters to stop. Hosea Williams asked to parley but Cloud refused, declaring instead that they had two minutes to disperse. Andrew Young had told a reporter on Friday that, if the authorities were reasonable, the marchers would "probably turn around and go back to church. If they try to bully us," he had added, "we'll have to stand our ground and refuse to cooperate" (Garrow 1988: 396). Seeing no immediate compliance with his order, Cloud ordered his men to advance with their masks ready to protect them from tear gas. In tightly formed ranks with batons braced to push the protesters aside, the troopers hit the waiting column like a steamroller. Knocked to the ground, the demonstrators screamed with pain and fear as blows rained down. Clark's cheering posse spurred their horses after the fleeing men, women, and children, forcing them to crowd together for protection. Seeing the retreat paused, Clark himself fired the first in a volley of tear-gas canisters into the already panicked crowd.

Through the clouds of gas, reporters could hear the striking sound of police night-sticks. One blow fractured John Lewis's skull, making him one of around eighty casualties. Hosea Williams picked up 8-year-old Sheyann Webb to carry her to safety, but she remembers shouting for him to put her down because he wasn't running fast enough (Webb 1980: 97). Somehow, the marchers found their way back to Brown Chapel, where a furious Wilson Baker demanded that Clark and his posse withdraw before local residents added gunfire to the bottles and bricks that were already flying. Andrew Young never forgot trying to dissuade local blacks from getting their guns. "You had to be grimly specific, asking them what guns they had and how their firepower compared to the carbines and high velocity rifles available to the white authorities massed outside," he recalled. Baker, a moderate segregationist, in combination with Young and others, averted a shoot-out, but Wallace's original plans were in ruins. Already, jaw-dropping footage was on its way to ABC, which interrupted its evening movie *Judgment at Nuremberg* with a news-flash that looked like a Gestapo raid. The events on the Edmund Pettus Bridge would go down in history as the United States' "Bloody Sunday."

Dominating Monday's newspapers, Bloody Sunday massively increased the pressure for legislation. A month earlier, President Johnson had privately assured King that a voting rights bill would be introduced, but Attorney-General Katzenbach had initially favored a constitutional amendment (a slow process, which required a two-thirds Congressional majority and ratification by three out of every four states). After Bloody Sunday, with the national media demanding action, it was confirmed that Katzenbach's bill was under Senate minority leader Everett Dirksen's scrutiny as a bi-partisan measure. Despite these developments, King did not rescind his national call for more recruits to march from Selma on March 9. Instead, his attorneys sought an injunction against further state interference from federal judge Frank Johnson. The Johnson in Montgomery, like his namesake in the White House, saw avoiding any repetition of Sunday's violence as his first priority. To march again on Tuesday seemed reckless to him, and on Monday evening King's lawyers warned him that, pending hearings on their desired injunction, Judge Johnson wanted no further marches.

King's Obedience To Federal Law

Perceived and presented in white circles as the Movement's leader, King was expected to control its actions, but this presupposed that he knew what to do and would be obeyed. Publicly committed, King explained privately to LBJ that he needed grounds to call it off, and urged the government to increase and publicize its mediation efforts. President Johnson dispatched CRS Director Leroy Collins to Selma to signal that negotiation was more profitable than protest at this stage. By the time Collins arrived, the SCLC leader's vacillations had first bewildered, and then incensed Movement insiders. First, despite remonstrations from SNCC's James Forman that the Movement must not allow white judges to timetable its actions, King said he would obey the federal court order and postpone the march. Then, on arrival at Brown Chapel's exuberant mass meeting, he seemingly changed his mind. To the surprise of those with whom he had privately caucused, he told the congregation to get out their walking shoes ready for the next morning's march.

For hours after midnight, SNCC and SCLC debated the decision to march. Having previously derided the March to Montgomery as a publicity stunt, SNCC was now adamant that no external authority, be it Governor Wallace, Judge Johnson, or President Johnson, should stop people from protesting against injustice. Court orders had always been used to block and exhaust Movement forces. Overturning them took time and money, and the associated delay and frustration had weakened past campaigns. If King called off the march, SNCC would proceed unilaterally. Thus, going ahead seemed essential to avoid a damaging public split. On the other hand, Justice Department officials confirmed that Judge Johnson, in the interest of public safety, would issue a federal court order banning the march. Were King to defy it, he would be sinking publicly to the same level of illegality as his segregationist opponents. How could he expect the due process of federal law ever to protect African American rights effectively, they argued, if he himself was prepared to disobey a federal judge? Thus, a postponement seemed vital to ensure that the Movement's most basic demand for legal redress remained viable.

Some SCLC staff had more immediate misgivings. The logistical challenges of a mass march had not lessened. Instead, due to the influx of supporters from across the country, the task of marshaling sufficient support services had ballooned. A further delay, as Judge Johnson's scheduling of hearings about the safety of the march for Thursday seemed to demand, would enable them to strengthen the march's supply lines. To their dismay, when the meeting broke up in the early hours of March 9, King seemed persuaded that he needed to take his stand at the head of Tuesday's march. His inner circle knew he remained concerned at the likelihood of white violence and was considering a token march that stayed within the terms of Judge Johnson's order. Sensing King's willingness to compromise, CRS Director Collins advised him that he would seek assurances from state authorities. King wished him luck.

With barely any sleep, King continued to wrestle with his dilemma on Tuesday morning. A conference call with advisors gave no help. According to Bayard Rustin, King had no choice but to violate the injunction, a view contradicted equally emphatically by the Legal Defense Fund's Jack Greenberg. He advised King to wait for Johnson's ruling to be overturned on constitutional grounds. Hanging up, King gloomily said he would proceed. Collins had meanwhile consulted Al Lingo and Jim Clark over how to avoid renewed violence. Stung by Governor Wallace's angry recriminations over Sunday's debacle, Lingo and Clark saw Collins's suggestion of a symbolic march to the bridge as a ploy that might appease their angry master. So King could signal that he had agreed to Collins's plan, they gave the CRS Director a hand-drawn map of the route King must take and where he must stop.

The wrangling over the previous twenty-four hours ensured that the never punctual civil rights leadership was not ready to march until nearly 2.30 p.m. Then, King emerged from Brown Chapel at the head of 2,000 marchers, many of them white newcomers, moved to action by Sunday's dreadful newscast. Collins pressed a map into the SCLC leader's hand and quietly assured him that if he stuck to this route there would be no trouble. "I'll do my best to turn them back," King murmured discreetly. "I won't promise you but I'll do my best" (Garrow 1988: 403). To underline King's predicament, when the march reached the Edmund Pettus Bridge, a federal marshal read Judge Johnson's order, thus ensuring that King could be sued for contempt if he disobeyed its terms. Descending the bridge's span, King could see the state troopers ahead. With the map to guide him, he halted the procession fifty yards from the officers and secured permission to pray. A succession of preachers led prayers and then the marchers joined in singing "We Shall Overcome."

As King turned to lead the marchers back, the troopers withdrew to the roadside, leaving Highway 80 open and clear. Despite this attempt at entrapment, successive ranks of bemused marchers followed King's lead and headed back across the bridge into Selma. It was only when they were back at Brown Chapel that SNCC workers and Selma teenagers gave vent to their anger at this unexpected retreat. Surrounded by militants and journalists demanding an explanation, King struggled to respond. If he revealed his collusion with Collins, it would fuel SNCC charges that he listened to and valued federal authorities more than he did his Movement colleagues. If he insisted that he had intended to proceed, he risked contempt charges from Judge Johnson. "We knew we would not get past the troopers," he told the press. But the conspicuous, last-minute withdrawal of the highway patrol undercut his words. By Thursday, under hostile questioning in Judge Johnson's courtroom, the SCLC leader was obliged to admit that Collins had brokered what he termed "a tacit agreement" (Garrow 1988: 404).

Mistrust of King intensified. James Forman summed up SNCC's feelings by denouncing the "Tuesday turnaround" as a classic example of trickery against the people. Press reports spoke of "open contempt" for King among other Movement figures and pointed out that he had "stayed in seclusion" throughout Wednesday. Feelings were so strong that King temporarily withdrew to a friend's house in Montgomery. Two separate, well-informed articles on the unfolding campaign pointedly took the Freedom Song "Ain't Gonna Let Nobody Turn Me Round" as their title (Kopkind

1965; Ulmer 1965). King told celebrity supporter Harry Belafonte that SNCC's James Forman was pushing the Movement to the brink of violence that might sabotage King's public diplomacy (Joseph 2014: 84). With SNCC barely speaking to him, King tried to mend his strained relations with federal officials, who had been shocked by his apparent willingness to disobey a federal court order. By phone, he explained that his leadership would otherwise have been seriously compromised and in court he justified Tuesday's march by arguing that without such an outlet, "the pent-up emotions ... would have exploded into retaliatory violence" (Garrow 1988: 406).

The President Joins The Movement

Further violence in Selma ultimately resolved King's predicament. On the evening of March 9, three Northern clergymen, including James J. Reeb, a white Unitarian minister from Boston, drew catcalls as they walked past a known meeting place for racists, the Silver Moon Café. As they moved away, the full force of a baseball bat smashed Reeb's skull from behind. Doctors judged his survival chances slim. Fearing further embarrassing violence, Selma authorities established a police cordon to restrict all Movement activities to the black neighborhood around Brown Chapel. But Reeb's condition, continuing reverberations from Sunday's televised attack, and fresh photographs of police denying peaceful protesters, even nuns, the right to march to the courthouse, ensured that the media remained fixated on Selma. On Friday March 12, they reported that Reeb had died the previous evening and that President Johnson had immediately phoned personal condolences to Reeb's family. Indicative of the tensions inside the Movement, Johnson's and the nation's response to Reeb's death evoked resentment because it far surpassed the attention given to Jimmie Lee Jackson's murder in February.

The President was even more widely rebuked, however, for what he had failed to do rather than for what he had done. Johnson and Justice Department officials had met repeatedly with Congressional leaders about a far-reaching voting rights bill since "Bloody Sunday," but the public chorus of complaint over "an unbelievable lack of action" grew (Fairclough 1987: 247). Summoning Wallace to the White House on March 13, Johnson took the opportunity to restore his reputation with mainstream liberals. First, in private conversation, he told Wallace that the present crisis was not due to King or "outside agitators," but to Alabama's denial of voting rights and Wallace's own failure to protect peaceful demonstrators. With a nervous governor beside him, Johnson was equally blunt to the waiting press. "It is wrong to do violence to peaceful citizens in the streets of their town," he declared. "It is wrong to deny Americans the right to vote. It is wrong to deny any person full equality because of the color of his skin." A bill to ensure the right to vote would go to Congress next week, he explained, and if Wallace took his advice, he would publicly endorse the principle of universal suffrage, guarantee the right of peaceful assembly in Alabama, and hold bi-racial meetings to nurture interracial cooperation. The crestfallen Governor made no comment (Garrow 1988: 407-8).

King declined an invitation to be present on March 15 when Johnson would address a special joint session of Congress to urge passage of the administration's bill without compromise or delay. Instead, in his first public appearance in Selma for six days, King spoke at a brief memorial service for James Reeb outside the courthouse. Sharing the dais with religious and secular dignitaries of different creeds and races, the civil rights leader alluded mournfully to the "agonies and lonely moments of leadership." Earlier, he had complained that clashes with SNCC produced "agonies of the spirit" that sapped his morale. Listening to the President's speech on television that evening, King showed his SCLC colleagues how deeply the campaign was affecting him. In a powerful address, Johnson referred to Reeb's death, the brutality of local officials, and the courage of African Americans, which had placed Selma on a par with Lexington, Concord, and Appomattox as "a turning point in man's unending search for freedom." He called upon the nation to overcome its "crippling legacy of bigotry and injustice" and, after a pointed rhetorical pause from a man renowned more for his powers of private persuasion than for his platform oratory, he concluded: "And We Shall Overcome." Live TV cameras captured the ensuing standing ovation while in a crowded Selma living room, King's friends observed tears trickling down his face. They had never seen him cry before. But emotion overwhelmed him now as he sensed that this speech – even more than his own "I Have a Dream" speech – would secure a tangible legislative gain (Garrow 1988: 408-9).

Movement Divisions Deepen

This euphoric moment, and the words that inspired it, could not bridge the growing mistrust of mainstream liberals among some activists, nor calm their irritation at King for what they perceived to be his courtship of Johnson. Aggravating the situation, white resistance also stiffened after what segregationists saw as a fellow Southerner's betrayal. The day after Johnson's speech, a Montgomery posse beat SNCC protesters in scenes reminiscent of Selma's Bloody Sunday. Observing the savage beatings from an upstairs hotel room, a trapped Stokely Carmichael broke down. His co-workers hurried him to the airport so that he could get help away from the front line (Joseph 2014: 84). SNCC's James Forman was already incensed by what he perceived to be the self-interested inertia of Montgomery's middle-class blacks, including Dexter's deacons and the Improvement Association (MIA). After the brutal assault, Forman told a church mass meeting that if black people were not to be allowed to sit at the "table of government", then they should "blow the fucking legs off" (Garrow 1988: 409). In town to learn Judge Johnson's final ruling on the Selma march, King intervened, personally leading a march to the county courthouse where Montgomery's sheriff publicly apologized for the previous day's attack. Nonetheless, King was already worried that black retaliatory violence, inflamed by rhetoric like Forman's angry call for revolutionary violence, could quickly reverse the nation's shallow commitment to reform.

While SNCC's emergent leadership interpreted King's continued commitment to nonviolence as naive in the face of America's persistent racism, it was actually bolstered by his own mistrust of white liberals. He was unsure of the coalition of conscience that recent events had created. From Montgomery's courthouse steps on March 17, he summarized part of the hard-nosed strategy that SCLC had adopted when he declared: "we will no longer let [white men] use their clubs on us in dark corners. We are going to make them do it in the glaring light of television" (Garrow 1978: 111). All the same, King was never entirely comfortable with a strategy that relied so heavily on televised black suffering. In Birmingham, he had initially hoped to use economic leverage, and if the Selma-to-Montgomery march served to strengthen the coalition of conscience that was pressing the Johnson administration to enact voting registration, he hoped to be able to return to economic and political pressure tactics to address the many inequities that remained.

Despite his fine words, Johnson, King suspected, would ultimately value order above justice, like Kennedy before him. An archetypal electoral politician, LBJ was hostile to a politics of demonstration, and his management of the War on Poverty was already signaling a tendency to let entrenched forces protect their turf at the cost of the disadvantaged. Effective enfranchisement of African Americans in the South might ultimately improve the election prospects of New Deal liberals like Johnson, if the race card ceased to be central to the region's politics. It should also end the international embarrassment of these racial clashes by directing black grievances into the formal institutional channels of American government. But judging by the recent urban clashes, African American impatience and white fears could equally inflame reactionary tendencies. Johnson avidly read opinion polls which regularly asked Americans if they felt demonstrations "hurt the Negro's cause." Gallup found that 60 percent had felt they did in June 1963 (after Birmingham) and 74 percent had felt so by May 1964. The trend would continue upwards with 85 percent of respondents agreeing in October 1966 (Jackson 2007: 222). In the spring of 1965, King retained some hope still that the vote could act as a springboard for the far-reaching social and economic changes that he increasingly saw as essential for the securing of racial justice. But the electoral cycle would have to be continuously informed by ongoing protests by the disadvantaged. Nothing would be given by the powerful willingly. In this respect, Judge Johnson's ruling in support of the Selma march, which worried some conservative jurists, was encouraging to King. At its heart was what the judge called his "commensurity theorem": namely, "that the right to assemble, demonstrate and march peaceably along the highways and streets in an orderly manner should be commensurate with the enormity of the wrongs that are being protested and petitioned against."

King had written in his "Letter from Birmingham Jail" that "Injustice anywhere is a threat to justice everywhere" (Carson 1998: 189) and he consistently interpreted the right to protest in this light. SCLC announced that the court-sanctioned Selma-to-Montgomery march would begin on Sunday March 21. The chief remaining problems were its logistics and the serious threat from white terrorism en route. With funds from innumerable sympathizers, SCLC overcame the former and, once it became clear that Governor Wallace would not afford protection, President Johnson federalized the Alabama National Guard to provide a mass armed escort and reconnaissance parties. Despite fears for his safety, a tired-looking King walked with the other marchers for the first three days. Like many of his companions, he had badly blistered feet by Wednesday, when he left the march for an Ohioan fund-raiser. He rejoined the procession's front rank on the outskirts of Montgomery the next day (March 25), surrounded by proud black preachers who, according to Andrew Young, did not realize that their prominent position was to ensure that a white assassin would find it harder to single out King himself.

Swelled by sympathizers from across the country, an estimated 25,000 people swept up the gentle slope of Dexter Avenue past the church that King had pastored to the state capital's plaza where once Confederates had listened to their new president. Looking out over an interracial sea of faces, King could not help but note how far the Movement had come since Rosa Parks refused to give up her bus seat in December 1955. As at the Lincoln Memorial in 1963, his oratory rose to the occasion, buoying up his audience with the theme that they were on the move and "no wave of racism" could stop them (Carson 1998: 284-86). They would have to march against segregated housing and schools and against poverty, he declared in an address that hinted at how much more was needed for "the realization of the American dream." But if they marched on the ballot boxes, he urged them, with a glance toward the Governor's mansion, "the Wallaces of our nation" would have to "tremble away in silence" to be replaced by "men who will not fear to do justice, love mercy, and walk humbly with their God." That battle lay ahead.

Before them, King warned, loomed further difficulties and suffering. Mindful of the appeal of Black Nationalism, he urged his fellow African Americans not to try "to defeat or humiliate the white man," but to seek "a society at peace with itself, a society that can live with its conscience." For that would mark the triumphal "day not of the white man, not of the black man," but "of man as man." Finally, to reaffirm the faith of his followers, who understandably wondered "How long will it take?" he built to a final crescendo that balanced the repetitive call and response of "How long?" and "Not long" through a succession of climactic, moral affirmations. It would not be long "because truth pressed to earth will rise again," "because no lie can live forever," "because you still reap what you sow," and "because the arc of the moral universe is long, but it bends towards justice." While his audience still cheered at the grandeur of that last phrase, he carried them with him into the familiar cadences of the "Battle Hymn of the Republic" so that they too felt as if they had "seen the glory of the coming of the Lord" and that "His truth is marching on." It was a virtuoso performance that set the seal on a remarkably peaceful demonstration.

As the rapturous crowds dispersed and Martin and Coretta King safely caught a plane home, nervous federal officials watched with premature relief. SCLC organizers had stressed that participants should not linger since white racists might attack stragglers. A team of volunteer drivers, including a white housewife from Detroit, Mrs. Viola Gregg Liuzzo, was on hand to carry Selma marchers back home. As Mrs. Liuzzo and a young local SCLC volunteer, Leroy Moton, returned from Selma on a deserted Lowndes County stretch of Highway 80, they were overtaken by a carload of Klansmen, who opened fire. The mother of five died instantly and the blood-splattered Moton only escaped death by feigning it when the murderers returned to check the car. An undercover FBI informant Gary Rowe was in the Klan car and informed his control agent within hours of the shooting. To conceal his role, Rowe and his three Klan companions were arrested together less than twenty-four hours after the murder. President Johnson told a live television audience that the FBI had the murderers in custody. Setting aside his own feelings about Hoover, King sent a congratulatory telegram, but SNCC militants reflected bitterly on the different reaction to black deaths like Jimmie Lee Jackson's and white ones, like Reeb's and Liuzzo's.

National disgust at the latest outrage added to the already considerable Congressional support for the voting rights bill. Wrangling centered on whether an automatic trigger mechanism of a less than 50 percent voter registration among eligible adults in any county that used literacy or other voting tests was either too broad or too narrow a criterion for the deployment of federal registrars. Some felt that it allowed too much federal interference, while others felt that poll taxes and other obstacles to voting would preserve large pockets of disenfranchisement. Justice Department officials tried to placate the former by considering possible "escape clauses," and the latter by reluctantly addressing the constitutionally vexed poll tax question. Despite overtly bipartisan consultations, legislation that might change the electorate faced close scrutiny from incumbent politicians, especially in the House, where two-year terms induced near permanent electioneering. Whereas the Senate approved its version of the Voting Rights Act on May 26, the House took until July 9, and the final Act only emerged from a conference committee for Congressional approval on August 4; President Johnson signed it into law two days later. Meanwhile, King faced fresh challenges and disappointments.

The Next Steps Fail: Economic Coercion And Political Organizing

On Sunday March 26 King announced that, to ensure that Governor Wallace was forced to end the "reign of terror," Americans must boycott Alabama products. Unions should refuse to ship Alabama goods and the US Treasury should withdraw federal funds and withhold federal grants. As originally conceived, this boycott, coupled to a month-long direct action campaign in Montgomery itself, was intended to topple Wallace and instigate federally supervised elections with genuinely universal suffrage. Reminding King of their limited commitment to social change, liberal newspapers such as the *New York Times* and liberal politicians such as Jacob Javits roundly criticized this boycott call. As a black civil rights organization largely devoted to lobbying business for better treatment, the National Urban League also condemned King's proposed blanket assault on Alabama.

Bayard Rustin feared that a general boycott would unduly penalize Alabama's black poor. Although King conceded that any boycott should be selective and progressive, he refused to abandon the idea since it demonstrated the key economic component within racial injustice. This was becoming increasingly important in his thinking as he strove to develop programs for the Northern ghettos. Despite objections, the SCLC board meeting (April 1-2) had approved a significant expansion of the organization's purpose on the grounds that "many so-called Southern problems are national and require a national solution." Endorsing objectives such as a higher minimum wage and national health insurance, SCLC signaled that for King, civil rights included the goals of "full employment, decent housing and quality education" (Garrow 1988: 414-15). The new national goals, allies warned King, would require King to foster a class coalition as donations from middle class whites dried up as he attacked their interests (Jackson 2007: 230-31).

Among those who wanted SCLC to remain "Southern" focused was Hosea Williams, a hard-drinking, hard-talking staff member who competed with Bevel for the title "SCLC firebrand," and teased Andrew Young as an "Uncle Tom." Williams argued that SCLC should prepare for the new politics that an effective Voting Rights Act would bring to the South by launching a "Summer Community Organization and Political Education" (SCOPE) program. Modeled on the Mississippi Freedom Summer campaign, SCOPE would recruit a thousand Northern students to work with SCLC field staff in 120 Black Belt counties to register and organize potentially decisive black majority electorates. Fundamentally sound, and popular with the often neglected SCLC affiliates, SCOPE marked a return to the idea of a Crusade for Citizenship that SCLC had failed to realize in 1958. It was also a continuation of its grassroots Citizenship Schools program, which, according to its experienced coordinator, 67-year-old Mrs. Septima Clark, had never received the staff support it deserved because of the competing appeal of direct action campaigns. Despite these discouraging precedents and staff resentment at Williams's self-aggrandizing, maverick style, King persuaded the board to approve SCOPE as well as Bevel's double-pronged attack on Alabama including the escalating national boycott.

Both initiatives inclined King to heal his relations with SNCC. Now directing SNCC's Lowndes County project, the handsome and articulate Stokely Carmichael perceived SCLC's overall goals as "very radical" and applauded King's realization that "the real issues" were "economic problems." He did not think that King knew "how to get to" these problems, but SNCC's efforts to organize independent black "Freedom Democratic" parties in Lowndes and similar counties could still profit from King's mass appeal. Despite unresolved differences, the two sides publicly espoused cooperation on April 30. But a truce with SNCC did not help Bevel's poorly supported Montgomery campaign which by the end of May, along with the boycott, had fizzled out. SCOPE was also grievously disappointing. It was smaller (about 300 volunteers in fifty-one counties) and registered fewer voters than anticipated, partly because the delayed August enactment of the Voting Rights Act gave student volunteers little time before they returned to college (Fairclough 1987: 260-63).

In the six Alabama counties around Selma where federal examiners were symbolically dispatched to implement the Act, black registration rose markedly: from 0 to 1,496 in Lowndes, for instance, and 320 to 6,789 in Dallas County itself. But to King's vocal dismay, the Justice Department had sent examiners to only twenty-four counties across the entire South by late October. Discrimination, intimidation, and violence still blocked black political participation, with Southern courts consistently refusing to punish the perpetrators. In Selma itself everyone who attended an SCLC Citizenship class reportedly lost their job as a result. Such reprisals seemed intended to eliminate black voting power before it could be used (Jackson 2007: 233). When an Alabama jury acquitted the alleged killer of Viola Liuzzo on October 23, King launched a campaign to demand legislation reforming jury selection and making homicide a federal crime. In this instance, active cooperation from SNCC might have helped SCLC to attract vital publicity through demonstrations in Lowndes, where not just Liuzzo but a white seminarian, Jonathan Daniels, had been murdered. But focused on launching the Lowndes County Freedom Democrats, SNCC obliged King to rely on his own, increasingly disaffected affiliates and discontented field staff.

The national and short-term orientation of his mobilizing strategy came back to haunt King. The organizations he had left in old Alabama battlegrounds – Montgomery, Birmingham, and now Selma – were riven with dissension and painful memories of the cost of protest. Warned by King that they were just "shacking up" with rather than marrying the local communities to which they were assigned, SCLC staff did not know where they would be from one week to the next (Fairclough 1987: 269). Once the Voting Rights Act enabled African Americans to vote, Movement attention turned to the selection of candidates and the exercise of office since practical political power was wielded daily by office-holders rather than electors. This required a level of permanent organization alien to all three direct action organizations – CORE, SNCC, and SCLC. While scholars have criticized King and cele-brated the "organizing" tradition evident especially in SNCC's work in Mississippi, they have tended not to examine too closely the latter's claim that "organizing" secured more tangible gains than King-style "mobilizing" in places like Albany or Selma. The truth seems almost certainly to be that both were required – indefi-nitely. During a much-needed week's vacation in Jamaica in June, King had wondered aloud whether he could take a year away to ready himself for the struggles ahead, before wearily admitting that the people's need for a symbol and SCLC's never-ending financial needs were shackles he could not escape.

Under King's leadership, dramatic protests had pressurized a liberal President and Congress to address the chief deficiency of the 1964 Act by strengthened federal protection of voting rights. When King claimed, from the steps of the Alabama state capitol in March 1965, that the arc of the universe bends towards justice, his supporters had nodded agreement. But to others, the gains came at too high a price. The Selma campaign of 1965 was in key respects the culmination of the nonviolent tactics that King had developed over the previous two years. The Birmingham pattern of staging a dramatic confrontation with a violence-prone segre-gationist adversary was reprised. Local African American grie-vances were used as a foundation for a primarily nationally orientated campaign. Sympathetic media coverage was courted to mobilize national support for federal action, while efforts to defuse the crisis prematurely by minimal local concessions were evaded.

At the same time, the most dramatic events of the Selma campaign — its three murders, the Bloody Sunday attack on the Edmund Pettus Bridge, and the mass march from Selma to Montgomery itself — reawakened criticisms leveled against King during the St. Augustine campaign. Did SCLC tactics needlessly jeopardize local people? Jimmie Lee Jackson had been fatally wounded during a risky night march in an already inflamed racist community as King tried to maintain media pressure. Was the staging of spectacular protests essential to securing the aims of the Movement? By March, the time of Bloody Sunday, and the subsequent murders of the two Northern white supporters, James Reeb and Viola Liuzzo, King already had President Johnson's promise of voting rights legislation and several indications of full support. Finally, had King become so ensnared by his own national politicking, and the media circus that accompanied it, that he failed to communicate openly and honestly with Movement followers? When King decided to abort the mass march from Selma on Tuesday March 9, having seemingly assured the rank and file that he was going ahead, he protected his ties to the federal government, but inside the Movement, he simultaneously frayed bonds of trust.

The bruising disappointment of the MFDP's convention challenge of the previous summer and the volatility of the Northern ghettos meant that militants in 1965, especially in SNCC and CORE, did not share King's tears of delight at Johnson's symbolic embrace of the Movement's cause. When the President quoted "We Shall Overcome" in his speech to Congress on March 15, radicals suspected that perhaps the Movement was settling for too little. A black mayor would not replace Joe Smitherman in Selma for another thirty-five years, thanks largely to Smitherman's skillful adaptation to African American reenfranchisement. Politically, King's success seemed partial in 1965, and was derided by increasingly vocal militants as "selling out." He had reached a career peak. No subsequent campaign had as clear-cut and positive an outcome as Selma did; yet the evils of racism, poverty, and violence constituted a challenge he chose not to ignore.

8 King's Call

Organizing And Mobilizing Chicago, 1965-66

As King urged protest in the South of the early 1960s, thousands of African Americans chose instead to flee. The *Chicago Daily News* referred to the city's West Side ghetto as "the part of Mississippi that got away" (Connolly 1989: 60-61). Between 1940 and 1960 the black population living outside the states of the old Confederacy exploded from 4 million to 9 million people, making the 1960s the decade in which African Americans became predominantly non-Southern urbanites. King always knew that racial injustice affected both North and South. An April 1965 visit to Boston saw him denounce the residential segregation that produced black slums and *de facto* segregated and unequal education. An abiding memory of his days as a Boston University student, he told reporters, was the ordeal of trying to find somewhere to live. He had inquired wherever he saw "Rooms to Rent" signs, but once landlords discovered he "was a Negro," "suddenly [the rooms] had just been rented" (Garrow 1988: 423).

Northern Ghetto Problems

Prejudice and institutional racism produced ghetto poverty and at the same time were bolstered by it. Disproportionately, black migrants headed for the nation's twelve largest cities and overwhelmed the ghettoes into which they were funneled. Driving into the city, white suburbanites were appalled by the ghetto's dereliction. They shook their heads at the large number of youths on the streets and in the parks, and shuddered at radio reports of ghetto murders, delinquency, and crime. Living in these ghettos,

African Americans resented the high rents they paid for shame-fully neglected tenements. But they knew that they could not escape because white vigilante attacks enforced the color line between neighborhoods. Financial institutions used racial compo-sition as a key criterion of "blight" and whites feared any black influx that would reduce property values. Using the same criter-ion, loans were made infrequently and on tougher terms to African Americans, or for properties in predominantly black neighbor-hoods. Work-wise, African Americans were last hired and first fired and concentrated in the ranks of the unskilled whose future was being eroded by automation. Employers could buy black labor cheaply and white unions, especially in construction, operated a color bar in apprenticeships that ensured their unions' "closed shop" prevented African American advancement. Institutional racism lay behind much of the ghetto's squalor, but most whites attributed it to personal vices. By 1965, King was determined to force a reappraisal.

Ghetto poverty was a product of interlocking, discriminatory processes and King had to decide at what point in a cycle of cumulative, negative causation he should intervene. Education was one. Northern cities could not build classrooms quickly enough to accommodate the African American influx. To maximize existing capacity, Boston and Chicago, among others, introduced tempor-ary double shifts, putting many black students out of school during the day, and on the street again heading home late at night. At the same time, white relocation to the suburbs left other nearby schools underutilized. For black parents, the only explanation for their child's consignment to a crowded night school rather than a comfortable day school was the racism that made the transfer of black pupils to historically white schools with declining numbers unthinkable.

But the white, often Catholic, parents in these blue-collar, ethnic neighborhoods reacted to the idea of "busing" just as white Southerners resisted the *Brown* desegregation ruling. Neighbor-hood schools, like parish churches, were crucial to their communal identity. Busing in black students, they contended, meant importing delinquency, disease, and academic underachievement. As in the South, the Movement in the North faced a counter-movement, which ultimately fed into a powerful neo-conservatism that questioned state interference in what it considered the private sphere of home and family. Since King's death, such views have ensured that the United States has not become the beloved community of which he dreamed, but displays still the prejudices he deplored.

The *Brown* decision assumed that schools could engineer solutions to deep-seated social problems, but teachers themselves were often less confident that they could easily or consistently redress the negative impact of households in poverty and communities in crisis. Slum housing, low incomes, and frequent unemployment did not help black parents who wanted their children to excel. If King attacked housing or employment discrimination, he might ultimately address educational inequalities too. Some liberal, religious, and labor organizations worked for open housing and equal employment opportunity, but education, always a key African American concern, remained a springboard for northern protest. In 1963-64, massive school boycotts in Boston, Chicago, and New York demonstrated black anger at unresponsive education authorities. In Chicago, nearly 225,000 students had stayed home in protest in October 1963.

King hoped during 1965 to build on these protests. But school boycotts, unlike bus boycotts, could not be sustained indefinitely without damaging the formal education of the children involved. King also felt that he needed to attack ghetto poverty on a broader front. The limited education of migrants tended to restrict their job prospects to unskilled positions, even in states that had fair employment laws. By the 1960s, technological and organizational changes were already reducing the number of unskilled and semiskilled, industrial jobs available. Successive generations of African Americans in the North faced technological redundancy, unemployment, and underemployment. With low levels of seniority and limited access to training and promotion, they were set to be laid off or fired. Their children, too, had fewer local job opportunities as firms relocated, restructured, and automated. Black unemployment had remained twice the white level during the supposedly prosperous 1950s, and that fed other problems.

King agreed with Bayard Rustin, a key advisor, that together the Civil Rights Movement and the trade unions could reduce employment discrimination. From their Northern strongholds, national labor leaders had generally backed the Southern freedom struggle financially and politically. But the liberal stance of progressive AFL-CIO leaders offered a poor guide to rank and file sentiment. With their own jobs threatened, Northern white workers typically responded with hostility to black aspirations. King's increasing emphasis on better homes and jobs for African Americans during the mid-1960s generated loathing among many such workers. He was threatening to devalue their homes, and take away their jobs and prospects. He seemed to expect them to stand by while teenagers from schools with a history of violence and delinquency were transferred to study alongside their own sons and daughters. Despite King's advocacy of nonviolence, Northern whites did not associate African Americans with self-control and stoical resistance, but with crime and self-indulgence. So powerfully embedded were these negative connotations that by the 1980s, crime and other symbols of irresponsibility, such as unmarried mothers, became code words for a new rhetoric that mobilized racist sentiment without using explicitly racist language (Edsall and Edsall 1992).

King's Decision To Go North

At a Virginia retreat in mid-June 1965, SCLC staff and King's Northern advisors debated the case for a Northern campaign. Bayard Rustin and Norman Hill, a progressive trade unionist, jointly tried to persuade King not to go North. The SCLC's fundraising coordinator, New Yorker Stanley Levison, warned that a Northern campaign would probably see donations plummet and confirm the shallowness of his fellow Northern whites' liberal principles. With the Voting Rights Act before Congress, Hosea Williams called for SCLC to concentrate on Southern voter registration. Randolph Blackwell, a vociferous critic of Williams's cavalier management of the SCLC's new voter registration initiative, SCOPE, nonetheless seconded his call.

Others, however, supported the move North. Shortly before King's visit to Boston, James Bevel had told a Chicago audience that "the nonviolent movement" would soon demand the city eradicate "the racist attitude that is denying Negroes the right to live in adequate housing" (Ralph 1993: 1). As SCLC's most imaginative tactician, Bevel was already considering a permanent move to Chicago to join his ex-SNCC colleague Bernard LaFayette as a community organizer. A native Mississippian, Bevel empathized with his transplanted brethren on the West Side and knew that their frustrations needed an outlet. During the previous summer, Andrew Young had been sent with Bevel to calm violent disturbances in Rochester, New York. Usually seen as cautious, he too backed the idea of a Northern campaign. If they could mobilize the same proportion of Chicago's million-strong black population to engage in active protest as they had in smaller, Southern population centers, he observed, they would have a formidable force.

Always aware that racism was national not sectional, King was convinced that he had to move beyond the South, not least because of his commitment to nonviolence. By 1965, King knew that Northern ghettos were on the brink of civil conflagration on a scale unmatched since World War II. If he failed to act, interracial violence would not only cost lives but also damage the prospects for racial comity that his nonviolent approach sought to promote. To some, King's willingness to tackle Northern problems reflected renewed ambition after Selma. With the voting rights bill nearing passage, King hoped that the coalition of conscience created by the Selma campaign would be prepared to confront Northern injustices. "It is not a constitutional right that men have jobs," he told new audiences, "but it is a human right" (Jackson 2007: 244).

On Independence Day, 1965, King preached at Ebenezer about how his 1963 dream of justice had been "shattered" by the realities of poverty he had witnessed. "I still have a dream," he declared, "that one day all of God's children will have food and clothing and material well-being for their bodies, culture and education for their minds, and freedom for their spirits." Elsewhere, he urged massive public works alongside a more generously funded War on Poverty to tackle unemployment, which among ghetto youth exceeded 70 percent in some cities (Jackson 2007: 246, 249). As Americans celebrated July 4 in 1965, King's white confidant Stanley Levison reminded him of the generally hostile reaction to his recent call for a boycott of George Wallace's Alabama. According to Levison, the outcry disproved Rustin's naive proposition that a "majority liberal consensus" had emerged, capable of supporting "a radical program" to "alter the social structure of

America." On the contrary, there was "basically a coalition for moderate change" that wanted "gradual improvements" and dreaded "excessive upheavals." Only fanatical and well-publicized conduct by Alabama's segregationists had made this moderate coalition temporarily militant. King had better realize, Levison warned, that "not even the appeal of equality" would tear this deeply centrist coalition away from "their essentially moderate tendencies." Like the labor movement of the 1930s, this was a reformist not a revolutionary movement. King needed to accept this, Levison admonished, to optimize its potential. As long as he heeded their moderation, Americans might undertake "perhaps major, reforms," but if King demanded a revolution, he would find that whites were "not inclined to change their society to free the Negro" (Garrow 1988: 420).

Unlike SNCC militants like Stokely Carmichael, who felt that African American leaders had tried too hard to tailor their words for white consumption, King understood the political perils of pursuing revolutionary goals in a conservative nation. While King shared Levison's skepticism on American liberalism, however, he refused to limit his goals. His faith in a Social Gospel demanded that he contest injustice, whether it took the form of ghetto poverty or US foreign policy in Vietnam. Despite cogent arguments against a move North, he had essentially resolved to do so, before the Voting Rights Act was passed or the Watts riot in Los Angeles in August. The latter, the most serious race riot since World War II, simply accelerated his plans. Raging for four days after an incident of typically insensitive policing, the disturbances left thirty-four dead, around a thousand injured, and an estimated $200 million worth of property destroyed. Cutting short what he had hoped would be a recuperative holiday King joined Bayard Rustin in Los Angeles on August 17 to see the devastation at first hand.

King's efforts to calm the 1964 Harlem disturbances had been vilified as Uncle-Tomism by local blacks. Now, in meetings with an unsympathetic Mayor Sam Yorty and an openly hostile Police Chief William Parker, he argued the case for a civilian review board to investigate allegations against the police. He warned reporters not to expect ghetto-dwellers to be appeased by the Movement's gains in the South since these did not address the key economic issues that oppressed them. In private, a distraught Martin told Rustin: "You know, Bayard, I worked to get these people the right to eat hamburgers, and now I've got to do something ... to help them get the money to buy it" (Garrow 1988: 439). A sentiment shared by many activists, the comment shows that King's move North reflected his sharpened, though always present, desire for economic justice.

According to Andrew Young, King also reacted to Robert Kennedy's remark that the Watts riot reflected how the Movement's Southern focus had caused it to neglect Northern city problems. Young thought it preposterous for Kennedy, a millionaire and former US Attorney-General, to imply that somehow the Movement was at fault. "But Martin took it seriously," he writes. "He never thought he had done enough and Bobby Kennedy's words ate at him" (Young 1996: 380). Acknowledging the risks, King told Levison that it was a case of "damned if you do, damned if you don't. If we don't go North, we're damned, but if you go you've got some problems" (Ralph 1993: 38). At the 1965 SCLC convention, King spoke out against the "violence of poverty" within which ghetto blacks were imprisoned, and urged colleagues to break the cycle of powerlessness. He also warned them that the jobs available to middle-class blacks within the War on Poverty might tempt them to "forget their brothers in the teeming ghettos" (Jackson 2007: 250, 262). A week after returning from Watts, he held a three-day emergency staff meeting. "A bankruptcy of leadership," he warned, would prompt Northern blacks to turn to violence, unless he provided a meaningful alternative. To do so, SCLC must prepare to work in Chicago. "Chicago is on fire with a nonviolent movement," King declared. "They want us to come in September. We must not ignore their call" (Fairclough 1987: 275).

Why Chicago?

According to James Bevel, King chose Chicago because Bevel had already chosen to work there. But it was not that simple. A frequent destination on King's endless fund-raising circuit, Chicago's huge school boycott, organized by a consortium of civic groups, the Coordinating Council of Community Organizations (CCCO), had caught his imagination. In late July 1965, he began a five-city fact-finding tour in Chicago. Guided by the CCCO, King appeared before such a succession of cheering crowds and militant meetings that he was barely able to continue on to his next stop, Cleveland. "The doctors tell me I can't get by on two or three hours of sleep a night," he told reporters. "I try to do it and learn I just can't" (Garrow 1988: 434).

The SCLC was looking for a cooperative Northern beachhead and, even allowing for King's weakened condition at later stops, none of the other cities on his tour matched Chicago. Open hostility to King's visits from black Congressman Adam Clayton Powell in New York and local NAACP president Cecil Moore in Philadelphia ruled them out. Black mayoral candidate Carl Stokes in Cleveland was also wary of King's plans because his electoral success probably depended on white votes that direct action might alienate. Finally, in Washington, DC, African American grievances were inextricably tangled up with the issue of ending Congressional oversight of the city in favor of home rule, a unique situation that argued against it serving as a site for dramatizing ghetto problems in general. By comparison, the nation's second-largest city, Chicago, had already organized mass nonviolent protests via the CCCO, under the capable Al Raby, and Chicagoans had responded warmly during King's recent visit.

The power of Chicago's Mayor Richard Daley also attracted King. Elsewhere faction-ridden councils limited a mayor's power, but Chicago under Daley had a definite power center that King could target for redress. As a critical Earl Bush, Daley's press secretary, put it, "King thought that if Daley were to go before a microphone and say 'Let there be no more discrimination,' there wouldn't be." King did tend to believe that white power-holders could do more to root out racial injustice than they themselves believed was true, and initially, he may not have fully detected that the city which he saw as the most segregated in the United States was, for Daley, simply and proudly "a city of neighborhoods" (Cohen and Taylor 2000: 338).

Daley had seemed a King ally. He had praised the civil rights leader for his Nobel Peace Prize award, and declared that there was no disagreement between them that: "we must root out poverty, rid the community of slums, eliminate discrimination and segregation wherever they may exist, and improve the quality of education." A better gauge of Daley's position, however, came with his reaction to a series of marches into his home neighborhood of Bridgeport, organized by local black activist Dick Gregory in late July 1965. Although Daley mostly ensured that precinct workers kept his white neighbors from confronting African American marchers, after a minor riot in early August, he declared: "I don't think it helps their cause to be marching in residential districts. I think they are surely trying to create tension" (Cohen and Taylor 2000: 342).

King and Young announced Chicago as SCLC's next target on September 1. A Northern counterpart to Birmingham, Chicago epitomized ghetto problems. If "Northern problems can be solved there," Young remarked, "they can be solved everywhere." The powerful Mayor Daley machine could help the process. The Democratic boss and his followers, Young claimed, "can make changes in behalf of the people if their conscience is sharpened and the issues clearly raised before them." Judging the city by the white liberal clergy who had backed SCLC past efforts, Young suggested that the new campaign would enjoy influential religious support. He stressed that the presence of the CCCO had been central to SCLC's choice, and King concurred, identifying its aim of "quality integrated education" as the joint campaign's initial focus (Garrow 1988: 444).

Young's comments disguised the fact that, by late August, he had private misgivings, although he was never as forthright in his opposition to King's decision as he suggests in his memoirs. Well aware of Bevel's maverick tendencies, he did emphasize the importance of working with Chicago's CCCO, and of carefully preparing the ground. A diplomat by inclination, he wanted to cultivate white allies before launching any campaign. King, however, dismissed calls for delay by insisting that the Movement had already proved that direct action campaigns recruit people, educate the press, and attract white allies as they develop. "We cannot expect such allies in the beginning," he remarked. With Watts in mind, he added that the "present mood dictates that we cannot wait" (Garrow 1988: 442-43).

Only in his memoirs does Young forcefully argue that SCLC "had neither the resources nor the staff to sustain" a crucial

Southern campaign to mobilize black voters and a massive Northern assault on ghetto poverty. With Williams anxious to be rid of Bevel, it was left to Rustin and Randolph Blackwell to argue that SCLC should concentrate on transforming Southern politics, hoping to remove a key conservative bastion. Thirty years later, Young appreciated that many SCLC's field workers, although graduates of Southern campaigns, were freshmen in Chicago and that their reassignment took strength from the South while adding little to the Northern campaign. It was not Young but Levison who warned that a Chicago campaign would over-tax the SCLC's limited resources, both in the expenses it entailed and the donations it lost (Young 1996: 381-85). The key point remains that, from whatever source they came, King knew the arguments against his proposed campaign, and yet he went ahead. It was very much his call to demonstrate the power of nonviolence to the powerless and, as the next chapter makes clear, he made the decision to try to loosen the suburban "white nooses around the black necks of the cities" at the same time as he accepted the political cost of speaking out on Vietnam (Jackson 2007: 277).

A New Challenge: Organizing Rather Than Mobilizing

In Chicago, SCLC was embarking on a campaign of intense and sustained organizing to create a mass movement. It was this grassroots' approach that attracted SNCC veterans like Bernard LaFayette and, to some extent, James Bevel, but organizing in this sense had never been King's forte. Under his charismatic leadership, SCLC had thrived as a mobilizing agency, moving into a community like an evangelical mission, building up short-term fervor through dramatic events, but relying extensively on other institutions, including other civil rights groups as well as churches, to do the initial organizing and pick up that task in the longer term. The large, foundation grants consumed by SCLC's Citizenship School program should have warned King that local organizing ate up resources and took time. Unfortunately, the CCCO was itself primarily a mobilizing rather than organizing framework, with weak links with individual neighborhoods. In key respects, it reinforced King's weaknesses.

SCLC's principal advance agents, James Bevel, and an equally mercurial new recruit, Jesse Jackson, correspondingly did not strengthen the CCCO. Recruited by a Chicago outreach ministry, the West Side Christian Parish (WSCP), rather than the CCCO itself, Bevel never warmed to Al Raby's consortium, which included many civic groups from the older South Side ghetto. With an emphasis on neighborhood organizing rather than metropolitan politicking, the WSCP operated largely independently of the CCCO. Similarly, a Ford Foundation project was Jesse Jackson's Chicago base from October 1965, as he helped to found the Kenwood-Oakland Community Organization (KOCO). Jackson subsequently led Operation Breadbasket, which used the threat of consumer boycotts to negotiate job openings for blacks, via Chicago's black churches. Both roles enhanced his capacity for independent action. It had been difficult for thirty-six black civic groups and several white religious organizations to form the CCCO, and Bevel's and Jackson's cavalier style revived centrifugal tendencies that Raby had struggled to contain. This was especially so because SCLC quickly abandoned the CCCO's primary goal of ousting Chicago's long-serving Superintendent of Education Benjamin Willis for his racially insensitive defense of white neighborhood schools. In its place, SCLC proclaimed Bevel's crusade to eliminate the slums.

Underestimating the task, King announced in early January 1966 that the first part of his Chicago battle plan would be to educate and organize on a block-by-block basis. The schedule indicated that by March 1, "community response and live issues should have evolved to the point where some consensus has been reached about specific targets." The proposed timetable not only implied that King believed that SCLC could organize the supply lines for its "nonviolent army," in two months, it also suggested that it had abandoned a key lesson of the 1961-62 Albany campaign, namely, targeting a limited, specific issue. A staff document justified this change by referring to "the probability of a ready accommodation to many of the issues in some token manner" in Chicago, "merely to curtail the massing of forces and public opinion around those issues." This recognized that Mayor Daley would avoid the crude confrontational tactics of Birmingham's Bull Connor or Selma's Jim Clark. But SCLC's corollary – "Therefore, we must be prepared to concentrate all our forces around any and all issues" – was inherently contradictory and utopian (Garrow 1988: 456-57). Forces cannot be concentrated along an infinite front line, unless they, too, are infinite, and King never had the luxury of unlimited resources.

Attempting Too Much With Too Little?

In spring 1965, the Selma campaign had produced a financial windfall for SCLC. Between September 1964 and June 1965, income doubled over the previous year's to exceed $1.5 million. On the strength of this, 125 new staff joined the organization, bringing its personnel to around 200 people. Then, due to lax financial controls, Hosea Williams's SCOPE program and other staff initiatives generated a torrent of bills that ate up the Selma windfall, even before the Chicago campaign began. Most of the money had come as small donations (averaging $10). A mistaken belief among many whites that the Voting Rights Act removed the one remaining obstacle to equal black participation in American society, combined with King's criticisms of US military involvement in Vietnam, and his sharper emphasis on national problems of racialized poverty, slowed the flow of small, one-off contributions over the next financial year. Unable to clear SCOPE's debts or impose financial discipline on his colleagues, King had to cancel a second summer of student voter registration efforts in the South. "I just can't have this hanging over my head," he told Levison wearily in February 1966. With a huge deficit looming in May, a worried Levison concluded that King was "trying to turn his back on" the SCLC's financial crisis (Fairclough 1987: 255-56, 286-87).

The financial freefall proved that the SCLC did not have the resources to fight on two fronts. King's decision to help transplanted black Southerners and their offspring in Chicago meant that he was less able to assist their counterparts in Natchez, Mississippi, for instance, or sustain the continuing struggles in Birmingham or Selma. These communities had looked to King for assistance and had received either an ill-judged or inadequate response from SCLC. Given that King was quick to see that President Johnson could not sustain both the War on Poverty and the war in

Vietnam, it is ironic that he was unable to see the crucial importance of focusing his own efforts. Not only was he unwilling to accept Rustin's charge that the Chicago protest movement he hoped to lead risked damaging the effective political development of the Southern Movement, he was also reluctant to select a clear focus for the Chicago campaign.

Admittedly, by the time of the Chicago Freedom Movement's launch, the CCCO's focus on schools and Superintendent Willis attracted faltering support. By 1966, Willis's school-building projects had expanded ghetto classroom capacity sufficiently to end the hated double shifts. A CCCO complaint against the school district under Title VI of the 1964 Civil Rights Act had prompted the new Department of Health, Education and Welfare to freeze $34 million in federal aid on October 1, 1965, but Mayor Daley's clout ensured that President Johnson ordered the grants released just five days later. Despite Daley's obvious support of Superintendent Willis, King was reluctant to personalize his campaign as an attack on the mayor. To most commentators, his claim to be fighting the system but not Daley's machine was either transparently disingenuous or desperately naive.

Initially, slum landlords seemed to be King's primary targets, with a secondary attack on racist employers. Despite a calendar littered with commitments, King had agreed to live in Chicago for three days each week. Without disclosing his identity, SCLC rented a four-room apartment on the third floor of an aging apartment house in North Lawndale. But before King moved in on January 19, word leaked and quickly repairmen appeared to mend the apartment's more egregious faults. Nevertheless, when she joined her husband, Coretta King was shocked by the insecure outer door, the ground-level dirt floor, and the "overpowering" smell of urine on the stairs (Scott King 1969: 278-79).

The local press debated this publicity stunt's effectiveness. Mike Royko looked back cynically: "Chicagoans already knew about slums. Whites were indifferent and Negroes didn't have to be reminded where they lived" (Fairclough 1987: 290). Though equally sardonic, the Chicago *Sun-Times* was positive. King should move into other neighborhoods, it editorialized. If his presence continued to draw the same swift action, he might produce "an elimination of blight that would amaze even the most optimistic of city planners" (Connolly 1989: 57). Unfortunately, the token repairs were limited to just King's apartment. His colleague Ralph Abernathy recalls that no one bothered to fix up his West Side apartment (Abernathy 1989: 371). King himself felt that his arrival raised local morale, as he walked the neighborhood, visited a school, and even shot pool in a neighborhood dive. Hopefully, this would help SCLC to organize tenants' unions.

Symptomatic of the campaign's scattershot approach, however, the main organizing thrust was not in North Lawndale, where King was securing headlines, but in neighboring East Garfield Park, where Bevel strove to create his Union to End Slums. King joined him there in late January for an emotional church mass meeting, with Southern-style singing and testifying. Eventually, the union was established with an elaborate structure rooted in individual building stewards and street block delegates. Modeled on Chicago organizer Saul Alinsky's The Woodlawn Organization (TWO), Bevel's team sought to generate solidarity under the slogan "We Are Being Robbed!" But unlike TWO, Bevel's Union to End Slums was not content to "organize people on the basis of their hate." It tried to educate them as to the structural basis of their oppression so that they would learn "that the struggle to which they are being called is not merely the besting of an enemy, but the renewal and re-democratization of the social order itself" (Ralph 1993: 59, 62).

Unfortunately, the churches, which had been central to SCLC's Southern campaigns, were an unreliable means of reaching black Chicago's slum-dwellers, and most East Garfield Park residents did not respond. Such apathy proved soul-destroying for Bevel's assistants, who recalled how months of their door-to-door canvassing "went by with nothing seemingly happening." Expectations had been unrealistic. Not "even top-notch professional organizers," staff member Billy Hollins concludes, "could have organized this community of 70,000 in just a few months" (Ralph 1993: 63). It was late March before the union was able to mobilize against just one pair of landlords, and mid-July before it compelled their lawyers to accept an unprecedented collective bargaining agreement. However important, this small beginning could not match the burden of expectation King carried. Meanwhile, Mayor Daley used War on Poverty monies to demonstrate how he was addressing the practical needs of Chicagoans with Head Start kindergartens and neighborhood youth corps jobs (Jackson 2007: 283).

Without Parallel?

The scale and complexity of Chicago's ghettos, King eventually conceded, required "organizing people into permanent units, rather than on a temporary basis just for demonstrations." To establish tenant unions in dozens of neighborhoods would require an unprecedented SCLC commitment, taking eighteen months, perhaps, compared to earlier, Southern campaigns of three to six months. The closest parallel to Chicago in King's career was not Birmingham or Selma, but Montgomery during the Bus Boycott. But that comparison reveals that he really had nothing to guide him. King could not lead the nearly 1 million black Chicagoans by preaching at church mass meetings. In Chicago, there would have to be not one, but many boycotts, as well as rent strikes and other forms of direct action. Unlike King's Montgomery adversaries a decade earlier, Mayor Daley would seek to calm inflammatory situations. When King called for the elimination of slums, the wily mayor concurred, and listed city programs already in place to advance that goal. Ultimately, Montgomery's buses had been desegregated by federal court order on constitutional grounds. In Chicago, litigation challenging de facto school segregation was flagging by 1966, and a 1963 municipal fair housing ordinance ensured that the city was judged to comply with Supreme Court rulings outlawing agreements that restricted sale or tenancy on the basis of race.

In Chicago, King was as ill equipped for what confronted him as he had been in Albany in 1961. Once again, he acted impulsively. Learning of a sick baby in a nearby, rundown apartment house with a faulty heating system, he announced on February 23 that SCLC was taking the property into "trusteeship" and would collect the rent and spend it on repairs. When challenged, King insisted that the "moral question is far more important than the legal one" (Ralph 1993: 56). He had hoped to corner a greedy landlord but, embarrassingly, owner John Bender was "very old, very sick, and almost as poor as the tenants." During its three-months' trusteeship, the SCLC collected $200 in rent but spent

$2,000 on repairs. This hardly dramatized the exploitative nature of ghetto landlordism, especially when the octogenarian landlord died shortly afterwards. King's SCLC, Levison fumed, came across publicly as "a gang of anarchists" (Fairclough 1987: 290).

Like Chief Pritchett in Albany, Mayor Daley had allies inside the black community, and worked to ensure that King did not gain significant outside sympathy by being seen as the victim of unreasonable repression. Rustin had tried to warn King about the mayor's power over black Chicago, but King seems only to have understood, once he had experienced it. Movement activists were particularly hostile to the so-called "Silent Six" – the six black aldermen who acted as a buffer between Daley and growing black discontent. Patronage did not completely explain their loyalty to Daley. The mayor had supported national civil rights legislation and had ensured that not just black Congressman William Dawson but white members of Chicago's Congressional delegation backed such bills. He had lobbied for a state fair employment practices law and continued to advocate fair housing legislation to bolster the municipal ordinance of 1963. A Democratic kingpin, Daley had organized quickly to secure massive federal antipoverty grants under Johnson's Great Society programs, and this ensured that federal patronage augmented the local patronage his Cook County machine could dispense.

The African American share of jobs and contracts under Daley was never quite commensurate with their growing importance within his electoral coalition. But from Daley's perspective, the need to retain white ethnic votes dictated this. It was a delicate balancing act, to which King seemed oblivious. Since the 1920s, the confinement of blacks to certain neighborhoods had produced a residential pattern that had facilitated the Democratic machine's control of the city. Ward captains had cultivated a concentrated African American vote in the so-called plantation wards. If blacks scattered across the city, not only would this bloc vote become diffuse, but white flight from the currently stable Bungalow Belt would undermine the machine in these wards as well. As early as February 1966, King heard rumors that Daley was rattled. But the mayor was not worried that King would outwit him, rather he feared that King's blundering "would create a political maelstrom beyond his control" (Ralph 1993: 85). To contain King, Daley trumpeted his own campaign to end slums by 1967. By July 1966, he boasted that over 16,000 buildings in North Lawndale and East and West Garfield Park had been inspected and re-inspected. Using federal War on Poverty grants, seven Urban Progress centers were established, mainly in competition with the movement on the West Side, and staffed by people from community organizations. This surge of official activity significantly dampened SCLC's progress, making the Chicago campaign a time of mounting frustration for King. Andrew Young complained that no sooner had the movement organized a neighborhood than "Daley's forces would come in and offer a preacher a contract for subsidized daycare in his church" (Cohen and Taylor 2000: 364).

The proliferation of issues and strong factionalism inside the black community also resembled King's Albany experience. While he tried to highlight tenants' housing problems on the West Side, Operation Breadbasket focused on black unemployment, using black consumer leverage. King promoted the scheme successfully at a large gathering of priests and ministers on the South Side on February 11. Shortly after this meeting, King joined Al Raby at a CCCO rally for parents and teachers unhappy with the white principal of an overwhelmingly black school, thus appearing to identify quality education as an active movement goal. On issues that might require a direct confrontation with Mayor Daley, King found local black clergy hesitant. The location of SCLC's campaign headquarters at Warren Avenue Congregationalist Church, which had a white pastor, reflected the reality that Chicago's black clergy were not solidly King's men.

Multiple goals reinforced rather than reduced divisions. A source of patronage, Operation Breadbasket attracted local clergy partly by boosting their competitive rivalry within individual communities, and its successes enhanced Jesse Jackson's autonomy to such a point that King became concerned about his young lieutenant's eagerness to operate independently. The Chicago Freedom Movement was supposed to be a joint SCLC-CCCO venture with common policies determined by an Agenda Committee. But, in practice, the initiative seemed to lie primarily with King's staff on the so-called Action Committee, particularly Bevel and Jackson, who largely ignored what they regarded as a moribund CCCO. Neither King nor SCLC executive director Andrew Young had the time or energy to overcome these internal divisions.

Based largely on the South Side, Chicago's black elite worried about King's protest plans. With business and political ties to the status quo and assets to lose, they generally favored a philosophy of self-help and the NAACP's legalistic tactics, which conspicuously had not joined the Freedom Movement. One particularly vociferous critic was the Reverend Joseph H. Jackson, pastor of Olivet Baptist Church on the South Side and, since 1953, President of the National Baptist Convention (NBC). Rooted in King's past efforts to oust him from the NBC presidency, Jackson's animosity also articulated a significant, black conservative position that deplored mass civil disobedience as a form of intimidation. His public opposition ensured that King did not enjoy the whole-hearted support of Chicago's black Baptists.

Unreliable Allies

Unlike the militants who dominated CORE and SNCC by 1966, King still believed in an interracial coalition for black advancement. In Chicago, despite his initial concentration on black neighborhood organizing, King was counting on the active support of white religious groups and organized labor. Members of the Chicago Conference on Race and Religion (CCRR) listened attentively to King in late January, although some quietly warned that their assistance might not match the aid sent to Selma. White Chicago was predominantly Catholic, and so King was careful to meet with Archbishop John Cody and to liaise with John McDermott of the Catholic Interracial Council (CIC), a founding member of the CCCO. As Bishop for New Orleans, Cody had previously faced Southern segregationist fury for his desegregation of parochial schools, while McDermott, a lay militant, had told a New York colleague in 1964 that "the time for an education-only approach in race relations is long past. Chicago CIC is a social action as well as an educational organization. We are committed to the direct action movement" (McGreevy 1996: 143).

King misjudged the prelate's liberalism and the layman's influence. Briefed by the FBI on King's communist ties and "hypocritical behavior" in sexual matters, Cody tried to keep his distance, while still applauding King's goal of social justice. In August, when King had generated a genuine crisis, Cody called for the open housing marches' suspension because of the violent reaction they provoked. The 1966 campaign revealed a vehement racism among the white Catholic laity and, by November, McDermott could only confirm sadly the gulf between liberals like himself and most Chicago Catholics. The latter, he wrote, "are particularly bitter towards priests, bishops and organizations who tell them that they are in conflict with their religion. 'Since when?' they retort" (McGreevy 1996: 187-90).

On racial matters, white Catholics would not obey their priests, and King's hopes of white religious leadership were again unfulfilled. His dreams of a powerful labor alliance proved similarly illusory. In late March, he fashioned a framework for labor cooperation with senior members of the AFL-CIO's Industrial Union Department, UAW leaders, and local leaders from the United Packinghouse Workers of America (UPWA), whose members worked in Chicago's famous meat-packing plants. This support was more than offset, however, by the hostility of Chicago's most powerful workers' organization, the Chicago Federation of Labor and the Industrial Union Council (CFL-IUC), which had close ties to Mayor Daley. The CFL-IUC included affiliates from the traditionally lily-white building trades, who accepted few black apprentices. Rank-and-file trade unionists were more often counter-demonstrators than open housing marchers in Chicago and, although representatives of organized labor did give King support, they, like Archbishop Cody, conspicuously pressed him for a settlement in late August to end the violent neighborhood clashes. They never appreciated King's key point that nonviolent protest-generated "creative tension" was the prime lever available to the poor.

King Switches Back To Mobilizing

Shuttling between Atlanta and Chicago, and beset by problems of mounting SCLC debts, falling staff morale, and the hostility of the Johnson administration, King eventually decided that he could not sustain a marathon organizing campaign but must revert to a shorter-term mobilization strategy. On May 26, he announced a mass rally at Chicago's Soldier Field in one month's time to launch the campaign's "action phase." The deteriorating situation forced his hand. In early June, the *Chicago Daily News* quoted one local resident's description of King and his lieutenants as "romantic, disorganized little tin gods who don't know the city" (Ralph 1993: 91). But even before King could try to rescue the stumbling campaign, news broke on June 6 that James Meredith had been shot as he attempted to walk from Memphis to Jackson, Mississippi. As the next chapter explains, King felt obliged to continue Meredith's "Walk against Fear" with CORE and SNCC, both to keep a media spotlight on Mississippi and to rally support for a federal protection of civil rights workers' clause in the civil rights bill currently before Congress.

King headed for Memphis. For almost three weeks, his priorities switched back to the South, with Chicago activists raising money and joining the Meredith march rather than working to ensure a huge turnout for their own rally, scheduled for June 26. The Black Power controversy that erupted during the march is also discussed in the next chapter, but its impact on the Chicago campaign was negative. The media portrayed King as an embattled leader in decline, whose message of nonviolence had been superseded by Stokely Carmichael's strident calls for Black Power. SCLC workers, like James Orange, had been working hard to persuade Chicago's gang members that nonviolence was the best strategy. But his efforts balked after some of his recruits went to Mississippi and heard Carmichael, SNCC's new leader, re-articulate Malcolm X's view that African Americans should not be constrained by nonviolence. CORE's formal endorsement of a Black Power strategy at its July 4 convention was also significant because Robert Lucas, its Chicago chapter head, was already abandoning CORE's tradition of nonviolence and interracialism.

Involvement in the Meredith march required King to postpone the Chicago mass rally to July 10 and increased the pressure on him to find a way to demonstrate nonviolence's continuing viability. To facilitate a dramatic direct action campaign, King changed the Freedom Movement's goal from "ending the slums" to "creating the Open City." For African Americans, Chicago was a closed city. Its realtors generally ignored the municipal fair housing ordinance and did not show black customers properties in all-white neighborhoods. African Americans who did breach the residential color line faced a response of Mississippi-like virulence. William Moyer, a white Freedom Summer veteran working in Chicago, pointed out that, while the Ku Klux Klan burnt churches in Mississippi in 1964, Chicago arsonists simultaneously attacked three non-ghetto houses in the city purchased by African Americans. This blatant racism suggested that here was an issue that King could use to make local injustice into a national issue, and which would secondarily boost his own flagging reputation.

The July Riot And King's Despondency

Soaring temperatures and poor promotional work meant that 30,000, rather than the projected 100,000, attended the July 10 rally. Drawing on rhetoric from his Montgomery days, King declared: "We are here today because we are tired ... tired of being seared in the flames of withering injustice." Floyd McKissick, CORE's national director, had preceded King with a speech that portrayed Black Power as neither inherently violent nor anti-white, and the relieved SCLC leader took up the theme to defend his nonviolent philosophy. "Our power does not reside in Molotov cocktails, rifles, knives and bricks," he proclaimed, but in the "powerful and just weapon" of nonviolence: "a sword that heals" (Ralph 1993: 106-7). Critics carped that King led his 5,000 marching followers that day from the comfort of a limousine, and that his demands, nailed Martin Luther-like to the City Hall door, were too general, enabling Mayor Daley to finesse them the next day as goals he was already pursuing.

A graver threat to King's position came on July 12 when insensitive policing provoked widespread violence in the West Side ghetto. Molotov cocktails were thrown, bricks shattered store windows, and gunfire sounded, notwithstanding King's efforts to restore calm. After three days of nightly disorders, Mayor Daley asked Governor Kerner to mobilize Illinois's National Guard, and complained publicly that SCLC staff had been "showing pictures and instructing people in how to conduct violence" (Ralph 1993: 111). The accusation mixed the truth that Jim Bevel had shown clips of the Watts riot at workshops with the fiction that the motive had been to nurture violence rather than to show the superiority of nonviolence. Without blaming King directly, Daley capitalized politically on the public's conflation of protest with disorder. A worried Andy Young admitted privately that some Chicago movement members were so hostile to the police that he had struggled to prevent them from encouraging the riots. Stanley Levison also worried that if African Americans once saw King as the white man's riot-stopper, they *would* reject him.

A shaken King signaled his agitation at press conferences. "I need some victories. I need some concessions," he implored. Otherwise, the Chicago movement was "in deep trouble" (Ralph 1993: 113). Emotionally overwrought and physically exhausted, King nonetheless tried to open a dialogue with some of Chicago's gang leaders. They demanded "power to the people" and King sensed their wounded dignity from police harassment (Jackson 2007: 287). Roger Wilkins of the federal CRS recalled that he was kept waiting until 4.00 a.m., while King tried to "convince these kids that ... the way to change a society was to approach it with love of yourself and mankind and dignity in your own heart" (Fairclough 1987: 296). Ironically, while the idea of buying a house in an all-white neighborhood had little relevance to such gang members, the overtly confrontational character of marching into these "no-go" areas appealed. On Sunday July 17, however, it was a group of 200 largely middle-class demonstrators who strolled through the all-white residential district of Gage Park on the Southwest Side and, ignoring the teenage hecklers, held a vigil outside a Catholic church.

Confrontations For The Cameras

In late 1965, historian and activist August Meier had dubbed King "the conservative militant," capturing his ambiguous role as the vital center of the Civil Rights Movement. In July 1966, King felt the pressure of being a paradox. "I have to be militant enough to satisfy the militant," he told one interviewer, "yet I have to keep enough discipline in the movement to satisfy white supporters and moderate Negroes." As the mainstream media continued to stress the threatening connotations of Black Power, whose advocates rejected the need to cultivate an interracial consensus, King accepted that his role was "to interpret to the white world" since there had to be "somebody to communicate to two worlds" (Garrow 1988: 496-97). In practice, this meant that he tried to satisfy militants by marching in Chicago and hoped that extreme racist reactions would communicate the ghetto's immorality to sympathetic whites. Andrew Young summarized the campaign's tactics when he said it needed the kind of confrontation that interrupted TV schedules.

By month's end, successive marches into Gage Park were attracting a white reaction that newsmen could not ignore. Local whites hurled cherry bombs, rocks, and bottles and explicitly identified themselves in hate-songs with Alabama's state troopers, wishing that they too "could hang a nigger legally." The July 30 marchers returned to their Marquette Park starting-point to find many of their cars torched, but no suspects apprehended, despite a police presence (Ralph 1993: 120). The next day, a white nun, Sister Mary Angelica, was struck by a rock as she marched in sympathy. As her head wound began to bleed, the white Catholic residents cheered and raised cries of "White Power!" Similar marches into Northwest Side neighborhoods the following week drew hundreds of angry, jeering whites, but police restrained them. By August 4, "the reaction of the white community was so virulent and so fearful," John Dermott recalled, "it made a terrific story on television" (Ralph 1993: 122).

Creating A Crisis

For a Negro, staying in your place, King reminded his August 4th congregation, meant essentially living "on a reservation," and accepting a "low paying job," and "overcrowded, inadequate schools." He demanded better. "My place is in the sunlight of opportunity. My place is in the dignity of a good job and livable wages," he intoned. "My place is in the security of an adequate quality education." With 2,000 voices joining his litany, King continued: "My place is in comfort and in the convenience and in the nobility of good, solitary living conditions and in a good house." To cheers he concluded, "My place is in Gage Park" (Ralph 1993: 122). The next day, King led 500 marchers into another white neighborhood, Marquette Park. Thirty demonstrators were injured and King himself was struck by a rock that dropped him to his knees. Had it not been for the 1,200 police, few movement people doubted that there would have been fatalities. The mob – over 4,000 strong in places – dwarfed the crowds that SCLC had confronted elsewhere. Dazed more by the venom of his reception than by the rock, King told reporters afterwards that he had "never seen anything so hostile and so hateful" (Garrow 1988: 500). He left Chicago to recuperate before SCLC's annual convention.

In their leader's absence and without consultation, Bevel and Jackson announced further marches, even into the notoriously anti-black community of Cicero. Many Chicagoans saw the marches as needlessly provocative and, keen to minimize violence, Mayor Daley stepped up police protection. When the movement marched into the Northwest Side on August 7, police literally formed "a wall between the march and the people in the community" and, by preempting counter-violence, made the protests less dramatic (Ralph 1993: 133). Nevertheless, Daley realized that the marches were damaging the Democrats politically in the run-up to the 1966 state and Congressional elections. Increased police protection for the demonstrators might permanently alienate voters to whom Daley and his associates must appeal in next year's municipal elections. The Daley machine needed a settlement.

Daley's six black aldermen had sought a compromise with King on August 4. Readily, they endorsed movement calls that the fair housing ordinance be enforced and for financial institutions to consider loan applications without bias. King stressed that he was reasonable, but his nonviolent strategy needed victories if it was to provide an alternative to the July riots. Over the following week, Chicago's liberal press called for the marches to halt, claiming King had made his point. More influentially, Walter Reuther of the UAW, a key labor supporter of King, phoned him at the SCLC convention to discuss Chicago, and the UAW's Midwest director Robert Johnston conferred with both Raby and Daley before urging negotiations on August 11. Johnston's intervention strengthened Archbishop Cody's call the previous day for a suspension of demonstrations to allow talks to "achieve a just and lasting resolution of the present crisis" (Ralph 1993: 146). The cleric's admonition drew an acid response from Jim Bevel: if Cody lacked "the courage to speak up for Christ, let him join the devil" (Jackson 2007: 290).

Bed-ridden with a fever at SCLC's convention in Jackson, Mississippi, King appeared fatalistic, but resolute to journalists. "If some of us must die," he said softly, "then we will die" (Garrow 1988: 502). Back in Chicago, Bevel led another, heavily policed, march into the Southwest community of Bogan on August 12. When the CCRR announced that it would host talks in five days' time, the Freedom Movement reacted by expanding rather than curtailing its marches. On August 14, there were three simultaneous marches, with Jesse Jackson and Al Raby revisiting Bogan and Gage Park respectively, while Bevel targeted another Northwest community, Jefferson Park. Adding to the turmoil, a white supremacist rally in Marquette Park spawned a mob that attacked passing black motorists. Local leaders and SCLC militants remained wary of the proposed negotiations but, as in earlier campaigns, King knew he needed to prepare the ground for SCLC's withdrawal.

Negotiations Begin

When King returned for the CCRR-sponsored "summit" conference, it seemed to Andrew Young that the campaign was following SCLC's classic formula: "challenge, conflict, crisis, confrontation, communication, compromise, and change" (Ralph 1993: 151). The open housing marches constituted the confrontation that had generated a sense of crisis, but white moderates, like Ed Marciniak of the city's Human Relations Commission, doubted whether this had improved communication since Chicago race relations now had a rancor unmatched since World War II. In King's absence, the Chicago movement's demands on open housing had been hastily drafted on the mistaken assumption that they could be refined and made more substantive during lengthy negotiations. By itself, the movement could not unite the divided city, King declared as the conference opened, "we need the help of the people with real power" (McKnight 1989: 113).

Reading the written demands, the tactically adept and well-briefed Mayor Daley quickly committed his administration to a more vigorous enforcement of the fair housing ordinance, which had yet to penalize a realtor. Chicago Housing Authority head Charles Swibel equally swiftly promised to build as much "non-ghetto

low-rise" public housing "as is feasible," a step which might eventually reverse the CHA's current predilection for high-rise ghetto
housing projects. President of Chicago's Mortgage Bankers' Association, Clarke Stayman, then accepted the Freedom Movement's
demand for mortgages to be available regardless of race. King had
not expected such quick apparent concessions. As Daley intended,
they left the realtors isolated as seemingly the only major obstacle
to a resolution (Ralph 1993: 149-54).

Ross Beatty and Arthur Mohl of the Chicago Real Estate Board
(CREB) tried to exonerate their members. Beatty complained that
the brokers were being scapegoated. "We must represent our cli-
ents," he explained, most of whom opposed open occupancy. Mohl
asked for realism and empathy. Like "mirrors," the realtors simply
reflected "the bigoted attitudes in the neighborhoods." If brokers
were bullied into an open occupancy stance, they would be bankrupted as Chicagoans would simply lease their properties without
using a broker. King responded that before the 1964 Act, Southern "restaurant owners and hotel owners" had told him essentially
the same thing (McKnight 1989: 115, 118-19).

As the CREB representatives continued to insist that they could
not "bargain with the civil righters for something that we don't
have the power to give," King wearily asked them to act as "men
confronted by a moral issue." How could they suggest they were
neutral when they were spending millions lobbying and litigating
against open housing? Others, especially from the churches, joined
in this criticism. Eager to expedite a settlement, Mayor Daley
urged the realtors to "get on the phone to their members and do
something about these demands now." Adjourning the meeting
until 4.00 p.m., chairman Ben Heineman told the CREB delegation bluntly: "The monkey, gentlemen, is right on your back, and
whether you deem it as fair or not, everyone sees that the monkey
is there" (McKnight 1989: 120-22).

When the talks resumed, Beatty read a convoluted CREB
statement, which, amidst complaints about the movement's tactics
and weasel words to permit continued opposition to open housing,
contained two small concessions. CREB "would withdraw all
opposition to the philosophy of open occupancy legislation at the
state level" and "remind all members to obey the city's fair housing ordinance." When he denounced the testing of realtors'

practices by white and black movement volunteers as "unwarranted harassment," however, a dismayed King whispered to a colleague: "This is nothing," and asked Beatty to clarify. Beatty began rereading the prepared statement, provoking other movement leaders to demand real concessions. Mayor Daley countered by trying to talk up the significance of the CREB's pledge to end its opposition to state legislation, which it had effectively blocked since 1957. But King wanted to know: when would black Chicagoans be able to buy homes anywhere? "We need a timetable, something very concrete," he declared (Garrow 1988: 508-9).

As Daley and his allies pressed for an immediate suspension of protests, Raby and other movement leaders insisted on clear commitments with verifiable implementation before they stopped marching. It seemed that negotiations would collapse, especially after Raby snarled at Daley that he wished there was a Mayor of Chicago who would do justice because it was right instead of trying to trade it for a protest moratorium. Referring to the recently successful drive to pass a municipal bond proposal, Raby demanded the same backing for the "Open City" program. There should be action against those "who are acting like Fascists in the neighborhoods." If "an employee stole something and was arrested," he fumed, "they would be fired immediately, but when they're stoning Negro cars and innocent Negro people, nothing happens at all." Only "a moratorium on discrimination," he dramatically concluded, "will bring a moratorium on marches" (McKnight 1989: 132-33).

At this point, King impressively calmed the situation. Calling the meeting "a constructive and creative beginning," he sought to reestablish a bond of sympathy between the two sides. "[If] you are tired of demonstrations," he observed, "I am tired of demonstrating." Shaming his adversaries, he personalized the issue by adding: "I am tired of the threat of death. I want to live. I don't want to be a martyr. And there are moments when I doubt if I am going to make through ... But the important thing," he went on, "is not how tired I am; the important thing is to get rid of the conditions that lead us to march." Pressing his advantage, he stated candidly that the movement could not surrender its right to march cheaply since it had no other comparable source of influence. For King, the CREB's denunciation of the marches highlighted a basic failure to understand. "A doctor doesn't cause a cancer when he finds it," he told Beatty and his colleagues. "In fact, we thank him for finding it, and we are doing the same thing. Our humble marches have revealed a cancer." Addressing the wider city negotiating team, he went on in quiet condemnation,

> We have not used rocks. We have not used bottles. And no one today, no one who has spoken, has condemned those that have used violence. Maybe there should be a moratorium in Gage Park. Maybe we should begin condemning the robber and not the robbed.

He defended the marches as a means of making "the issue so alive that it will be acted on. Our marching feet have brought us a long way." He urged the negotiators to continue (McKnight 1989: 133-34).

The tension dropped once King had spoken and, to carry matters forward, the chair proposed forming a subcommittee to draft written recommendations on how to achieve an Open City for the larger conference's approval in ten days' time. The twelve-man subcommittee would have five Freedom Movement representatives. On this basis, the meeting dispersed without an agreed press statement. The next day, a somber King privately warned colleagues not to expect too much since Daley and other leaders had only a limited understanding of the race problem. "They see it as a matter of individual intent," he explained, "rather than a societal sin" (Ralph 1993: 159). Informed by Reinhold Niebuhr's neo-orthodox Protestantism, King thus recast theologically the crucial distinction between personal and institutional racism that was to bedevil the politics of affirmative action for decades to come.

Although a fervent mass meeting raised his spirits a little that Thursday night, King confessed his weariness to the packed church. With the stress of recent weeks etched on his face, he declared that he was "tired of marching for something that should have been mine at first." As he had told the summit conference, so he assured this congregation: he had "no martyr complex." He wanted "to live as long as anybody in this building tonight," although sometimes he doubted that he would make it. References to premature death can be found in earlier speeches, but this

Chicago address revealed the soul-sapping, relentless pressure that consumed King's days. Knowing the criticism that would be leveled at him, he declared, almost in frustration: "I don't march because I like it, I march because I must" (Garrow 1988: 515). More mischievously, Jim Bevel taunted Mayor Daley by telling the audience that the movement should march "until every white person out there joins the Republican Party" (Cohen and Taylor 2000: 412).

King also warned in his speech that efforts to block the protests would ultimately rebound against Mayor Daley as they had against Southern officials. But the next day Daley responded shrewdly to Bevel's threats. Realizing that a blanket ban on marches would contravene the First Amendment, he secured a state court injunction requiring the movement to give the police at least twenty-four hours' prior notice, to restrict its marching to no more than 500 participants in one city district on any one day, and to march only in daylight outside of the rush hours. In a strong TV address, the mayor explained that he was trying to balance the right of petition with the right to safety by reducing the strain that the protests placed on Chicago's police. With only one dissenting vote out of fifty, the city council applauded the move. King denounced the August 19 injunction, imposed while negotiations proceeded, as "a very bad act of faith." But although he threatened defiance, his lawyers advised that violating this injunction would not produce arrests to fill the jails and embarrass the mayor, but a succession of fines that might break SCLC's already feeble treasury.

No National Gains In Prospect

Outmaneuvered, King agreed that negotiations via the subcommittee should continue as the most likely source of progress in local terms. Since the 1961 Freedom Rides, King had usually been sensitive to the national as well as the local dimension of protest, but now he seemed to discount the national. After all, Congress was considering a civil rights bill, which included a clause outlawing discrimination in the sale and rental of housing (Title IV). The SCLC board in early August had pointed to the Chicago neighborhood marches as proof that Title IV was urgently needed and a black newspaper, the *Cleveland Call and Post*, argued that King's stoning in Gage Park on August 5 might yet reverse weakening amendments to Title IV passed in the House. But neither King nor President Johnson made a determined effort to use the Chicago situation to save the civil rights bill. Of the Chicago protagonists, it was Daley who phoned LBJ on August 16, the day before the CCRR conference meeting, and his priority was restoring order, not securing legislation (Ralph 1993: 180, 182).

By the time the House passed the bill on August 9, amendments had lifted any threat of anti-discrimination charges from nearly 60 percent of private homes on the basis of size and, thanks to concerted pressure from the National Association of Real Estate Boards, from all brokers selling single-family homes. CORE's Robert Lucas believes that, had King broken the injunction and rallied thousands of black Chicagoans and their sympathizers to his cause, the Chicago crisis could have reached the same intensity as Selma's. But given the injunction threat, this seems dubious. More importantly, King had gone to Chicago with a different approach from the mobilizing strategy he used in Selma. Federal prohibition of housing discrimination via the 1966 bill had not been his identified goal. Only when the practicalities of organizing black Chicago against the complex problems of ghetto poverty threatened to engulf SCLC did open housing emerge as a key mobilizing issue. King was thus more committed to securing an agreement to break down local ghetto barriers than to resuscitating a federal measure that was so watered down that he himself described it as "virtually meaningless" (Ralph 1993: 179).

After August 19, marches in Chicago itself, limited by the injunction, and demonstrations in neighboring suburban communities outside the court order's remit, maintained pressure and publicity. But these protests were mainly symbolic, expressing and exciting the Chicago Movement's militancy. This made the proposed Cicero march especially significant. Ever since 1951, when local whites had rioted after a single black family moved into the community, Cicero had been a talismanic racist town. As recently as May 1966 a young African American job-seeker had been murdered there. When King announced that he would lead a march into Cicero, Governor Kerner immediately placed the National Guard and state police on red alert. "We can walk in outer space," King commented, "but we can't walk the streets of Cicero without the National Guard" (Lewis 1978: 344). Robert Lucas of CORE, Monroe Sharp of Chicago's small SNCC group, and other militants like Chester Robinson of the West Side Organization (WSO) enthusiastically endorsed King's plans.

The Summit Agreement

On Thursday August 25, despite pleas from Archbishop Cody and others, King was still insisting that Sunday's Cicero march was going ahead. At the same time he knew that the subcommittee had drafted an accord for the full Summit Conference's considera-tion. The CCCO leaders, including Raby and other members of the Agenda Committee, favored acceptance. The marches had been nerve-wracking and, fearful that Chicago might erupt again with the violence that had claimed two lives in July, they were inclined to settle for the best deal available. Bevel and other members of the Action Committee, however, believed that demonstrations should continue until white good intentions had been fleshed out into tangible black gains. In the subcommittee, chairman Thomas Ayers had blocked Bevel's efforts to introduce targets and time-tables by insisting that the movement could not add to the demands it had listed at the start of negotiations.

The subcommittee proposals codified the undertakings made at the initial conference session. The city undertook to enforce the fair housing ordinance vigorously, with all licensed brokers being required to post the ordinance prominently in their offices. The CHA promised to seek scattered, lower-density public housing sites and the County Department of Public Aid agreed to solicit "the best housing" for welfare recipients irrespective of existing racial residential patterns. The financial institutions consented to a nondiscriminatory loans policy, and as a regulator and guarantor, the federal government undertook to investigate this policy under existing law. The CREB's written commitments, however, remained deliberately opaque. The Chicago Board – but by implication, no other board in Illinois – withdrew its opposition to state open housing legislation in principle provided any pro-posed measure applied to owners as well as brokers. It still expressly reserved "the right to criticize detail as distinguished from philosophy," a qualification that justified test litigation as well as hostile lobbying. On the basis of these concessions, the neighborhood marches must end.

At Friday's Summit meeting, the CREB's equivocation threatened the deal. King complained that Beatty had declared on the radio that if brokers had "to sell and rent to Negroes, the real estate industry will go out of business" (McKnight 1989: 139). Only the apparent willingness of other parties, particularly the churches, to work actively to implement the agreement induced King to follow his Agenda Committee colleagues and accept the proposals. Daley's injunction was a final obstacle, especially after one white cleric blithely suggested that the Movement could overturn this by appealing to the US Supreme Court. With incredulity, King responded sharply that this would take at least three years and cost $200,000. He warned Daley that if the injunction stayed, at some point he would have to break it. Although Daley refused to consider withdrawing the injunction as part of the accord, he did suggest that its terms might be amended through subsequent negotiation. After a brief caucus, King accepted this offer under the auspices of the CCRR's continuing body, which was to oversee the agreement's implementation.

Despite the Freedom Movement delegation's considerable misgivings, the Summit Agreement was adopted unanimously. In closing remarks, King stressed that the white city leadership had better make the agreement work quickly. "Our summers of riots have been caused by our winters of delay," he declared. He then cautioned his own side to interpret the agreement "as a victory for justice and not a victory over the Chicago Real Estate Board or the city of Chicago." Relieved that the marches were over, Mayor Daley told the press that it was "a great day for Chicago." Modeling his own advice, King praised the agreement as "far-reaching and creative" (Garrow 1988: 523). With hindsight, one can detect hints of desperation in King's final conference remarks, as if he sensed that the white leaders' past conduct did not warrant his faith. In the summer of Black Power, King also knew that there was a chorus of angry black voices at which white moderates could take fright. The same voices were unlikely to celebrate a King victory over white power, but instead to condemn him as a blunderer who allowed Mayor Daley to escape just when black

Chicagoans had him on the ropes. Within days of the agreement SNCC members in Chicago were circulating flyers that read "Daley blew the whistle and King stopped the marches" (Cohen and Taylor 2000: 422).

A Failure?

The Summit Agreement spoke of a cessation of marches as long as its program was being implemented, but it had no timetables or targets to gauge implementation. The least powerful body economically and politically, the CCRR was the principal implementation body, with little beyond moral suasion to compel compliance. At the end of October, tests of real estate offices in white neighborhoods still found routine discrimination. And what did open housing gain in any case? Historian David Lewis asks: how could Chicago's ghetto blacks, with low average family incomes, purchase homes in white areas where the average income range was twice as high (Lewis 1978: 350)? After the marches had exposed the vicious race hatred of white residents, why would they want to? As one activist observed, "the low income Negro has other problems to deal with first," and King had seemingly abandoned them (Ralph 1993: 212).

A West Side activist, Chester Robinson, immediately denounced the Summit Agreement as selling out "the poor Negro." He declared that the Cicero march would go ahead on September 4. King was subsequently able to restrain him by promising to battle for better public housing and welfare reforms of more direct relevance to ghetto residents. Chicago CORE militants ensured that the Cicero march happened, nonetheless, as an act of defiance with no strategic goal. Linda Bryant Hall recalls that it attracted local community people rather than trained nonviolent activists. When whites threw bricks or bottles, these marchers readily threw them right back. The security operation, involving thousands of police and National Guardsmen, was clearly more organized than the 200-strong protest. Interviewed many years later, CORE leader Robert Lucas declared proudly that the march confirmed that nonviolence "wasn't about to work in the North," which sadly suggests that he still relished point-scoring against King.

But Lucas was not alone in seeing King's Chicago efforts as failing. When blizzards in January 1967 helped to ensure that SCLC's city voter registration campaign failed dismally, and when Mayor Daley secured a fourth term in April with an increased majority and a still considerable black vote, there were few, even at SCLC, prepared to trumpet positive achievements. Bevel always thought they had settled too early and King himself later conceded that it might have been better to have marched into Cicero to expose the full scope of white racism. There were some benefits, however, in the longer term. Operation Breadbasket continued to secure jobs and provided a power base for Jesse Jackson, initially in Chicago, and later in his presidential campaigns. Despite Daley's victory, the election of two independent black aldermen in 1967 indicated his loosening grasp of the "plantation" wards. Black political independence culminated in Harold Washington's becoming Chicago's first black mayor in 1983, and community organizing on the far South Side was the starting point for Barack Obama's political journey to the White House.

Thinking back, Bernard LaFayette has observed: "We started a marathon, but it ended up being a sprint." The Summit Agreement, King himself conceded, was "the first step in a 1,000 mile journey." It was neither King's style nor choice to be a constant participant in such a long march. There were too many other journeys to be begun. He had answered Chicago's call not because it was politic but because it was right. By 1967, he seemed increasingly to embrace ethical imperatives over political calculations. Back in December 1965, King had interrupted Rustin's efforts to stop him from going to Chicago by declaring that he must now consult God over "what he wants me to do." A furious Rustin railed then that this "business of King talking to God and God talking to King" would not resolve the Movement's strategic dilemmas. A diminished counselor of King's, Rustin in September 1966 judged the recent campaign "a disaster." But if poverty still dominated the lives of many black Chicagoans, it was not primarily because King listened to God, but because others did not. White votes for Republican candidates gave the GOP (Grand Old Party) control of the Cook County Board and robbed Mayor Daley of 18,000 patronage jobs. Like numerous other politicians, Daley heard the seductive voice of the election returns and cursed King

(Cohen and Taylor 2000: 426). Heeding "a voice saying 'Do something for others'," and realizing that poverty was no accidental product of a capitalist economy, Martin Luther King was set to be an increasingly rejected hero for the remainder of his life (Garrow 1988: 455, 524, 530).

9 Shrinking Options

"Black Power" And Vietnam, 1966-67

By the autumn of 1966, the momentum generated by the Selma campaign seemed a distant memory for Martin Luther King. A lack of progress regarding implementation of August's Chicago Summit Agreement strengthened critics' claims that King's application of nonviolent tactics to a Northern target had failed. Stokely Carmichael's call for "'Black Power'" during the Meredith march in June was attracting fresh headlines after Carmichael's arrest on September 6 for allegedly inciting a riot in Atlanta. Although King resisted pressure to join others in condemning Carmichael, the latter's rhetoric and King's own efforts to confront Americans nationally with the realities of racism alienated some sympathizers, and galvanized many more mainstream whites into active support of the status quo. With their mailbags filled with letters from frightened and angry constituents, politicians who had supported earlier civil rights measures, including Republican leader Senator Everett Dirksen of Illinois, changed their stance and the 1966 civil rights bill failed.

To underline the reactionary trend, an outspoken segregationist Lester Maddox won Georgia's Democratic gubernatorial primary on September 27. King was deeply troubled by this. With African American militants advocating armed self-defense, and whites reacting more to their fears and prejudices than to their hopes and moral principles, the situation was becoming increasingly difficult for King who had previously operated primarily as a strategist of the center. At the same time, the escalating Vietnam War revealed that memories of how the Republicans had smeared the Truman administration for failing to stop communist expansion continued to haunt President Johnson. Such "Red Scare" tactics still poisoned the atmosphere for political debate, ensuring that few prominent figures voiced public criticism. Despite deep misgivings, King himself tried to limit his comments on the war in 1966 to complaints about its negative impact on domestic social programs. Nevertheless, a year after the Voting Rights Act's passage, King was a virtual outcast in LBJ's eyes due to his failure to back the President on Vietnam. After April 1967, critics would charge that his anti-war stance was a mistake, born of his desperation to secure a new following, now that the militant cry of "Black Power" was resonating powerfully with his core African American constituency.

"Black Power"

Stokely Carmichael's call for "Black Power" grew from his experiences as an organizer in the Deep South, and it enjoyed greater influence because it spoke directly to the sensation of powerlessness endured by the black poor. It was also the paradoxical product of SNCC's interracial history. For all King's advocacy of integration, his SCLC was essentially a black organization. It welcomed white support for its campaigns and had a few white advisors and peripheral staff members but, like the black churches from which it sprang, it was an African American institution. By comparison, SNCC had white members from the outset and although its leading figures were black, its more open, democratic way of working gave white staff access to its inner circle. This became especially problematical after the Mississippi Freedom Summer of 1964 produced a sudden influx of whites.

In St. Augustine and Selma, King demonstrated that white volunteers could be valuable in short-term protest campaigns. As potent symbols of national support for black Southerners, they helped to mobilize public opinion. Even before Freedom Summer, however, some SNCC staff had questioned white involvement in organizing campaigns intended to develop indigenous black leadership. Patterns of black deference and white assertion, rooted in racism and class privilege, impeded a process that for many SNCC workers rested on the overturning of precisely these patterns. At the same time, between 1960 and 1965, the traumas of the struggle itself made both SCLC and SNCC wary of white liberals' promises. Death and the threat of death psychologically shook Movement workers in the Deep South, including Carmichael, like soldiers on the front line. Ironically, the death of white seminarian Jonathan Daniels strengthened a personally grieving Carmichael's commitment to independent black politics (Joseph 2014: 88, 90-92).

For SNCC, the failure to seat the MFDP at the Atlantic City Convention in 1964 proved liberals' perfidiousness. Working in areas like the Mississippi Delta, with potentially black majority electorates, SNCC workers began to believe that their construction of parallel institutions should no longer be a primarily symbolic demonstration against exclusion. Instead, they believed that tactical separatism offered a surer route to African American empowerment through self-determination. King's maneuverings during the Selma campaign deepened SNCC misgivings over the cultivation of white allies. Selma coincided with SNCC's application of the MFDP third-party political model to Lowndes County, Alabama. The then project director, Stokely Carmichael, explained to local people that since the majority of eligible voters were black, it was both feasible and fitting that Lowndes's elected representatives should be African American also.

Both Carmichael and James Forman had grown up in the North, and had a less religious approach to the Movement than Southerners like John Lewis. After they ousted Lewis as chairman of SNCC in May 1966, SNCC essentially ceased to be the philosophically Gandhian organization that it had been in April 1960. Indian independence had become a less fashionable model of decolonization. Armed struggle, seemingly proven in China, Algeria, and Cuba, attracted greater attention from black intellectuals. The writings of Mao Zedong and Frantz Fanon, and the efforts of Che Guevara to export the Cuban revolutionary model in Latin America, captured their imagination. Such influences mixed with the more potent legacy of Malcolm X to weaken King's appeal. Thanks especially to the posthumous publication of *The Autobiography of Malcolm X*, Malcolm's defiant stance and his later calls for an internationalization of the struggle provided a powerful alternative to King for disillusioned, young African Americans. In death, as in life, Malcolm's words resonated especially in the non-Southern ghettos, where unemployment, poor housing, and police brutality indicated that the African American plight was worsening rather than improving, despite the civil rights gains in the South. Unfortunately, Malcolm's speeches, however inspirational, could not provide an effective tactical guide for African American militants, even while they fanned angry frustration toward desperate action. King sensed this desperation too, but could not assuage it.

The shooting of James Meredith in June 1966, near the beginning of his March against Fear in Mississippi, provided Carmichael and his supporters with an ideal opportunity. The continuing march attracted African American support, both on the ground in counties where SNCC was well established and, largely due to the media interest surrounding King, in the nation at large as well. King's call for nonviolence had always attracted some criticism among African Americans on the basis that it denied the fundamental right to self-defense. In Mississippi, particularly, SNCC had found that most local people had no hesitation in using arms to defend their homes and their lives. In neighboring Louisiana, white efforts to quash CORE's voter registration drives prompted local blacks to organize a paramilitary organization, the Deacons for Defense. For both SNCC and CORE, therefore, Meredith's shooting not only dramatized the continuing need for armed self-defense, but also provided the occasion for them to strike a more militant stance that captured the seething ghetto discontent.

Ironically, the SNCC and CORE of the early 1960s had been the true exemplars of nonviolent direct action. By comparison, among Movement insiders, King's status had dropped sharply after he refused to participate in the Freedom Rides of 1961, and fallen again when, in their view, he failed to abide by the "Jail, Not Bail" principle in Albany. The Birmingham and Selma campaigns with their unpunished murders did not entirely restore King's reputation inside the Movement. It was a former SNCC member, Jim Bevel, who had ensured that Birmingham's children filled the jails, and by the time he did so, King had already made bail. King's jail stays in Selma had been similarly transient and it had been left to others to confront the state troopers on "Bloody Sunday." When King himself led the marchers the following Tuesday, he had turned them around, at the behest of the Johnson administration, to avoid a confrontation. Thus, while King loftily extolled nonviolence as a philosophy and a way of life, in the eyes of many SNCC and CORE members, he was actually highly pragmatic and tactical (some put it less kindly) when it came to applying it. For Carmichael and others, despite King's pronouncements, nonviolence remained a tactical option, not a sacred dogma, and they used the Meredith march to publicize their position.

Ostensibly a rejection of King's approach, Carmichael's "Black Power" strategy was also an imitation. While it moved away from King's principles of nonviolence and racial integration, it embraced the media dimension of King's mature strategy of "creative tension." Although some Movement workers resented the media attention King drew, no one doubted by 1966 that enthralling the nation was a key element in King's protest style. White opponents and black rivals agreed that King's career depended on publicity. His more astute, white opponents urged their associates to counter King with a strategy of avoiding public confrontations, while discreetly increasing legal and political harassment. During 1966, Mayor Daley of Chicago proved adept in this respect.

Other Movement leaders had always competed for the limelight with King, although Ella Baker had tried to moderate this tendency in SNCC's early years. As a newly appointed leader in 1961, James Farmer had clearly seen the Freedom Rides as a means of establishing CORE's Movement credentials before a national audience, and to some extent, the Mississippi Freedom Summer of 1964 had been SNCC's attempt to attract national media attention in order to reduce local white violence. As early as 1964, CORE protests at the New York World's Fair had suggested the increasing competition for publicity. The national outcry over the Freedom Summer murders and then the killings during the Selma campaign seemed to confirm that dramatic violence was vital for publicity. Nor were Southern Movement workers alone in drawing this bitter conclusion. King recalled that when he toured the devastated Watts neighborhood of Los Angeles after the 1965 disturbances, he heard local people declaring that they had won. Incredulous, he pointed out that African Americans constituted the overwhelming majority of the dead and injured, and that their own neighborhood lay in ruins. But one youth had responded: "We made them pay attention to us." This demand for attention was always one paradoxical part of the "Black Power" rhetoric whose essence was to choose words to affirm black rather than white sensibilities (Carson 1998: 293).

The Meredith March

After the Meredith shooting, Carmichael, King, CORE's new leader, Floyd McKissick, and the Movement's conservatives, Roy Wilkins of the NAACP and Whitney Young of the Urban League, caucused in Memphis on June 7. Continuing the March against Fear to press for greater federal powers to protect civil rights workers seemed a logical point of consensus. But the 25-year-old Carmichael objected. With curses, he told Wilkins and Young that their limited, lobbyist approach was contemptible. He later claimed that his insults were intended to separate these conservatives from King, who remained silent while Carmichael showered the two with expletives. Disgusted with Carmichael, and unhappy about the participation of the armed Deacons of Defense, Wilkins and Young returned to New York, leaving King to negotiate with SNCC and CORE over the purpose of the march.

King was happy to couch the march as a call for stricter enforcement of the Voting Rights Act and a truly "adequate budget" for the War on Poverty, rather than just the current civil rights bill. He shared some of SNCC's and CORE's misgivings about the Johnson administration and white liberals generally. When he announced on June 9 that the march was actually going to concentrate on voter registration en route, the shift reflected not just SNCC's preference for grassroots organizing, but his own current ambivalence. On the one hand, he acknowledged the need for what might be called the "ground war" of organizing, but on the other, he sensed that the "air war" of mobilizing via short-term, dramatic, well-publicized confrontations was still needed, and better suited to his strengths. He was concurrently dealing with this same dilemma of "organizing" versus "mobilizing" in the Chicago campaign, and its demands made him an irregular participant in the march itself.

Rejoining the march briefly on June 12, after two days in Chicago, King tried to synthesize the two strategies by telling reporters that the voter registration drive (organizing) would generate pressure (mobilizing) for the deployment of federal registrars into these counties and for legal protection of civil rights workers. While King remained determined to extract national gains from local projects, Carmichael seemed intent on reversing the equation in favor of the local. On June 16, with King absent again in Chicago, the march reached a SNCC stronghold, Greenwood. There, Carmichael tested his new slogan. The city council had refused permission to camp at the local black school and arrested Carmichael for trespassing. Released on bail, the angry SNCC leader told an evening rally that only taking power would remedy such injustice. He would not have been arrested, he declared, if black sheriffs had been elected in Delta towns like Greenwood. When he shouted "We want 'Black Power'," the crowd took up the chant (Garrow 1988: 481).

King returned in time for the next evening rally and heard one of Carmichael's lieutenants, Willie Ricks, lead an enthusiastic crowd in repeated calls for "Black Power." The chord struck by the new slogan sprang from the Mississippi movement experience. It drew on memories of unavenged white violence that were sharpened by the marchers' eerie encounters with both Byron de la Beckwith (the unconvicted killer of Mississippi's NAACP leader, Medgar Evers) and Sheriff Cecil Price (who had similarly escaped punishment for the Freedom Summer murders in Neshoba County). King himself recalled how unsettling it had been to hold a memorial service for James Chaney and his two white colleagues with Sheriff Price standing mockingly behind him. He agreed that blacks needed the power to bring men like Price to justice. Shouting "Black Power" might work in the Delta, but it contradicted a basic tenet of King's national approach. Instead of driving a wedge between extreme racists and white moderates, as King's nonviolent campaigns had done, "Black Power" strengthened a hostile, conservative white coalition.

King And "Black Power"

If "Black Power" had simply denoted an electoral strategy to mobilize a solid black vote for maximum political advantage in black majority areas of the country, King would have endorsed it.

He had been preaching that message since 1956. If "Black Power" had comprised nothing more than an exhortation for African Americans to take pride in their race and use their economic and cultural resources for collective advantage, King would have had no quarrel with it. In countless sermons, he had sought to rekindle what he referred to as the "somebodiness" that racism systematically tried to weaken, and with Operation Breadbasket especially, he had attempted to flex black economic muscle. Beginning with consumer boycotts to pressurize reluctant white employers to hire more black workers, Operation Breadbasket was growing under Jesse Jackson's direction into a broader effort to ensure economic development in black neighborhoods. Supermarkets were pressed to stock the products of black manufacturers, and businesses that operated in black communities were "encouraged" to deposit their takings in African American banks. Although King never believed that a separate black economy was viable, he did believe that African Americans could achieve improvements through unity. Most of all, King's recent experience in impoverished communities across America made him realize the corrosive effects of powerlessness.

His primary misgiving lay with the new militants' rejection of nonviolence. King had no qualms about their demand for power. Within the Movement, sentimental white liberals, often from a religious background, were uneasy with the very concept of power. Prompted by the furore over "Black Power," King took pains to remind them that power was not inherently immoral. It represented the capacity to act purposefully and effectively. But power and violence were not inextricable. At a Mississippi rally on June 21, King embraced the goal of power but insisted that violence would prove counter-productive. The next day, he tried unsuccessfully to persuade Carmichael and McKissick to abandon the new slogan. Toward the end of their discussion, Carmichael confided that he had deliberately used the media circus around King to project the new separatist agenda nationally. "I have been used before," King responded phlegmatically. "One more time won't hurt" (Garrow 1988: 485).

King understood "Black Power's" appeal, just as he was able to appreciate how the hopelessness of ghetto life spawned the civil disturbances that had rocked American inner cities each summer

since 1964. Empathy did not alter the fact that these developments limited his options. King did not believe that the slogan
"Black Power!" could be fleshed out into a genuinely satisfactory
program of action, and it was certainly not a sound strategy with
which to reverse the authoritarian trends that he already detected
in the nation. Its inflammatory tone added to the always fraught
task of leadership.

On June 23, the sheriff in Canton refused to allow the marchers
to camp at the local black school. When they refused to move,
highway patrol officers fired tear gas into their encampment before
beating the dazed demonstrators with clubs. This wanton assault
was an outrage. Only their gassed state prevented Carmichael and
McKissick from leading a retaliatory attack, and even the normally
cool Andrew Young recalled thinking to himself: "If I had a
machine gun, I'd show those mother-fuckers!" (Fairclough 1987:
318). King, however, retained his composure. Not only did he
remind the marchers to keep their nonviolent discipline, he also
sought to interpret the event for a dazed press corps. They had
witnessed, he said, "one of the best expressions of a police state I
have ever seen." He upbraided news photographer Flip Schulke for
getting sucked into the clash rather than capturing it on film.
"I'm not being cold blooded about it," King explained, "but it is
so much more important for you to take a picture of us getting
beaten up than for you to be another person joining in the fray"
(Garrow 1988: 703). The absence of any national outcry over the
incident underlined the Movement's fraying relations with external allies. As King and his physically and emotionally shaken
comrades spent a restless night at Canton's Catholic mission, the
only response they received from US Attorney-General Katzenbach
was a lecture against trespassing.

Internal Movement dissension seemed the lead story rather than the
violence protesters faced. By the time of the final rally in Jackson
on June 26, press interest seemed divided between an expectation
that Carmichael and McKissick's "Black Power" rhetoric would
eclipse King and a cynical longing for a dramatic climax. When
the rally passed off with no more than white jeers, the press pursued the "movement divided" storyline. A weary King faced a
battery of questions about "Black Power" rather than his own
agenda or the continuing need for racial reform in Mississippi.

Baited, he eventually let his irritation at Carmichael show. Because Carmichael had launched "a debate over 'Black Power'" during the march, King declared, "we didn't get to emphasize the evils of Mississippi and the need for the 1966 Civil Rights Act" (Garrow 1988: 489). He acknowledged that his once optimistic vision of American democracy was now clouded by "broken promises" and "deferred dreams," but lamented that SNCC's impulsive language and actions would have damaging political consequences (Joseph 2014: 123).

King could not deny that Carmichael had upstaged him. The July edition of *Ebony* captured the intensity of interest that Carmichael aroused. "Hour in and hour out – on TV, in print media, in the slums and in the mortgaged fortresses of the black and white middle-class," it proclaimed, "men and women condemned 'Black Power', praised it, drew back from it in horror or embraced it with hope and fierce pride." It added that "wherever 'Black Power' was hailed or damned, there also Stokely Carmichael was praised or blamed." Ironically, by exploiting a local campaign to capture national headlines, Carmichael had behaved in precisely the way that SNCC had often condemned King for doing, but with the distinction that Carmichael believed that his rhetoric of defiance would excite African Americans to a grassroots militancy that would compensate for the loss of white allies and the surge in white reaction. Senator Bobby Kennedy publicly described the term "Black Power" as "very damaging," while privately an angry Lyndon Johnson predicted that Carmichael would be murdered within three months (Joseph 2014: 126).

Carmichael had set his course, prompting King's advisors to warn that SNCC was no longer viable, and King must distance himself. In mid-October, A. Philip Randolph, Bayard Rustin, Roy Wilkins, and Whitney Young condemned "Black Power" in the *New York Times*, but King refused to add his name. Nonetheless, the media's fascination with "Black Power" continued to thwart King's efforts to redirect attention to issues of economic justice. SNCC militants, working in their Atlanta-based Vine City project, successfully proposed that all whites should be expelled from the organization in December 1966. Carmichael made the reasonable point that there was plenty of work for whites to do tackling racism inside their own communities, but the move sharpened the wider public's perception of an anti-white trend inside the Movement. Carmichael's own declarations, such as: "I know black power is good because so many white folks came out against it" reinforced this view (Joseph 2014: 167).

Violent disturbances in Chicago and other cities that summer of 1966 swelled the reactionary tide, but King felt that he could not go too far in his comments against the "riots" without seriously damaging his own credibility. Men like Wilkins and Young, who condemned the rioters unequivocally, were denounced in the black community as "Uncle Toms," and their inability to control the disturbances simultaneously weakened their standing among whites. If he was to have any chance of channeling black frustration, King realized that he needed to retain ties to those in the black community who had rallied to "Black Power." His own Chicago experiences had deepened his anger at a society which could tolerate such extremes of wealth and poverty, and at a Congress that could commit billions of dollars to developing weapons of mass destruction, defending suspect foreign regimes, and reaching the moon, yet show hesitancy and mean-spiritedness over anti-poverty spending. Congressional conservatives targeted the Child Development Group of Mississippi (which provided much needed employment as well as preschool childcare) because of its connections with the Freedom Democratic Party. King had to lobby hard for the continuance of federal funding, and Carmichael-style rhetoric complicated the task.

While King tried to defuse white prejudice against the "Black Power" slogan, Carmichael elaborated on the new stance by suggesting that it remedied flaws in King's leadership style. Writing in the *New York Review of Books* in September 1966, Carmichael complained that by tailoring its "tone of voice" to a liberal white audience, the Movement had become little more than "a buffer zone between [whites] and angry young blacks." Since the Movement's preeminent voice was King's, he was Carmichael's key implicit target when he observed: "An organization which claims to speak for the needs of a community – as does the Student Nonviolent Coordinating Committee – must speak in the tone of that community, not as somebody else's buffer zone." For Carmichael, this was central to the significance of "Black Power." "For once," he declared, "black people are going to use the words they want to use – not just the words whites want to hear." Behind this rhetoric of speaking truth lay a more dubious assumption that African Americans could independently define social, political, and cultural phenomena. King stressed humanity's interdependence. He certainly did not disagree with Carmichael's assertion that "the economic foundations of this country must be shaken if black people are to control their lives," but sensed that African American resources alone were insufficient for all that was needed and that "liberation must come through integration" (Joseph 2014: 149-51; Jackson 2007: 299-300).

More worrying for King than these jibes, was how "Black Power" rhetoric seemed to facilitate a conflation of protest demonstration on the one hand and public disorder on the other. Carmichael did not cause the ghetto disturbances but his oratory was presented as their spark. At a press conference in Chicago on March 24, 1967, as King resisted calls for him to condemn last summer's disorders, he declared that the best response was:

> not a speech by Martin Luther King saying don't be violent ... but a program on the part of the city and the federal government to remove the conditions that make people so cynical and frustrated and desperate that they engage in this kind of misguided activity. In the final analysis, a riot is the language of the unheard.[1]

In the six months after Carmichael's September arrest for incitement, King honed his response to such questions so that the emphasis was not on the condemnation of ghetto disturbances. The latter were misguided, but not meaningless. By the time he appeared on *Face the Nation* on April 16, 1967, he was able to turn around the charge that "Black Power" had provoked a "white backlash" that damaged the political prospects for racial reform.

It was wrong to speak of a backlash, King argued, since there had always been "vacillation and ambivalence ... on the part of large segments of white America towards the whole question of Negro equality." Commentators needed to examine the sequence of events. "There were no shouts of 'Black Power'," he pointed out, and "there had been no riot in Watts when the people of California voted out of existence a fair housing bill. It may well be that 'Black Power' and riots are the consequences of the white backlash," King concluded, "rather than the causes of them." On the same program, he parried efforts to induce him to condemn Carmichael and others. The "cry of 'Black Power'," King explained, while he did not agree with many aspects of it, needed to be seen as a cry of disappointment, hurt, even despair, and overall as "a reaction to the failure of white power."

At the same time, the demagoguery of Carmichael and others continually reduced King's room for maneuver. In mid-March 1967, a fresh series of church bombings in the South prompted Carmichael to issue an angry press release. "The bombing of our churches and homes will only unify us more," the SNCC leader avowed, "and make us more determined than ever to fight back." Carmichael's threat of retaliation and outspoken criticism of Johnson's Vietnam escalation echoed Malcolm X's insistence that African Americans had the right to self-defense and no automatic loyalty to the American state; an impression bolstered during 1967 by the increasing notoriety of the paramilitary Black Panther Party of Oakland, California. Established by Huey Newton and Bobby Seale in October 1966, the Black Panthers took their name from the dramatic symbol adopted by the Lowndes County Freedom Party to identify its candidates in the upcoming local elections in Alabama. Whereas the LCFP channeled its energies into independent electoral politics, however, the Oakland Black Panthers seemed initially focused on confronting state and local police, and proclaiming their commitment to the armed struggle by parading their weapons.

King also had to be concerned over Black Power's impact on white financial supporters. Respondents to SNCC mail appeals to regular contributors in early 1967 stated plainly that they were terminating their support because they viewed "Black Power" as a rejection of nonviolence, as anti-white, and as tactically inept. Some added that SNCC's opposition to the Vietnam War had alienated them. A few indicated that they were redirecting their support to King's SCLC; but too few. In the wake of King's open housing campaign and his own anti-war comments, SCLC was a net loser of financial support, with the NAACP being the chief beneficiary among the major civil rights groups after 1966 (Haines 1988). What made this loss of income so telling was that it coincided with both an expansion of Movement activity from the South to the nation and a renewed emphasis on the labor-intensive tasks of community organizing. King was struggling to do more with less.

SCLC's Problems

Through his exhausting itinerary of public appearances, King raised over half of SCLC's income. Stanley Levison and his New York colleagues came up with schemes to market the SCLC leader's speeches through radio syndication and recording deals. But, in general, efforts to secure more reliable sources of income, notably via churches, never really proved effective. This meant that the few major sources of funding had to be cultivated. The United Church of Christ, whose Board of Home Missions (for tax reasons) acted as recipient for a large Field Foundation grant in support of SCLC's Citizenship Education Program, demanded assurances in late 1966 that this money was being spent appropriately rather than being siphoned off to maintain SCLC's general operations. It raised particular questions about the role of Andrew Young, whose salary had been paid on the basis that he was a key CEP staff member whereas by 1966 he was SCLC's executive director.

As the pot shrank, major donors' influence grew. Ann Farnsworth, a wealthy heiress, gave SCLC nearly $100,000 in eighteen months, a significant contribution but one partly predicated on King's visible support for a range of New Left causes involving Farnsworth's husband, Dr. Martin Peretz. Organized labor had also given important financial support, sometimes via union headquarters but at other times on a local basis. Here, too, there were strings. Walter Reuther of the UAW had pointedly mentioned his past support of SCLC when asking King to lobby on behalf of the compromise proposal on the seating of MFDP delegates at the 1964 Atlantic City Democratic National Convention. American unionism was a maze of local affiliations with a recurring problem of inter-union competition. Accepting support from one union risked alienating another. As King embraced the task of organizing poorly paid and currently nonunionized workers, such as hospital and municipal employees, or when he supported wildcat strike actions by black workers in an overwhelmingly white union, as he did in the case of Atlanta's firefighters in 1967, he confronted these jurisdictional disputes and jeopardized future support.

The white flight from "Black Power" compelled financial retrenchment and this, in turn, exacerbated internal SCLC tensions. King had always struggled to contain these personality clashes, which fueled staff turnover and organizational inefficiency. By the end of 1966, Randolph Blackwell, Harry Boyte, Robert Green, and C. T. Vivian had all tendered their resignations. Affiliates Director Vivian was the longest serving of the four and, while his attention to the needs of existing affiliate organizations might be questioned, he was an inspiring advocate of nonviolence who encouraged local centers to align themselves with King. He left to head a Ford Foundation training center for black ministers. Programs Director Blackwell was arguably the greatest loss since he had taken on some of the disciplinary functions that Andrew Young shirked. Blackwell had indicated as early as February 1966 that his feud with fellow executive Hosea Williams had reached crisis point, and in August he pleaded with King to terminate Williams' SCOPE project before it embroiled SCLC in scandal. In his candid opinion, the project had "degenerated in the main to an experiment in liquor and sex, compounded by criminal conduct, no less than a series of reported rapes." Despite pleas from King for him to stay, Blackwell left to found Southern Rural Action, a nonprofit organization intended to promote cooperative enterprises.

On top of external challenges, King was wracked during 1967 by internal organizational problems born of a dispirited field staff and the incessant clash of executive egos. One of the few white staffers, Harry Boyte, had urged tighter management at SCLC, but to little effect. Seconded for a year from his post on the Education Faculty of Michigan State University, Robert Green had formally been head of the CEP, although he had been quickly swept up by the excitement of racial confrontations during the Meredith march. His scheduled departure, alongside the others, served to underline the lack of organizational acumen around King by early 1967. James Bevel, too, was leaving. To the annoyance of some, King granted him a paid leave of absence to work on the Spring Mobilization, a massive anti-Vietnam War demonstration. His tactical inventiveness was greatly missed.

Designated King's successor, Ralph Abernathy stayed. As SCLC's treasurer, he paid the bills – eventually. But few initiatives flowed from him. He commanded no great respect within SCLC and could never, no matter how hard he tried, hold a national audience in the King style. The setbacks of 1966 revealed the limits not only of King's leadership but, even more so, of those around him. Exhausted and depressed, Andrew Young felt like quitting by the end of the year. Accompanying King on his travels, he had become so absorbed in the tasks of executive assistant that he could not perform his duties as executive director. Critics charged that he was just not tough enough to manage the larger-than-life personalities at SCLC. Despite a reputation for pragmatism and moderation, Young was so much in sympathy with King's new priorities of economic justice and international peace that he ceased to be an effective counterbalance to the militants. On Vietnam in particular, Levison complained that Young was pulling King into the New Left camp.

In some respects, two of the strongest figures around King by 1967 were Hosea Williams and Jesse Jackson. Despite his mis-management of SCOPE and failure to mobilize an effective voter registration campaign in Chicago in January 1967, Williams's position as SCLC's chief political organizer was unassailable because of the need to capitalize on the South's re-enfranchised black elec-torate. Colleagues complained that he could manipulate King better than anyone. A relative newcomer, Jackson had rapidly become a force by virtue of his astute management of Operation Breadbasket. No other aspect of the Chicago campaign had yielded as many tangible gains, and Jackson had significantly expanded the project beyond its initial aim of boosting black employment. Both Williams and Jackson had developed personal fiefdoms, with Williams as the main contact for an increasingly disgruntled Southern field staff, and Jackson as the leader of a largely Northern-based economic development program. Significantly, neither man shared King's misgivings about capitalism as an inherently exploitative economic order. Jackson had the greater potential for autonomous action, while Williams's established links to the field staff made him integral to any future SCLC campaigns in the South.

Buffeted by internal bickering and external demands, by accusations of complicity with whites from "Black Power" spokesmen, and of irresponsibility from the mainstream white media, King struggled on. Pressed to offer solutions to the deepening racial crisis, he spent the winter of 1966-67 trying to complete a new book, *Where Do We Go From Here? Chaos or Community?* By February 1967, he was so desperate to finish that he tried to reuse whole chunks from his previous book, *Why We Can't Wait.* Published in June 1967, thanks to extensive editorial assistance, *Where Do We Go From Here?* was a somber work that could not help but reflect the weariness that King felt, as he had watched his "dream turn into a nightmare."

In trying to stress the need for measures against economic discrimination, King minimized the importance of his previous achievements. A journalist with New Left sympathies, Andrew Kopkind, offered the harshest review in the *New York Review of Books,* arguing that, for all its rhetoric, the book had no consistent idea of what "structural change" was needed and even less understanding of the processes by which America could be changed. King had "been outstripped by his times, overtaken by events which he may have obliquely helped to produce, but could not predict." Even King's basic assumptions had been invalidated. He had believed that liberals, out of moral conviction, would act as a wedge demanding entry for poor blacks into the mainstream. He had believed that the Democratic Party would be "the effective agent of change" with "a marching army of blacks" to spur the country's conscience. Once an already unsupportable Southern feudalism had been overturned, however, King's strategy had faltered conspicuously. The Chicago campaign showed that liberals and Democrats were too wedded to the status quo to destroy it. After various digs at King's middle-class status, Kopkind dismissed his proposals for a guaranteed annual income, for a jobs program to tackle ghetto unemployment, for better schools, and more black elected officials as not just "unexceptionable," but as unlikely to produce the changes that King insisted the United States needed (Kopkind 1969: 55-70).

Dwindling resources kept the pressure of fund-raising on King. Day after day was spent in travel and in duels with a more cynical press. There was little time for home and family life, yet the remorseless demands upon him increased King's need for relaxation, for at least some respite from the pressure. Sexual liaisons that may have once marked the triumph of desire over ethics in his early career served now as solace, allowing King to shed the public persona that imprisoned him. He had long-term mistresses and one-night stands, and all in the certain knowledge that the FBI had him under close and hostile surveillance. It seems almost as if he was courting exposure – as if he would welcome the fall.

Vietnam – King's Initial Vacillation

By 1967, King's reckless private life had a nobler parallel in his public outspokenness, particularly in relation to the Vietnam War, the viciousness of which was brought home by the nightly news, which carried grim tallies of Americans killed each day and eventually pictures of villages, jungle, and even a fleeing girl on a road, set ablaze by napalm. King's public opposition to militarism was longstanding and so it is a mistake to see his 1967 stance as a major shift. As early as March 1, 1965, King had called for a negotiated settlement, but he did not immediately become an anti-war leader. Thus, while he publicly urged the government to seek a diplomatic solution on July 2, 1965, he backtracked, under press questioning, from the idea of staging peace rallies on the scale of the 1963 March on Washington or the more recent Selma march. Internal opposition fueled his circumspection. Ahead of SCLC's convention in August 1965, he had agreed with advisors that he would write personally to all parties to the Vietnam conflict urging negotiations. He had assumed the convention would endorse his stance, but several board members felt it unwise of him to venture into international relations. The upshot was a resolution that acknowledged King's right to speak as a matter of personal conscience, but affirmed that SCLC's aim was "to secure full citizenship rights for the Negro citizens of this country." It added pointedly that the organization's resources were insufficient for other purposes (Garrow 1988: 438).

When King did announce to the press that he would send letters calling on the leaders of the Vietcong, North and South Vietnam, the USSR, and China as well as President Johnson "to bring their grievances to the conference table," it made front-page headlines. He also urged Johnson to "seriously consider halting the bombing" and to indicate unequivocally a US willingness to negotiate with the Vietcong. He simultaneously dismissed, however, Jim Bevel's suggestion to the press that, once the Voting Rights Act was passed, a "peace army" would replace the Civil Rights Movement's nonviolent army. King was under no illusions that President Johnson would tolerate criticism. Even in the immediate aftermath of the 1965 Watts disturbances, Johnson had taken time to chide King for comments on Vietnam. Ambassador to the United Nations, Arthur Goldberg, was ordered to brief the SCLC leader to bring him "on-side." But when King appeared unconverted, a close ally of the President, Senator Thomas Dodd of Connecticut, lambasted King and warned that it was a criminal offense for private citizens to negotiate with foreign powers to influence US policy.

Dodd's attack deterred King as the first salvo in what could be a whole-hearted assault that would drain his energies for the vital civil rights struggles ahead. He assumed the FBI sex tapes would be made public. "I really don't have the strength to fight this issue *and* keep my civil rights issue going," he confided. "I'm already overloaded and almost emotionally fatigued," he went on, and so the only sensible step seemed to be to withdraw from the peace issue at least temporarily in order to restore the emphasis to civil rights (Garrow 1988: 445). King's New York advisors, Stanley Levison, Clarence Jones, Harry Wachtel, and Cleveland Robinson, as well as SCLC executive director Andrew Young, listened to a distraught Martin talk through the reasons for a tactical retreat on Vietnam during a telephone conference call (caught by the FBI's bug on Levison's phone), and voiced no dissent. The letter-writing campaign would be quietly dropped. It was a difficult decision to take, one that troubled King for months, and about which he later felt guilty.

In late November 1965, King shared a plane flight with renowned pediatrician, Dr. Benjamin Spock, who had already spoken out against the war. Spock urged King to be the leader around whom a peace movement could develop, but King refused to be drawn. This was not easy since he regarded seeking peace among men as an integral part of his ministerial calling. He continued to condemn the war's escalation, especially when it prompted cutbacks in anti-poverty programs, both directly via reduced appropriations and indirectly via spiraling inflation. King also warned audiences that "an ugly repressive sentiment" was taking shape that wrongly depicted "advocates of immediate negotiation" like himself "as quasi-traitors, fools, or venal enemies of our soldiers and institutions" (Garrow 1988: 453).

Confirming this reactionary trend, in January 1966 the Georgia state legislature refused to seat newly elected assemblyman Julian Bond, SNCC's former press secretary, because he had endorsed SNCC's opposition to US involvement in Vietnam. King condemned the exclusion, and on January 15 he spoke at a protest rally outside the state capitol building. Nevertheless, he remained politic. On the one hand, he endorsed opposition to the military draft in principle. Were it not for his ministerial exemption, King declared, he himself would be a conscientious objector. But on the other hand, he denied his enemies grounds for prosecution by declaring that he had never, nor was he now, encouraging draft evasion. The vast majority of Americans supported the administration's current actions in Vietnam, he conceded, and lamentably, as long as they remained ignorant of the origins and present character of the Vietnamese conflict, they were likely to continue to do so. For his part, he would begin by educating his Ebenezer congregation about why the country's hands were dirty in Vietnam and why killing Vietnamese was just as evil as killing Americans.

The faltering Chicago campaign and fund-raising efforts, including appearances at benefit concerts by Harry Belafonte in Europe, kept King busy in early 1966. He continued to speak critically against the war, but almost in passing. In mid-March, the magazine *Christian Century* accurately commented that "King seems to be trying to walk a tortuous middle path: opposing the war as a matter of form but doing so as quietly as possible." It added that the escalating US military role would probably make this stance untenable. Sure enough, at the SCLC's April board meeting in Miami, King won approval for a resolution that condemned the "immorality and tragic absurdity" of uncritical US support for the South Vietnamese military junta and complained that Johnson's anti-poverty programs were among the war's casualties. It recommended a prompt withdrawal followed by free elections in Vietnam to replace the military oligarchy. "The intense expectations and hopes of the neglected poor of the United

States," the resolution concluded, "must be regarded as a priority more urgent than the pursuit of a conflict so rapidly degenerating into a sordid military adventure" (Garrow 1988: 469-70).

While the latter statement spelt out the links that made SCLC's anti-war stance appropriate for an organization committed to domestic social justice, journalists quickly slanted their coverage around the question of how much damage King's opposition to the war would do to the Civil Rights Movement. The *New York Times* reported on its front page that 41 percent of Americans polled felt that black criticism of the war made them less sympathetic on civil rights. This still left nearly 60 percent seemingly unaffected at a time when African Americans more generally were starting to turn against the war. SNCC and CORE had also condemned what they termed an imperialist war, which sent African Americans abroad to fight other people of color. Limited education concentrated black soldiers in the fighting front ranks of the US armed forces and the growing casualty list grimly reflected this fact. As King's Chicago campaign highlighted, African Americans had also been among the prime, potential claimants under Johnson's Great Society programs, and so the domestic cutbacks that accompanied the surge in war costs also hit them disproportionately.

Taking up this point at a late May press conference, King called for the expenditure of at least $100 billion over the next decade to eliminate acute social and economic deprivation by radical measures, including a guaranteed annual income for the poor. Vietnam, he conceded, made these ambitious plans economically as well as politically utopian. To signal that his anti-war stance was far from uninformed, a South Vietnamese dissident Buddhist monk, Thich Nhat Hahn, joined King at this Chicago news conference. Despite King's pleas to end the bombing and seek a negotiated settlement that included the Vietcong, however, the Johnson administration continued to escalate US military operations in Southeast Asia.

By the time of the SCLC's 1966 convention in August, a resolution that denounced the war as "corrupting American society from within and degrading it from without" readily received approval, even though King himself was too ill with a throat infection to speak. In the convention hall, Andrew Young read King's annual report aloud. It warned that "the cries of warning and shouts of desperation of our ghettos fall on deaf ears," and using the current vocabulary of militancy linked African American discontent with other liberation struggles. "Self-determination for an oppressed people," it declared, "requires power" (Garrow 1988: 502). But the power of the oppressed was controlled and diffused by a hegemonic complex of social and ideological forces, as King was simultaneously discovering in Chicago. To break that control and concentrate the power of the lower classes required a combination of long-term organizing and tactically focused mobilization.

At the end of the year, King remained unsure how to meet these requirements for revolution. The concurrent experiences of Chicago and the "Black Power" controversy during the Meredith march suggested that organizing could not keep pace with African American frustrations sufficiently to channel communal anger into sustained nonviolent action. The rhetoric of King's rivals added to the difficulties by fanning the flames of black impatience, which in turn sharpened white fears and resentments. What they considered to be damaging and shallow demagoguery from SNCC spokesmen incensed King's colleagues and advisors. Bayard Rustin was particularly vociferous. The long-time pacifist was so committed by now to his dream of a labor-civil rights coalition that as long as the AFL-CIO remained pro-war, he would oppose a heightened anti-war stance. SNCC's claim that African Americans were forced to fight in Vietnam was simply untrue, Rustin complained to King. Most black soldiers were volunteers, he declared. But as he went on to explain that the young men enlisted because they could not find jobs, and that they chose to join the paratroopers in their quest for higher pay and thus suffered higher casualties, Rustin unwittingly revealed the structural forces that impelled African Americans to fight in Vietnam.

On December 15, 1966, US Senator Abraham Ribicoff provided King with an influential platform from which to call for a reordering of the nation's priorities from war to domestic reform. At the hearings of the Senate Committee on Government Operations, liberal committee members like Ribicoff and Robert Kennedy heard King press for the guaranteed income scheme as a more direct and effective solution to the problem of poverty than current government initiatives. Instead of dividing anti-poverty efforts into separate programs that attacked the problem from the different angles of education, or housing or unemployment, the government should embrace economist J. K. Galbraith's assumption that in the contemporary economy, the key principle was "enabling people to consume." From this Keynesian premise, King explained, flowed the fact that as "standards of life rise for affluent Americans, we cannot peg the poor at the old levels of 'subsistence' without producing socially explosive levels of relative deprivation." The Vietnam War and the Cold War's concurrent arms and space races squandered resources that could eliminate poverty. By comparison, King complained, "the war on poverty is not even a battle, it is scarcely a skirmish" (Garrow 1988: 539).

King's eloquent exposition of how the Vietnam War hurt the domestic War on Poverty understandably encouraged liberal activist Allard Lowenstein, Yale chaplain William S. Coffin, and veteran socialist leader Norman Thomas to ask King (via Stanley Levison) to consider a third-party presidential candidacy in 1968. In early January 1967, the wiretaps on Levison's phone noted King's response that running for President, not to win, but in order to offer a real alternative, "would be an interesting idea." Earlier in December, SCLC had announced that King would take two months' leave to work on the book that became *Where Do We Go From Here?* and to that end, he flew to Jamaica on January 14. At the airport, he picked up a copy of *Ramparts*, a New Left magazine, which featured a gruesome photo essay on the child victims of the US bombing in Vietnam. The sickening photos convinced King that he must do all he could to end the war.

King Takes His Stand

In this rare Jamaican interlude from the daily pressures of leadership, King resolved that he could no longer remain "silent about an issue that is destroying the soul of our nation and destroying thousands and thousands of little children in Vietnam." He recalled it as "an existential moment" when he decided that he must speak out (Carson 1998: 335). Pushing him to make this stand was a highly agitated James Bevel, who arrived, uninvited, at King's secluded holiday home with news that he had been told by God that they must stop the war. King reported that Bevel sounded crazy, but he gave him paid leave from SCLC to work on

the Spring Mobilization, a massive anti-war demonstration scheduled for April 15 in New York. King shared Bevel's objectives
and, while he did not immediately commit himself to speak at the
Mobilization, he was determined to speak out against the war at a
late February forum on the war, organized by liberal magazine
editor, Carey McWilliams.

As King prepared for this February 24 conference, his first
public appearance in over two months, he warned Levison that, no
matter how much financial support SCLC lost as a result, he was
now keen to take an active role in the peace movement. At the Los
Angeles seminar, King was the main speaker on a program that
included four anti-war US Senators – Ernest Gruening, Mark Hat-
field, Eugene McCarthy, and George McGovern. This was the
kind of respectable company that Levison advised King to cultivate. If he wanted to generate a serious challenge to LBJ's war,
King needed to be associated publicly with substantial figures like
Walter Reuther and Bobby Kennedy rather than fringe celebrities
like Dr. Spock, or fringe politicians like Norman Thomas. Bevel's
"Spring Mobe" was likely to attract precisely this fringe. But
despite warnings that he risked being identified with hippies,
pacifists, Trotskyites, and communists, King chose to speak at
Bevel's march to the UN Building scheduled for April 15.

Ironically, given the FBI's conviction that King was a tool of
the alleged communist agent Levison, it was King who insisted
that what the peace movement needed was mass mobilization in
the streets. Levison, on the contrary, believed that King's core
African American constituency and, indeed, the administration's
policies would be more swayed by a conspicuous alliance between
King and power-brokers like Kennedy and Reuther. Although
virtually all his advisors continued to plead with him not to march
in the Spring Mobe, King now possessed a determination that he
had not had in 1965. "I just know, on the war in Vietnam," he
explained, "that I will get a lot of criticism, and I know it can
hurt SCLC. But I feel better, and I think this is the most important thing. Because if I lose the fight then SCLC will die anyway"
(Fairclough 1987: 337).

A remarkable facet of King's mature personality was his integ-
rity in the face of adversity. Many public figures would have
tacked their course to try to protect their current status and

interests, but King believed by 1967 that unless he did what he believed was right, he would actually have nothing in the end. It was not an easy position to sustain since he recognized that so many people were depending upon him and that the consequences of his actions – staff lay-offs at a cash-starved SCLC, for instance – hit other people beside himself.

The Riverside Speech

King had resolved to follow his conscience. He announced on March 24 that he would take a much stronger stand against the Vietnam War and, accompanied by Dr. Spock, led 5,000 anti-war demonstrators through downtown Chicago. He had warned Levison that the war had become so evil that he could not remain cautious. The "time had come for real prophesy," he declared, "and I'm willing to go that road" (Garrow 1988: 550). Although SCLC donations were holding steady, Levison wanted King to present his case against the war in a more controlled and respectable setting than the Spring Mobe. Accordingly, King agreed to preach to a prominent anti-war group, Clergy and Laymen Against the War, on April 4. The venue chosen was New York's Riverside Church, which had hosted many of the country's most famous Protestant preachers for nearly a century.

If Levison expected King's Riverside address to mollify critics, he was to be roundly disappointed. In his sermon that day, King began by commending those among the nation's religious leaders who had moved "beyond the prophesying of smooth patriotism to the high grounds of a firm dissent," and explained why he felt called to denounce US conduct in Vietnam. The most obvious reason was the way the war had sucked vital resources from domestic anti-poverty programs. "I was increasingly compelled to see the war," King declared, "as an enemy of the poor and to attack it as such." This feeling had been reinforced by the recognition that it was the black and white sons of the poor doing most of the fighting; dying, ironically, side by side, while "they would hardly live on the same block in Chicago." King had been discomforted further by the anomaly of having to preach nonviolence to frustrated ghetto youths, who rightly perceived force to be the keystone of US foreign policy. King no longer felt able to speak out against the oppressed's resort to violence until he had condemned "the greatest purveyor of violence in the world today," his own government.

The SCLC motto, King reminded the congregation, was "To Redeem the Soul of America," and that mission ensured that he could not ignore this poisonous war. Opposition was not only his patriotic duty, it was also his obligation as a Nobel Peace Laureate, and part of his ordained vocation as a Christian minister. The personalist theology that King had embraced in college rested on the conviction that God was in every person. It was not enough for the government to identify enemies of the United States, "for no document from human hands can make these humans any less our brothers."

In what some took to be a treasonable identification with America's foes, King spoke of the traumas of the Vietnamese people at the hands of their "strange" liberators. The United States had supported French attempts at recolonization after 1945 and had blocked unification and free elections under the 1954 Geneva Agreement. It had stopped land reform and imposed, first, Premier Diem, whom King described as "one of the most vicious modern dictators," and then a succession of military juntas. As matters stood, with ever increasing casualties and environmental destruction from American bombing, there was every reason for the Vietnamese peasantry to regard Americans as their enemy. King likened the relocation of peasants in "fortified hamlets" to the Nazi concentration camp policy, implicitly accusing his country of crimes against humanity. While King did not condone the Vietcong's actions, he urged his listeners to "understand their feelings," and argued that, since America's "own computerized plans of destruction simply dwarf[ed]" Vietcong atrocities, the latter's mistrust and reluctance to negotiate were predictable.

Having spent so long empathizing with the enemy, King sought next to remind his audience of his concern for US troops as well. But, even here, the tone was critical as King foresaw the psychological difficulties ahead for veterans of this dishonorable war. He was in no doubt that the United States was at fault, and like a stern confessor, he urged five immediate steps to end the war and begin the process of atonement. The US should end all bombing; declare a unilateral ceasefire as a trust-building measure;

curtail her military buildup in Thailand and interference in Laos; and accept that the Vietcong's substantial support in South Vietnam made the National Liberation Front an inevitable part of any meaningful negotiations and any future Vietnamese government. Finally, the United States should set a date for the removal of all foreign troops from Vietnam in accordance with the 1954 Geneva Agreement.

Before this sympathetic audience, his demands won sustained applause. This was not the general reaction, however, especially since King went on to explain why ending the war might require widespread protest and marked only the first step in a wider revolution. Articulating the sentiments of the emerging counter-culture of the New Left, King urged the country to move from a "thing-oriented society" to a "person-oriented society." If people became truly more important than commodities to Americans, US foreign policy would be driven more by human rights than by the protection of overseas investments. If Americans perceived the person in all people, they would be unable to countenance the use of weapons of mass destruction that indiscriminately maimed and killed civilians, especially children. Reiterating points he had made elsewhere, King spelt out that racism, like militarism, was predicated on the denial of personhood, on the reduction of a person into something less than human. To the clergymen inside Riverside Church, King's words were an affirmation, but outside they drew widespread condemnation.

White House aide John Roche shared President Johnson's disgust at King's speech. Describing King to the President as "inordinately ambitious and quite stupid," Roche explained that in his "desperate search for a constituency," the SCLC leader had "thrown in with the commies." Firing the usual cheap shots that King's public career was fed by a need for applause and "money to keep up his standard of living," Roche declared that "Communist oriented 'peace' types have played him (and his driving wife) like trout." The FBI had consistently suggested that King was under communist influence, and in a private memo Hoover stated that after Riverside, it was clear that King "is an instrument in the hands of subversive forces seeking to undermine this nation" (Garrow 1988: 554-55).

Another White House aide, Bill Moyers, recalls that the President agreed with Roche, regarding King as just "a naive black preacher

[who] was being duped by a Communist" (Fairclough 1987: 340). Ironically, the Riverside speech, drafted largely by Spelman College professor and preacher Vincent Harding, met with little approval from King's alleged communist manipulator, Stanley Levison. It had been ill considered and unbalanced, Levison complained, and he warned again that King risked reducing his leadership, if he associated with fringe figures. As a damage-limitation measure, Levison and fellow attorney Harry Wachtel would prepare a more measured speech for the upcoming Spring Mobe. Underlining just how far Roche's analysis missed the mark, King responded that he felt he had "a role to play which may be unpopular." He expected hostility, not plaudits and donations, over Vietnam.

While King had foreseen that his speech would be slated as "politically unwise," he could hardly have anticipated the scale of the backlash, which greatly exceeded the reaction that had prompted his retreat on Vietnam in the autumn of 1965. Roy Wilkins' and Whitney Young's swift disassociation of their respective organizations from King's remarks was predictable. But fellow Nobel Laureate and UN diplomat Ralph Bunche's view that King had made a "serious tactical mistake" by trying to merge the civil rights and peace movements, shocked him.

Other African American sources joined the chorus of disapproval. The influential black newspaper, the *Pittsburgh Courier*, editorialized that King was "tragically misleading" black Americans on issues that were "too complex for simple debate." With active encouragement from the White House, black journalist Carl Rowan immediately attacked King in his newspaper column, lamenting his decline from the politically sensitive, Bus Boycott leader of 1956 to "the King of today who has very little sense of, or concern for, public relations, and no tactical skill." Months later, Rowan renewed his attack in the widely read pages of September's *Reader's Digest*. King was no longer "the selfless leader of the 1950s," Rowan lamented. Communist influence and "an exaggerated appraisal" of himself had prompted King's "tragic decision" to denounce the US Vietnam policy, and as a result he had "alienated many of the Negro's friends and armed the Negro's foes" (Garrow 1988: 554-55, 577).

Rowan's *Reader's Digest* piece largely repeated hostile comments from the nation's main newspapers. The *Washington Post* complained that King's "bitter and damaging allegations and inferences" were unsubstantiated. By indulging in "sheer inventions of unsupported fantasy," he had damaged both himself and "his natural allies." The Riverside speech constituted "a great tragedy," the *Post* averred, because it diminished King's authority, and thereby "his usefulness to his cause, his country and his people." The *New York Times*, mindful of its Jewish American audience, censured King for "recklessly comparing American military methods to those of the Nazis," and gave prominent coverage to claims that King was detrimentally merging the Civil Rights Movement with the peace movement. With every appearance of a concerted campaign against him, King fretted that "J. Edgar Hoover's old stuff" (especially the sex tapes) would be made public (Garrow 1988: 553-54, 556).

With the media aroused, King's appearance at the Spring Mobe demonstration on April 15 was likely to attract hostile scrutiny. Levison and Wachtel had drafted a much more moderate speech than the Riverside sermon, one which took pains to state explicitly that King did not want "a mechanical fusion" of the civil rights and peace movements. Nevertheless, as Levison feared, the event associated King with figures already smeared, like Stokely Carmichael, whose SNCC contingent sported Vietcong flags. Typically combative, Carmichael condemned US hypocrisy and declared that as black men: "We will not support LBJ's racist war in Vietnam" (Joseph 2006: 181). Appearing on CBS's *Face the Nation* the next day, King was asked: how could he share a platform with Carmichael and listen to him call the President a buffoon, the Secretary of State a fool, and the Secretary of Defense a racist? King responded by pointing out that he had shared a platform recently with South Carolina's veteran segregationist Senator Strom Thurmond, and he certainly had more in common with Carmichael than Thurmond. At the same time, he added (somewhat ambiguously) that he would never call the President a fool since he preferred to deal with issues rather than personalities.

Despite this claim, King was fully aware that both personalities and issues shaped American politics. Securing a cessation of American bombing meant dealing with the personality of President Johnson, whose own insecurities made any such policy reversal difficult. Older colleagues with vivid memories of McCarthyism, like Levison, doubted the ability of protest actions to shape foreign policy decisively. When King suggested that the administration would be compelled to halt its bombing raids, if he and thousands of other Americans went voluntarily to Hanoi and took up position near strategic targets like bridges or steel plants, Levison was aghast. King had better realize that "he is dealing with the State Department and the Pentagon," Levison complained to Harry Wachtel, "and not some stupid sheriff in the South" (Fairclough 1987: 340).

King For President?

For its part, the Johnson administration took due note of the potential influence of King's personality on politics. While King was speaking on CBS, Secretary of State Dean Rusk told NBC's *Meet the Press* that recent anti-war demonstrations had received support from the "Communist apparatus." Through the FBI wiretaps, officials tracked King's plans, especially his response to calls that he run as a third-party "Peace" candidate for President the next year. King gave the proposal serious thought and there was speculation over his candidacy in April's newspapers. He eventually decided not to run, and on April 25 called a press conference to explain that he wanted to operate "outside the realm of partisan politics." Accordingly, he declared: "I have no interest in any political candidacy," and two days later he reiterated his position. "Being a peace candidate is not my role," he said emphatically, "I feel I should serve as a conscience of all the parties and all of the people, rather than be a candidate myself" (Garrow 1988: 559).

King's desire to be the country's conscience was symptomatic of his inflated preacher ego, according to black militants, and of his extraordinary hypocrisy, in the eyes of J. Edgar Hoover. King sensed that there were some in the black community who would read a presidential campaign as pretentious and he knew that at any time the FBI's record of his sexual indiscretions could destroy his reputation, especially as a Christian minister. There were already some who felt that the peace movement had damaged African American interests by redirecting the energies of young activists and liberal donations. Contributions to SCLC plummeted in April and May. Its staff had been cut back to eighty-five by that stage, less than half of them in the field, with only fourteen workers across six Southern states. A "Peace" candidacy by King would be seen as a further siphoning away of dwindling resources that the Civil Rights Movement desperately needed. It seemed more politic not to run.

The grim course of events in the summer of 1967 sharpened King's focus on African American domestic problems. In quick succession, first Newark (July 12-15) and then Detroit (July 23-27) were wracked by violent ghetto disturbances that left a combined total of sixty-one dead. "There were dark days before," King told Levison gloomily, "but this is the darkest." King had still to prove that nonviolence would work as a means to secure economic justice in a complex metropolis. A Chicago activist had written in April to complain that the empty Summit Agreement had broken the back of the movement there. If King planned to return, he should come better prepared. "We need no more empty promises," the letter declared, "no more betrayals." Reporters detected a faltering of the SCLC leader's power to stir a crowd. In Cleveland, Ohio, one wrote: "There were times during his most impassioned moments when teenagers in the audience laughed or simply ignored him and began talking among themselves" (Garrow 1988: 560, 569, 571).

King's foreign policy stance similarly did not sway the general public. A May poll had shown that 73 percent of Americans disagreed with his position on the Vietnam War and only 25 percent of African American respondents actually endorsed it. The Six Day War between Israel and the Arab states in June not only deflected attention from Vietnam, but forced many Jewish Americans to reappraise their position. "Half of the peace movement is Jewish," reported Levison from New York, "and the Jews have all become 'hawks'" (Fairclough 1987: 343). In July 1967 President Johnson increased the level of US troops in Vietnam from 480,000 to 525,000, and the bombing continued. Against this dispiriting backdrop, Martin Luther King resolved to go for broke.

Note

1 Unless otherwise indicated, quotations are taken from the press clippings and speech files at the King Center in Atlanta.

10 Going For Broke

Memphis, 1968

The problems that King had confronted throughout 1967 showed little sign of abating as the year neared its close. The hostile, coordinated press reaction to his Riverside speech against the Vietnam War was proof of his rift with the Johnson administration. The violent July disorders in Newark and Detroit revealed not only the unwillingness of many African Americans to rely on King's nonviolent protest methods, but also how the deteriorating ghetto conditions fed the culture of violence from which King still hoped to redeem the United States. The fragility of SCLC's financial position, the low morale of its field staff, the wrangling between King's lieutenants, and the open antipathy between moderate civil rights organizations, like the NAACP, and the militant Black Power groups, eagerly reported by the media, compounded his difficulties.

At a senior staff retreat in mid-September, Marian Wright, an attorney who had backed the Child Development Group of Mississippi, sold King on the idea of bringing the poor to Washington to demand a real war against poverty. She claimed that it was Bobby Kennedy's idea, and thus had some political traction. Poll data suggested whites both favored federal construction projects to reduce unemployment and believed that ghetto reconstruction might stifle racial unrest, and this encouraged King to pursue the strategy (Jackson 2007: 333, 335). That autumn, as King pondered the practicalities of a campaign that targeted the federal, rather than local or state, government, he could point to some gains. With low-key SCLC help to get out the vote, Carl Stokes was elected as the first black mayor of Cleveland, Ohio in

November. Almost simultaneously, King learned that the Ford Foundation had approved a $230,000 grant for SCLC to train cadres of black ministers as community leaders in at least fifteen cities (Garrow 1988: 581). If these ministers could embrace the revolutionary values that King increasingly espoused openly within SCLC – values that recognized the necessity for "a radical redistribution of power," as he put it – then the Ministers' Leadership Training Program could provide a framework for a Poor People's Campaign (PPC). Economic justice was now a conspicuous part of King's measure of empowerment.

Planning for the PPC began in earnest at a retreat in late November. To secure definite economic gains in terms of incomes and jobs, King declared, the Washington protests needed to be "as dramatic, as dislocative, as disruptive, as attention-getting as the riots without destroying life or property." The fundamental requirement was to recruit well-trained activists in sufficient numbers, and King envisaged 200 from each of ten or twelve different locations converging on the capital. This "March on Washington" would be very different from its 1963 namesake. Its purpose would not be "to have a beautiful day" but to dislocate governmental functions until the nation gave priority to the needs of the underprivileged. "This is a kind of last, desperate demand for the nation to respond to nonviolence," King confessed. He could not guarantee success, but he added,

> We've got to go for broke this time. We've gone for broke before, but not in the way we're going this time, because if necessary I'm going to stay in jail six months – they aren't going to run me out of Washington.
>
> (Garrow 1988: 582)

Doubts About The PPC

Some staff members were enthusiastic about the PPC, provisionally scheduled for April 1968. Freed from his executive director duties, Andrew Young, for one, almost gleefully told the press that the SCLC had plans to close down the US capital, if necessary; and he sharpened the threat by warning that for many in the underclass, a spring jail term in Washington would be more comfortable than their current lives in Mississippi or Chicago. Other colleagues had reservations, however, not least because King insisted they make their own initiatives secondary to the PPC.

Still obsessed by the Vietnam War, Jim Bevel wanted SCLC's explicit target to be the Johnson "war machine." Jesse Jackson was concerned that the effort might drain resources from the Operation Breadbasket program, which was his own power base. As a sign of his lack of interest in PPC plans, Jackson failed to attend bimonthly staff meetings. For this oversight, William Rutherford, whom King had appointed SCLC executive director to restore some discipline to an increasingly chaotic organization, issued a formal reprimand. Though needed, Rutherford's blunt warnings to staff that they faced the sack, unless their performance improved and they accounted for their expenses, fueled resentment. Staff who felt that King's proposed, apocalyptic descent on Washington was too vague in its objectives to attract the nonviolent army that they were ordered to recruit, were particularly incensed by Rutherford's tough line. SCLC's previous campaigns had begun with local grievances that had already prompted action, but the PPC was to be launched from scratch and pursued ardently, amidst continuing problems caused by SCLC's frequent assignment of staff to communities with which they had had little prior contact.

King brought in Bevel's former SNCC colleague, Bernard LaFayette, to coordinate plans for the PPC. LaFayette had strong links to the American Friends Service Committee (AFSC), which could provide additional financial support as well as a network of local Quaker contacts, for a project that sought to mobilize not just African Americans, but other poor communities, including Hispanic, Native American, and white Appalachian groups. When Jackson and Bevel renewed their criticism of the PPC at the December 27 executive staff meeting, LaFayette endorsed their complaint that the campaign's objectives needed to be more specific. More sharply defined goals would both help field staff to recruit effectively and reassure the AFSC that the organizational costs would result in real gains. "What is more basic an issue than jobs and incomes?" was King's rejoinder, but his assertion did not really address Jackson's supplementary argument that federally funded jobs and incomes could breed a dependency that might cow future militancy; a view which reflected Jackson's larger suspicion of King's socialist solutions (Fairclough 1987: 362).

King also rejected Bevel's claim that the PPC would not evoke enough "creative tension" unless it was set up "to get the war machine to attack us rather than us attacking the war machine." Whereas Bevel insisted that the cause of stopping the war demonstrably attracted young activists in large enough numbers to confront the national government, King believed that their commitment was still relatively shallow, and might fade, given the prison terms draft-resisters might face. By focusing his proposed campaign on domestic issues, King believed that he was choosing to work at the salient "second level." Since the 1966 Chicago campaign, he had doubted the continued effectiveness of "first level" or purely local campaigns, but he did not believe that the Movement was ready yet to move to the "third" or international level, which he believed Bevel's focus on Vietnam and desire to take the fight directly to the federal authorities logically entailed. He asked again for the staff's unreserved commitment to the PPC (Garrow 1988: 590).

Although these exchanges clarified certain issues, Bevel and Jackson continued to grumble. In response to what he perceived as a challenge to his leadership, King called another meeting for his 39th birthday, January 15, 1968. He reiterated his belief that jobs or income for the poor provided a clear and simple focus around which to mobilize support but, in an effort to pacify Bevel, he added that this did not require SCLC to ignore other evils, like the draft. Just days earlier, King had condemned the government's prosecution of anti-war campaigners, including Dr. Benjamin Spock and Yale chaplain William Sloane Coffin, for urging young men to resist conscription, and he had visited singer Joan Baez and other protesters, who had been jailed for sitting-in at the Oakland Military Center in California. "Everyone is on welfare in this country," he had also told the press, but when white or rich people benefitted, "we call it subsidies" (Jackson 2007: 332). King's eloquence temporarily generated a semblance of unity but, in discussions held in his absence the next day, factionalism resurfaced, with Jackson and Bevel's sympathizers reasserting that the PPC was ill-conceived.

Alerted to this fresh dissension, King tried again to ensure unity and lift morale on January 17. To those who charged that there was not enough time before April to plan an effective campaign, he retorted that they were taking far more time than it had taken to launch the year-long Bus Boycott in Montgomery. To those who complained that the demands were too few and too vague, he replied that SCLC had gone into Selma without "one thing on paper in terms of demands." Long lists of demands, especially if they involved complex compensatory mechanisms like negative tax relief, King argued, would not mobilize ordinary people as effectively as a simple slogan, and he was confident that the slogan "Jobs or Income" could "rally more people than almost anything else." Even its vagueness might help, he claimed, making a tactical withdrawal easier, once enough partial gains had been secured to boost popular confidence in nonviolence. Thus, King tried to persuade his critics that he remained a realist. The ultimate goal of freedom, or whatever they wanted to call it, was not going to be achieved in one year, he reminded them. "Let's find something," he pleaded,

> that is so possible, so achievable, so pure, so simple that even the backlash [in Congress] can't do much to deny it, and yet so non-token and so basic to life that even the black nationalists can't disagree with it that much. Now that's jobs or income.
>
> (Garrow 1988: 593)

A key part of SCLC's mission was to keep hope alive, he explained, and the essence of hope was the refusal to give up.

For many of King's contemporaries, however, fear was more potent than hope by 1968. On December 11, 1967, King's old theology tutor, Harold DeWolf, warned in a letter that the mass civil disobedience King was reportedly planning for 1968, an election year, would probably produce "an even more reactionary Congress," and if the protests degenerated into aimless disorder, they might even provoke "a Fascist-type revolution," putting "the country under the direct rule of the military-industrial complex, ending civil liberties and civil rights and precipitating World War III" (Fairclough 1987: 364). With similar misgivings about the PPC's potentially negative impact, Bayard Rustin and white Socialist Michael Harrington warned King on January 29 that he needed a tactical victory to revive his own credibility, not a spectacular confrontation that increased repression. Others raised practical issues. Mississippi activist R.B. Cottonreader pointed out that the poor would struggle to find the money to get to Washington and after the campaign was done, where would these evicted sharecroppers go then? (Jackson 2007: 344). King had heard successive Presidents tell him that his protests would make matters worse rather than better; and he believed that he had proved them wrong. Now, he heard similar arguments from acknowledged reformers with far less reason than Kennedy or Johnson to urge restraint, yet he was unpersuaded.

Meetings with officials from the National Welfare Rights Organization (NWRO) and with followers of Stokely Carmichael, who had relocated to Washington, DC, showed that black militants were skeptical about King's current ability to secure gains. The NWRO's women board members grew irritated at King's shocking ignorance of the actual details of current welfare policy debates, especially the struggle to roll back the restrictions attached to welfare by "P.L. 90-248," effective from January 2, 1968. How could this ignoramus pretend to be their leader? In Andrew Young's words: "They jumped on Martin." To his credit, King subsequently insisted that eliminating the hostile changes to welfare form part of the PPC, despite internal SCLC opposition (Jackson 2007: 345-46). Still shaken by this challenge to his claim to lead the poor, King attended a meeting with local Washington activists. There, a young black nationalist woman charged that King had sold out the Movement during the Selma campaign and roundly accused him of being untrustworthy. A livid King denied the accusation (Garrow 1988: 594-95).

Despite criticisms, King's aims for the PPC were genuinely radical and would have transformed the American welfare state. Besides seeking an overall appropriation of $30 billion in anti-poverty spending, King declared that his "absolute minimum" was a legally binding, federal commitment to full employment; passage of a guaranteed annual income law; and funds to construct a minimum of 500,000 low-income housing units each year. In private, he was willing to characterize his proposals as socialistic, to applaud Scandinavia's social democratic regimes, and to bemoan America's knee-jerk anti-communism that prevented serious public debate over the need to redistribute wealth and power. At the same time, even though in numerous speeches he labored the fact that he expected much more profound opposition than he had faced during the struggle for desegregation and voting rights, King's tactics had not become proportionately more radical.

Admittedly, in initial staff meetings and press comments, there was a radical emphasis on dislocating the US capital's functions. Government buildings would be occupied. The sick would demand treatment at federal hospitals; the hungry – food at the Department of Agriculture; the unemployed – jobs at the Labor Department; and the homeless – decent shelter at the Department of Housing and Urban Development. SCLC might even mimic the ill-received, New York CORE chapters' tactic of the "stall-in," and block the Potomac bridges to produce gridlock inside the Beltway. Similarly, seeking to pacify Bevel, King implied that he had no objection to the PPC's laying nonviolent siege to the Pentagon. There was even talk of concurrent campaigns in other cities and nationwide strikes. At this stage, King seemed to have moved to a blatantly coercive mode of nonviolence in the form of mass civil disobedience in order to precipitate negotiations against a background of acute crisis. Such a strategy required mass mobilization, since the pressure would have to be sustained, even if the authorities resorted to large-scale internment and legal harassment. King's initial recruitment target of over 2,000 demonstrators would have to be met not just once, but exceeded several times.

The strategy's underlying premises were either that the regime's internal divisions would be widened by the crisis to such a point that key elements would favor concessions, or that the legitimacy of the regime would become so discredited that the people demanded its destruction. Given the growing conservatism of Congress, the likelihood of liberals forcing through a reform agenda that went beyond Johnson's Great Society initiatives was not great; instead, the immediate response seemed likely to be repression. Much would then depend on King's ability to present the Movement positively and to cultivate any groundswell of discontent against the authorities. Only at that stage might a liberal agenda of a guaranteed income, full employment, and massive public works appeal as a recipe for the restoration of stability.

Such speculations seem justified when one considers the fact that the Nixon administration did consider the guaranteed income as a possible way forward in 1969 at a time when the disorder and violence of recent years had frightened many powerful figures in the United States.

Nevertheless, King was intrinsically a radical reformer who sought resolution rather than protracted conflict. He had backed away from potential bloodbaths in Birmingham in 1963 and Chicago in 1966. By the end of January 1968, he was already retreating from his genuinely revolutionary program of nonviolent disruption, which seems to have been a rhetorical maneuver to appeal to militants and agitate moderates. By early February, he was publicly disavowing any desire to disrupt the capital; perhaps, the symbolic presence of the poor on the Mall, and carefully orchestrated lobbying of federal offices and Congress, would generate a national consensus behind his call to shift national priorities. Fatefully, King's abandonment of his planned mass disruption did not prompt him to reduce the scale of what was becoming a moral spectacle. He rejected the idea that the campaign could include the donation of a transported Mississippi sharecropper's shack to the Smithsonian to dramatize that such poverty should really be a thing of the past. Instead, he clung to the idea of creating an actual tent city of the poor in the heart of government.

King was moving back to the Selma campaign model in which concessions came due to pressure from a coalition of militants with moderate sympathizers, mobilized by a moral spectacle that induced the latter to side with the Movement. But the Movement he was trying to create was more diverse. King desperately wanted to improve the lot of his fellow African Americans, but he had learned from his advisors that numerically the majority of the nation's poor were white. Native Americans and Hispanics were also disproportionately among the disadvantaged. Their protest movements, however, did not always have identical priorities to King's. Native Americans had many concerns over tribal land use and Hispanics wanted bilingual education, for instance. Such diversity complicated the task of effective organization (Chase 1998).

Making visible the multi-racial character of poverty, King believed, might rally popular support for universal entitlement programs, like the guaranteed income, more effectively than could a demand for exclusively African American benefits, even if these were couched as reparations for slavery. In the context of 1968, organizing diverse racial and ethnic constituencies behind a common campaign ran headlong into the reality that race relations were already inflamed to the point of separatism and interracial violence. Crime figures that showed how readily the poor turned on each other in their desperate struggle to survive made King's vision of a multi-ethnic commune of the poor, a high-risk strategy. If federal authorities moved aggressively and clumsily to evict the poor from their unauthorized shantytown, there was a chance that popular sympathies would rally behind the PPC, or at least become more critical of the federal government. On the other hand, if the authorities were patient, the logistics of sustaining and supervising the tent city would exhaust SCLC, or violent protest or disorder could discredit King's entire campaign.

By seeking a confrontation with federal authorities, King was seeking to apply nonviolence in a way he had not done before. In Birmingham and Selma, the creative tension produced by King's nonviolent confrontations with local adversaries had compelled federal intervention. In both cases, King had exploited divisions within the local white power structures, but subsequent events in Birmingham and Selma scarcely suggested that his tactics facilitated the immediate establishment of more liberal regimes. The PPC's political logic rested on the questionable assumption that a crisis involving King's nonviolent army and the federal government would ultimately strengthen the position of progressive rather than conservative elements in government.

Inside the Johnson administration, the PPC was taken very seriously, especially by its conservative elements. Attorney-General Ramsey Clark subsequently remembered official apprehension as "a paranoia, literally." Inflaming fears was integral to J. Edgar Hoover's strategy for defending and expanding the FBI's budget. After the 1967 disturbances, the White House had asked the FBI to recruit ghetto informants to provide early warnings of future outbreaks. On January 4, 1968, more than 3,000 informants were urged to report on the activities of PPC recruiters in order to assess their significance in terms of the FBI's so-called "rabble-rouser index." James A. Harrison, SCLC's financial comptroller and a paid FBI informant, provided the list of recruiters, but virtually none of them really qualified as a rabble-rouser. Wire-taps on the phones of King's trio of New York advisors, Levison, Rustin, and Clarence Jones, ensured that the FBI also knew of the doubts and divisions around King. Nevertheless, Hoover did nothing to assuage administration fears about the PPC, and nationally his agents continued a campaign of intimidation, disinformation, and disruption (McKnight 1998: 22-28).

The covert FBI campaign had some impact, but the challenge of rapidly mobilizing the nation's poor would have exceeded SCLC's resources in any case. On February 11, King openly considered calling the whole thing off because his staff "had not recruited twenty folks that are people who will go and stay with us." As matters stood, SCLC might be able to get a lot of people to Washington briefly but they would not be "the hard-core poor people" whom King felt were essential (Fairclough 1987: 366). Postponing the campaign's start by three weeks, King accepted staff promises of greater effort. That same day in Memphis, sanitation workers voted in favor of strike action to secure union recognition in their fight against harsh city management. A local conflict, initially, albeit one involving impoverished black workers, the Memphis strike was destined to have a decisive impact on both the PPC and King. In late February and early March, King began to hear more encouraging reports from PPC recruitment workers but as he tried to grab a short break in Jamaica to shake off the despondency that increasingly afflicted him, the Memphis strike escalated.

King's Depression

During what proved to be the last year of his life, King sometimes teetered on the brink of despair. His increasing sensitivity was revealed by an unusually public clash with National Urban League Director Whitney Young at an early 1967 Long Island reception. Young complained that King's strong condemnation of Johnson's war policy in a recent speech had adversely affected the whole Movement. "Whitney, what you're saying may get you a foundation grant," King replied, "but it won't get you into the kingdom of truth." Since King suspected that his anti-war remarks might have damaged the chances of the then pending SCLC application to the Ford Foundation, his words had a special edge (Garrow 1988: 546).

But the encounter did not end there. Irritated by King's moral superciliousness, Young pointed to the SCLC leader's protuberant stomach, a product of too much airline food, too many pre-speech dinners, and too little exercise, and remarked scathingly: "You're eating well." It was a telling body blow, and further undignified cat-calling ensued before colleagues pulled the two apart. King later phoned Young to apologize and they spoke at length about Vietnam. King had always been somewhat sensitive about his personal appearance. He had to use a special depilatory cream on his tough beard and was sufficiently embarrassed by his short stature to have "boosts" in his shoes. Although he angered his wife and father by his increasingly abstemious approach to material matters such as the family home and car, his celebrity status ensured that he never lived as frugally as Movement field workers did. Nor did his embrace of nonviolence as a way of life include Gandhi's strict vegetarianism. He and Ralph Abernathy displayed the traditional love for "soul food" with its emphasis on heavily seasoned pork and chicken with long-, some say, over-cooked greens. It was not a diet designed for slimness, low blood pressure or longevity.

The pervasive armed conflict around the world in 1967 from the Holy Land, to which King had intended to lead a pilgrimage, to the streets of major US cities, so depressed the SCLC leader that caring colleagues grew worried. Old enough to be Martin's grandmother, Septima Clark tried to persuade him to hire a reliable administrator, like Randolph Blackwell. He should delegate more, she declared, not just for his own sake, but to encourage his staff to be less dependent on him. "You are certainly more valuable healthy than sick," she warned, "and God help us all if you become exhausted to the point of a non-active person." Coretta, too, was worried by her husband's depression, which by early August 1967 "was greater than ever before." Everyone was looking to him for answers, King remarked sadly, but "I don't have any answers." Folk singer Joan Baez recalled hearing him at a September staff retreat with "a couple of whiskies in him" saying how sick of it he was: "the Lord had called him to be a preacher, and not to do all this stuff" (Garrow 1988: 565, 571, 572, 576, 578).

In November 1967, King told an old family friend that he felt that everything that he had tried to do to reform the country had been in vain. In many of his Sunday sermons, he sounded deeply despondent, although he would tell his congregation that whenever he got weary and felt his work was in vain "the Holy Spirit revives my soul again." Both his wife Coretta and long-time SCLC colleague Dorothy Cotton knew that behind the public facade, King felt that he did not deserve the adulation he frequently commanded. As criticisms multiplied in the winter of 1967-68, they fed his guilt and self-doubt. When he attended a meeting of his New York advisors on January 29, 1968, Michael Harrington was struck by how the exuberance and equanimity that had once characterized King was now missing (Garrow 1988: 594).

Normally able to retain his composure, King became visibly angry during some meetings in early February, eruptions that Bill Rutherford took to be symptomatic of physical and emotional exhaustion. As problems continued to beset preparations for the PPC in March, King became increasingly sensitive to opposition from those close to him. An SCLC board member, Marian Logan, was so convinced that the campaign would backfire that she circulated a memo urging its cancellation. King responded first with a succession of phone calls asking Logan to withdraw the memo and finally visited her New York home in late March. Exhausted and increasingly drunk, he badgered Logan to change her position with barely concealed anger. Eventually, in the early hours of the morning, Marian's husband, Arthur, told Martin to "drop it."

Returning to SCLC in late February after a three-week tour of the Far East, King's closest colleague, Ralph Abernathy, felt the sad figure whom he found on his return to be "just a different person." King's desperate attempts to steal a break largely failed. Phone calls and intrusive celebrity-hunters spoiled his Jamaican vacation and a three-day break with Abernathy in Acapulco secured little rest or relaxation. On both the outbound and homeward flights, a clearly agitated King told Abernathy how he wanted to be remembered as a "Drum Major for Justice," a theme that he had used in a sermon at Ebenezer a few weeks earlier. To Abernathy's discomfort, King kept returning to the subject of what Abernathy must do when he succeeded King at SCLC. Back in the United States, the exhausting schedule of public appearances resumed, leaving King looking, as one staff member put it, "dark, gaunt, and tired." She added: "He felt that his time was up ... He said he knew that they were going to get him" (Garrow 1988: 599, 602).

The Memphis Strike

Race and labor relations in the city of Memphis had involved an abundance of small brutalities, but no major race riot since 1866. Black minister Samuel Kyles summed up the local police's policy as being that whenever "the niggers are getting out of hand ... the only way to put them back in their place is to crack them across their skull" (McKnight 1998: 33). Industrial relations in the bustling river town exhibited a similar savagery, with instances of kidnap, murder, and wrongful imprisonment. For one of the country's fastest growing unions, the American Federation of State, County, and Municipal Employees (AFSCME), Memphis had already proved recalcitrant. Municipal authorities refused to recognize AFSCME Local 1733 and broke a 1966 strike with a court injunction that affirmed that municipal workers had no right to strike.

Among black city workers, those who collected the garbage and fixed the drains and sewers faced particularly harsh conditions. As "unclassified" employees, they were not covered by workmen's compensation rules in cases of injury or lay-offs, and they were paid such a low hourly rate (less than $70 for a full week) that any loss of hours was devastating. In January 1968, heavy rains prevented work in the city sewers. Twenty-one black workers received just two hours of "show up" pay per day, but what triggered a strike among previously docile workers was the fact that their few white co-workers and supervisors received full pay. Black anger intensified further when two African American sanitation workers were crushed to death in their own garbage truck. Forbidden to loiter on the porches of white residences, they had taken shelter in the back of the truck from a torrential rainstorm. Although the accident was due partly to defective equipment and racist city policies, as the dependents of "unclassified" workers, the men's bereaved families were not entitled to any benefits.

The heavy-handed approach of the newly elected white Republican mayor, Henry Loeb III, and the demeaning treatment of an overwhelmingly African American workforce ensured that the strike escalated into a racial as well as labor confrontation. When police broke up a strikers' march to City Hall on February 23, they used MACE gas against ministers and other respectable leaders. This united the black community behind the strike support group, Community on the Move for Equality (COME). Through old friends of King's, Reverend Kyles and veteran nonviolent activist James Lawson, COME and SCLC became linked and, for old times' sake, King reluctantly agreed to speak on March 18, en route to a PPC recruitment drive in Mississippi. In the event, the reception he received from a 15,000-strong capacity crowd at the Mason Temple genuinely lifted his spirits.

In support of the strike, COME had launched a boycott of downtown stores, and this tactic, plus the euphoria of the mass meeting, revived happy memories of past victories for King. Applauding their use of economic leverage, he suggested that if Loeb remained obdurate on the issue of union recognition, the black community should escalate the campaign by calling a one-day general strike. Delighted by the rapport King shared with COME's followers, Lawson quickly asked him to lead a march and they set the date for March 22. Announcing this to the crowd, King urged everyone to stay away from work or school that day. The PPC, he declared, would start in Memphis. "I've never seen a community as together as Memphis," King enthused, as he chatted late into the night at his Lorraine Motel room (Garrow 1988: 606).

A Disastrous Detour

King's decision to get involved in Memphis paralleled his sudden involvement in the 1961 Albany campaign, and his colleagues, whom he had been scolding for not staying focused on the PPC, were understandably dismayed. Andrew Young, for one, felt that the dispute was a dangerous distraction, especially since PPC preparations were far from well advanced. King himself was soon complaining that his Mississippi tour had generated few volunteers or dollars, and bad weather and plane delays adversely affected similar trips to Alabama and Georgia. The SCLC's income no longer covered its costs, with field staff regularly reporting the imminent closure of offices or loss of phone lines due to nonpayment. Little wonder that many SCLC recruiters proved unable to fill their quota of volunteers willing to go to Washington. In addition, the FBI continued to do all it could to obstruct and derail King's plans. When a freak snowstorm hit Memphis on March 22, forcing the scheduled protest's postponement, it seemed that even the weather was against King.

Impressed by the mass meeting he attended and local leaders' accounts of peaceful neighborhood rallies, King and his SCLC colleagues left arrangements for the rescheduled march in the hands of Lawson and other COME leaders. They did not apply the lessons of past campaigns about double-checking the sometimes over-sanguine claims of community solidarity made by local leaders, or consider the local impact of the continuing challenge of "Black Power" to King's nonviolent protest model. As a result, they were unaware of the existence of a small black nationalist youth faction, the Invaders, whose leaders Charles Cabbage and John Burrell Smith had gained a certain standing among black high school and college youth by urging blacks to "get guns," instead of marching and praying, as the "Tom" ministers on the COME committee advised. What Memphis needed, according to the Invaders, was a "good race riot." When they demanded a bigger role in COME, Lawson rebuffed them. Thanks partly to the presence of Marrell McCollough, an undercover officer who infiltrated the Invaders as the strike impasse lengthened, the Memphis Police Department knew of these intracommunal tensions before King did (McKnight 1998: 48-50).

The day of the protest (March 28) was unseasonably hot and the late arrival of King's plane forced Lawson to hold the march's front columns for nearly two hours. Protest placards, mounted on hefty sticks, had been distributed by inexperienced parade marshals before they moved forward to man the route to City Hall. The Invaders used the delay to denounce nonviolence, unchallenged, to several hundred restless teenagers at the march's initial staging area of Clayborne Temple Church. Members of the crowd, McCollough reported, had already torn off the placards and were waving the sticks as clubs. Unfortunately, news of this development was relayed neither to the march organizers, who were preoccupied by King's tardy arrival, nor to King himself, even though the police knew exactly when his plane would land. As King and

Abernathy at last forced their way to the front of the march, they sensed that all was not well, but Lawson was anxious to proceed.

The front rank of dignitaries set off down Memphis's famous Beale Street but, as they turned right into Main Street, from several blocks to the rear came the sound of plate-glass windows being smashed. Bystanders quickly joined stick-wielding youths in opportunistic looting from shattered storefronts. As police called for back-up, their commanders instructed King and Lawson to curtail the march. Accordingly, Lawson borrowed a police bull-horn and instructed the marchers to return to Clayborne Temple. Simultaneously, worried colleagues urged King to leave the increasingly chaotic scene quickly for his own safety. In a borrowed car with a police motorcycle escort, he was rushed, not to his regular hotel since it was too close to the unfolding disturbances, but to the Hilton Rivermont, where his aides booked a suite. In mounting anguish at the turn of events, King took to his bed.

Instructed to clear the area, the Memphis police did so brusquely, without distinguishing between those directly engaged in crime and those simply returning to the staging area as instructed. When a handful of stone-throwing youths sought refuge in Clayborne Temple Church, the police fired tear gas inside. In the ensuing turmoil, sixty-two people were wounded, $400,000 worth of property was destroyed, and 16-year-old Larry Payne was shot dead by police. The black-owned *Memphis Tri-State Defender* carried a photo of the dead youth slumped against the wall with his mouth and eyes still open and both hands raised above his head, an image sharply at odds with police claims that, armed with a butcher's knife, he had menaced a patrolman, who shot in self-defense. At Mayor Loeb's request, 4,000 Tennessee National Guardsmen arrived to enforce a dusk-to-dawn curfew.

The FBI was determined to use the march's violence to damage King's reputation as much as possible. J. Edgar Hoover hoped that it might even force the PPC's cancellation. In his hotel suite, a despondent King foresaw a storm of public criticism, much of it to the effect that, if he could not control a small march in Memphis, his grandiose plans for mass demonstrations in Washington constituted a reckless courtship of disaster. Although still deeply upset by the debacle and the spirit of violence it represented, he quickly realized that the best way to restore his own credibility was to return to Memphis and lead another, disciplined, and dignified protest. Such a move was essential to prove the continuing viability of nonviolence in an inflamed racial climate. He even considered undertaking a classically Gandhian penitential fast in order to shame the Memphis black community and his critics.

Press accounts of the Memphis disorder were much as King feared. The *New York Times* editorial for March 31 urged the PPC's cancellation as the only sure way to avoid "another eruption of the kind that rocked Memphis." Given the likelihood of violence, it concluded, any SCLC campaign in the capital risked damaging the very policies that King claimed to support. Prompted by the FBI, the *Memphis Commercial Appeal* made the most of King's hasty departure from the scene, with a cartoon of the fleeing SCLC leader, captioned "Chicken à la King." Its editorial declared that he had "wrecked his reputation as a leader as he took off at high speed when violence occurred, instead of trying to use his persuasive prestige to stop it." Drawing on an unsigned FBI press release, the St. Louis *Globe Democrat* lambasted the "real Martin Luther King" as "more dangerous than Stokely Carmichael because of his non-violent masquerade" (Jackson 2007: 352). The paper castigated King as "a man who hides behind a facade of 'non-violence' as he provokes violence." A cartoon showed King shooting up "trouble," "violence," and "looting" from his pistol, even while protesting in the caption that "I'm not firing it. I'm only pulling the trigger" (Oates 1994: 480).

Before this denunciation had even begun, King was rebuking himself for the Memphis debacle. A distraught James Lawson shifted the blame to the Invaders when he visited King's hotel suite on the afternoon of March 28. Charles Cabbage, one of three Invaders who came to the hotel the next morning, denied responsibility and argued that, if Lawson had included the Invaders in COME's deliberations, they might have been able to contain the outbreak. Realizing too late how little he really knew about black Memphis, King was downcast. But he told Cabbage that he would be in touch because he would have to lead a peaceful march in Memphis, and he put on a brave face for the press when he announced that there would be a second Memphis strike march which, unlike the first, the SCLC would organize, just as it would continue to prepare for the PPC in Washington.

Back in Atlanta, a weary King faced his executive staff. Bevel and Jackson remained openly hostile to the Washington project. Young and others were now equally opposed to further involvement in Memphis, which they argued was already interfering with efforts to make the PPC a success. After several hours of bickering, with one side saying that King had to go back to rescue his credibility and that this meant canceling the PPC and the other side defending the Washington project, but urging King to have nothing more to do with the Memphis strike, King was in despair. He rounded on his colleagues, complaining that he had always supported their efforts, but now when he needed them, they were not displaying the same loyalty. He was particularly incensed at Jackson. "If you want to carve out your own niche in society," he told him, "go ahead, but for God's sake don't bother me." And with that, he stormed out of the meeting and, knowing that he might face complaints and recriminations on other matters from Coretta at home, he hurried to a girlfriend's apartment (Garrow 1988: 616-17).

By the time he returned, his lieutenants had settled their differences. Bevel, Jackson, and Hosea Williams, together with James Orange, a young staff member who had worked with Chicago gangs, had been selected to go to Memphis to ensure black unity prior to a fresh march. Other staff would continue preparations for the Washington protests. After preaching at the capital's National Cathedral the next day, March 31, King announced to the press that the PPC would go ahead on schedule. Later that evening, his gloomy mood was lifted by President Johnson's surprise announcement that he would not seek reelection. The move seemed to open the way for Robert Kennedy to secure the Democratic nomination. Kennedy's public misgivings about the Vietnam War and his senatorial efforts to investigate the problems of poverty made the prospect of a new Kennedy presidency appealing to the battle-weary SCLC leader.

King Returns To Memphis

Over the next few days, while his advance team tried to ensure that the Invaders were fully committed to nonviolence for the April 5 march, King remained in Atlanta at PPC planning meetings.

On April 3, he boarded an American Airlines plane for Memphis, only to be held at the gate for an hour while all baggage was searched because of a telephoned bomb warning. King had grown accustomed to such scares. By 1968, the FBI had logged fifty assassination plans and was aware that two St. Louis-based supporters of George Wallace's American Independent Party had placed a bounty of between $70,000 and $100,000 on King's head. Among the disaffected white Southerners who knew of this reward was a small-time crook and drug peddler, James Earl Ray, who also arrived in Memphis on April 3. Ray checked into Room 5B of Mrs. Bessie Brewer's seedy rooming house on South Main. The small room with a wire coat-hanger for a door handle, a stained bed, ripped sofa, greasy pillows, a strong odor of disinfectant, and a solitary naked light bulb had little to commend it, except perhaps its only window, which offered a partial view of the Lorraine Motel, where radio reports indicated that King would stay. A better view was available from the bathroom down the hall (Posner 1998: 26).

According to Ralph Abernathy, King was in good spirits when they checked into Room 306 at the Lorraine and met with COME leaders. Word that a federal court order had been issued, temporarily prohibiting King and his allies from any mass protest for ten days, did not faze him. At a subsequent legal conference, King agreed that Movement lawyers should argue for permission to have a limited, tightly disciplined march. Being easier to control, it would better serve King's purpose of proving the continuing feasibility of nonviolent protest. Even the delay of a legal wrangle might work to his advantage, allowing national labor groups to join a march on Monday April 8 that they couldn't make earlier. Before the press, King sounded militant, promising to march whether the court order was changed or not.

Back at the Lorraine, King met the Invaders with colleagues to see if the young militants backed the goal of a peaceful march. Having previously been frozen out of community action grants to a large extent by older, more established, black leaders, the Invaders' priority was a piece of the action. James Orange acted as their intermediary and, while Abernathy and others bridled at what they took to be blackmail, King gave the youths' proposals a respectful hearing. With no clear commitment to nonviolence from them, however, he remained circumspect. Unable to promise direct SCLC funding, he agreed to make some phone calls to organizations that funded community projects, and said that Andrew Young would help the Invaders couch their initiatives in terms likely to find favor with grant-awarding bodies. If they committed themselves to peaceful protest, the Invaders could serve as parade marshals at Monday's march.

After the meeting, the rain that had been threatening came down with a vengeance, and the radio warned of tornadoes. The scheduled rally at the Mason Temple seemed likely to attract a small crowd so King dispatched Abernathy to make his apologies and speak in his place. He was right. The audience was far smaller than the nearly 15,000 to whom King had spoken on March 18, but Abernathy sensed that the 2,000 souls who had braved the storm were the real core of the Memphis movement. They yearned to see King and, given his recent emotional fragility, Abernathy suspected that King probably needed to see them as well. "I really think you should come down," he told Martin over the phone. "The people want to hear you, not me. This is your crowd." Wearily, King dressed and sped to the rally through rain-soaked streets (Oates 1994: 484).

Relieved to see their hero, the crowd gave him a euphoric reception, and he, in turn, gave them an extemporaneous address of great poignancy and emotional power. Although he would have loved to have seen Moses parting the Red Sea or to have witnessed his namesake Martin Luther nail his ninety-five theses to Wittenberg Cathedral's door, King declared, he was content that God had allowed him to be with them in the second half of the twentieth century. He reminded his audience of how close he had come to death after his stabbing in 1958. Just a sneeze would have killed him, apparently, and then he would have missed so many great events: the student sit-ins of 1960, the Freedom Rides of 1961, the Albany struggle of 1961-62, the Birmingham confrontation, and his chance to tell the country about his dream in 1963. He would have been absent from Selma in 1965 and unable to be part of this Memphis movement of "brothers and sisters who are suffering. I'm so happy that I didn't sneeze," he said, smiling to the applauding crowd.

Of course, the threat of death lingered as the morning bomb scare showed, but that didn't matter anymore because, King told his rapt audience, "I've been to the mountaintop." With a voice suffused with sadness, he went on amidst a chorus of cries and sobs:

> Like anybody, I would like to live a long life. Longevity has its place. But I'm not concerned about that now. I just want to do God's will. And He's allowed me to go up to the mountain [*go ahead*]. And I've looked over [*yes, doctor*]. And I've *seen* the Promised Land [*go ahead, doctor*]. I may not get there with you [*yes, sir, go ahead*]. But I want you to know tonight that we as a people will get to the Promised Land [applause, cries, *go ahead, go ahead*]. So I'm happy tonight. I'm not worried about anything. I'm not fearing any man. Mine Eyes Have Seen the Glory of the Coming of the Lord!

As King sat down his audience was near tears. He retained an extraordinary capacity to move people by his oratory, especially in a nation in which the Bible remained a core cultural text. Unlike his famous 1963 address before a huge interracial audience, the Memphis speech was for a predominantly Southern black audience with strong church ties that inclined them to empathize potently with King's message of struggle and deliverance in the face of death (Dyson 2008).

Abernathy and Young had heard King deliver essentially this same peroration several times before, but the emotional intensity of tonight's delivery and the backdrop of the storm outside made his morbid, spiritually charged reflections more striking, and a few colleagues asked pointedly if Martin was okay. But King appeared happy and relaxed after the speech. He enjoyed a late meal and was pleased to see his brother, A.D., who had come down from Louisville. He joked around until daybreak and slept in till near noon.

The Assassination

While King slept on the morning of April 4, Young and Lawson testified in federal court that a limited, disciplined march was not only guaranteed them under the First Amendment, but was more likely to preempt a race riot, born of the accumulated frustrations of black Memphis with Mayor Loeb and the local police. The legal proceedings were protracted and, when King eventually arose, he grew impatient at the lack of news from the courtroom. Adding to his irritation, he learned that Hosea Williams had suggested adding Charles Cabbage of the Invaders to SCLC's staff, even though Cabbage was not committed to nonviolence. "Hosea," King fumed, "no one should be on our payroll that accepts violence as a means of social change. The only way to have a world at peace is through nonviolence" (Garrow 1988: 622).

The intensity with which King rebuked Williams suggested that he was still ill at ease but, after lunch with Abernathy, he strolled along the motel's balcony and downstairs to his brother's room. Jointly, Martin and A.D. phoned their mother and talked for about an hour. This improved King's mood but, as time passed without news, he became agitated. It was after 5.00 p.m. when Young and the legal team eventually returned. In mock anger, King belabored his assistant with a pillow for his failure to call. This kind of fraternity play-fighting was common in King's inner circle and a full-scale pillow fight ensued before Young could properly report that the judge would allow a limited, heavily supervised march on Monday.

Relieved, King reminded his friends that they were scheduled to go to Reverend Kyles's house for dinner: soul food, cooked just the way King liked it. They had best start getting ready, he said, and he and Abernathy returned to Room 306 upstairs. The time-consuming process of taking a shave using his "Magic Shave" depilatory powder ensured that King was not ready an hour later when Kyles knocked at his door. Invited in, Kyles found Martin struggling vainly to button up his shirt collar. They bantered about weight, while Martin found a larger shirt and looked for his tie. He wanted to be sure that Mrs. Kyles would give him some real soul food, and not some awful, cold ham salad, like he had once had at another preacher's house.

Down in the courtyard, the white Cadillac that King was allowed to borrow from a Memphis funeral director whenever he was in town was waiting, as were Young, Bevel, Jackson, Williams, and others. Leaving Abernathy to splash on his cologne, King and Kyles emerged onto the balcony and called to their friends below. The driver Solomon Jones suggested that King bring a coat, as it was turning chilly. "Solomon, you really know how to take good care of me," King replied, turning to ask Abernathy to grab his coat. Kyles had headed for the stairwell, when the sound of what some took to be a firecracker or a car backfiring rang out across the courtyard. As Kyles turned, he saw Martin lying on the balcony floor, and Abernathy could see his fallen friend through the doorway. They both knew that the sound was a gunshot.

Abernathy took Martin in his arms and saw the three-inch gaping wound that the high-velocity rifle had made through the right side of the jaw and neck. The blood was gushing and King had little ability to move as the bullet had severed both the jugular artery and the spinal cord before lodging in his shoulder. As he patted Martin's left cheek, Abernathy tried desperately to get his friend's attention: "Martin, Martin, this is Ralph," he called, "Do you hear me? This is Ralph." For an instant, it seemed as if King was trying vainly to speak, but the shattered jaw, nerve trauma, and spewing blood had stilled his voice forever. Others converged. They tried to staunch the bleeding with a towel, tried to find a pulse, tried to phone for help, tried to keep the man they loved warm and comfortable, tried to point out to arriving police the direction from which they thought the shot had come, and tried not to accept the horror they knew was fact.

The Memphis police had a surveillance unit watching the Lorraine from Fire Station No. 2, half a block away. They, along with other officers and firemen, converged rapidly on the motel, moving away from South Main Street itself from where the shot was fired. An ambulance arrived and raced King, with Abernathy in attendance, to St. Joseph's Hospital. In its emergency room, a trauma team tried to spark or sustain a flicker of life, although a neurosurgeon quickly established that King had already suffered irreparable brain damage. At 7.05 p.m., on April 4, 1968, doctors pronounced Martin Luther King, Jr. dead. His parents heard the news on the radio and sat silently weeping. By phone, Coretta King was informed that her husband had been shot. With Atlanta's Mayor Ivan Allen, she had already raced to the airport when word came that Martin was dead. In shock, she returned home to be with her four children.

Who Killed Martin Luther King?

In his eulogy on April 9, Morehouse College President Benjamin Mays declared bluntly "the American people are in part responsible for Martin Luther King, Jr.'s death. The assassin heard enough condemnation of King and of Negroes to feel that he had public support. He knew millions hated King" (Lewis 1978: 392). Today, with King venerated as a national hero, it is necessary to recall that around the United States in 1968, many ordinary whites cheered at the news of his murder. Known white supremacists like J.B. Stoner of the National States Rights Party were, of course, jubilant. Stoner was giving a speech in Meridian, Mississippi, when word came through. "I told the people that 'Martin Lucifer Coon is a good nigger now'," he gloated in an interview in the mid-1970s (Raines 1983: 323).

Understandably, as news of the murder spread through the country's black communities, it excited not just sadness, but rage. Campaigning for the Democratic presidential nomination, Bobby Kennedy told a stunned crowd and appealed especially to African Americans not "to be filled with hatred and mistrust," although as someone who had lost a brother to an assassin, he knew that feeling in his own heart. While the crowd responded to Kennedy's eloquence, the next day a coldly incandescent Stokely Carmichael reminded reporters that as Attorney General, Kennedy had responded to black murders with indifference lest he lose votes. "Bobby Kennedy pulled that trigger just as everyone else," he declared. The next day he amplified the charge. When white America "killed Dr. King last night," he said, "she killed the one man of our race that this country's older generations, the militants and the revolutionaries and the masses of black people would still listen to." He then advised Howard University students to stay off the streets unless they were armed and interviewed on Radio Havana declared that King's death necessitated revolution. Predictably, this added to the media hysteria, and prompted some to call for Carmichael's arrest and others to urge the press to give him less coverage (Joseph 2014: 257-60). Disturbances shook well over a hundred cities, with Washington, DC, where Carmichael was speaking, being particularly badly affected. When Under-Secretary of Labor James J. Reynolds flew out with instructions from the President to secure a quick settlement of the Memphis strike, he could see buildings ablaze barely blocks from the White House. It looked like a war zone. Between April 4 and 9, thirty-nine people were killed in clashes nationwide, eleven in the capital itself, a bitter by-product of the murder of the nation's most famous advocate of nonviolence.

Trying to unite the nation, President Johnson proclaimed Sunday April 7 a national day of mourning. By then, the FBI had already traced the murder weapon to a Birmingham gun shop and had a description of the man who bought it. More than 3,500 agents were on the case, and the driver of a white Mustang, seen leaving South Main shortly after the murder, was already their prime suspect. A six-minute drive would have carried him across the Arkansas state line to the West; a fifteen-minute one would have taken him into Mississippi.

The list of groups with the desire to do King harm in 1968, and the means to inflict it, was long. Official reaction to his opposition to government policy in Vietnam has prompted speculation about the role of the CIA, or angry super-patriots in the military. The entrenched antipathy of the FBI is well documented. Among King's aides, Andrew Young has always believed that administration fears over the PPC were grave enough to prompt the consideration, at least, of extreme measures. Given the racism that characterized its police department in 1968, it would not be surprising if some Memphis officers were less than wholehearted in their efforts to protect King. But at the same time, no sane police chief or mayor would want his city to be the site of King's murder. When news of the assassination reached Mayor Loeb, observers reported that his face crumpled like a bombed building. Within days, he was forced to recognize the AFSCME union and to settle the strike.

King's increasing support for African American unionization not only antagonized business interests, especially in the South with its strong anti-union tradition, but also ensnared him in American labor's murky turf wars within which criminal syndicates were involved in both union-busting and labor-racketeering. Like John F. Kennedy's assassination, King's offers ample scope for conspiracy theories. But while the Mob, the Memphis Police Department, the FBI, and the CIA may have had the greater means, they did not exceed in terms of motivation King's most obvious enemy, the white supremacists. According to those who knew him previously in prison, or those who spoke to his brothers, James Earl Ray, the man eventually arrested at London's Heathrow

Airport on June 8, while trying to catch a flight to Brussels using a Canadian passport under the alias Raymon George Sneyd, hated blacks.

Ballistics tests on the .30-06 bullet that killed King cannot prove conclusively that it came from the rifle found near the scene; but neither can they rule it out. What can be established is that Ray bought the rifle and a telescopic sight under another alias in Birmingham and that, after a stay in King's hometown of Atlanta, he drove a white Mustang to Memphis and checked into a rooming house where he chose a room with a view of the Lorraine and spent a noticeable amount of time in the bathroom, which offered a good view of King's room. Shortly after arriving, Ray also purchased a pair of binoculars of the same magnification as his telescopic sight. His prints were found on the rifle, the sight, the binoculars, a newspaper, a bottle of aftershave, and a beer can, all found together in a bundled blanket outside a closed store on South Main. Within moments of the shooting, Ray was in the Mustang and headed back to Atlanta, where he dumped the car and began his flight out of the country. When police searched his rented Atlanta rooms, they found a map with King's home, church, and the SCLC's offices circled in pencil (Posner 1998: 326, 332).

This circumstantial evidence scarcely suggests innocence, but it does not prove that Ray acted alone. In the decades after his conviction, Ray himself insisted that he acted as a drug and gun smuggler under the instructions of a mysterious man known to him only as Raoul. While some have seen "Raoul" as the lynchpin in a high-level, government conspiracy that used Ray as a "fall guy," a less grand grouping of racists may equally have used him. According to his son, a Gainesville, Florida man, Henry Clay Wilson, in collusion with two other men (all now deceased), may have been King's assassin. As legal counsel to the King family and chief proponent of the government conspiracy theory, William Pepper dismissed Wilson's belatedly publicized confession but backed the contradictory claims of Loyd Jowers that King was a victim of a professional "hit," which culminated in a 1999 civil suit. There are holes in Ray's and Jowers' changing accounts, but Ray's limited education and incompetence as a career criminal seem at odds with the profile of a competent assassin, able to plan and execute the deed, escape the scene, and travel to Canada,

Britain, and Portugal using forged passports (Sides 2010). Despite a 2000 Justice Department report that rejected Jowers' conspiracy claims as unreliable, one can conclude, as the Memphis jury did in 1999, that King was the victim of an, as-yet-unexposed, plot. Others, besides Ray, are stained by King's blood.

The PPC Goes Ahead

By the time Ray was apprehended on June 8, the United States was reeling from Bobby Kennedy's assassination by Sirhan Sirhan on June 5, and the PPC that SCLC had launched in Washington in pursuit of King's dream of justice was headed for disaster. In the weeks after King's murder, African Americans had muted their criticisms of the PPC and contributions to SCLC had provided a budget in excess of $1 million. After two days of lobbying in Washington, Abernathy led a rally in Memphis to launch the PPC on May 2. The first contingents of protesters were expected to arrive in the capital by May 11 for a Mother's Day march of welfare recipients, led by Coretta King.

In sharp contrast to the liaison between government and the civil rights leadership that had largely nudged the 1963 March on Washington into position behind the 1963 Kennedy bill, PPC leaders had little contact with liberal Senators and Congressmen. In Congress, reactionary lawmakers, warning of subversion and urging a clampdown, dominated the days prior to the arrival of the poor. Criminally inclined black militants had already infiltrated the PPC, warned Senator John McClellan of Arkansas inaccurately on May 7, and from the planned shantytown on the Mall they would launch waves of looting, rioting, and lawlessness (McKnight 1998: 88).

The violence that had rocked Washington and other cities immediately after King's assassination was a more potent memory in the minds of the nation's senior politicians than any grief-sparked sympathy for the fallen SCLC leader's dream of a more equal and just society. Senator McClellan had set the tone by earlier declaring that "willful civil disobedience" leads inevitably to wanton law-breaking and Congress passed his Omnibus Crime Control Act in the wake of King's death (Jackson 2007: 334). Other segregationist Senators echoed McClellan's implicit charge. Robert Byrd of West Virginia pronounced that: "one cannot preach nonviolence and at the same time, advocate defiance of the law. ... For to defy the law is to invite violence, especially in a tense atmosphere." Strom Thurmond of South Carolina joined the chorus to say in essence that King had it coming (Chappell 2014: 18-19).

When aides proposed to President Johnson that he address Congress on the domestic crisis and call for increased social welfare expenditures, the tired Texan, a lame duck by his own admission, dismissed the move as futile. With an outraged "silent majority" fueling both George Wallace's maverick campaign and the political resurgence of Republican Richard Nixon, politicians with an eye on the November elections favored actions that served to placate their constituents' anger at inflation, a pending 10 percent tax hike, crime, and the interminable war in Vietnam. The Civil Rights Act of 1968, presented as a tribute to King, did extend federal protection to civil rights workers and outlaw blatant housing discrimination, but it also made the crossing of state lines with a view to fomenting unrest a federal offense and allocated fresh appropriations for riot control. The *Pittsburgh Courier* pointed out that no one had predicted the measure's passage until King's assassination and the rioting in 110 cities that followed (Chappell 2014: 24). Like other laws passed as a result of King's life's work, the 1968 Act needed judicial interpretation and reinforcement before it effectively tackled housing discrimination. Just as the employment provisions of the 1964 Act and the franchise protections of the Voting Rights Act can be seen as best serving the black middle class, ensuring its growth in the professions and the election of more African Americans to high office, so the housing provisions have protected those with money to spend and a decent credit rating. The 2008 collapse of the subprime mortgage market brought ruin disproportionately to the African American poor who had been duped into buying these products.

As Congress embodied the myth of the "outside agitator" into law, and prominent figures applauded Mayor Daley of Chicago's recent call for local police to shoot rioters, the political tide was running against King's hopes of a radical program to redistribute power and resources to the poor. Even those White House aides who sympathized with the PPC, like Joseph Califano, knew that in practice their goal was to soothe with words since there was little political scope for real concessions. Others, like Roger Wilkins of the CRS, could help to ensure that the PPC bus caravans arrived without mishap, but could do little to advance the purpose of their journey (McKnight 1998: 92, 100-106).

A Mismanaged Campaign

Getting its army of the poor to Washington was only the first phase of SCLC's ambitious project, although it had consumed many of the planning meetings held while King was alive. What decisively destroyed the project, however, was not King's absence, but the enormity of sustaining the Washington encampment for six increasingly desperate weeks. Attorney-General Ramsey Clark managed to block demands for the PPC to be banned, or for troops to be pre-positioned around key federal buildings. When SCLC applied for a campsite permit in West Potomac Park between the Reflecting Pool and Independence Avenue, from the Lincoln Memorial to 17th Street NW, Clark ensured that the National Park Service approved it. Like Chief Pritchett in Albany, Georgia, he realized that the gravest error would be overreaction.

After the assassination, grieving SCLC leaders regarded Clark's sympathetic response as genuinely helpful, even though it postponed the moment of confrontation that past campaigns had shown to be crucial in determining success or failure. On Monday May 13, with extensive media coverage, Abernathy officially opened "Resurrection City" by driving in the first nail for the A-frame wooden homes to be built in what he averred would be a model community of love and brotherhood. Since it symbolized the poverty that needed to be eliminated, however, Resurrection City could not be a utopia. Other errors followed. If the city's radical political significance was to be conveyed effectively, it needed astute press management. Instead, the press corps was free to keep the community under round-the-clock surveillance and young camp marshals, often one-time gang members from Chicago or Memphis, were permitted to harass white reporters without regard for the negative media fall-out. James Orange recalled that Washington's "wild side" also came into the site "starting trouble" (Jackson 2007: 354). After the first week, press coverage of the

PPC turned hostile, and Abernathy and other SCLC officials, such as Bernard LaFayette, had proved that they lacked King's public relations skills.

The schedule for the campaign had called for small-scale demonstrations building up to a mass rally on May 30 – Solidarity Day. Like the 1963 March on Washington, this was planned to be a huge interracial gathering, with extensive middle-class involvement, to promote the call for jobs and income. Unfortunately, Abernathy had become so fixated on the idea of his own great day on the Mall that, as progress at the site slowed, he first announced that Solidarity Day was postponed and then scaled down demonstrations in an attempt to avoid trouble before the mass rally itself. The campaign lost momentum and there was too much time for people to focus on the mundane monotony of camp life. Compounding this mismanagement, the rains came on May 23 and continued for eleven out of the next fourteen days. Waterlogged conditions added greatly to the already overwhelming burden of running the tent city and seriously lowered morale. Whereas in other campaigns, King and his aides had refined their targets to generate confrontations and crises, the PPC remained literally bogged down.

To ensure that Solidarity Day was worthy of comparison with King's "I Have a Dream" moment, Abernathy appointed Bayard Rustin, the logistical mastermind behind the 1963 march, to coordinate preparations. It was Rustin who insisted that Solidarity Day be postponed until June 19. But more positively, he tried to identify specific legislative goals for a campaign that currently demanded jobs, incomes, land, access to capital, and the empowerment of people within the government programs that affected them. To the anger of others in the PPC, on June 5 Rustin unilaterally issued a statement that effectively scaled down the campaign's goals to the restoration of budget cutbacks in welfare, education, and employment imposed since 1967; a demonstrable commitment to full employment; the extension of collective bargaining rights to agricultural workers; and the passage of pending legislation on housing and urban development. This was a liberal reform agenda that no longer resonated with those attracted by King's increasingly radical agenda. Denounced by his PPC colleagues, Rustin resigned on June 7. His departure increased the national media's hostile presentation of Resurrection City, a trend that SCLC tried to mollify on June 13 by approving a somewhat larger, though far from revolutionary, list of demands – many of them administrative actions to improve the delivery of existing food, jobs, health, education, welfare, and work programs – as the goals of the PPC (McKnight 1998: 125-28).

Solidarity Day passed without serious incident on June 19. Underlining the fateful implications of King's choice of Abernathy as his successor, the speech that came closest to King's in power was delivered by Jesse Jackson (Chase 1998). It could not equal King's cadences, but Jackson's reminder that Lincoln had freed African American slaves "into capitalism without capital" and that they now lived "in a land of surplus food with 10 million starving citizens" and "in a land in which some men swim in wealth while others drown in tears from broken promises, destroyed dreams and blasted hopes" captured the slain leader's spirit for the 50,000 crowd. When Jackson declared, "America can afford a job or an income for all men if she has the will to put healing programs over killing programs," he channeled King's spirit. Others might argue that the most potent speech was by King's widow Coretta who reminded Americans that theirs was a violent society in which violence took many forms. "I remind you," she declared:

> that starving a child is violence; suppressing a culture is violence; neglecting schoolchildren is violence; punishing a mother and her child is violence; discrimination against a working man is violence; ghetto housing is violence; ignoring medical needs is violence; contempt for equality is violence; even a lack of will power to help humanity is a sick and sinister form of violence.

Less than two months after the funeral, King's widow explained why Martin's dream risked lapsing into nightmare.

By Solidarity Day, Resurrection City's population was already falling. Most of those who remained were ghetto youths, who considered police-baiting a recreational activity. They added to official apprehension at Abernathy's announcement of a fresh round of protests. Initially, efforts to expose the inequity of allowing bigoted local authorities to deny federal food surpluses to the hungry, while paying wealthy landowners, like Senator James Eastland of Mississippi, $13,000 a month *not* to grow food, generated positive press comments. But these quickly disappeared after violent clashes outside the Supreme Court Building involving Hispanic and Native American demonstrators protesting judicial denial of communal land and fishing rights (McKnight 1998: 130-31).

Too late, SCLC adopted a direct action imperative that Jim Bevel summed up as getting "Ralph's ass in jail." There were some chaotic clashes with police on June 21, but no real strategy emerged and Abernathy removed himself to the safety of a private Washington residence after death threats circulated. The permit for Resurrection City was set to expire on the evening of June 23, and the escalating problems of maintaining order and basic amenities encouraged SCLC to abandon the site. Beginning at 10.00 a.m. on June 24, up to 2,000 police oversaw the dismantling of Resurrection City, which took roughly ninety minutes. It was a dispiriting occasion and, despite Abernathy's arrest during one last protest at the capitol, it excited little positive media interest (McKnight 1998: 132, 137-38).

Assessing King's Later Career

The bleak, political landscape for liberal and progressive forces by the end of 1968 has helped to sustain the illusion that the Civil Rights Movement's rise and fall was largely determined by the life and death of Martin Luther King, Jr. In support of this claim, there is the fact that no other figure could fill the void after King's assassination. The reality, however, was that King himself could not meet the unrealistic and contradictory expectations of race leadership by 1968. In terms of the Southern freedom struggle, signs of organizational decay were evident in the wake of the Mississippi Freedom Summer of 1964, and the increasing ineffectiveness of SNCC in the field by the end of 1965 was a portent of things to come. For African Americans outside the South, the growing sense of insurgency found expression in ongoing local struggles and uprisings. King strove to address their grievances, but Malcolm X best captured their mood.

The Martin Luther King murdered in Memphis was in many respects a more heroic figure than the one who stood before the applauding thousands at the Lincoln Memorial in 1963. To the dismay and fury of several colleagues, he had come increasingly to believe that he must act in accordance with his beliefs, rather than conduct himself with a wary eye for the political main chance. It was not an easy path, and King was both hesitant and fallible. He hesitated more than figures like Stokely Carmichael before championing opposition to the Vietnam War in 1966 and he was still uncertain what tactics to employ during the PPC. Despite SCLC efforts to get out the vote, he did not fully exploit the opportunities of the Voting Rights Act of 1965 by embracing the different demands of long-term political organizing that could win office for black candidates across the South. He did not think strategically enough about the implications of his Chicago campaign, which shifted from organizing to mobilizing imperatives, was slow to find its target, expected too much white support, and was too loosely related to immediate legislative goals, when compared to earlier successes.

As King came to see how entwined were the failings of America's domestic and foreign policies, he found it hard to move from analytical exposition to sustained mass protest. At a time when Vietnamese Buddhist monks burned themselves alive in protest, King, acclaimed as Gandhi's heir, did not announce a penitential fast or other symbolic protest. Finally, having decided to risk everything on a Washington showdown, he allowed himself to be deflected into the Memphis morass. Thomas Jackson has offered a valuable summary of King's significance as part of a continuing struggle that challenged economic inequalities "as much as it pursued civic equality and political citizenship." He celebrates King as a proponent of democratic socialist alternatives and as a critic of Lyndon Johnson's Cold War liberalism, which cherished stability more than justice and ultimately aligned government with the powerful rather than the truly disadvantaged. Jackson also acknowledges the key contribution of new scholarship in highlighting that "integration and black power, northern and southern movements, civil rights and human rights were never so much neat binaries defining phases of historical development than they were intertwined aspects of ongoing struggle" (Jackson 2007: 363-64).

King recognized the enormity of the structures of oppression, and he saw the bleak cruelty of poverty and powerlessness in ghetto tenements and rural backwaters. At the end of his life, he was a haunted man, driven by the imperatives of the Gospel that was his rock. During a supposed holiday in Acapulco, Abernathy had found a deeply desolate King, reciting the words of the old hymn "Rock of Ages" as he stared out at a rock being battered by the waves. To others, King confided how he longed to be simply a pastor, and in his sermons at Ebenezer he seemed sometimes a tormented soul. When that small church filled for King's funeral on April 9, 1968, it was wisely decided that only King's voice could meet the challenge of delivering his eulogy. The mourners listened to a tape of King's sermon "The Drum Major Instinct."

The sermon begins by warning how the human yearning for recognition has been exploited by advertisers and perverted into a desire to feel superior; a desire, King explains, that finds its sickest expression in racism and militarism. It can even cause a man who feels he is a nobody to take up a gun and kill. But after explaining how Christ transformed this need for recognition into a positive force, when He told His disciples that if they wished to be first in His kingdom, they must be servants of all, King reflects on how he would like to be remembered. A somber church full of celebrities listened to King's unheeded request for a simple funeral and a short eulogy with no reference to his Nobel Peace Prize or other awards. Many wept openly as King's voice continued:

> I'd like somebody to mention that day that Martin Luther King, Jr., tried to give his life serving others. (*Yes*)
> I'd like for somebody to say that day that Martin Luther King, Jr., tried to love somebody.
> I want you to say that day that I tried to be right on the war question. (*Amen*)
> I want you to be able to say that day that I did try to feed the hungry. (*Yes*)
> And I want you to be able to say that day that I did try in my life to clothe those who were naked. (*Yes*)
> I want you to say on that day that I did try in my life to visit those who were in prison. (*Lord*)
> I want you to say that I tried to love and serve humanity. (*Yes*)
> Yes, if you want to say that I was a drum major, say that I was a drum major for justice. (*Amen*) Say that I was a drum

major for peace. (*Yes*) I was a drum major for righteousness. And all of the other shallow things will not matter. (*Yes*) I won't have any money to leave behind. I won't have the fine and luxurious things of life to leave behind. But I just want to leave a committed life behind. (*Amen*) And that's all I want to say.

By this standard, many of us will be rightly forgotten, but he will be remembered.

11 Epilogue

In Memoriam – Remembering King

The shock of King's murder reverberated around the world. In London *The Times* spoke of a great loss for the world. Pope Paul VI expressed his "profound sadness." The *Daily Graphic* in Ghana's capital, Accra, which King had visited nearly a decade earlier, was particularly outraged. The American "affluent society," it declared, was actually "a fraudulent society – a human jungle wherein the black man is the target for destruction, even extermination." Noting that King had been scheduled to visit their war-torn country on April 15, Nigerian officials condemned "this sad and inhuman killing," and declared that, like Gandhi's murder, King's would "have meaning only if US Negroes achieve equality and human dignity in the shortest possible time and without resorting to a bloody struggle." In a rare tribute to a foreign citizen, the Indian Parliament observed a minute's silence.

The Reverend Trevor Huddleston, at that time expelled by the apartheid regime in South Africa, declared that King's death was a tragedy unmatched since Gandhi's assassination. In South Africa itself, the Afrikaans newspaper *Die Vaderland* remarked that King was a victim of "evil racial passions" that he had helped to excite but ultimately could not control, while the Anglophonic *Johannesburg World* condemned the "senseless killing" and declared: "One trembles for the future of the race relations of the United States." In Rhodesia (what is now Zimbabwe), another bastion of white rule in Africa in 1968, the *Salisbury Times* limited its coverage of King's murder, preferring to dwell on the racial disturbances that followed, complete with a photograph of looters in a supermarket, captioned "SELF-SERVICE under ironic sign."

Across Western Europe, King's death was linked to the 1963 assassination of John F. Kennedy and seen as indicative of America's general instability. In West Germany, the federal Parliament in Bonn held a silent tribute and a thousand mourners marched behind Berlin's Mayor Klaus Schutz to a ceremony in John F. Kennedy Square. Germans regarded King's death at a time when there were fresh peace initiatives over Vietnam as deeply suspicious, and fretted that "the evil deed" might have "incalculable consequences." The *Neue Zurcher Zeitung* envisaged a spiral of increasingly radical protest and violent repression, and warned: "even Bismarck realized that one does not sit comfortably on bayonets in the long run." Denmark's *Berlingske Tidende* quoted the Danish Prime Minister Hilmar Baunsgaard as saying that the assassination was especially tragic because it might result in African Americans abandoning their nonviolent stance that had won them respect everywhere in the world and in the Scandinavian countries in particular. King's "I Have a Dream" speech was printed in Danish on the paper's front page. Fears of an incipient race war in the United States were by no means confined to Denmark. Israeli newspapers stressed that every indication suggested that the assassin was a white man and the Lebanese press warned of a "Negro revolt."

African American militants were quick to announce that the revolt had begun and that it would follow H. Rap Brown's axiom that "violence is as American as cherry pie." Washington-based black activist Julius Hobson was quoted by the *New York Times* as saying that King's "concept of non-violence died with him. It was a foreign ideology – as foreign to this violent country as speaking Russian." Inside the communist bloc, King was extensively celebrated as a martyr. The Soviet newspaper *Isvestia* discussed the assassination under the headline "United States is a Nation of Violence and Racism." In East Germany, the government newspaper *Neues Deutschland* declared that the White House lay behind King's murder, largely because he had "highlighted the indissoluble link between Washington's external politics of aggression and its internal terror." Just as the murder of Nobel Laureate Carl von Ossietzky by German fascists had once rallied international opposition, the paper claimed, so King's assassination would prompt "hundreds of thousands to join the international front against the barbaric imperialism of the US and its allies." While openly propagandistic, this sentiment did foresee that King's reputation would grow in the 1970s as increasing numbers of Americans ceased to support the Vietnam War.

At the same time, the rhetoric of militant groups like the Black Panthers in the Nixon era reinforced King's importance as their supposed antithesis (his nonviolence being misunderstood as simply the disavowal of armed struggle tactics). The appeal of his 1963 "I Have a Dream" speech grew with repetition so that, by the time fellow Georgian Jimmy Carter entered the White House in 1977 and appointed King's close aide, Andrew Young, as his ambassador to the UN, there was a cultivated illusion that King's brand of peaceful racial reform had been embraced by the nation. This foreshadowed what historian Glenn Eskew has termed the "Won Cause" version of the Movement. Whereas once the white South cultivated the myth of the "Lost Cause" to ennoble their Civil War memories, with largely uncritical support from the mainstream media, it has now developed the myth of the "Won Cause" with King at its heroic center in a narrative that stresses the progress made. King can be sanctified in this account because its implicit message is that the past is past. David Vann, former Birmingham mayor and backer of that city's Civil Rights Institute, commemorating the 1963 campaign in particular, revealed perhaps more than he intended in 1992 when he commented that: "I've always said that the best way to put bad images to rest is to declare them history and put them in a museum" (Dwyer and Alderman 2008: 28-31, 77).

In the 1970s, African Americans confronted bad realities rather than just bad images, and in numerous local struggles, they fought to continue the battle rather than declare a false victory. While there remained a tension between the pragmatism of the increasing number of black elected officials and lobbyists who stressed the need to cultivate interracial coalitions and the vehemence of militants who prioritized African American sentiments even if they alienated whites, both groups attempted to present themselves as Martin's heirs. King's death was seen to have left a "leadership void" that had to be filled collectively and institutionally in order to avoid the perils of over-reliance on a single charismatic leader. As actor-activist Ossie Davis told the National

Black Political Convention (NBPC) in 1972: "It's not the rap, it's the map. It's not the man, it's the plan." Striving to develop an agenda that would unify African Americans, the Convention organizers gave both Coretta King and Betty Shabazz (Malcolm X's widow) prominent places on the podium. But unity was not easily achieved. Gains were more the product of local activism than national campaigning as the 1960s legislative achievements slowly and partially were translated into everyday life through boycotts and legal challenges to those who did not adapt to desegregation and black re-enfranchisement. Nevertheless, in 1974, as a souring economy began to threaten the economic hopes of the poor once more, the NBPC's chair Mayor Richard Hatcher of Gary declared that since King's death, "black America has not had a spokesman to ... articulate its dreams" (Chappell 2014: 37-38, 44-45, 56).

The main talking point in relation to King himself during the 1970s was the assassination which, after revelations in mid-decade about the clandestine operations of the FBI's COINTELPRO project, seemed plausibly to have been a conspiracy that might, indeed, reach to the heart of government. The 1974 murder of King's mother, killed by a deranged, black gunman while playing the organ in Ebenezer church, certainly added to the public fascination. COINTELPRO had involved illegal surveillance, the use of *agents provocateurs* and other infiltrators to destabilize radical groups like the Black Panthers, and countless other illegal acts. These revelations coming on top of President Nixon's resignation over the Watergate scandal, made many people wary of the federal government's capacity for illegal action. While exposure of official repression fueled radical outrage, many mainstream Americans in the Carter years began to see the 1960s as a time when things went wrong; a sentiment that the current economic malaise and faltering détente with the USSR deepened. In this cultural landscape, King's memory became a contested commodity deployed in contradictory ways.

Some conservative white preachers, like Jerry Falwell, who had denounced King as a communist tool in 1965, perceived the political advantage of a different approach. Falwell founded the Moral Majority in 1979 and he began to see that its crusade against abortion, gay rights, the Equal Rights Amendment, and other perceived threats to traditional "family values" could co-opt King's arguments in favor of protest against unjust laws. Speaking in 1981, he defended the anti-abortion campaign by saying: "I feel that what King was doing is exactly what we are doing." Cal Thomas, Moral Majority's PR director, commended King's willingness to go to jail for what he believed. It was an example that Falwell's crusaders should follow (Baldwin and Burrow 2013: 11-12).

At the same time, communities with strong associations with the slain civil rights legend tried to perpetuate his memory by renaming or founding new institutions. The new King Center in Atlanta sponsored the first commemoration of King's birthday in 1969, and the King Site of Entombment was opened in 1976. King's church in Montgomery became Dexter Avenue King Memorial Baptist Church and Andrew Young opened the Martin Luther King International Memorial Chapel at Morehouse College in 1978; the latter's international dimensions resonating with not just King's life but Young's then role as UN Ambassador. The US Postal Service honored King with a stamp in 1979 and the same year saw a formal memorial to King unveiled outside Selma's Brown Chapel, the protest movement's headquarters in 1965. By 1980, the main sites associated with King in Atlanta, including his parents' home and Ebenezer church, were designated the Martin Luther King Jr., Historical Site, managed by the National Parks Service.

Naming or renaming a street in honor of King became a common practice, especially in the South. The controversy surrounding such decisions illustrates the contested nature of King's memory. In January 1981, for instance, the Chattanooga City Commission received a petition for the renaming of Ninth Street. At the time race relations in the Tennessee city were still tense following the acquittal of two out of three defendants in a Ku Klux Klan-related shooting that not coincidentally had occurred on Ninth Street. While the street ran through "Soulville," the African American business district, it extended beyond it to the west. A white real estate developer T.A. Lupton who owned property in the western portion protested that the renaming would adversely affect his plans to build and rent commercial offices. His counter-proposal was essentially a segregated one: the renaming should apply to East Ninth Street alone and West

Ninth should retain its name. This would protect his redevelopment plans and the job opportunities they would provide would be of more tangible benefit to the neighborhood's black residents than the symbolic re-naming would be. George Key of the local NAACP retorted that Lupton symbolized why downtown Chattanooga was struggling: "There's lots of people, both tourists and business persons," he stated, "who don't want to come to an area where there are racist attitudes and racial problems." Black Congressman Parren Mitchell, a former chair of the Black Congressional Caucus weighed in by declaring that renaming the whole street would underline the fact that King's historic and international significance was not just for African Americans.

The City Commission vacillated. It first refused the renaming request, then tried a compromise of creating a plaza nearby in King's name, but after community protests that involved pasting "Dr ML King Jr. Blvd." on street signs, it reversed itself and agreed that the whole of Ninth Street would be renamed for King. Property developer Lupton got around this outcome by creating a private drive leading to his complex, which he perhaps mischievously named Union Square. Largely outside of the South, there was a trend to designate a local high school in King's honor and here too, controversy has erupted when white parents have complained that the designation "blackens" the school's reputation by sparking the assumption that the school is a "black majority" one. While the African American freedom struggle was waged during King's life-time in communities across the country, its commemoration is more marked by museums and monuments in the South. Its Northern battles are less celebrated. Sometimes, the dedication of monuments has affirmed African American political leverage. Kelly Ingram Park, where the children of Birmingham confronted Bull Connor's water cannon and attack dogs, was re-dedicated as "A Place of Revolution and Reconciliation" in 1992 by Richard Arrington, the city's first African American mayor (Dwyer and Alderman 2008: 3-10, 18).

Whereas outside of the South, naming streets in King's memory is common only in metropolitan areas, King Street has become a feature of the Southern small town. Overall, America's King streets are typically neighborhood roads, a mile or so long, and often in neighborhoods that are more African American and poorer than the citywide averages. Too often such areas in metropolitan areas also have a reputation for crime. African American comedian Chris Rock has remarked: "If a friend calls you … and says they're lost on Martin Luther King Boulevard and they want to know what they should do, the best response is, 'Run'." Journalist Jonathan Tilove writes that a "Martin Luther King street" has become "a generic marker of black space and not incidentally, of ruin, as a sad signpost of danger, failure and decline. … (Dwyer and Alderman 2008: 84). If civil rights museums such as those in Birmingham or Atlanta tend to venerate the "Won Cause," life on the streets renamed in King's memory tends to underline the injustices which King was fighting right up to his death. Opponents of the creation of the National Civil Rights Museum in Memphis charged that his memory would have been better served by building a homeless shelter, a school or job training center rather than a cultural complex to serve primarily the tourist traffic (Dwyer and Alderman 2008: 54-55, 65). King's commemoration in the years after his death has thus reflected his followers' efforts to sustain his legacy and more general efforts to accommodate the changes that the movement set in motion, including efforts to resist them and minimize the concessions made to African American claims.

As King sensed at the end of his life, black political empowerment was coming too slowly and incompletely to transform social and economic realities in the South, and national trends were still less progressive. When King's widow testified in support of the Humphrey-Hawkins bill to secure full employment on the seventh anniversary of his death, she rightly said she was continuing her husband's work. She lobbied Congress again the following year warning that the low priority given to job creation threatened "the repeal of the civil rights acts of the 1960s. …" Mrs. King explained: "What good is the legal right to sit in a restaurant if one cannot afford the price of its food? And what good is the promise of fair employment when there is no employment for black Americans?" Ella Baker had made the first point about lunch counters in 1960 to remind SNCC activists of the movement's larger goals and President Kennedy had used the same argument in 1963 as he urged Birmingham businessmen in private meetings not to panic at the prospect of lunch counter desegregation (Chappell 2014: 73, 79).

Hubert Humphrey, the full employment bill's Senate sponsor, died in 1978, two days before King's birthday. The bill's co-sponsor, Congressman Augustus Hawkins, whose district included the Watts neighborhood of Los Angeles, tried to use Humphrey's death to expedite passage. "Like the late Dr. Martin Luther King," he told the *Los Angeles Sentinel*, "Hubert Humphrey had a dream. His dream was simply to make sure that every man, who is able, has a job and is able to stand on his two feet as a man. We cannot afford to let that dream die, just as we cannot afford to let Dr. King's dream die." The sole African American in the Senate, Edward Brooke also linked the two men. "Just as Dr. King was the father of the civil rights revolution," he declared, "Hubert Humphrey was its legislative father." With eviscerating amendments, the Humphrey-Hawkins Act was signed by President Carter with Coretta King standing beside him on October 13, 1978. Channeling her husband's realism she defended the measure to reporters: "We got the first step, but if you don't get the first step, you don't ever move" (Chappell 2014: 83-84).

For most of the decade after King's death, the employment opportunities provided by the 1964 Civil Rights Act had gone to better-educated African American professionals and women of all races, but not all classes. The Nixon administration in particular had witnessed the development of "affirmative action." This sparked a heated debate about racial preference as a criterion for hiring and promotion and the growing neo-conservative movement sought to place Martin Luther King on their side. King's dream in 1963 that one day his children might be judged not "by the color of their skin but by the content of their character" was seen as endorsing their insistence on "color-blindness." Appointed to the Civil Rights Commission by Ronald Reagan, Clarence Pendleton announced that its goal was to secure "a color blind society" and Assistant Attorney General William Bradford Reynolds maintained in his confirmation hearings that the Constitution was "color-blind" on every question relating to civil rights. Reagan himself summed up the conservative position in 1986. "We want what I think Martin Luther King asked for," he told the press: "We want a colorblind society" (Rodgers 2011: 129-30). What the Reagan administration definitely wanted was a smaller regulatory state. Their stated position ignored evidence that the US free labor market economy did not operate in a non-discriminatory way and that without checks to counteract existing patterns, disadvantaged groups needed legal protection. Nevertheless, as political rhetoric, "color-blindness" was highly astute since it appealed to whites who were worried that they were more vulnerable in the job market and yet worked to disarm liberal critics by branding them as the perpetuators of racism.

The commitment to full employment in the 1978 Humphrey-Hawkins Act had been so watered down that its effects were limited. When Reagan replaced Carter as President in 1981, black unemployment (14.3 percent) was more than double white unemployment (6.3 percent). By the time of the Reagan landslide in 1984, both indices had worsened to 15.9 and 6.5 percent respectively, and the core aspiration of the New Deal state that the power of government should protect the underprivileged and enhance their security, always hesitantly extended to African Americans, had been diminished. Government, as Reagan famously phrased it, was not the solution. It was part of the problem. Reagan's political career had blossomed as King's faltered. His 1966 gubernatorial victory in California had been a symbol of the backlash to the Watts uprising and the Berkeley campus protests, and foreshadowed the emergent tax revolt. The last had achieved national prominence in 1978 with the passage of the California ballot initiative, "Proposition 13" that put a 1 percent ceiling on property taxes as a means of forcing governmental cutbacks. Reagan's presidential victory in 1980 indicated that taxcuts were to be a hallmark of the increasingly conservative Republican Party that found favor among disaffected white southern voters. Reagan himself signaled his courtship of what he called "George Wallace-inclined voters" by attending the Neshoba County Fair in Mississippi in August 1980. Not normally included in GOP presidential candidate schedules, Neshoba was known to the rest of the nation as the place where the bodies of the three murdered Freedom Summer volunteers were found buried. Reagan did not mention that detail, but did declare his support for states' rights and complained: "we've distorted the balance of our government today by giving powers that were never intended in the Constitution to the federal establishment" (Crespino 2007: 1-2).

Mississippi, with its once majority black population reduced to little more than a third of the state's total by the 1980s, remained one of the country's most impoverished areas, and refugees from it struggled to find a better life elsewhere since poverty and deprivation continued to stalk African American communities nationwide. The largely forgotten "War on Poverty" that had so disappointed King by 1968 would wither further as Reagan mobilized support through racially coded attacks on "welfare queens." The embers of King's movement to achieve economic justice still burned in local battles but less brightly than the sparks of the neo-conservative tax revolt. Embittered black ghetto youths in the 1990s sometimes wondered what progress the Civil Rights Movement had achieved and scorned the expanded African American middle class who seemed its primary beneficiaries. The ghetto still identified more with Malcolm X's anger than King's supposed moderation (Dyson 2000). While some communities signaled their commitment by commemorating Malcolm (Lenox Avenue in Harlem was renamed in his honor in 1987), many more also marked King's birthday and supported the campaign to establish a national public holiday in January that would link the civil rights leader's birthday to the earlier African American tradition of celebrating the day of "Jubilee" when their slave forbears learned of their emancipation. However, this also increased the likelihood that the real-life radical King would be forgotten in favor of a less controversial, national icon. As ghetto life remained harsh, King's appeal to young and poor African Americans logically faltered whereas his memory was equally reasonably cherished by the enlarged black middle class, who wanted his achievement honored and his dream of justice pursued. King's status among whites was equally ambiguous with most publicly applauding his idealism; in part, because acknowledging King's moral example formed part of their efforts to place discrimination in the past and implicitly declare the new America less culpable and more legitimate in racial matters.

The Making Of King Day

Efforts to secure a national holiday for King began just four days after the assassination, when black Congressman John Conyers introduced a bill into the House. But the momentum behind the campaign strengthened during the Carter presidency; ironically, just as prospects for King's goal of economic justice diminished further. Carter, who had won in 1976 thanks to African American voters, faced a nomination challenge from Senator Edward Kennedy and the holiday became an issue over which each man courted the black vote (Chappell 2014: 95). Several Northern states had already adopted a paid holiday for state employees in honor of Dr. King. In 1978, the National Council of Churches urged Congress to pass national holiday legislation, and millionaire pop star Stevie Wonder became a particularly strong backer of the campaign, releasing his hit single "Happy Birthday" in 1980, to rally support. The following year, Wonder funded the holiday coalition offices in Washington, DC, to lobby Congress, and by 1982, the coalition had secured over 6 million signatures on petitions calling for a federal public holiday for presentation to House Speaker Tip O'Neill (Wiggins 1987).

Previous committee hearings on the proposed holiday had seen conservative Congressmen, notably Larry MacDonald of suburban Atlanta and John Ashbrook of rural Ohio, question whether King was worthy of such an honor. The old allegations of King's courtship of violence, and of communist influence, were aired anew. Equally telling, however, were suggestions that a King holiday would devalue the status and increase the economic cost of such holidays. Honoring the black civil rights leader would set a precedent that would inevitably lead to the proliferation of holidays, either because a case could be made for similarly honoring numerous other figures or by encouraging token holidays for different American social groups in a nation increasingly aware of its fragmentation. But praising King had become valuable to conservatives. Cannily using the "Won Cause" narrative, President Reagan issued a public statement on King's birthday in 1983. He declared: "History shows that Dr. King's approach achieved great results in a comparatively short time, which was exactly what America needed. ... What he accomplished – not just for black Americans, but for all Americans – he lifted a heavy burden from this country." Implicitly, this burden – racism – was now gone (Chappell 2014: 114).

In August 1983, the House of Representatives, which had voted down previous King holiday proposals, passed a bill to establish the third Monday in January as the Martin Luther King national holiday by the overwhelming margin of 338 to 90 votes. One factor noted by House committee members was renewed interest in the ideals of nonviolence generated by the Oscar-winning movie of that year, "Gandhi." This strengthened holiday proponents' claims that a King holiday would have universal appeal and would celebrate peaceful democratic citizenship. The battle proved more intense in the now Republican-controlled Senate. The bill's chief opponent Senator Jesse Helms of North Carolina delighted in pointing out to its Senate sponsor Edward Kennedy that Ted's own brothers, Robert and John, had ordered FBI surveillance of King because of his suspicious communist connections. But Helms was in the minority. Most of his Southern senatorial colleagues – even former Dixiecrat presidential nominee, Strom Thurmond – felt that attacking King's reputation courted electoral difficulties in Deep South states with potentially large African American voting blocs. Helms found more solid support in state delegations from Idaho, Iowa, and New Hampshire than from Alabama, Georgia, or Mississippi (Chappell 2014: 117-19).

By the time the Senate passed the bill in October 1983 by a vote of 78 to 22, support for King Day had been further boosted by a huge turnout of nearly 750,000 people to commemorate the twentieth anniversary of the 1963 March on Washington. In the White House Rose Garden, President Reagan signed the measure into law in the presence of King's widow Coretta. Asked to comment on the significance of the holiday, which would not be formally celebrated until 1986, Mrs. King expressed hope that the United States would forge "a new commitment to nonviolence." Pressed for his own view on King, particularly whether he was a communist agent, the genially right-wing Reagan alluded to the sequestered tapes and records that will not be made available until 2027, saying: "We'll have to wait and see" (Chappell 2014: 120).

Securing the King holiday has proved an ambiguous victory since it has involved a seemingly inevitable dilution of King's specifically African American and radical legacy in favor of more uncontentious national platitudes. Further legislation reinforced this tendency in 1994 when President Bill Clinton signed the King Holiday and Service Act which defined King's legacy as one of service to the community. Each King Day is marked by a presidential proclamation, initiated in 1995 when Clinton summed up King's central imperative as the question: "What are you doing for others?" The majority of proclamations have predictably cited the "I Have a Dream" speech; George W. Bush being the most consistent in this respect, referencing the speech in all eight proclamations even in the context of his 2002 call for Americans to remain united against terrorism in the wake of the 9/11 attacks. The change instigated by the 1994 Act does seem to confirm the threat that Michael Dyson detected in the cession of control of King's image to "the federal government" (Seay in Baldwin and Burrow 2013: 244-46; Dyson 2000: preface, x).

As the nation's first African American president, Barack Obama, has taken a different tack to his predecessors in his King Day proclamations (2010-14). He has referenced King's final Memphis address more often to indicate that the Promised Land lies ahead and so the struggle for justice continues. Like Clinton, he has spoken of the moral imperative to help others. In 2010 he commended specifically efforts to help the victims of the Haitian earthquake. The following year with economic issues paramount, Obama referred again to the mountaintop of justice to which King led Americans and extolled them to work for "economic security for all." Obama inevitably did refer to the 1963 March on Washington as its fiftieth anniversary loomed and the King Monument, complete with a truncated reference to his status as a "drum-major," was unveiled on the Mall, but he also recognized "the quiet heroes whose names never appear in history books," urging collective engagement in the continuing quest for justice. He echoed this reference to "the multitudes of men and women who struggled for justice and equality" the following year and continued to stress mutual obligations that formed part of the march to freedom and justice. This culminated in his speech at the 50th anniversary of the March itself where Obama declared: "The tireless teacher who gets in early and stays late and dips into her own pocket to buy supplies because she believes that every child is her charge – she's marching" (Obama 2013). While more nuanced and truthful about the movement's collective character, Obama's rhetoric nevertheless has taken King's memory away from protest and misapplied it to the daily tasks of life that make an unjust society bearable.

Just as the holiday has become much more an affirmation of America's civil religion, the insurgent Right has continued to try to co-opt King's memory, even while its cruder elements still denounce King as unworthy of respect. In 2010, Fox News pundit and right-wing activist Glenn Beck organized a mass rally in front of the Lincoln Memorial that deliberately invoked King's memory, even while it espoused a conservative agenda that attracted an overwhelmingly white audience. Beck's controversial opinions have appealed most readily to the harshest critics of the Obama administration and his vision of limited government runs contrary to King's vision of state-underwritten guarantees of equal employment, education, housing, justice, and healthcare in the context of a guaranteed minimum income. Organizing a counter-rally to Beck's, New York's flamboyant, activist preacher Al Sharpton declared: "We ain't giving them this day! This is our day!" Beck's marchers chanted "U-S-A, U-S-A" and Sharpton's shouted "M-L-K! M-L-K!" To the neutral observer, neither side was edifying (Baldwin and Burrow 2013: 21-27).

The conservative embrace of King the symbol of moral activism against the state and of color-blindness has required their spokesmen to de-emphasize his personal failings which otherwise they would foreground, but in practice conservative voices decrying those faults, especially if they involve sex, have never been silenced. The 1990s' controversy over King's plagiarism of his doctoral thesis is discussed in Chapter 12, but rumors of King's womanizing had circulated for a long time before David Garrow's 1988 award-winning biography confronted them directly. He offered a psychological interpretation that suggested that King's abiding sense of being unworthy of the exalted position into which he was cast inclined him to indulge his promiscuity as a rejection of saintly pretensions. Simultaneously, guilt over his adultery prompted him to return to the trials of leadership to expiate his sins. When King's closest SCLC associate Ralph Abernathy published his memoirs in 1989, the relationship between the venal and the virtuous in King's personality was sharply highlighted when Abernathy revealed that King's last night alive had included casual sexual encounters and a somewhat violent confrontation with one of his long-term girlfriends. Even while he remained circumspect about his own foibles, King's best friend Ralph apparently wanted to show how human the real King had been. As the first of King's paramours to kiss and tell, Georgia Davis Powers offers some confirmation of Abernathy's claims. Significantly, others have remained silent (Davis Powers 1995).

King's Successors

Revelations about King's love life have not fatally damaged his heroic standing. In the holiday's civic gatherings and in the huge number of short biographies for children, they simply do not feature. Hence, it seems unlikely that the taped materials gathered by the FBI (if ever released) will prompt the kind of serious public criticism of the civil rights leader in death that they threatened to do while he was alive. Although the sexual peccadilloes of President Bill Clinton ultimately led to his impeachment, a surprisingly large portion of the American electorate was more embarrassed than outraged by the revelations. A more pointed parallel with King's predicament, however, has been the experience of the Reverend Jesse Jackson, whose public championing of African American complaints about ballot irregularities during the 2000 presidential election was effectively ended by the suspiciously opportune revelation that he had fathered a love child with one of his senior staff. This should not eclipse Jackson's significance as one of King's successors.

Back in 1968, the young Jackson had been quick to present himself as a potential successor to Dr. King in the aftermath of the assassination. He had even told the Chicago City Council that the sweater he wore to a special memorial session for the fallen SCLC leader some time after the murder was stained with King's blood. He was one of several SCLC figures who questioned the succession of Ralph Abernathy, although he played a full role in the PPC that he had previously opposed. In 1971 Jackson developed his own organization, People United to Serve Humanity (PUSH), drawing on the base of support he had mobilized during King's 1966 Chicago campaign. Using his powerful evangelical speaking style, Jackson spent the increasingly Black Nationalist years of the early 1970s urging the broad-based economic development programs associated with Operation Breadbasket and get-out-the-vote efforts for black candidates. His stellar performance at the NBPC in Gary also enhanced his leadership claims. While other Movement veterans, like Julian Bond, John Lewis, Hosea Williams, and Andrew Young, sought elected office, and militants like Stokely Carmichael found a home of sorts in troubled African states, Jackson's public campaigning established him as a recognizable national figure in the eyes of the media, a prominence he both used and strengthened during his presidential candidacies of 1984 and 1988. The latter campaigns seemed to hark back to Dr. King's PPC by proposing a multi-ethnic "Rainbow Coalition" of the disadvantaged at a time when Reaganite social policies were reversing the welfare improvements of the 1960s.

Like King, however, Jackson had difficulty appealing to the white working-class rank-and file. When he contested the Democratic nomination with Michael Dukakis in 1988, urging a "Rainbow Coalition," he received 92 percent of black votes but only 17 percent of white votes; a warning that Obama's campaign managers took to heart in 2008. "White" remains a difficult color to fit into any rainbow. In other respects, Jackson's public career has taken a King-like path. During the Gulf War of 1991, he argued that the billions of dollars spent on hi-tech weaponry inevitably drained funds from under-resourced domestic programs, and complained that a dearth of civilian employment opportunities was making African Americans the "cannon-fodder" of the US armed forces. Blacks formed 23 percent of US military personnel, but little more than 12 percent of the total US population in 1990.

One key difference with King has been that Jackson has exhibited a fascination for the dynamism of capitalism, even while complaining about its inhumanities. On Martin Luther King's birthday in 1997, he launched the "Wall Street Project" in order to build bridges to corporate America that would carry capital to underserved markets whose labor forces were underutilized. He insisted that the project's aim "to include all and to leave none behind" was a continuation of King's fight for a job or an income for all Americans. Dr. King would be proud, he declared, "to see the lions and the lambs lying down together – multiracial, multicultural, corporate executives, labor, Democrats, Republicans, Appalachia, ghetto, barrio – under one big tent overlooking Wall Street – the capital of capital" (Dyson 2000: 98-99). Jackson embraced the very

1990s' notion of public-private partnership, and of a more compassionate capitalism. In doing so, however, his enthusiasm was more reminiscent of Booker T. Washington in 1895 than of the grimly revolutionary Martin Luther King of 1967-68. King had tried to galvanize the poor, while Jackson wooed the rich. In this respect, Louis Farrakhan's 1995 "Million Man March" in Washington with its emphasis on African American self-reliance and self-respect could also claim King as an inspiration, even while its underlying conservatism ran counter to King's radicalism.

After the 2000 scandal, Jackson's relative silence prompted Reverend Al Sharpton to mount a challenge to be the preeminent spokesman for African Americans. By engaging in a prolonged hunger strike against the imprisonment of protesters opposed to US bombing trials in Puerto Rico, Sharpton attracted media attention by his nonviolent tactics and cultivated the black-Hispanic alliance that both he and Jackson saw as vital to effective mass action against ghetto injustice. Sharpton's reputation was severely tarnished by a spectacular rape trial in which he supported the ultimately disproven claims of the alleged African American victim, Tawana Brawley; at what one point he implied that whether the assault took place was immaterial since Brawley deserved reparations for what whites had done. Along with black attorney Johnny Cochran, who successfully defended O.J. Simpson, Sharpton emerged branded as an example of someone who uses the "race-card" to polarize debate and advance his own interests. His recent clash with Glenn Beck in 2010 is read by American audiences in this light. In an earlier tussle between Jackson and Sharpton, the latter's supporters publicized claims that Jackson had received "donations" from corporations such as "Burger King" that he had previously targeted for anti-discriminatory boycotts. Both men emerged from such arguments diminished, and the arguments leveled against King that African Americans do not need one great leader but many leaders were heard anew. By 2008, however, the great leader had seemingly arrived.

Barack Obama

In 1983, the King federal holiday law passed, Jesse Jackson planned his first run for the White House, and a young Barack Obama graduated from New York's Columbia University with a Political Science degree. As the economic hardships for working-class Americans sharpened, Obama worked as a community organizer in Chicago's South Side, experiencing his "first deep immersion into the African American community." The product of a short-lived marriage between a black Kenyan father and white mother from Kansas who met as students at the University of Hawaii in 1960, Obama's eclectic heritage was compounded when his mother's career as an anthropologist and her re-marriage took him to live in Indonesia from the age of six to ten. He feels that he benefitted from the multiplicity of cultures he encountered, but his African American experience, unlike King's, was an adult one. Wrestling with complex bureaucracies on behalf of poor people convinced Obama that he needed a law degree. He entered Harvard Law School in 1988 and became the prestigious *Harvard Law Review's* first non-white president in 1990. He had already met his future wife Michele Robinson, a Chicago native and Harvard Law graduate. Obama directed Illinois's Project Vote designed to increase turnout in the 1992 elections and, having married Michele, he worked for a local civil rights law firm and lectured part-time at the University of Chicago (Miller Center 2014).

Given the frequency with which Obama is compared to King, it is worth highlighting the contrasts. King was swept into protest leadership by the bus boycott after barely a year in Montgomery. Despite returning to Chicago with electoral contacts in 1992, Obama did not seek office there until 1996. He was thirty-five years old when he became an Illinois state senator (the same age King was when he received the 1964 Nobel Peace Prize). Obama would first secure national recognition, aged forty-three, with his speech to the Democratic National Convention. Had he died, like King at the age of thirty-nine, he would have remained unknown. It is true that both men were educated to graduate school level in Boston. But King was a product of African American church culture and the presence of his father loomed large. Obama was a multicultural global citizen haunted in some ways by his absent father and his incomplete identification as an African American. King was rooted in the black community and reached out to white America. Obama had to find his place in the black community and his life story enabled him to charm what Abraham

Lincoln had called "the better angels" of the American nation (Obama 1995).

King blended the African American preaching tradition in which he was schooled with a broader American tradition so that his dream became inexorably attached to the American dream. When Obama drew applause from Democratic Party delegates by declaring that the "true genius of America" was its "faith in dreams," he was primarily invoking the American dream of social mobility, but it was easy for his interracial audience to think of King's dream, too. Obama's eloquence has sparked glib comparison with King. But the importance of oratory in Obama's political ascent should not prompt us to overstate and assume the continuities between Obama and the 1960s struggles. Obama's election defeat in the 2000 Congressional race by former Black Panther Bobby Rush demonstrated that he could not win in a majority black district if the criterion were African American authenticity as measured by engagement in those struggles. Obama's Harvard Law background and professorial style undercut his street credibility. Rush was able to portray him negatively as the protégé of local white liberals, and thus untrustworthy to black voters. Since King's anti-war stance and overtly radical demands for jobs and a guaranteed income after 1965 had been largely forgotten, his remembered nonviolence and integrationist goals still failed to resonate with ghetto residents. In contrast, the media still portrayed the Panthers as King's armed and separatist antithesis. Chicago's First District had elected Rush, the ex-Panther as a symbol of that still active, Black Power impulse in 1992, and voters were not convinced that they should swap him for Obama, whose style contained little of Malcolm X's anger. After the success of Obama's 2004 convention speech and his US Senate victory, his position as a charismatic speaker in the King mold ironically became a political asset in mobilizing a national interracial vote rather than just a local black one; an asset rooted in the general public ignorance of how radical King had actually been in comparison to Obama.

To be fair, despite the parallels drawn by others due to his charismatic oratory, Obama has never pretended that he is Martin reincarnated. When he spoke out against the Iraq War in 2002, he made it clear that he was no pacifist. He told an anti-war rally in Chicago bluntly "I do not oppose all wars." He then added to cheers "What I am opposed to is a dumb war." King felt the Vietnam War was a dumb war, but he opposed war as an instrument of policy and decried US militarism. While Obama's early opposition to the Iraq War gave him an advantage over Hillary Clinton in the 2008 primaries, it was not clear that he could appeal to African Americans as their standard bearer as Jesse Jackson had done and simultaneously appeal to the wider electorate in order to overtake Hillary, the initial front-runner. At the start she enjoyed support from civil rights legends like John Lewis and Andrew Young and Obama was wary of seeking support from Jackson. But in a contest that coincided with the fortieth anniversary of King's death there was always likely to be an opportunity for Obama to draw support away from Clinton, if he could tap the King connection. In Atlanta's Ebenezer church on January 21, 2008, the day before King Day, Obama did so in virtuoso style by recapping the history of the civil rights movement as a victory for unity.

> What Dr. King understood is that if just one person chose to walk instead of ride the bus, those walls of oppression would not be moved. But maybe if a few more walked, the foundation might start to shake. If a few more women were willing to do what Rosa Parks had done, maybe the cracks would start to show. If teenagers took freedom rides from North to South, maybe a few bricks would come loose. Maybe if white folks marched because they had come to understand that their freedom too was at stake in the impending battle, the wall would begin to sway. And if enough Americans were awakened to the injustice; if they joined together, North and South, rich and poor, Christian and Jew, then perhaps that wall would come tumbling down, and justice would flow like water, and righteousness like a mighty stream.
>
> (Obama 2008a)

Affirming King's status as Moses, Obama stepped smoothly into Joshua's shoes. At the same time, he reminded not only his immediate audience but the wider public that interracial as well as racial unity had been integral to the movement's success. In contrast, Hillary Clinton drew fire by unsubtly telling a Harlem congregation that Republican leaders had run the House of Representatives "like a plantation, and you know what I'm talking about." The slavery analogy did not work.

As the contest sharpened, the question of Obama's racial loyalties arose again. He was obliged to respond to media coverage of sermons given by his Chicago pastor Jeremiah Wright that seemed to espouse an anti-white position that included such controversial claims as attributing the AIDS epidemic to a federal government attempt to exterminate people of color and seeming to justify the 9/11 attacks. Obama's March 18 speech "A More Perfect Union" was a thoughtful rebuttal of Wright's angry rhetoric. It carefully explained why Obama could no more disown his pastor than he could the black community. It asked people to recall that for Wright's generation "memories of humiliation and doubt and fear" of the racist America of the 1950s, "have not gone away; nor have the anger and the bitterness." He reminded them that there was abundant, racist bitterness in white communities, concealed behind a public veneer, and he charged, this bitterness had been exploited by coded Republican rhetoric since the Reagan era. There were no direct invocations of King in this crucial speech but his spirit was there, most notably in Obama's insistence that his pastor's main fault was that he saw race relations as "static." "This union may never be perfect," he declared, "but generation after generation has shown that it can be perfected" (Obama 2008b).

The skill with which Obama dealt with the Wright controversy has been seen as crucial to his victory in the nomination race. Equally significant, in later speeches, his confidence that positive change could occur was conveyed by using King's famous line from his 1965 speech at the end of the Selma-to-Montgomery march: "that the moral arc of the universe is long, but it bends towards justice." Obama added the important proviso that the arc did not "bend on its own. It bends because each of us puts our hands on that arc and bends it towards justice." This emphasis has remained in later presidential speeches.

Once he secured the Democratic nomination in August 2008, Obama felt able to reduce his direct allusions to King so that in his acceptance speech he referred, almost archly, to a young preacher from Georgia who told Americans that their destiny was "inextricably linked" and that "together, our dreams can be one." The spiralling financial crisis ensured that his campaign addresses concentrated on the economic issues that threatened the dreams of all, and sparked a repudiation of the Republican White House that increased the likelihood that as the Democratic nominee, Obama would become the first black president of the United States. The historic significance of that outcome ensured that when he gave his victory speech in November, he inevitably referred back to the civil rights movement and his indebtedness to it. He did so by summarizing the events in the long life of a black voter, Ann Nixon Cooper, who was 106 years old. She had lived, he told the crowds, through "the buses in Montgomery, the hoses in Birmingham, a bridge in Selma, and a preacher from Atlanta who told a people 'We Shall Overcome'" (Obama 2008c; Obama 2008d).

The burden of expectation that Obama might be the fulfilment of King's legacy was magnified further by the decision to award him the 2009 Nobel Peace Prize. The main reason for the award seemed to be nothing Obama could possibly have done on taking office but rather all that his internationally unpopular predecessor George W. Bush had come to represent in terms of American unilateral use of military force. When Obama accepted the prize in December in Oslo, he acknowledged that he was standing in King's footsteps, quoting King's statement that violence cannot secure peace, but instead creates new and more complicated problems. However, he then proceeded to defend the use of force on the basis of the principle of self-defense, which was made essential by the presence of evil in the world. In short, while he revered King for the nobility of his ideals and his personal courage, he declared that, as a head of state, he could not be guided by his example, if he was to abide by his oath to defend the United States (Obama 2009).

By maintaining the legitimacy of national self-defense, Obama was aligning himself with the majority of Americans, some of whom had viewed his Nobel Prize as confirming their fears that he would not be as determined a defender of American interests as his predecessor. In effect, Obama's unwillingness to adopt King's nonviolence mirrored the reluctance of most African Americans to do so, and underscored the radicalism of King that saccharine celebrations of the holiday have concealed. Obama's frequent invocation of the many nameless individuals who marched with King and contributed to the Freedom Struggle similarly rehashes the SNCC critique that it is historically false and counter-productive to believe in a Messiah figure, when the outcome of the struggle largely hinges on everyone's willingness to get involved. Ella Baker's maxim – "Strong people don't need strong leaders" – still carries weight, but ultimately King's life deserves acclaim and remains an inspiration.

King's Lasting Significance

King's own call to activism seems to have sprung more from his religious and philosophical conviction rather than any conscious emulation of earlier leaders, even Gandhi, although his philosophy of nonviolence was a vital discovery. Given that his relatively comfortable background is sometimes cited in order to diminish his achievements – in comparison to the harsh early life of Malcolm X, for example – it is worth reiterating that King did not have to take up the challenge of race leadership in the way that he did. The African American church has been central to both accommodation and resistance, and King would have joined the ranks of the majority (both then and now) if he had been a more circumspect preacher. His first legacy, then, is an exhortation to take risks for what you believe to be right.

King's media image, and the way in which the mass media focused upon him, has also become a stick with which to beat him. By creating the impression of King as the supreme commander of the Movement, the media image was a distortion that did both King and the Movement a disservice. At the same time, it should be evident that King's image advanced the cause. His powerful oratory and persuasive presentation of the African American case both sustained local struggles from Birmingham to Memphis and gave key concerns a vital public prominence. In this respect, he was also an important transitional figure who took presentational skills nurtured in the older public sphere of direct oratory and showed how they could be powerfully transferred to the new medium of television. The now iconic "I Have a Dream" speech is partially misleading in this respect since the highly theatrical, set podium speech underutilized television's special advantages. Combining the cinematic power of photomontage and the domestic intimacy of radio, television placed King's emotive voice in a special context. His calm, yet emotionally charged voice of reason in countless press conferences was juxtaposed in newscasts to scenes of brutal disorder and viewed by people as they sat in what was supposed to be the moral sanctuary of their own homes.

After 1965 especially, TV news showed that it could dilute and distort as well as reinforce King's message. Nonviolence, for instance, could be made to appear hopelessly idealistic and crudely hypocritical. Sound bites of the "I Have a Dream" speech, even today, can create the false impression that King saw the eradication of racism as simply a matter of goodwill, whereas his nonviolent tactics were rooted in the need for action in the context of proven resistance. As early as the Freedom Rides, media commentators had been ready to question the legitimacy of nonviolent tactics that seemed to court violence, a recurring feature that obliged King to articulate the merits of conflict to a regime that venerated consensus. Between 1963 and 1965, his unwelcome message served as a foil for President Johnson's promotion of reform as the surest source of stability. By 1966, however, King's message that creative tension was the essential prelude to positive action was increasingly hard for a white mainstream audience to accept, especially when what the media presented them with were pictures of massed police protecting civil rights demonstrators from enraged white homeowners, or when the press discussion centered on how King's efforts could easily spark civil disturbances. By the time of his ill-fated march in Memphis, King knew well that his exhortations for nonviolence would be replayed against scenes of African Americans looting, or fighting with police, in ways that undercut his position. At the same time, while King may ultimately be viewed as being as much a victim as a beneficiary of the media, the fact remains that his presentational skills as a national figure surpassed those of his African American contemporaries and rivals. The tragedy for the overall Movement was not just that the media pack was obsessed with King but that mainstream reporters and newsmen cynically refocused their attention on figures like

Stokely Carmichael, H. Rap Brown, and Huey Newton, whose words more readily elicited the alarm that framed press story-lines.

King's career, particularly after 1965, was made more difficult by the mistakes and limitations of others, whether it be the ineptness of Hosea Williams's SCOPE voter registration program or the shallowness of Carmichael's Black Power program as a practical strategy of empowerment. Carmichael's analysis of white faults could be acute, but his ability to develop and implement an alternate and organized protest strategy, as he toured the country, was far less evident, as his SNCC colleagues complained.

King's pursuit of racial justice had always been hampered by the inertia and trepidation of his supposed white allies, and when he focused on issues of economic inequality, their doubts about his realism resurfaced. He himself had been hesitant (he would have said, cowardly) in his opposition to the Vietnam War. The hostile reaction to his 1965 anti-war comments deepened his fear that he might jeopardize the hopes of men like Bayard Rustin, who believed that support for the Johnson administration would ensure the consolidation of racial reform and eventually the expansion of social welfare programs. By the time King embraced the anti-war cause in 1967, the unpopularity of US policies was obvious internationally, in papal condemnations and UN appeals for a ceasefire. But in the strictly American context in which a virulent, domestic Red Scare had accompanied the last major war (the Korean War, 1950-53), few politicians of stature shared King's courage to speak out before 1968. The majority remained wedded to the idea that to propose conceding ground to communism internationally was politically suicidal. By speaking out, King aligned himself with the younger African American militants like Carmichael, and white student groups who were seen as increasingly wedded to protest almost as an end in itself rather than to institutional politics. A harsh critic could complain that King allowed himself to be unduly swayed by the charge that he was damaging African American interests by speaking out on the war. After all, those black leaders levying the charge, chiefly Roy Wilkins, seem to do so for little better reason than a desire to appease Lyndon Johnson. The logical thrust of King's own analysis of the war should have led him to adopt Jim Bevel's almost monomaniacal obsession with ending the war. But King always had a tendency to listen more than Bevel and to seek a compromise position that was consistent with his basic principle of contesting injustice.

When the National Civil Rights Museum opened in Memphis on the site of the Lorraine Motel in 1991, Mohandas Gandhi's grandson offered the opinion that it was a disservice to King's memory. King and Gandhi, he declared, "didn't want people to erect statues and museums in their memory. It's a waste of money." Certainly, the memorialization that has occurred over the last half century has been a mixed blessing, and has largely obscured the overtly radical King of his final years. The monument dedicated in his honor in Washington has been controversial because its stern standing figure conflicts with popular perceptions of King and nonviolence, and because it truncated a quotation about how King wanted to be remembered as "a drum major for justice," and made it into a seemingly boastful declaration of his own worth. This certainly did not capture the character of the man, who at the same time as he told his congregation how he hoped to be remembered, was wrestling with the depressing thought that he could not meet the extravagant expectations that others had of him nor provide the answers for the problems that the world seemed to expect him to solve.

Although historians mistrust biography because it tends to celebrate exceptional individuals and exaggerate their historical significance, it can also serve to give the past a human face, enabling us to see that choosing to act and failing remains superior to the act of failing to choose. While carried along by developments far larger than himself, King played his part as a symbolic figure, protest leader, and public spokesman. King did not make the Movement and he did not realize his Dream, but he also did not forsake the Movement nor abandon his ideals. He continued to apply pressure to the moral arc of the universe so that it did bend towards justice. In many of his sermons in small black churches across the South, he preached a gospel of sacrifice by declaring that any man who has found nothing for which he is prepared to die has not yet found a reason to live. He would invoke the traditional African American virtue of persistence by urging the congregation to "keep on keeping on." They would respond: "Amen," and so can we.

Glossary of Organizations

ABC	American Broadcasting Company
ACLU	American Civil Liberties Union
ACMHR	Alabama Christian Movement for Human Rights
AFL-CIO	American Federation of Labor-Congress of Industrial Organizations
AFSC	American Friends Service Committee
AFSCME	American Federation of State, County and Municipal Employees
CBS	Columbia Broadcasting Company
CCCO	Coordinating Council of Community Organizations
CCRR	Chicago Conference on Race and Religion
CEP	Citizenship Education Program
CIA	Central Intelligence Agency
CIC	Catholic Interracial Council
CIO	Congress of Industrial Organizations
COFO	Council of Federated Organizations
CORE	Congress of Racial Equality
CRS	Community Relations Service
FBI	Federal Bureau of Investigation
FOR	Fellowship of Reconciliation
ICC	Interstate Commerce Commission
MFDP	Mississippi Freedom Democratic Party
MIA	Montgomery Improvement Association
NAACP	National Association for the Advancement of Colored People
NBC	National Broadcasting Company

NCC	National Council of Churches
NWRO	National Welfare Rights Organization
PPP	Poor People's Campaign
SCEF	Southern Conference Educational Fund
SCHW	Southern Conference for Human Welfare
SCLC	Southern Christian Leadership Conference
SCOPE	Summer of Community Organization and Political Education
SNCC	Student Nonviolent Coordinating Committee
UAW	United Auto Workers
UN	United Nations
UPWA	United Packinghouse Workers of America
VEP	Voter Education Project
WSCM	West Side Christian Ministry
YWCA	Young Women's Christian Association

Guide to Further Reading

General Textbooks

Martin Luther King's career should not be seen in isolation. Readers seeking to place his life in the broad context of American history may wish to read such standard US history textbooks as Eric Foner's *Give Me Liberty* (2013) or Darlene C. Hine *et al.*'s account of African American history, *African American Odyssey* (2013). One of the by-products of the passing of the segregation era in the American South has been increased scholarly interest in the origins and fluctuating character of American apartheid. C. Vann Woodward's *The Strange Career of Jim Crow* (1974, or earlier editions), itself originally a product of the *Brown* decision of 1954, launched the debate on why the post-Civil War South came to have segregation by law. A vivid picture of life under segregation is provided by William Chafe *et al.* in *Remembering Jim Crow* (2013). Pete Daniel's *Lost Revolutions* (2000) captures well the profound material changes at work in the 1950s' South. Charles Bullock *et al.*'s *The New Politics of the Old South* (2014) offer the most wide-ranging assessment of the political implications of what the movement did. Numan Bartley's *The New South, 1945-1980* (1995) still provides an excellent regional overview. At the same time, the biggest shift in recent scholarship has been to focus attention beyond the South, and the key text in this respect is Thomas Sugrue's *Sweet Land of Liberty: The Forgotten Struggle for Civil Rights in the North* (2008).

Students might also like to consult one of the many textbooks on the classic civil rights struggle. As an African American Marxist, Manning Marable offers one interpretation in *Race, Reform and Rebellion* (2001) and Jack Bloom's *Class, Race and the Civil Rights Movement* (1987) offers a similar perspective. Doug McAdam's *Political Process and the Development of Black Insurgency* (1999) explains the Movement's rise and fall largely in terms of its inter-action with ultimately more powerful, external factors, whereas Aldon Morris's *The Origins of the Civil Rights Movement* (1984) emphasizes the role of internal African American community resources. Steven Lawson's *Running for Freedom* (2008), Harvard Sitkoff's *The Struggle for Black Equality* (2008), and Robert Cook's *Sweet Land of Liberty?* (1998), all offer sound liberal overviews of the Movement's course. For high school students, Vivienne Sanders's *Race Relations in the USA since 1900* (2000) and John Kirk's *Martin Luther King and the Civil Rights Movement* (2013) seem excellent starting-points. However, here, too, the major shift has been towards what is termed the "long civil rights movement," a frame-work laid out in 2005 by the then president of the Organization of American Historians, Jacqueline Dowd Hall, who stressed cor-rectly that the struggle began long before Montgomery and con-tinued beyond the gunshot in Memphis. This is highly visible in the proliferation of local studies, but also informs textbook accounts. One strand within this shift is a reevaluation of Black Power, decrying what Peniel Joseph has called the tendency to see it as civil rights' "evil twin" and to position it in a narrative of the movement's rise and fall. Joseph, too, rightly insists that African Americans resented and rejected their powerlessness and fought for power. Certainly, Martin Luther King did. An indication of how events look differently from this perspective is offered by Joseph's *Waiting 'Til the Midnight Hour* (2006). Other scholars, however, feel the need to acknowledge change and discontinuity so that we get a better sense of why progress was made in the 1960s that was not possible before, and why conservative forces have been gen-erally stronger than liberal ones in the decades since King's death. The overall effect of "long civil rights movement" studies has been to contest the previous over-emphasis on King.

How The King Literature Has Developed

The main biographies published in King's lifetime were by indi-viduals with personal connections to King. The author of *Crusader*

Without Violence (1959), Lawrence Reddick, knew King from Montgomery. The editor of the black magazine *Ebony*, Lerone Bennett, wrote *What Manner of Man* (1966) about a fellow Morehouse graduate, and William Miller's *Martin Luther King, Jr.* (1968) was the work of a supporter of nonviolence. The results were predictably laudatory. When C. Eric Lincoln put together a profile of King in 1970, the most probing treatments remained journalistic with white scholar activist August Meier's "The Conservative Militant" (1965; see Lincoln 1970) being easily the most insightful.

Lincoln's anthology was quickly joined by the work of one of Meier's students, David Levering Lewis, who wrote *King: A Biography* within a year of King's death. On publication in 1970, it was a rare, substantive voice of criticism as Lewis began the process of publicizing the SNCC critique of charismatic leadership that has increasingly informed scholarship on the Civil Rights Movement in general in the last twenty years. For all his considerable gifts, Lewis concluded, King's "singularity of leadership initially, and almost until the end" was "derived from forces external to himself" (Lewis 1978: 393). Prominent among those forces, Lewis believed, was a national, political establishment that could cope with King's moralizing against Southern segregation, but not his condemnation of both US militarism and structured economic inequality.

By securing access to FBI materials under the Freedom of Information Act and tapping both the King and SCLC papers and oral histories that were becoming available in the late 1970s, David Garrow placed himself at the forefront of King studies, beginning with his *Protest at Selma* (1978), the first thorough case study of how King's strategy of nonviolent direct action worked. His exposé of J. Edgar Hoover's obsessive pursuit of the SCLC leader, *The FBI and Martin Luther King, Jr.* (1981), followed, and in 1988 he was rightly awarded a Pulitzer for *Bearing the Cross*, which remains in key respects the definitive work on the details of King's career. Stephen Oates's *Let the Trumpet Sound* (1994) is highly regarded for its literary qualities, but has been supplanted in that respect by Taylor Branch's award-winning trilogy of works (1988; 1998; 2007). Clayborn Carson, editor of the King Papers project at Stanford has also presented King's life through a skillful compilation of writings published under King's name, in *The*

Autobiography of Martin Luther King, Jr. (1998 [2001]), and that has proved especially popular. Alongside Garrow's work, Adam Fairclough's study of the SCLC, *To Redeem the Soul of America* (1987) has also proved of enduring value for its lucid portrait of King as a conductor and orchestrator, whose achievements should be understood only alongside those of his associates. Michael Dyson's *I May Not Get There With You* (2000) captures important elements of King's intellectual style and his reflections on King's death *April 4, 1968* (2008) are thought-provoking. Of works published in the last decade, however, the most important has been Thomas Jackson's *From Civil Rights to Human Rights* (2007). He impressively argues that economic justice was a key element of King's agenda from the start and reveals King's radicalism more fully than earlier work.

Personal recollections have perpetuated internal Movement divisions. From the King camp, the autobiographical accounts of Scott King (1969), King Sr. (1980) and Benjamin Mays (1987), predictably give a positive depiction of the martyred King, and later family memoirs, sometimes pitched for a children's audience, have continued in this vein: for example his sons, Dexter Scott King (2003) and Martin L. King III (2013); and King's sister Christine King Farris (2009). Squabbles within the family and money-making maneuvers have damaged the King image. Ralph Abernathy's autobiography (1989) shocked some colleagues by its portrait of King's sexual appetites, especially as the author remained studiously silent about his own failings. Similarly, Andrew Young's excellent memoir, *An Easy Burden* (1996), by far the best civil rights memoir by a major figure, cannot resist settling a few old scores with both SCLC and SNCC rivals, and attorney Clarence Jones's two books (2008 and 2011) seem intent on securing some recognition and boosting his own views by suggesting they were Martin's. SNCC criticisms of King exist mainly in oral history interviews, but there are a few memoirs. Cleveland Sellers's *The River of No Return* (1973), James Forman's *The Making of Black Revolutionaries* (1997), and Stokely Carmichael's *Ready for Revolution* (2005) spell out the feeling that SNCC's work in the field, rather than King's platform oratory and high-level diplomacy, represented the heart of the Movement. Their recollections of organizing efforts in the Deep South and of a growing disaffection with the United States have been enriched by John Lewis, whose *Walking with the Wind* (1998) offers the viewpoint of a genuine practitioner of Gandhian nonviolence. White SNCC activist Bob Zellner (2008) also offers fascinating reminiscences on early SNCC while Bernard Lafayette (2013) and Chuck Fager (2005) recall the Selma campaign in detail. The works of two white feminists, Sara Evans's *Personal Politics* (1980) and Mary King's *Freedom Song* (1987), raise the important issue of how white female activists in SNCC moved from racial to gender discrimination issues in the mid-1960s. Subsequent scholarly studies have generally indicted the Movement's male leadership, but have tended to exonerate SNCC, prior to Stokely Carmichael's takeover, and to castigate Martin Luther King and his SCLC colleagues (Crawford *et al.* 1990; Robnett 1997; Grant 1998; Ling and Monteith 1999; Holsaert *et al.*, 2010).

Specialized studies of the different phases of King's career have proliferated. Stewart Burns crafted a wonderful account of the Montgomery Bus Boycott from original documents (Burns 1997) and African American lawyer Fred Gray (1999) and white preacher Robert Graetz (1999) have added their memoirs to King's *Stride Toward Freedom* (1958). Other accounts of the boycott have appeared courtesy of the editorship of David Garrow, including those of prominent participants Jo Ann Robinson and Ralph Abernathy (Robinson 1987; Garrow 1989b). Troy Jackson (2008) has explained how the campaign affected King, and most recently Jeanne Theoharis has provided a much more rounded account of the life of activist Mrs. Rosa Parks, both before and after the boycott (Theoharis 2013).

For the early unproductive years of the SCLC, Garrow's *Bearing the Cross*, Fairclough's *To Redeem the Soul of America*, and Branch's *Parting the Waters* provide the essential details. These can be usefully supplemented by Ralph Abernathy's generally disappointing memoir, *And the Walls Came Tumbling Down* (1989), Aldon Morris's *The Origins of the Civil Rights Movement* (1984), Joanne Grant's biography of Ella Baker (1998); and the range of studies on the relationship between the Cold War and US race relations in the 1950s has grown extensive (Dudziak 2000; Krenn 1999; Meriwether 2002; Lieberman and Lang 2011; Frederickson 2013). A vivid study of NAACP militant Robert Williams, Tim Tyson's *Radio Free Dixie* (1999), shows how fragile King's nonviolent leadership was in the late 1950s and Numan Bartley's older study of Southern segregationists, *The Rise of Massive Resistance* (1999), has been augmented by a cluster of excellent studies of the white opposition that King faced (Morgan Ward 2014; Wallace 2013; Cunningham 2012; Webb 2010; Walker 2009; Lewis 2004).

King remained a minor player in both the sit-ins and the Freedom Rides, although he participated to a degree in both (Ling 2000, 2001; Arsenault 2011). Among the subsequent King battlegrounds that have yet to receive full-length treatment, Albany, Georgia, stands out. Branch catches its spiritual intensity nicely in *Parting the Waters*, building on contemporary accounts by journalist Pat Watters and by academic/activist Howard Zinn (Watters and Cleghorn 1967; Watters 1993; Zinn 1965). Garrow's biography and Fairclough and Morris (cited above), as well as Stephen Tuck's broader history of the struggle in rural Georgia (2003), effectively analyze the Movement's shortcomings and Chief Laurie Pritchett's strengths, but, despite a special issue of the local *Journal of South-West Georgia History* (Fall 1984), defeat in Albany has received nowhere near the scrutiny that "victory" in the Birmingham campaign has attracted. Albany does feature in other studies such as Wesley Hogan's account of SNCC (2007), Charles Cobb's study of armed self-defense in relation to the nonviolent movement (2014), and Maurice Daniels's study of black attorney Donald Hollowell (2013).

For Birmingham, Andrew Manis's biography of Fred Shuttlesworth (1999) adds to our understanding of the Movement side, and Glenn Eskew's somewhat overstated critique of King's class bias and national orientation (1997) should not blind anyone to the importance of his contribution, not least for his account of Bull Connor's power. Some later works valuably extend our understanding of white Birmingham, notably J. Mills Thornton's *Dividing Lines* (2006), which dissects municipal politics in Montgomery, Birmingham and Selma, and Diane McWhorter, a Birmingham native, exorcising a few family ghosts as she probes the Klan network in a richly textured, gossipy narrative, *Carry Me Home* (2001). S. Jonathan Bass offers a sensitive reappraisal of the white, and by Alabama standards, progressive clergy whose public letter to King prompted his more famous reply from Birmingham Jail (Bass 2001), while Jonathan Rieder's *Gospel of Freedom* (2013) analyzes the wider significance of King's letter. Cynthia Levinson's lavishly illustrated children's book, *We've Got a Job* (2012) details the children's marches, and can be read alongside Horace Huntley and John McKerley, *Foot Soldiers for Democracy* (2009) which is a collection of oral histories of the protest.

David Colburn's excellent case study of St. Augustine pulls no punches in its criticisms of King (Colburn 1991). It has been supplemented by white intermediary, Dan Warren's memoir (2008). King's claim of a simple causal connection between the protest campaigns in Birmingham and St. Augustine and the 1964 Civil Rights Act warrants close scrutiny. The Act's fiftieth anniversary has prompted two journalistic accounts of the complex Congressional politics behind Lyndon Johnson's securing of the 1964 Act (Purdum 2014; Risen 2014). Garrow's *Protest at Selma* (1978) remains the most insightful study of that campaign, although see also the final volume of Taylor Branch's trilogy, *At Canaan's Edge* (2007) and J. Mills Thornton's work (cited above). J.L. Chestnut and Sheyann Webb provide local memoirs from the experienced and the youthful black perspective respectively (Chestnut 1991; Webb 1980).

James Ralph's *Northern Protest* (1993) remains the best assessment of the Chicago campaign, the failings of which, he argues, should not obscure its achievements. It can be supplemented by Garrow's edited collection of documents and essays related to the Northern campaign, by Robert McKersie's insider account (2013) and by biographies of the notorious Mayor Daley (Garrow 1989d; Royko 1971; Cohen and Taylor 2000). The most succinct discussion of King's decision to come out against the Vietnam War is available in Adam Fairclough's short biography (1995a) with Garrow's *Bearing the Cross* giving the most detailed account of King's last year of ruminations, and Peniel Joseph's biography of Stokely Carmichael (2014) showing how Carmichael ran ahead of King on Vietnam. Michael Honey's *Going Down Jericho Road* (2008) has supplanted Joan Beifuss (1985) as the fullest account of the ill-fated Memphis campaign. Gerald McKnight (1998) remains the main study of the Poor People's Campaign but it can be supplemented by Thomas Jackson's broader account of King's pursuit of economic justice (cited above).

Accounts of the assassination and investigations of James Earl Ray's guilt substantially begin with William B. Huie (1997).

Ray's own account was published most extensively as *Who Killed Martin Luther King Jr.?* (Ray 1997). Having failed to convince a Congressional investigation into the King and Kennedy assassinations, attorney Mark Lane, with civil rights activist Dick Gregory, published their conspiracy theory as *Code Name "Zorro"* (1977). More recently, the King family's efforts to establish the existence of a conspiracy have been aided by lawyer William Pepper (1998). Nonetheless, the most careful and even-handed examination of the evidence remains Gerald Posner's (1998), and the evidence in the 1999 civil suit has not persuaded me to depart from his conclusions. Hampton Sides (2010) has provided a study of the man-hunt that led to James Earl Ray's capture.

Three other aspects of the King literature deserve special mention. The first relates to his intellectual development and preaching skill. Some of the best early articles on King's theological position are available in David Garrow's three-volume anthology *Martin Luther King, Jr.: Civil Rights Leader, Theologian, Orator* (1989a) and King's thought is also scrutinized skillfully in Richard H. King's *Civil Rights and the Idea of Freedom* (1996). An erudite examination of the significance of personalism as the framework for King's world-view can be found in the work of Rufus Burrow (2006; 2014). Lewis Baldwin similarly sensitively investigates King's prayer life (2010). The Martin Luther King Papers Project, which began publication in 1992 under the general editorship of Clayborne Carson, had to confront the fact that King's academic work from undergraduate essays through to doctoral thesis in systematic theology was frequently characterized by the unattributed use of direct quotations from the written work of others. With Carson's cooperation, the *Journal of American History* published a roundtable discussion of King's plagiarism in the summer of 1991 (vol. 78, no. 1). No participant denied the facts, but their significance was widely interpreted. Some argued that King was following an African American practice of "voice-merging" that did not adhere to the Eurocentric concept of intellectual property rights, while others argued that the persistence of plagiarism in his doctoral thesis suggested that King had been poorly supervised by Boston University's benignly racist, white academic staff. The "culture wars" within American intellectual circles, particularly the renewed backlash against multiculturalism and affirmative action during the early 1990s, vitally shaped this discussion, with press suggestions that the revelation was symptomatic of inequities perpetrated on behalf of certain African Americans under the auspices of affirmative action. King did not deserve his doctorate, the most hostile critics claimed, arguing that Boston should rescind its degree award to its most famous student.

Scholar Keith Miller showed that King's subsequent sermons were often constructed from the rhetoric of others (Miller 1992). He also discussed the related topic of the balance of "black" and "white" cultural influences within King's oratory, which was also a key concern of Lewis Baldwin (1991). Richard King subsequently published a rebuttal of their efforts to minimize Euro-white influences on King (Ward and Badger 1996). An expert in the academic study of preaching (homiletics), Richard Lischer, provides a useful alternative to Miller's largely text-focused discussion by emphasizing that preaching is a performance (Lischer 1995). He shows that King varied his performance from audience to audience. When he addressed huge interracial audiences, King's rhythmic rhetoric employed what one might characterize as "crossover" music. Further studies of King's virtuosity as a speaker include Jonathan Rieder (2010) and Gary Selby (2008).

Another theme in the recent literature has been a comparison between King and his African American contemporary, Malcolm X. James Cone gives the topic its most extensive treatment (Cone 1991) and others, notably Carson and Dyson, take up his suggestion that the common practice of contrasting the two is simplistic (Carson *et al.* 1991; Dyson 1995). Britta Waldschmidt-Nelson's *Dreams and Nightmares* (2012) is the most recent comparative study. In doing so, Cone and Carson probably push the argument that King and Malcolm X were on convergent paths beyond the historical evidence. Dyson has published a study of King that seeks to emphasize his current relevance, and includes valuable critiques of efforts by the New Right to claim that King would have opposed affirmative action (Dyson 2000). Also useful for students wishing to compare King to other black leaders are two older collections of essays that include short profiles of King and Malcolm X, *Black Leadership in America* (1992) by John White, and John Hope Franklin and August Meier's *Black Leaders of the Twentieth Century* (1982).

Finally, as part of a larger discussion of the role of women in the Civil Rights Movement, King has been indicted as a male chauvinist. Veteran female activist Septima Clark (Stokes Brown 1990; Charron 2012) corroborated Ella Baker's complaint that King largely dismissed women's views. An anthology edited by Vicki Crawford and others takes up this theme, which has been amplified by Belinda Robnett's sociological analysis of women's concentration in an organizing, intermediate tier of Movement leadership, and by an anthology of original essays co-edited by Sharon Monteith and myself (Crawford *et al.* 1990; Robnett 1997; Ling and Monteith 1999). The latter includes my own essay on the relationship between nonviolence and the macho culture of King's SCLC. The importance of masculinity is more fully explored in Estes (2005).

Related Studies

As already indicated, the current scholarly consensus is that the role of Martin Luther King has been exaggerated as part of a narrow focus on the 1950s and 1960s and the struggle in the Southern states. Consequently, the number of studies of the freedom struggle's other eras and locations continues to grow exponentially. We now have important works on the civil rights battles in Northern and border cities like Milwaukee (Jones 2010), New York (Biondi 2003), Oakland (Self 2003), Philadelphia (Countryman 2005), and St. Louis (Lang 2009). In the first edition I noted the growing number of community case studies that showed the classic Southern movement's long roots and complicated local evolution that proceeded largely without King or the national media's presence. Bill Chafe's and Robert Norrell's studies of Greensboro, North Carolina, and Tuskegee, Alabama, respectively (Chafe 1981; Norrell 1986), have been amplified by Christina Greene (2005) and Fergus (2009) for North Carolina and by Jefferies (2010) in Alabama. John Dittmer (1994) and Charles Payne's (1995) work on Mississippi has been enriched by subsequent studies by Andrews (2004), Crosby (2005), Hamlin (2012), and Moye (2004). All four new local studies amplify Payne's argument that it is a distortion to see the Movement through the lens of the mass media and its fascination with Martin

Luther King, and demonstrate how important were the years after 1968 in securing movement gains. New studies of the movement in the Deep South have also punctured the legend that it was characterized by nonviolence. Umoja's *We Will Shoot Back* (2013), alongside Cobb (cited earlier), Hill (2004), and Wendt (2007), convincingly show the importance of armed self-defense as a deterrent to racist terrorism.

Other Movement figures have gained attention, although none to rival the library on King himself. Among King's co-workers, Grant's biography of Ella Baker (1998) has been superseded by Barbara Ransby (2003) and Todd Moye (2013). Similarly, Anderson (1998) offers a disappointing summary of Bayard Rustin's extraordinary career in comparison to D'Emilio (2003). David Halberstam offers vignettes of early SNCC activists such as Diane Nash and Jim Bevel in his study of the Nashville movement, *The Children* (1998) and Houston (2012) looks at the movement's local story. Wesley Hogan (2007) represents the first major reconsideration of SNCC's evolution since Carson (1981). Eric Burner's study of the enigmatic SNCC leader Robert Parris Moses (1994) remains valuable, although Moses deserves more attention. We lack a study of James Forman, and need more works like Cynthia Fleming's portrait (1998) of a key, but tragically short-lived member of SNCC's inner circle, Ruby Doris Smith Robinson. With characteristic panache, Peniel Joseph (2014) presents the case for placing Stokely Carmichael alongside Malcolm X and Martin Luther King as the movement's star figures. Chana Kai Lee (1999) and Kay Mills's (1994) remain the best of several sympathetic biographies of the redoubtable Mississippi activist, Mrs. Fannie Lou Hamer.

Oral histories of the Civil Rights Movement have also proved insightful about the experiences of activists, and provide a real flavor of the Movement. Howell Raines's classic collection, *My Soul is Rested* (1983), can now be supplemented with later interviews collected by the producers of the *Eyes on the Prize* television series, and by Cheryl Greenberg at one of SNCC's annual reunions (Carson *et al.* 1991; Hampton and Fayer 1994; Greenberg 1998). Interviews have also provided vivid accounts of local movements; for instance in Perry County Alabama (Evans 2012) and Holmes County Mississippi (Youth of the Rural Organizing and Cultural

Center 1991). Much of this material is now being digitalized and kept on-line in collections such as the Southern Oral History Program at the University of North Carolina-Chapel Hill. Local studies beyond the South have increased interest in the Congress of Racial Equality which, apart from Meier and Rudwick (1973), had been discussed in relation to the Freedom Rides, which it launched (Arsenault 2011), and Mississippi Freedom Summer (Watson 2010) where three of its volunteers were murdered. Purnell (2013) examines the sometimes controversial actions of its Brooklyn chapter and Singler *et al.* (2011) recovers the Seattle chapter's efforts to fight job discrimination. At the same time, Greta de Jong's (2002) study of rural Louisiana and Kent Germany's (2007) study of New Orleans confirm CORE's Deep South contributions.

Like his father and grandfather, Martin Luther King, Jr., was a lifelong member of the NAACP. Despite Gilbert Jonas' 2004 study, there is still no single comprehensive study of this complex organization, whose reputation for bureaucracy is confirmed by its mountainous records at the Library of Congress. Its centennial does seem to have boosted scholarly recognition with Sullivan's monograph (2009) and Verney and Sartain's edited collection (2009) providing an excellent starting point for readers. Berg (2005) presents the NAACP's fight against black disenfranchisement, and Bynum (2013) offers the first study of NAACP youth councils. Another point of entry into NAACP efforts and achievements is Richard Kluger's definitive study of the *Brown* decision, *Simple Justice* (1975). One can also read autobiographies and biographies of its leading figures notably Roy Wilkins and Thurgood Marshall. Wilkins's (1984) autobiography can be supplemented by Ryan's biography (2013). Marshall's later career as a US Supreme Court justice has ensured greater attention and Williams (1998) offers a sound biography and Tushnet (1997) is a reliable guide to his jurisprudence. Litigation and lobbying were the twin pillars of the NAACP's national strategy, with the litigation increasingly undertaken by its quasi-independent legal arm, the so-called Inc. Fund. Jack Greenberg concentrates on the latter's achievements in *Crusaders in the Courts* (1994). Litigation case studies reveal the significance of federal judges to the racial struggle, and Jack Bass celebrates the brave men among them in his *Unlikely Heroes* (1990). The importance of NAACP lobbying is captured in

Denton Watson's account of Clarence Mitchell's career (1990). The NAACP's alliance with the National Urban League, which was similarly viewed as too moderate by black militants in the 1960s, is integral to Nancy Weiss's study, *Whitney M. Young, Jr. and the Struggle for Civil Rights* (1989). Young's astute courtship of corporate America in the context of African American employment discrimination has prompted a reappraisal (Dickerson 2004).

King's career spanned three American presidencies – Eisenhower, Kennedy, and Johnson – and each has received intense scholarly attention. The positive revision of Eisenhower's reputation continues to struggle to excuse his lack of leadership on racial matters, but the best recent defence is Nichols (2007). As Carl Brauer's *John F. Kennedy and the Second Reconstruction* (1977) shows, the Kennedys shared their predecessor's reluctance, being as alert to the political costs of pursuing the civil rights issue too far as they were aware of the impossibility of ignoring it. We are able to get a fuller sense of the Kennedy brothers' conflicted position from the White House recordings (Rosenberg and Karabell 2003), but the generally critical view of Kennedy civil rights policy, especially prior to May 1963, remains dominant (Niven 2003; Bryant 2006). Having told the story from King's perspective, my *John F. Kennedy* (2013) considers it more from the President's side. The tape recordings of LBJ's handling of civil rights in the summer of 1964 can be read and heard (McKee *et al.* 2011) and two close, domestic policy advisors Nicholas Katzenbach (2008) and Joseph Califano (1991) have written their memoirs. Mark Stern's *Calculating Visions* (1987) compares Kennedy and Johnson's approaches and a clear and largely positive evaluation of LBJ is also offered by Ellis (2013), which supplements Kotz (2005). The impact of the Voting Rights Act is evaluated positively by Gary May (2013) and negatively by King-Meadows (2011). Hugh Graham's *The Civil Rights Era* (1990) painstakingly elaborates the administrative revolution set in motion by the 1964 Act.

Thanks to the World Wide Web, more and more material on the Movement is available over the Internet. Since pathways change, the surest way to find these is to search for well-established sites such as the Library of Congress, the Martin Luther King Papers Project at Stanford University, or the Civil Rights Museum in Memphis, and they will have links to other sources of information.

Select Bibliography

Abernathy, R. (1989) *And the Walls Came Tumbling Down*, New York: Harper & Row.

Anderson, J. (1998) *Bayard Rustin: Troubles I've Seen: A Biography*, Berkeley: University of California Press.

Andrews, K.T. (2004) *Freedom Is A Constant Struggle: The Mississippi Civil Rights Movement and Its Legacy*, Chicago: University of Chicago Press.

Arsenault, R. (2011) *Freedom Riders: 1961 and the Struggle for Racial Justice*, New York: Oxford University Press.

Baldwin, L.V. (1991) *There is a Balm in Gilead: The Cultural Roots of Martin Luther King, Jr*, Minneapolis: Fortress Press.

—— (2010) *Never To Leave Us Alone: The Prayer Life of Martin Luther King Jr.*, Minneapolis: Fortress Press.

Baldwin, L.V. and Burrow, R.F. (eds.) (2013) *The Domestication of Martin Luther King Jr: Clarence B. Jones, Right-Wing Conservatism and the Manipulation of the King Legacy*, Eugene: Cascade Books.

Bartley, N.V. (1995) *The New South, 1945-1980*, Baton Rouge: Louisiana State University Press.

—— (1999) *The Rise of Massive Resistance: Race and Politics in the South during the 1950s*, Baton Rouge: Louisiana State University Press.

Bass, J. (1990) *Unlikely Heroes*, Tuscaloosa: University of Alabama Press.

Bass, S. J. (2001) *Blessed Are the Peacemakers: Martin Luther King, Jr., Eight White Religious Leaders, and the "Letter from Birmingham Jail,"* Baton Rouge: Louisiana State University Press.

Beifuss, J. (1985) *At the River I Stand: Memphis, the 1968 Strike, and Martin Luther King*, Memphis: B & W Books.

Bennett, L. (1966) *What Manner of Man: A Biography of Martin Luther King, Jr.*, London: Allen & Unwin.

Berg, M. (2005) *Ticket to Freedom: The NAACP and the Struggle for Black Political Integration*, Gainesville: University of Florida Press.

Biondi, M. (2003) *To Stand and Fight: The Struggle for Civil Rights in Post-war New York City*, Cambridge, MA: Harvard University Press.

Bloom, J. (1987) *Class, Race and the Civil Rights Movement*, Bloomington: Indiana University Press.

Branch, T.B. (1988) *Parting the Waters: America in the King Years, 1954-63*, New York: Simon & Schuster.

—— (1998) *Pillar of Fire: America in the King Years, 1963-1965*, New York: Simon & Schuster.

—— (2007) *At Canaan's Edge: America in the King Years, 1965-1968*, New York: Simon & Schuster.

Brauer, C. (1977) *John F. Kennedy and the Second Reconstruction*, New York: Columbia University Press.

Bryant, N. (2006) *The Bystander: John F. Kennedy and the Struggle for Racial Equality*, New York: Basic Books.

Bullock, C.S. III et al. (eds.) (2014) *The New Politics of the Old South: An Introduction to Southern Politics*, Lanham: Rowman & Littlefield.

Burk, R.F. (1985) *The Eisenhower Administration and Black Civil Rights*, Knoxville: University of Tennessee Press.

Burner, E. (1994) *And Gently He Shall Lead Them: Robert Parris Moses and Civil Rights in Mississippi*, New York: New York University Press.

Burns, S. (ed.) (1997) *Daybreak of Freedom: The Montgomery Bus Boycott*, Chapel Hill: University of North Carolina Press.

Burns, R. (2010) *Burial For a King: Martin Luther King Jr.s Funeral and the Week that Transformed Atlanta and Rocked the Nation*, New York: Scribner.

Burrow, R. Jr. (2006) *God and Human Dignity: The Personalism, Theology and Ethics of Martin Luther King, Jr.*, Notre Dame, IND: University of Notre Dame Press.

—— (2014) *Extremist for Love: Martin Luther King Jr.: Man of Ideas and Nonviolent Social Action*, Minneapolis: Fortress Press.

Bynum, T. (2013) *NAACP Youth and the Fight for Black Freedom*, Knoxville: University of Tennessee Press.

Cagin, S. and Dray, P. (1988) *We Are Not Afraid: The Story of Goodman, Schwerner and Chaney and the Civil Rights Campaign in Mississippi*, London: Macmillan.

Califano, J.A. Jr. (1991) *The Triumph and Tragedy of Lyndon Johnson: The White House Years*, New York: Simon & Schuster.

Carmichael, S. [Kwame Toure] (2005) *Ready For Revolution: The Life and Struggles of Stokely Carmichael (Kwame Toure)*, New York: Scribner.

Carson, C. (1981) *In Struggle: SNCC and the Black Awakening of the 1960s*, Cambridge, MA: Harvard University Press.

Carson, C. (ed.) (1991) *Malcolm X: The FBI File*, New York: Carroll & Graf.

—— (1998) *The Autobiography of Martin Luther King, Jr.*, New York: Warner Books.

Carson, C. and Halloran, P. (eds.) (1998) *A Knock at Midnight: The Great Sermons of Martin Luther King, Jr*, London: Little, Brown.

Carson, C., Burns, S., and Carson, S. (eds.) (1996) *The Papers of Martin Luther King, Jr.: Volume III: Birth of a New Age December 1955–December 1956*, Berkeley: University of California Press.

Carson, C., Carson, S., Clay, A., Shadron, V., and Taylor, K. (eds.) (2000) *The Papers of Martin Luther King, Jr., Volume IV: Symbol of the Movement January 1957–December 1958*, Berkeley: University of California Press.

Carson, C., Garrow, D.J., Gill, G., Harding, V., and Hine, D.C. (eds.) (1991) *The Eyes on the Prize Civil Rights Reader*, Harmondsworth: Penguin.

Carson, C., Luker, R., and Russell, P.A. (eds.) (1992) *The Papers of Martin Luther King, Jr.: Volume I: Called To Serve January 1929–June 1951*, Berkeley: University of California Press.

Carson, C., Luker, R., Russell, P.A., and Holloran, P. (eds.) (1994) *The Papers of Martin Luther King, Jr.: Volume II: Rediscovering Precious Values July 1951–November 1955*, Berkeley: University of California Press.

Carter, D.T. (1995) *The Politics of Rage: George Wallace, the Origins of the New Conservatism, and the Transformation of American Politics*, New York: Simon & Schuster.

Chafe, W.H. (1981) *Civilities and Civil Rights: Greensboro, North Carolina, and the Black Struggle for Freedom*, Oxford: Oxford University Press.

—— (2013) *Remembering Jim Crow: African Americans Tell About Life in the Segregated South*, New York: The New Press.

Chappell, D.L. (2014) *Waking from the Dream: The Struggle for Civil Rights in the Shadow of Martin Luther King Jr.*, New York: Random House.

Charron, K.M. (2012) *Freedom's Teacher: The Life of Septima Clark*, Chapel Hill: University of North Carolina Press.

Chase, R.T. (1998) "Class Resurrection: The Poor People's Campaign of 1968 and Resurrection City," *Essays in History*, vol. 40 (published by the Corcoran Department of History at the University of Virginia).

Chestnut, J.L. (1991) *Black in Selma: The Uncommon Life of J.L. Chestnut, Jr.*, New York: Anchor Books.

Cobb, C.E., Jr. (2014) *This Nonviolent Stuff'll Get You Killed: How Guns Made the Civil Rights Movement Possible*, New York: Basic Books.

Cohen, A. and Taylor, E. (2000) *American Pharaoh: Mayor Richard J. Daley, His Battle for Chicago and the Nation*, London: Little, Brown.

Colburn, D.R. (1991) *Racial Change and Community Crisis: St Augustine, Florida, 1877-1980*, Gainesville: University of Florida Press.

Cone, J.T. (1991) *Martin & Malcolm & America: A Dream or A Nightmare?*, Maryknoll: Orbis.

Connolly, K. (1989) "The Chicago Open Housing Conference," in D. Garrow (ed.) *Chicago 1966*, Brooklyn: Carlsen.

Cook, R. (1998) *Sweet Land of Liberty? The African-American Struggle for Civil Rights in the Twentieth Century*, London: Longman.

Cotton, D.F. (2012) *If Your Back's Not Bent: The Role of the Citizenship Education Program in the Civil Rights Movement*, New York: Atria Press.

Countryman, M.J. (2005) *Up South: Civil Rights and Black Power in Philadelphia*, Philadelphia: University of Pennsylvania Press.

Crawford, V., Rouse, J.A., and Woods, B. (eds.) (1990) *Women in the Civil Rights Movement*, Bloomington: Indiana University Press.

Crespino, J. (2007) *In Search of Another Country: Mississippi and the Conservative Counterrevolution,* Princeton: Princeton University Press.

Crosby, E. (2005) *A Little Taste of Freedom: The Black Freedom Struggle in Claiborne County, Mississippi*, Chapel Hill: University of North Carolina Press.

Cunningham, D. (2012) *Klansville, USA: The Rise and Fall of the Civil Rights Era Ku Klux Klan*, New York: Oxford University Press.

Daniel, P. (2000) *Lost Revolutions: The South in the 1950s*, Chapel Hill: University of North Carolina Press.

Daniels, M.P. (2013) *Saving the Soul of Georgia: Donald L. Hollowell and the Struggle for Civil Rights*, Athens: University of Georgia Press.

Davis Powers, G. (1995) *I Shared the Dream: The Pride, Passion and Politics of the First Black Woman Senator from Kentucky*, Far Hills, NJ.: New Horizons Press.

De Jong, G. (2002) *A Different Day: African American Struggles for Justice in Rural Louisiana, 1900-1970*, Chapel Hill: University of North Carolina Press.

D'Emilio, J. (2003) *Lost Prophet: The Life and Times of Bayard Rustin*, New York: The Free Press.

Dickerson, D.C. (2004) *Militant Mediator: Whitney M. Young, Jr.*, Lexington: University Press of Kentucky.

Dittmer, J. (1994) *Local People: The Struggle for Civil Rights in Mississippi*, Urbana: University of Illinois Press.

Dowd Hall, J. (2005) "The Long Civil Rights Movement and the Political Uses of the Past," *Journal of American History*, 91: 1233-63.

Dudziak, M.L. (2000) *Cold War Civil Rights: Race and the Image of American Democracy*, Princeton: Princeton University Press.

Dwyer, O.J. and Alderman, D.H. (eds.) (2008) *Civil Rights Memorials and the Geography of Memory*, Chicago: Center for American Places at Columbia College Chicago.

Dyson, M.E. (1995) *Making Malcolm: The Myth and Meaning of Malcolm X*, New York: Oxford University Press.

—— (2000) *I May Not Get There with You: The True Martin Luther King, Jr*, New York: Free Press.

—— (2008) *April 4, 1968: Martin Luther King Jr.'s Death and How It Changed America*, New York: Basic Civitas.

Edsall, T.B. and Edsall, M.D. (1992) *Chain Reaction: The Impact of Race, Rights, and Taxes on American Politics*, New York: W.W. Norton.

Ellis, S. (2013) *Freedom's Pragmatist: Lyndon Johnson and Civil Rights*, Gainesville: University of Florida.

Eskew, G. (1997) *But for Birmingham: The Local and National Movements in the Civil Rights Struggle*, Chapel Hill: University of North Carolina Press.

Estes, S. (2005) *I Am a Man! Race, Manhood and the Civil Rights Movement*, Chapel Hill: University of North Carolina Press.

Evans, S. (1980) *Personal Politics: The Origins of Women's Liberation in the Civil Rights Movement and the New Left*, New York: Vintage.

Evans, S.M. (2012) *Do What the Spirit Says Do: An Oral History of the Civil Rights Struggle in Perry County, Alabama*, Createspace Independent Publishing Platform via Amazon.

Fager, C. (2005) *Eating Dr. King's Dinner*, Fayetteville, NC: Kimo Press.

Fairclough, A. (1987) *To Redeem the Soul of America: The Southern Christian Leadership Conference and Martin Luther King, Jr.*, Athens: University of Georgia Press.

—— (1995a) *Martin Luther King, Jr.*, Athens: University of Georgia Press.

—— (1995b) *Race and Democracy: The Civil Rights Struggle in Louisiana, 1915-1972*, Athens: University of Georgia Press.

Farmer, J. (1985) *Lay Bare the Heart*, New York: Arbor House.

Fergus, D. (2009) *Liberalism, Black Power and the Making of American Politics, 1965-1980*, Athens: University of Georgia Press.

Fields, U.J. (1959) *The Montgomery Story: The Unhappy Effects of the Montgomery Bus Boycott*, New York: Exposition Press.

Fleming, C.G. (1998) *Soon We Will Not Cry: The Liberation of Ruby Doris Smith Robinson*, Lanham: Rowman & Littlefield.

Foner, E. (2013) *Give Me Liberty: An American History*, New York: W.W. Norton.

Forman, J. (1997) *The Making of Black Revolutionaries*, Seattle: University of Washington Press.

Franklin, J.H. and Meier, A. (eds.) (1982) *Black Leaders of the Twentieth Century*, Urbana: University of Illinois Press.

Frederickson, K. (2013), *Cold War Dixie: Militarization and Modernization in the American South*, Athens: University of Georgia Press.

Garrow, D.J. (1978) *Protest at Selma: Martin Luther King, Jr., and the Voting Rights Act of 1965*, New Haven: Yale University Press.

—— (1981) *The FBI and Martin Luther King, Jr.: From "Solo" to Memphis*, New York: W.W. Norton.

—— (1988) *Bearing the Cross: Martin Luther King, Jr. and the Southern Christian Leadership Conference*, London: Jonathan Cape.

Garrow, D.J. (ed.) (1989a) *Martin Luther King, Jr.: Civil Rights Leader, Theologian, Orator*, 3 vols., Brooklyn: Carlson.

—— (1989b) *The Walking City: The Montgomery Bus Boycott 1955-1956*, Brooklyn: Carlson.

—— (1989c) *Birmingham, Alabama, 1956-1963: The Black Struggle for Civil Rights*, Brooklyn: Carlson.

—— (1989d) *Chicago 1966*, Brooklyn: Carlson.

Germany, K. (2007) *New Orleans After the Promises: Poverty, Citizenship and the Search for the Great Society*, Athens: University of Georgia Press.

Goldfield, D. (1990) *Black, White and Southern: Race Relations and Southern Culture, 1940 to the Present*, Baton Rouge: Louisiana State University Press.

Graetz, R. (1999) *A White Preacher's Memoir: The Montgomery Bus Boycott*, Montgomery: Black Belt Press.

Graham, H.D. (1990) *The Civil Rights Era: Origins and Development of National Policy 1960-1972*, New York: Oxford University Press.

Grant, J. (1998) *Ella Baker: Freedom Bound*, New York: John Wiley & Sons.

Grantham, D. (1988) *The Life and Death of the Solid South: A Political History*, Lexington: University Press of Kentucky.

Gray, F. (1999) *Bus Ride to Justice: Changing the System by the System: The Life and Works of Fred D. Gray, Preacher, Attorney, Politician: Lawyer for Rosa Parks*, Montgomery: Black Belt Press.

Greenberg, C.L. (1998) *A Circle of Trust: Remembering SNCC*, New Brunswick: Rutgers University Press.

Greenberg, J. (1994) *Crusaders in the Courts: How A Dedicated Band of Lawyers Fought for the Civil Rights Revolution*, New York: Basic Books.

Greene, C. (2005) *Our Separate Ways: Women and the Black Freedom Movement in Durham, North Carolina*, Chapel Hill: University of North Carolina Press.

Greene, M.F. (1997) *The Temple Bombing*, London: Vintage–Random House.

Haines, H.H. (1988) *Black Radicals and the Civil Rights Movement, 1954-1970*, Knoxville: University of Tennessee Press.

Halberstam, D. (1998) *The Children*, New York: Random House.

Hamlin, F. N. (2012) *Crossroads at Clarksdale: The Black Freedom Struggle in the Mississippi Delta after World War II*, Chapel Hill: University of North Carolina Press.

Hampton, H. and Fayer, S. (1994) *Voices of Freedom: An Oral History of the Civil Rights Movement from the 1950s through the 1980s*, New York: Vintage.

Hill, L. (2004) *The Deacons of Defense: Armed Resistance and the Civil Rights Movement*, Chapel Hill: University of North Carolina Press.

Hine, D.C. et al. (2013) *African American Odyssey*, New York: Pearson.

Hogan, W. (2007) *Many Minds, One Heart: SNCC's Dream for a New America*, Chapel Hill: University of North Carolina Press.

Holsaert, F.S. et al. (eds.) (2010) *Hands on the Plow: Personal Accounts by Women in SNCC*, Urbana: University of Illinois Press.

Honey, M.K. (2008) *Going Down Jericho Road: The Memphis Strike, Martin Luther King's Last Campaign*, New York: W.W. Norton.

Houston, B. (2012) *The Nashville Way: Racial Etiquette and the Struggle for Social Justice in a Southern City*, Athens: University of Georgia Press.

Huie, W.B. (1997) *He Slew the Dreamer: My Search, With James Earl Ray, for the Truth About the Murder of Martin Luther King, Jr.*, Montgomery: Black Belt Press.

Huntley, H. and McKerley, J.W. (eds.) (2009) *Foot Soldiers for Democracy: The Men, Women and Children of the Birmingham Civil Rights Movement*, Birmingham AL.: Birmingham Civil Rights Institute.

Jackson, T. (2008) *Becoming King: Martin Luther King Jr. and the Making of a National Leader*, Philadelphia: University of Pennsylvania Press.

Jackson, T.F. (2007) *From Civil Rights to Human Rights: Martin Luther King Jr. and the Struggle for Economic Justice*, Philadelphia: University of Pennsylvania.

Jefferies H.K. (2010) *Bloody Lowndes: Civil Rights and Black Power in the Alabama Black Belt*, New York: New York University Press.

Jonas, G. (2004) *Freedom's Sword: The NAACP and the Struggle Against Racism in America 1909-1969*, New York: Routledge.

Jones, C.B. (2008) *What Would Martin Say*, New York: Harper Collins.

—— (2011) *Behind the Dream: The Making of the Speech that Transformed a Nation*, New York: Palgrave Macmillan.

Jones, P.D. (2010) *The Selma of the North: Civil Rights Insurgency in Milwaukee*, Cambridge, MA.: Harvard University Press.

Joseph, P. (2006) *Waiting 'Til the Midnight Hour: A Narrative History of Black Power in America*, New York: Henry Holt and Company.

—— (2010) *Dark Days, Bright Nights: From Black Power to Barack Obama*, New York: Basic Civitas.

—— (2014) *Stokely: A Life*, New York: Basic Civitas.

Katzenbach, N. deB. (2008) *Some of It Was Fun: Working with RFK and LBJ*, New York: W.W. Norton.

Kelley, R.D.G. (1996) *Race Rebels: Culture, Politics, and the Black Working Class*, New York: Free Press.

King, M. (1987) *Freedom Song: A Personal Story of the 1960s Civil Rights Movement*, New York: Morrow.

King, M.L., Jr. (1958) *Stride toward Freedom: The Montgomery Story*, New York: Harper & Row.

—— (1964) *Why We Can't Wait*, New York: New American Library.

—— (1967) *Where Do We Go from Here? Chaos or Community?*, New York: Harper & Row.

King, M.L., Sr. (with Clayton Riley) (1980) *Daddy King: An Autobiography*, New York: William Morrow.

King, M.L., III, (2013) *My Daddy, Dr. Martin Luther King Jr.*, New York: HarperCollins.

King, R.H. (1996) *Civil Rights and the Idea of Freedom*, Athens: University of Georgia Press.

King Farris, C. (2009) *Through It All: Reflections on My Life, My Family and My Faith*, New York: Atria Paperbacks.

King-Meadows, T.D. (2011) *When the Letter Betrays the Spirit: Voting Rights Enforcement and African American Political Participation from Lyndon Johnson to Barack Obama*, Lanham: Lexington Books.

Kirk, J.A. (2013) *Martin Luther King and the Civil Rights Movement*, London: Routledge.

Klarman, M.J. (1994) "How *Brown* Changed Race Relations: The Backlash Thesis," *Journal of American History* 81: 81-118.

Kluger, R. (1975) *Simple Justice: A History of Brown versus the Board of Education and Black America's Struggle for Equality*, New York: Alfred A. Knopf.

Kopkind, A. (1965) "Selma: 'Aint Gonna Let Nobody Turn Me Round'," *New Republic* 152: March 20, 7-9.

—— (1969) *America: The Mixed Curse*, Harmondsworth: Penguin.

Korstad, R. and Lichtenstein, N. (1988) "Opportunities Found and Lost: Labor, Radicals, and the Early Civil Rights Movement," *Journal of American History* 75: 786-811.

Kotz, N. (2005) *Judgment Days: Lyndon Baines Johnson, Martin Luther King, Jr., and the Laws that Changed America*, Boston: Houghton Mifflin.

Krenn, M.L. (1999) (ed.) *The African American Voice in U.S. Foreign Policy since World War II*, New York: Garland.

Kuhn, C.M. (1997) "'There's a Footnote to History!' Memory and the History of Martin Luther King's October 1960 Arrest and Its Aftermath," *Journal of American History* 84: 583-95.

Lafayette, B. (with Johnson, K.L.) (2013), *In Peace and Freedom: My Journey in Selma*, Lexington: University Press of Kentucky.

Lane, M. and Gregory, D. (1977) *Code Name "Zorro:" The Murder of Martin Luther King, Jr.*, Englewood Cliffs: Prentice Hall.

Lang, C. (2009) *Grassroots at the Gateway: Class Politics and the Black Freedom Struggle in St. Louis, 1936-1975*, Ann Arbor: University of Michigan Press.

Lawson, S. (2008) *Running for Freedom: Civil Rights and Black Politics in America since 1941*, New York: McGraw-Hill.

Lee, C.K. (1999) *For Freedom's Sake: The Life of Fannie Lou Hamer*, Urbana: University of Illinois Press.

Lentz, R. (1990) *Symbols, the News Magazines, and Martin Luther King*, Baton Rouge: Louisiana State University Press.

Levinson, P. (2012) *We've Got A Job: The 1963 Birmingham Children's March*, Atlanta: Peachtree Publishers.

Lewis, D.L. (1978) *King: A Biography*, Champaign-Urbana: University of Illinois Press.

Lewis, G. (2004) *The White South and the Red Menace: Segregationists, Anti-Communism and Massive Resistance, 1945-1965*, Gainesville: University of Florida Press.

Lewis, J. (1998) *Walking with the Wind: A Memoir of the Movement*, New York: Simon & Schuster.

Lieberman, R. and Lang, C. (eds.) (2011) *Anti-Communism and the African American Freedom Movement: "Another Side of the Story,"* New York: Palgrave Macmillan.

Lincoln, C.E. (ed.) (1970) *Martin Luther King Jr.: A Profile*, New York: Hill and Wang.

Ling, P.J. (1995) "Local Leadership in the Early Civil Rights Movement: The South Carolina Citizenship Education Program of the Highlander Folk School," *Journal of American Studies* 29: 399-422.

—— (2000) "Racism for Lunch," *History Today* 50 (February): 36-38.

—— (2001) "Rocky Ride to Freedom," *BBC History Magazine* (May): 28-33.

—— (2013) *John F. Kennedy*, London: Routledge.

Ling, P. J. and Monteith, S. (eds.) (1999) *Gender in the Civil Rights Movement*, New York: Garland.

Lischer, R. (1995) *The Preacher King: Martin Luther King, Jr and the Word that Moved America*, New York: Oxford University Press.

Manis, A.M. (1999) *A Fire You Can't Put Out: The Civil Rights Life of Birmingham's Fred Shuttlesworth*, Tuscaloosa: University of Alabama Press.

Mann, R. (1996) *The Walls of Jericho – Lyndon Johnson, Hubert Humphrey, Richard Russell, and the Struggle for Civil Rights*, New York: Harcourt Brace.

Marable, M. (2001) *Race, Reform and Rebellion*, Jackson: University Press of Mississippi.

May, G. (2013) *Bending Towards Justice: The Voting Rights Act and The Transformation of American Democracy*, New York: Basic Books.

Mays, B.E. (1987) *Born to Rebel: An Autobiography*, Athens: University of Georgia Press.

McAdam, D. (1999) *Political Process and the Development of Black Insurgency*, Chicago: University of Chicago Press.

McGreevy, J.T. (1996) *Parish Boundaries: The Catholic Encounter with Race in the Twentieth-Century Urban North*, Chicago: University of Chicago Press.

McKee, G.A. et al. (eds.) (2011) *The Presidential Recordings: Lyndon B. Johnson: Mississippi Burning and the Passage of the Civil Rights Act June 1 1964-July 4 1964: volumes 7 & 8*, New York: Simon and Schuster.

McKersie, R.B. (2013) *A Decisive Decade: An Insider's View of the Chicago Civil Rights Movement*, Carbondale: University of Southern Illinois Press.

McKnight, G. (1998) *The Last Crusade: Martin Luther King, Jr., the FBI, and the Poor People's Campaign*, Denver: Westview Press.

McKnight, J. (1989) "The Summit Negotiation," in D. Garrow (ed.) *Chicago 1966*, Brooklyn: Carlson.

McWhorter, D. (2001) *Carry Me Home: Birmingham, Alabama – The Climactic Battle of the Civil Rights Revolution*, New York: Simon & Schuster.

Meier, A. and Rudwick, E. (1973) *CORE: A Study in the Civil Rights Movement, 1942-1968*, New York: Oxford University Press.

Meredith, M. (1997) *Nelson Mandela: A Biography*, London: Penguin.

Meriwether, J.H. (2002) *Proudly We Can Be Africans: Black Americans and Africa, 1935-1961*, Chapel Hill: University of North Carolina Press.

Miller Center (2014) "Barack Obama: Life Before the Presidency," http://miller center.org/president/obama/essays/biography/2 [accessed August 13, 2014].

Miller, K. (1992) *Voice of Deliverance: The Language of Martin Luther King, Jr., and Its Sources*, New York: Free Press.

Miller, W. (1968) *Martin Luther King, Jr.: His Life, Martyrdom and Meaning for the World*, New York: Weybright & Talley.

Mills, K. (1994) *This Little Light of Mine: The Life of Fannie Lou Hamer*, New York: Plume Books.

Mills Thornton III, J. (1980) "Challenge and Response in the Montgomery Bus Boycott of 1955-56," *Alabama Review* 33: 163-235.

—— (2006) *Dividing Lines: Municipal Politics and the Struggle for Civil Rights in Montgomery, Birmingham, and Selma*, Tuscaloosa: University of Alabama Press.

Morris, A. (1984) *The Origins of the Civil Rights Movement: Black Communities Organizing for Change*, New York: Free Press.

Morrison, M. (1987) *Black Political Mobilization, Leadership, Power and Mass Behavior*, Albany: State University of New York Press.

Moye, J.T. (2004) *Let the People Decide: Black Freedom and White Resistance Movements in Sunflower County, Mississippi, 1945-1986*, Chapel Hill: University of North Carolina Press.

—— (2013) *Ella Baker: Community Organizer of the Civil Rights Movement*, Lanham: Rowman & Littlefield.

Nichols, D.A. (2007) *A Matter of Justice: Eisenhower and the Beginning of the Civil Rights Revolution*, New York: Simon and Schuster.

Niven, D. (2003) *The Politics of Injustice: The Kennedys, the Freedom Rides, and the Electoral Consequences of a Moral Compromise*, Knoxville: University of Tennessee Press.

Norrell, R.J. (1986) *Reaping the Whirlwind: The Civil Rights Movement in Tuskegee*, New York: Alfred A. Knopf.

Norton, M.B. et al. (1998) *A People and a Nation: A History of the United States*, Boston: Houghton Mifflin.

Oates, S.B. (1994) *Let the Trumpet Sound: A Life of Martin Luther King, Jr.*, New York: HarperCollins.

Obama, B. (1995) *Dreams from My Father: A Story of Race and Inheritance*, New York: Times Books.

—— (2008a) "Remarks in Atlanta: 'The Great Need of the Hour,' January 20 2008," http://www.presidency.ucsb.edu/ws/index.php?pid=77027 [accessed August 13 2014].

—— (2008b) "Address at the National Constitutional Center in Philadelphia: 'A More Perfect Union', March 18 2008," http://www.presidency.ucsb.edu/ws/index.php?pid=76710 [accessed August 13 2014].

—— (2008c) "Address Accepting the Presidential Nomination at the Democratic National Convention in Denver: 'The American Promise,' August 28 2008," http://www.presidency.ucsb.edu/ws/index.php?pid=78284 [accessed August 13 2014].

—— (2008d) "Address in Chicago Accepting Election as the 44th President of the United States, November 4, 2008," http://www.presidency.ucsb.edu/ws/index.php?pid=84750 [accessed August 14 2014].

—— (2009) "Remarks by the President at the Acceptance of the Nobel Peace Prize, December 10, 2009," http://www.whitehouse.gov/the-press-office/remarks-president-acceptance-nobel-peace-prize [accessed August 14 2014].

—— (2013) "Remarks at the 50th Anniversary of the March on Washington, August 28 2013" http://www.whitehouse.gov/photos-and-video/video/2013/08/28/president-obama-marks-50th-anniversary-march-washington [accessed August 13 2014].

Parker, F. (1990) *Black Votes Count: Political Empowerment in Mississippi since 1965*, Chapel Hill: University of North Carolina Press.

Payne, C. (1995) *I've Got the Light of Freedom: The Organizing Tradition and the Mississippi Freedom Struggle*, Berkeley: University of California Press.

Pepper, W. (1998) *Orders To Kill: The Truth behind the Murder of Martin Luther King, Jr*, New York: Warner Books.

Posner, G. (1998) *Killing the Dream: James Earl Ray and the Assassination of Martin Luther King, Jr.*, London: Little, Brown.

Purdum, T.S. (2014) *An Idea Whose Time Has Come: Two Presidents, Two Parties and the Battle for the Civil Rights Act of 1964*, New York: Henry Holt and Company.

Purnell, B. (2013) *Fighting Jim Crow in the County of Kings: The Congress of Racial Equality in Brooklyn*, Lexington: University Press of Kentucky.

Rabinowitz, H. (1992) *The First New South: 1865-1920*, Arlington Heights: Harland Davidson.

Raines, H. (ed.) (1983) *My Soul is Rested: Movement Days in the Deep South Remembered*, Harmondsworth: Penguin.

Ralph, J. (1993) *Northern Protest: Martin Luther King, Jr., Chicago, and the Civil Rights Movement*, Cambridge, MA: Harvard University Press.

Ransby, B. (2003) *Ella Baker and the Black Freedom Movement: A Radical Democratic Vision*, Chapel Hill: University of North Carolina Press.

Ray, J.E. (1997) *Who Killed Martin Luther King, Jr.? The True Story by the Alleged Assassin*, New York: Marlowe.

Reddick, L.D. (1959) *Crusader without Violence: A Biography of Martin Luther King, Jr.*, New York: Harper & Brothers.

—— (1970) "Martin Luther King and the Republican White House," in C. Eric Lincoln (ed.) *Martin Luther King, Jr.: A Profile*, New York: Hill & Wang.

Remnick, D. (2010) *The Bridge: The Life and Rise of Barack Obama*, New York: Alfred A. Knopf.

Ricks, J.A. (1984) "De Lawd Descends and Is Crucified: Martin Luther King, Jr. in Albany Georgia," *Journal of Southwest Georgia History* 2(Fall): 3-14.

Rieder, J. (2010) *The Word of the Lord is Upon Me: The Righteous Performance of Martin Luther King Jr.*, Cambridge, MA: Belknap Press.

—— (2013) *Gospel of Freedom: Martin Luther King, Jr.'s Letter from Birmingham Jail and the Struggle that Changed a Nation*, New York: Bloomsbury Press.

Risen, C. (2014) *The Bill of the Century: The Epic Battle for the Civil Rights Act*, New York: Bloomsbury Press.

Robinson, A. and Sullivan, P. (eds.) (1991) *New Directions in Civil Rights Studies*, Charlottesville: University of Virginia Press.

Robinson, J. A. Gibson (1987) *The Montgomery Bus Boycott and the Women Who Started It*, ed. D. Garrow, Knoxville: University of Tennessee Press.

Robnett, B. (1997) *How Long? How Long? African-American Women in the Struggle for Civil Rights*, New York: Oxford University Press.

Rodgers, D.T. (2011) *The Age of Fracture*, Cambridge, MA: Harvard University Press.

Rosenberg, J. and Karabell, Z. (eds.) (2003) *Kennedy, Johnson and the Quest for Justice: The Civil Rights Tapes*, New York: W.W. Norton.

Royko, M. (1971) *Boss: Richard J. Daley of Chicago*, London: Barrie & Jenkins.

Ryan, Y. (2013) *Roy Wilkins: The Quiet Revolutionary and the NAACP*, Lexington: University Press of Kentucky.

Sanders, V. (2000) *Race Relations in the USA since 1900*, London: Hodder & Stoughton Educational.

Scott King, C. (1969) *My Life with Martin Luther King, Jr.*, London: Hodder & Stoughton.

Scott King, D. (2003) *Growing Up King: An Intimate Memoir*, New York: Warner Books.

Selby, G. S. (2008) *Martin Luther King's Rhetoric of Freedom: the Exodus Narrative in America's Struggle for Civil Rights*, Waco, TX.: Baylor University Press.

Self, R.O. (2003) *American Babylon: Race and the Struggle for Postwar Oakland*, Princeton: Princeton University Press.

Sellers, C. (1973) *The River of No Return: The Autobiography of a Black Militant and the Life and Death of SNCC*, New York: Morrow.

Sides, H. (2010) *Hellhound on his Trail: The Stalking of Martin Luther King Jr. and the International Hunt for his Assassin*, New York: Doubleday.

Singler, J. et al. (2011) *Seattle in Black and White: The Congress of Racial Equality and the Fight for Equal Opportunity*, Seattle: University of Washington Press.

Sitkoff, H. (2008) *The Struggle for Black Equality*, New York: Hill & Wang.

Stern, M. (1987) *Calculating Visions: Kennedy, Johnson and Civil Rights*, New Brunswick: Rutgers University Press.

Stokes Brown, C. (ed.) (1990) *Ready from Within: Septima Clark and the Civil Rights Movement*, Trenton: Africa World Press.

Sugrue, T.J. (2008) *Sweet Land of Liberty: The Forgotten Struggle for Civil Rights in the North*, New York: Random House.

Sullivan, P. (2009) *Lift Every Voice: The NAACP and the Making of the Civil Rights Movement*, New York: The New Press.

Theoharis, J. (2013) *The Rebellious Life of Mrs. Rosa Park*, Boston: Beacon Press.

Tuck, S. G. (2003) *Beyond Atlanta: The Struggle for Racial Equality in Georgia, 1940-1980*, Athens: University of Georgia Press.

Tushnet, M. (1997) *Making Constitutional Law: Thurgood Marshall and the Supreme Court, 1961-1991*, New York: Oxford University Press.

Tyson, T.B. (1999) *Radio Free Dixie: Robert F. Williams and the Roots of Black Power*, Chapel Hill: University of North Carolina Press.

Ulmer, A. (1965) "Aint Gonna Let Nobody Turn Me Round," *New South* 20 (March): 11-13.

Umoja, A.O. (2013) *We Will Shoot Back: Armed Resistance in the Mississippi Freedom Movement*, New York: New York University Press.

Verney, K. and Sartain, L (eds.) (2009) *Long Is the Way and Hard: One Hundred Years of the NAACP*, Fayetteville AK: University of Arkansas Press.

Waldschmidt-Nelson, B. (2012) *Dreams and Nightmares: Martin Luther King Jr., Malcolm X, and the Struggle for Black Equality*, Gainesville: University of Florida Press.

Walker, A. (2009) *The Ghost of Jim Crow: How Southern Moderates Used Brown v. Board Of Education to Stall Civil Rights*, New York: Oxford University Press.

Wallace, D.J. (2013) *Massive Resistance and Media Suppression: The Segregationist Response to Dissent During the Civil Rights Movement*, El Paso, TX: LFB Scholarly Publishing.

Ward, B. and Badger, T. (eds.) (1996) *The Making of Martin Luther King and the Civil Rights Movement*, Basingstoke: Macmillan.

Ward, J.M. (2014) *Defending White Democracy: The Making of a Segregationist Movement and the Re-making of Racial Politics, 1936-1965*, Chapel Hill: University of North Carolina Press.

Warren, D.R. (2008) *If It Takes All Summer: Martin Luther King, the KKK and States' Rights in St Augustine, 1964*, Tuscaloosa: University of Alabama Press.

Watson, B. (2010) *Freedom Summer: The Savage Season That Made Mississippi Burn and Made America a Democracy*, New York: Viking.

Watson, D. (1990) *Lion in the Lobby: Clarence Mitchell, Jr. and the Struggle for the Passage of Civil Rights Laws*, New York: William Morrow.

Watters, P. (1993) *Down to Now: Reflections on the Southern Civil Rights Movement*, Athens: University of Georgia Press.

Watters, P. and Cleghorn, R. (1967) *Climbing Jacob's Ladder*, New York: Harcourt, Brace & World.

Webb, C. (2010) *Rabble Rousers: The American Far Right in the Civil Rights Era*, Athens, GA: University of Georgia Press.

Webb, S. (1980) *Selma, Lord, Selma: Girlhood Memories of the Civil-Rights Days*, Tuscaloosa: University of Alabama Press.

Weisbrot, R. (1990) *Freedom Bound: A History of the Civil Rights Movement*, New York: W.W. Norton.

Weiss, N.J. (1989) *Whitney M. Young, Jr. and the Struggle for Civil Rights*, Princeton: Princeton University Press.

Wendt, S. (2007) *The Spirit and the Shotgun: Armed Resistance and the Struggle for Civil Rights*, Gainesville: University of Florida Press.

White, J. (1991) *Martin Luther King, Jr. and the Civil Rights Movement*, Durham: British Association for American Studies.

—— (1992) *Black Leadership in America from Booker T. Washington to Jesse Jackson*, London: Longmans.

White, W. (1949) *A Man Called White: The Autobiography of Walter White*, London: Victor Gollancz.

Wiggins, W.H. (1987) *O Freedom!: Afro-American Emancipation Celebrations*, Knoxville: University of Tennessee Press.

Wilkins, R., with T. Matthews (1984) *Standing Fast: The Autobiography of Roy Wilkins*, New York: Viking–Penguin.

Williams, J. (1998) *Thurgood Marshall: American Revolutionary*, New York: Crown Publishing.

Woodward, C. V. (1974) *The Strange Career of Jim Crow*, New York: Oxford University Press.

Young, A. (1996) *An Easy Burden: The Civil Rights Movement and the Transformation of America*, New York: HarperCollins.

Youth of the Rural Organizing and Cultural Center (1991), *Minds Stayed on Freedom: The Civil Rights Struggle in the Rural South*, Boulder, CO: Westview Press.

Zellner, B. [with Curry, C.] (2008) *On the Wrong Side of Murder Creek: A White Southerner's Recollection of the Civil Rights Movement*, Montgomery: NewSouth Books.

Zinn, H. (1965) *SNCC: The New Abolitionists*, Boston: Beacon Press.

Index

Abernathy, Ralph: as pastor of First
Baptist 33–34; and Montgomery
campaign 40; house bombed 56;
assault case 61; as MIA president
68; sued for libel 71;
segregationist pressure against 78;
and Freedom Rides 79; and
Albany campaign 91–98, 101; and
Birmingham campaign 115,
117–18, 122, 124, 129, 131, 133;
and March on Washington 151;
and visit to Norway 184; and
Selma campaign 188–89, 191; and
Chicago campaign 225; and
Memphis 293, 296–97; and
King's assassination 299–300; and
PPC 304, 306–9; friendship with
King 33, 37, 115 288; jealousy of
King 59, 161, 179; as King's
successor 262, 327; on King's
depression 289, 311; memoirs
326–27, 344–45
ACMHR see Alabama Christian
Movement for Human Rights
Affirmative action 7, 8, 153, 180,
239, 320, 348, 349
AFL-CIO see Unions
AFSCME see American Federation of
State, County, and Municipal
Employees
Alabama: proposed boycott 160–61,
207–8; libel action against New
York Times 71, 92–93; see also
Anniston; Birmingham; Dallas
County; Gadsden; Huntsville;
Lowndes County; Marion; Mobile;
Montgomery; Selma; Tuscaloosa;
Tuskegee
Alabama Christian Movement for
Human Rights: cooperation with
SCLC 111–12, 131–32, 133;
receives affiliate of the year
161–62; Shuttlesworth's leadership
of 106, 110; violence against
56, 105
Alabama Council on Human
Relations 38
Alabama, University of 49, 138–39,
140, 143
Albany, Georgia: Albany Movement's
campaign (1961–62) 65, 89–104;
and SNCC 90–91, 95–99, 102–3;
and beating of Marion King 100;
reasons for campaign's failure
102–4; see also Anderson, William
Albert, Carl 145
Alinsky, Saul 225
Allen, Ivan 66, 300
American Federation of State,
County, and Municipal Employees
290, 302
American Friends Service Committee
(AFSC) 280
Americus, Georgia 94, 149

Anderson, William 90–91, 94–95
Anniston, Alabama 80
Arrington, Mayor Richard 318
Ashbrook, Congressman John 323
Atlanta Constitution, 20, 159
Atlanta Daily World, 26, 100
Atlanta, Georgia: and 1906 riot 12;
  segregation in 17; and civil rights
  gains by the 1940s 23; and bi-
  racial regime by 1960s 63–64, 66;
  and 1960 sit-in at Rich's
  department store 74; and
  downtown desegregation accord
  78–79; and SNCC activities in,
  165, 247, 256; King
  commemorative sites in, 317, 319;
  see also Ebenezer Baptist Church
Ayers, Thomas 242

Baez, Joan 281, 288
Baker, Ella: criticisms of King 1, 3,
  45, 51, 59, 61, 83, 142, 335; as
  SCLC temporary director 60–62
  and SNCC 3, 68, 70, 88, 95, 319;
  biography of, 345, 351
Baker, Wilson 186, 197
Baldwin, James 158
Bandung conference 53
Barbour, J. Pius 21, 23, 27
Baton Rouge, Louisiana: bus boycott
  27, 45
Beatty, Ross 237–39, 243
Beck, Glenn 326
Belafonte, Harry 70, 115, 120,
  201, 266
Bethel Baptist Church, Birmingham
  105, 109,
Bevel, Diane *see* Nash, Diane
Bevel, James: and Nashville
  movement 78; background and
  character 119; and Birmingham
  campaign 122–24, 127, 130; and
  Alabama "nonviolent army plan"
  160–61, 166–67; and Selma
  campaign 183, 188, 191, 194; and
  Chicago campaign 215–16, 218,

220–22, 225, 228, 232, 235–36,
  240, 242, 245; and Vietnam 261,
  265, 269–70, 280, 337–38; and
  the PPC 281, 284, 295, 309
Birmingham, Alabama: bus boycott
  56–57; and Freedom Riders
  80–81; and 1963 campaign
  105–40; and 1963 mayoral contest
  107, 109, 111, 116, 121; goals of
  campaign 111–12; bystander
  Leroy Allen bitten 117; "D-Day"
  children's march 124–26;
  Operation Confusion 129–30;
  desegregation agreement 130–31,
  134; Gaston Motel bombing and
  escalating violence 134–35;
  negative effective of campaign on
  King's reputation 136–37;
  significance of the campaign
  137–38; *see also* Connor, Eugene
  "Bull"; Bethel Baptist Church;
  Shuttlesworth, Fred; and Sixteenth
  Street Church
Black Panther Party 259, 315,
  316, 331
Black Power 2–5, 7, 8, 63, 231–34;
  243; 247–48; Carmichael's coining
  the slogan 253; and King 253–56;
  258–59, 292, 310, 337; and the
  media reaction 256–57, 278;
  negative impact on SCLC funding
  259–60; legacy of 331, 342;
  see also Carmichael, Stokely
Blackwell, Randolph 215, 221,
  261, 288
"Bloody Sunday" *see* Selma, Alabama
Bond, Julian 69, 70, 142, 266, 328
Boston University 24
Boutwell, Albert 109, 112–13,
  116–17, 121, 128, 131, 133, 138,
  157, 159, 162
Boynton, Amelia 183, 188
Boynton v. *Virginia* (1960) 78
Boyte, Harry 261
Branch, Taylor 33, 85, 94–95, 96,
  134, 142, 343, 347

Brightman, Edgar S. 22, 24
Browder v. *Gayle* (1956) 48–49,
    54, 56
Brown Chapel *see* Selma
Brown, H. Rap 314, 337
Brown v. *Board of Education* (1954)
    28, 38, 48, 52, 54, 59, 63, 214,
    341, 352 *Brown II* (1955)
    implementation decree 37
Bryant, Governor Farris G. 170, 172,
    174, 175
Bunche, Ralph 274
Burks, Mary Fair 34–35
Bus boycotts: Albany 97; Baton
    Rouge 27, 45; Birmingham
    56–57; Cape Town 53;
    Montgomery 35–56; Rock Hill
    57; Tallahassee 53–54
Bush, George W. 325, 334
Bus terminal segregation *see* Freedom
    Rides
Byrd, Senator Robert 171, 305

Cabbage, Charles 292, 294, 299
Califano, Joseph 305, 353
Canton, Mississippi 255
Capell, Arthur 187
Carmichael, Stokely: in Atlanta 247;
    and Black Power call 256–57,
    337; and SNCC interracialism
    248–49; in Lowndes County 249;
    in Selma 203; and King 209, 217,
    231, 251, 254, 257–59, 294, 351;
    and King's death 301; and
    Meredith March 250–56; and
    nonviolence 249, 251; and
    Vietnam 259, 275, 310, 337, 347;
    memoirs 344
Carson, Clayborne 348, 349, 352
Carter, Jimmy 315, 320–21, 323
Catholic Interracial Council (CIC) 229
CCCO *see* Coordinating Council of
    Community Organizations
Central Intelligence Agency (CIA) 302
CEP *see* Citizenship Education
    Program

Chaney, James 177, 253
Chattanooga: commemoration
    controversy 317–18,
Chicago: King threatened on 1963
    visit 113; Mayor Daley heckled at
    1963 NAACP convention 150;
    SCLC 1966 campaign 212–46;
    Bevel's role in 215–16, 218, 222,
    225, 232, 235–36, 240, 242, 245;
    school segregation 224, 226;
    housing discrimination 227, 230;
    Summit negotiations 236–44; and
    King's failure 244–46; *see also*
    Daley, Richard; Jackson, Jesse; and
    Obama, Barack
Citizens Council, White 29, 38, 43,
    45, 49, 159
Citizenship Education Program
    (CEP) 87–88, 102, 144, 208–9,
    221, 260; *see also* Clark, Septima;
    Cotton, Dorothy
Civil Rights Act (1957) 59–60, 73
Civil Rights Act (1960) 164
Civil Rights Act (1964): and
    President Kennedy 135, 145, 147,
    156; and President Johnson
    164–66, 176; and St Augustine
    169–71, 174–75, 192, 347;
    impact on black employment 320
Civil Rights Act (1968) 305
Civil Rights Commission 60, 61,
    116, 320
Clark, Ramsey 286, 306
Clark, Septima P. 87, 208, 288, 350
Clark, Sherriff Jim 135, 183,
    186–93, 196–97, 199
Clayborne Temple Church, Memphis
    292–93
Clergy and Laymen Against the
    War 271
Cleveland, Ohio 2, 219, 277, 278
Clinton, Bill 324–25, 327
Clinton, Hillary 332–33
Cochran, Johnny 329
Coffin, William Sloan 84, 269, 281
Colburn, David 175, 347

Cold War 22, 31, 53, 86, 134, 140, 269, 310, 345
Collins, Addie Mae 157
Collins, Leroy 189, 198–200
Colvin, Claudette 36–37
COME *see* Community on the Move for Equality
Communism, 43, 85, 106; and King 2, 87, 114, 146–47, 184, 229–30, 270, 273–74, 316, 323–24
Community on the Move for Equality 291–92, 294, 296
Community Relations Service 187
Congress of Racial Equality (CORE) 77, 149–50, 176–77, 229; and Black Power 231–32, 241; in Chicago 241–42, 244; *see also* Farmer, James and Freedom Rides
Connor Eugene "Bull," 8, and Freedom Rides 80–81; background of 106–7; and 1963 mayoral election 112–13; and his reaction to demonstrations 117–18, 124–26, 129–30, 137, 146; and Sixteenth Street church bombing 159
Conyers, John 322
Cooper, Annie Lee 188
Cooper, Ann Nixon 334
Coordinating Council of Community Organizations (CCCO) 218–22; 224, 228–29, 242; *see also* Chicago
CORE *see* Congress of Racial Equality
Cotton, Dorothy 88,117, 289
Council of Federated Organization (COFO) Mississippi 166–67
Crozer Theological College 20–22, 24, 61
Crusade for Citizenship 60–61, 69, 208
Curry, Izola Ware 62

Daley, Richard: black dissatisfaction with 86, 150, 220; black allies of 227, 235; union allies of 230; strength of his political machine

219–20, 224, 245; outmanoeuvres King 222, 225–26, 227–28, 232, 235, 236–37, 240–41, 243–44, 251; and July 1966 urban unrest 232–33; *see also* Chicago
Daniels, Jonathan 210, 249
Danville, Virginia 144, 156, 163
Davis, Ossie 315–16
Davis, Sammy, Jr. 189
Dawson, Congressman William 227
Deacons of Defense 252
De la Beckwith, Byron 144, 253
Deloach, "Deke" 186
Democratic Party: and the white "solid South" 16, 76, 98, 181, 247; and black voters in the New Deal coalition 16, 57–58, 73; 1964 national convention in Atlantic City 178–79; and Jesse Jackson 328; and Barack Obama 330–31, 333
Detroit: 1967 disturbances 277, 278
DeWolf, L. Harold 24–25, 282
Dexter Avenue Baptist Church 27–28, 33–35, 40, 58, 63
Dirksen, Senator Everett 176, 197, 247
Dixon, Governor Frank 31
Drew, John and Deenie 109, 112, 116, 123, 131
DuBois, W.E.B. 13
Dukakis, Michael 328
Durr, Virginia 32, 39, 50, 51, 73

Eastland, Senator James 38, 49, 309,
Ebenezer Baptist Church, Atlanta: A. D. Williams and 11; and King's childhood 11–12, 14; and Coretta Scott King's baptism 27; King's preaching on poverty and Vietnam 216, 266; and King's funeral 311; and mother Alberta King's 1974 murder 316; designated national historic site 317; and Obama's 2008 address 332
Edmund Pettus Bridge, Selma 195–97, 200, 211

Eisenhower, Dwight D. 59, 60, 61, 68, 73, 76, 155, 353
Elliott, Judge J.Robert 99–100, 101, 103
Employment discrimination 112, 149
Eskew, Glenn 111, 315, 346
Evers, Medgar 144, 168, 253

Face the Nation (TV series) 258, 275
Face to Face (TV series) 72
Fairclough, Adam 43, 103, 170, 344, 347
Falwell, Jerry 8, 316–17
Fanon, Franz 249
Farmer, James: at NAACP 70; and CORE's Freedom Rides 77–80, 84; in Louisiana 150; and 1964 civil rights debate 176; and President Johnson's 1964 call for a protest moratorium 178; and King 70, 184, 251
Farnsworth, Ann 260
Farrakhan, Louis 329
Faubus, Governor Orval 60
Fauntroy, Walter 189
Federal Bureau of Investigation (FBI): hostility to 1940s civil rights activists 32; hostility to King 7, 114, 124, 156, 184, 273, 286–87, 292–94; reluctance to protect Freedom Riders 79–80; bugging campaign against King 114, 171, 184–86, 229–30, 264–65, 276, 324, 327; required to investigate civil rights killings 158; use of Klan informers 206; and King's assassination 296, 302, 316; COINTELPRO 316; *see also* Hoover, J. Edgar
Fellowship of Reconciliation 48–49
Field, Marshall (Foundation) 87, 260
Fields, Uriah J. 54–55
First Baptist Church, Montgomery 33, 35, 57; 1961 siege of 81–83
Fisk University 47, 67

Flemming v. *South Carolina Electric and Gas* (1956) 54
Foley, Albert S. 116
Folsom, Governor Jim 29
Ford Foundation 222, 261, 279, 288
Forman, James: 91,117; in Birmingham campaign, 128–29, 133; in Selma campaign 198, 200–201; 203; and Black Power 249; memoirs 344, 351
Freedom Rides 77–78; 79–85; and King 81–83
Freedom Summer 166–67, 176, 208, 248, 251, 253, 309, 321, 352

Gadsden 144
Galbraith, J.K. 269
Gandhi, Mohandas K. 18, 48–49, 100, 160, 194, 324; comparison with King 50, 52, 58–59, 62, 83, 288, 336, 338; fasting 165, 294, 310, 313; and SNCC 226, 249,345
Gardner, William 24
Garrow, David 326, 343, 345, 348
Garvey, Marcus 114
Gaston, A.G. 108, 112, 116–17, 121, 123, 125, 130, 133, 162
Gaston Motel, Selma 114, 124, 129, 134, 194
Gayle, Mayor W.A. 36, 46,
Gayle v. *Browder* (1956) 48, 54, 56; *see also* Montgomery
Germany: reaction to King's death in the East (DDR) 314–15; reaction to King's death in the West 314
Ghana: King attends independence celebration 59; reaction to King's death 313
Ghettoes: 38, 69, 150, 211, 308; King's mixed reputation in 2, 184, 217, 244,249, 271, 322, 331; King's efforts to address problems in 4, 152, 181, 206, 212–14, 216, 218, 220, 226–27, 241, 267–68; disturbances in 5, 7, 178, 182,

232–34, 254–55, 258, 277–78;
see also Chicago, Poor People's
Campaign
Goldwater, Barry 145, 176–77,
178, 180
Goodman, Andrew 176
Graetz, Robert 57, 345
Grafman, Rabbi 159
Graham, Billy 121, 154
Granger, Lester 61
Gray, Fred 37, 345
Greenberg, Jack 190, 199
Green, Robert 261
Greensboro, North Carolina 64, 67,
78, 350
Greenwood, Mississippi 253
Gregory, Dick 220, 348
Guevara, Che 249
Gulf War 328

Halleck, Congressman Charles
155–56
Hall, Grover C. 31
Hall Linda Bryant 244
Hamer, Fannie Lou 178–79, 351
Hanes, Mayor Arthur 117
Hansen, Bill 98–99
Harding, Vincent 274
Hare, James 183
Harlem 19, 62, 195,322, 333
Harrington, Michael 282–83, 289
Harris, Don 149
Harrison, James A. 286–87
Harris, Rutha 93
Hartsfield, Mayor William 66,
74–75
Harvard University 26, 330
Hatcher, Mayor Richard 316
Hawkins, Congressman Augustus 320
Hayling, Robert B. 168–69, 174;
see also St Augustine
Helms, Senator Jesse 324
Henry, Aaron 179
Highlander Folk School, 39, 87–88
Hobson, Julius 314
Hollins, Billy 226

Holt Street Baptist Church,
Montgomery 35, 41–43
Hoover, J. Edgar 7, 114, 184–86,
206, 273, 276, 286–87, 293, 343
Horton, Myles 87
House Un-American Activities
Committee 32
Housing discrimination, 4, 7, 38, 73,
86, 205, 208, 214–15, 228, 230,
236–37, 241–42, 249, 258, 284,
305, 326
Huddleston, Bishop Trevor 313
Humphrey, Senator Hubert: 6, 31,
156, 192; Humphrey Hawkins
Act (1978) 319–21
Huntsville, Alabama 157
Hutchinson Street Baptist Church,
Montgomery 55, 57

"I Have a Dream" speech (1963)
151–56, 203, 307, 314–15, 325,
335–36
In Friendship 52
India 18, 62, 313
Indianola, Mississippi 38
Interstate Commerce Commission
(ICC) 86, 90, 92, 96; *see also*
Freedom Rides
Invaders, The (Memphis) 2, 292,
294–97, 299
Israel 277, 314
Izvestia (newspaper) 173

Jackson, Jesse 222, 228, 235–36,
245, 254, 262, 280–81, 295, 299,
308, 327–29
Jackson, Jimmie Lee 193, 195, 201,
206, 211
Jackson, Joseph H. 27, 229
Jackson, Mississippi 83, 144, 236,
255
Jackson, Thomas 310, 344, 347
Jacksonville, Florida 61, 168, 172
Javitz, Jacob 207
Jemison, Theodore J 27,45
Jet (magazine) 115, 159

Johnson, Governor Paul 177
Johnson, Judge Frank 192, 197–200, 203
Johnson, Lyndon: as vice-president 73, 139, 145–46, 168; and 1964 Act 165–66, 176, 347; and the MFDP 178–79; and Selma campaign 200–203, 205–6; and King 2, 177, 204, 211, 223–24, 241, 252, 295, 311, 336; and Vietnam 247–48, 264–67, 273–77, 337; King's assassination 301–2
Johns, Vernon 27–28, 33–34
Jones, Clarence 120, 147, 265, 287, 344
Jones, Solomon 299
Joseph, Peniel 4, 342, 347, 351

Katzenbach, Nicholas 143, 192, 195, 197, 255, 353
Kelsey, George D. 21
Kennedy, John F.: 1960 election 6, 72–76; ambivalence on civil rights 77, 353; support for voter registration rather than direct action 86–88; use of marshals to protect James Meredith in 1962 107; worry over King's Communist associates 115, 146–47; Birmingham campaign 120, 126, 129, 135–36; and Governor George Wallace 139; civil rights speech 143–44; March on Washington 149, 155–56; Birmingham church bombing 157–58, 160–62; assassination 163–64, 314
Kennedy, Robert F.: and Freedom Rides 6, 80–82, 84–85; Albany campaign 98–101, 149; Birmingham campaign 120–21, 128, 133, 135, 137; desegregation of University of Alabama 139–40, 143-; 1963 civil rights bill 139, 146; and Watts riot 218; and

Black Power 256; and poverty 268, 278; and Vietnam 270, 295; and King assassination 301; assassinated 304
Kennedy, Senator Edward 323–24
Kenwood-Oakland Community Organization (KOCO) 222
Kerner, Governor Otto 232, 241
King, C.B. 90, 95
King, Ed 179
King family: Adam Daniel (brother) 20, 116, 134, 184, 298–99; Alberta (*née Williams*; mother) 11, 14, 316; Bernice Albertine (daughter) 115; Christine King (sister) 14–15, 344; Coretta: (*née* Scott; wife) 25–27, 41; house bombed 48; and husband's jail sentences 74–75, 120–21; pressures on 92, 113, 164, 174, 181, 224, 296; and Nobel Prize award to Martin 179; reaction to FBI tape 185; and Martin's depression 288–89; and Martin's assassination 300; and PPC 304, 308; at 1972 National Black Political Convention 316; signing of the Humphrey-Hawkins Act (1978) 320; at signing of King Holiday Act 324; James (paternal grandfather) 14; Joel (uncle) 27; Martin Luther Sr. (father; a.k.a. Michael): early life and career 11, 13–14; attitude to racism 17–18; attitude to nonviolence 118; voter registration efforts 15; relationship with Martin 15, 20–21, 24, 27, 66; clashes with Coretta 26; tries to prevent Martin returning to Montgomery 50; Republican supporter 16, 73; 1960 Atlanta desegregation agreement 79; Martin Luther III (son) 60, 74, 344; Yolanda (daughter) 41, 48, 74; Dexter (son) 344; Williams,

Adam Daniel (maternal grandfather) 11–12, 13–14; Williams, Willis (maternal great grandfather) 10

King, Martin Luther, Jr.:

Events: birth and childhood 11, 14–19; name change 11; studies at Morehouse 18–20; studies at Crozer 21–24; studies at Boston University 24–27; licensed to preach 21; marriage 26; Minster at Dexter Avenue Church, Montgomery 28, 29, 33–35, 37, 58, 63; election as MIA president and Holt Street Church speech 41–43; arrested in Montgomery 47; kitchen table conversion experience 47–48; home bombed 48; found guilty of conspiracy 52; accusations of financial impropriety at the MIA 54–55; end of boycott 56; formation of SCLC 57; attends Ghana's independence celebrations 59; 1958 stabbing 61–62; moves back to Atlanta 63–64; Alabama tax case 69, 71; Atlanta sit-in, arrest and Kennedy-sparked release 73–76; role in Atlanta desegregation agreement 78–79; and Freedom Rides 81–83; Albany campaign 89–103; 1962 attack in Birmingham 108; Birmingham campaign 111–33; March on Washington 149–56; Birmingham church bombing 158–60; Kennedy assassination 163–64; St Augustine campaign 167–75; 1964 Democratic National Convention 178–79; Nobel Peace Prize 179–80. 183–84; Selma campaign 186–207; reaction to the Watts uprising 217–18; Chicago campaign 218–46; Meredith March and Black Power

252–60; Vietnam 264–77; Riverside address 271–75; reaction to 1967 ghetto uprisings 271; Poor People's Campaign (PPC) 279–89; Memphis 290–304; assassination 298–304; funeral 311–12

Personal Attributes: aloofness alleged 24; aural memory 14; hesitancy 41, 83; moderation 233–34; philosophical and intellectual 24–25; depression 58, 287–90, 297–98; exhaustion 63, 71, 142, 179, 219, 233, 239; financial probity 54–55, 71; love of food 20, 165, 288, 299; love of dancing 20; physical courage 48, 61–62, 108, 234–35; plagiarism 61, 348–49; sense of humor 191; sensitive about his height 288; womaniser 20, 25–26, 113–14, 185–86, 264, 295, 326–27

Relationships: Abernathy, Ralph 37, 59, 115, 179, 184, 225, 326–27; Baker, Ella 1–2, 3, 45, 51–52, 59, 61–62, 83, 142, 350; Bevel, James 124, 161, 218, 269–70, 280–81; Jackson, Jesse 280, 295, 327–28 Johnson, Lyndon 165, 177–78, 185, 202, 204, 265, 273; Kennedy, John F. 6, 76, 98, 120–21, 137–38, 145–46, 155, 160; Kennedy, Robert F. 6, 82, 84–85, 99–100, 120, 128, 133, 139, 218, 295, 301, 304; Levison, Stanley 51, 70, 71–72, 114, 146–47, 215, 216–17, 221, 233, 260, 265, 270, 274–76; Nixon, Richard 59, 73; Powell, Adam Clayton 59, 72, 139–40, 219; Rustin, Bayard 48–49, 56–57, 60, 73, 163, 178, 184, 199, 208, 214, 221, 224, 227, 245, 268, 282–83, 337;

Shuttlesworth, Fred 62, 105–6, 108, 111–12, 131–33, 179; Walker, Wyatt T. 83, 97, 114–15, 119, 127, 161, 165; Wilkins, Roy 59, 69, 139, 142, 149, 274, 337; Williams, Hosea 170, 179, 215, 261–62, 299; Young, Andrew 119, 142, 172, 185–86, 189–90, 205, 208, 218, 229, 261–62, 298, 299, 302, 317; Young, Whitney 287–88

Topics: arrests and jail terms 47, 61, 69, 74–75, 94–96, 118–23, 133, 172, 188–90; Black Power 3, 4–5, 7, 8–9, 63, 231, 233, 247–48, 251, 253–56, 257–59, 262, 278, 310, 337, 340; commemoration of King 2–3, 317–19, 322–26, 332, 335, 338; faith in economic leverage 109, 115, 128–29, 163, 204, 228, 254, 291; FBI bugging and smear campaigns 114, 146, 172, 185–86, 265; fund-raising role 50, 54–55, 61, 69, 71–72, 83, 99, 113, 118, 188, 205, 215, 218, 260, 263, 266; ghetto disturbances 258–59, 277; Martin Luther King Day 8, 322–25, 332–33; personalism 19, 22, 348; radical vision of economic and social justice 86, 183, 204, 208, 216–18, 221, 233, 258, 278–79, 282–83, 310; role of media in campaigns 58–59, 251, 335–36

Sermons and Speeches: Three Dimensions of a Complete Life 28; The Death of Evil upon the Seashore 52–53; Give us the Ballot 59; I Have A Dream 151–55, 314–15, 325; Nobel Prize lecture 184, 334; How Long Not Long 205–6; A Time to Break Silence 271–75; Been to the Mountaintop 297–98; Drum Major Instinct 289, 311–12, 338; threats and

plots against 71, 158, 170, 178, 195, 296, 300–302, 314, 316, 347–48; *see also* specific campaigns

King Holiday Act (1983) 324

King Holiday and Service Act (1994) 324–25

King, Slater 90, 100

Ku Klux Klan 38, 43, 69, 71, 79–80,105,122, 168–70, 175, 187, 196, 206, 232, 317, 346

Kyles, Samuel 290, 291, 299–300

Lafayette, Bernard 167, 183, 189, 216, 221, 245, 280, 307,345

Lawson, James 67, 70, 73, 78, 84, 88, 291–94, 298

LeFlore, John 167

Lentz, Richard 58–59

Levison, Stanley 6, 51, 56, 70–72, 86, 114, 138, 146–47, 164, 184, 215–18, 221, 222, 227, 233, 260, 262, 265, 269, 270–71, 274–77, 287

Lewis, David L. 96, 244, 343

Lewis, John 78, 151, 178, 187, 194–97, 249, 328, 332, 345

Lewis, Rufus 34–35, 40, 42

Lingo, Al 135, 157–58, 193, 196, 199

Little Rock, Arkansas 60, 68

Liuzzo, Viola Gregg 206, 209, 211

Loeb, Henry 290–91. 293, 298, 302

Logan, Marian 289

Lorraine Motel, Memphis 291, 296, 300, 303, 338

Los Angeles 19, 72, 270; *see also* Watts

Louisiana 67, 182, 352; *see also* Baton Rouge; Deacons of Defense; New Orleans; and Plaquemines Parish

Lowenstein, Allard 269

Lowery, Joseph 71, 189

Lowndes County Freedom Party (LCFP) 259

Lucas, Robert 231, 241, 244–45

Lucy, Autherine 49

Macdonald, Congressman Larry 323
Mao Zedong 249
Malcolm X 2, 135, 137, 148, 164,
  168, 194–95, 231, 249–50, 259
  322, 331, 335, 349, 351
Martin Luther King Center,
  Atlanta 317
Mboya, Tom 63
McCain, Franklin 67
McCarthy, Senator Eugene 270
McCarthy, Senator Joseph 51, 275
McClellan, Senator John 304
McCollough, Marrell 292
McComb, Mississippi 88–89
McDermott, John 229–30
McGovern, Senator George 270
McKissick, Floyd 232, 252,
  254–55 *see also* CORE and
  Black Power
McNair, Denise 157, 159
McNeil, Joseph 67
McWilliams, Carey 270
Maddox, Governor Lester 247
Malcolm X: 164, 259, 331,
  334, 351; criticisms of King 2,
  135, 137, 148, 349; influence
  of 148, 194–95, 231, 249–50,
  309, 322;
Mandela, Nelson 53
Manucy, Holstead "Hoss" 169–71
March on Washington 18, 138, 141,
  145, 150–55, 163, 265, 279, 304,
  307, 324, 325
Marciniak, Ed 236
Marion, Alabama 192–94
Marshall, Burke 82, 86, 98, 100,
  121, 126–27, 130, 132, 135,
  146–47, 158
Marshall, Thurgood 70, 352
Mason Temple, Memphis 291, 297
Massive Resistance 52, 87, 192, 346
Mays, Benjamin E. 18–19, 20–21,
  27, 155, 300–301, 344
Meier, August 233, 343, 349, 352
Memphis, Tennessee 2, 3, 8, 58,
  61, 124, 231, 252, 287, 290–94,

  296–300, 302, 304, 319,
  338, 347
Meredith, James 107, 250
Meredith March 231, 248, 251–56
MFDP *see* Mississippi Freedom
  Democratic Party
MIA *see* Montgomery Improvement
  Association
Million Man March 329
Mississippi: Freedom Summer
  166–67, 176; Black Power
  249–50, 252–53; Child
  Development Group 257; *see also*
  Medgar Evers, Greenwood,
  Indianola, Jackson, McComb,
  Robert Moses, Meredith March,
  Natchez, Emmett Till
Mississippi, University of 107, 140
Mississippi Freedom Democratic
  Party (MFDP) 167, 177–79
Mobile, Alabama 44, 71, 157,
  159, 167
Monroe, North Carolina 69, 89–90
Monson Motor Lodge, St Augustine,
  Florida 172, 173–74
Montgomery, Alabama: bus boycott
  29–58, 62–64, 345; violence
  against Freedom Riders 79,
  81–83; Selma march 182, 205–6;
  see also Dexter Avenue Baptist
  church; E.D. Nixon; Rosa Parks;
  JoAnn Robinson
Montgomery Improvement
  Association (MIA) 30, 42–60,
  61–64, 68, 167, 203
Moore, William 122
Morehouse College 11–12, 18–21,
  317 *see also* Benjamin Mays
Morgan, Charles 107, 159
Moses, Robert 89, 142, 167,
  179, 351
Mount Zion Baptist Church, Albany
  93, 100
Moyers, Bill 273–74
Muhammad, Elijah 164
Myrdal, Gunnar 19

NAACP *see* National Association for the Advancement of Colored People

Nash Bevel, Diane 67, 78, 81, 88, 99, 119, 351

Nashville, Tennessee 67, 78, 351

Natchez, Mississippi 223

Nation of Islam *see also* Malcolm X and Elijah Muhammad

National Association for the Advancement of Colored People (NAACP) 11, 13, 15, 18, 23, 28, 37–38, 44, 49, 53, 58, 60, 68, 70–71, 90–91, 103, 144, 150, 163, 168–69, 219, 229, 259, 318, 352: *see also* Ella Baker; Medgar Evers; John Leflore; E.D. Nixon; Rosa Parks; Roy Wilkins; and Robert Williams

National Baptist Convention 27; *see also* Joseph H. Jackson

National Civil Rights Museum, Memphis 319, 338

National Welfare Rights Organization (NWRO) 283

Nazi Party 187

Negro American Labor Council 147

New Orleans, Louisiana 41, 57, 58, 80, 229, 352

New York city 24, 72, 116, 158, 178, 186, 194, 214, 251, 284, 350; *see also* Harlem; Adam Clayton Powell and Riverside Church

New York Times 50, 71, 85, 92, 96, 102, 106, 112, 121, 138, 157, 173, 181, 189, 207, 256, 267, 275, 294, 314

Newark, New Jersey 7, 277, 278

Newton, Huey 337; *see also* Black Panther Party

Niebuhr, Reinhold 22, 23, 239

Nigeria 312

Nixon E.D. 34, 36, 39–42, 49, 59, 63

Nixon, Richard 6, 59, 72–73, 285, 305, 316, 320; 1960 election defeat 76

Nobel Peace Prize 142, 179, 180, 184, 219, 272, 311, 330, 334

Nonviolence 48–50, 67, 84–85, 108–9, 121–22, 135–36, 148, 169, 194, 203–4, 249–51, 254, 284–86, 288, 294, 296, 299, 305, 315, 324, 329, 334–35, 336

Obama, Barack 8–9, 245, 325, 328; and King 329–35

O'Boyle, Patrick 151

O'Dell, Jack 114, 146–47

Operation Breadbasket 109, 222, 228, 245, 254, 262, 280, 327

Operation Dixie 32

Orange, James 123–24, 193, 231, 295–96, 306

Organized labor: racism of rank-and-file 213, 215, 217, 230; AFL-CIO 32, 87, 92–93, 268; AFSCME 290–91; UAW 147, 151, 236, 260

Page, Marion 90, 95–96, 98

Parks, Rosa 36–37, 38–41, 42, 45, 48, 205, 332, 345

Patterson, Governor John 29, 80, 82–83

Paul VI, Pope 179, 313

Pendleton, Clarence 320

People United to Serve Humanity (PUSH) *see* Jesse Jackson 327

Personalism *see* Martin Luther King, Jr: topics

Philadelphia, Pennsylvania 16, 219, 350

Pitts, Lucius 108, 130, 162

Pittsburgh Courier [newspaper] 274, 305

Plessy v. *Ferguson* (1896) 13, 28, 36, 54

Poor Peoples Campaign (PPC) 279–87, 289, 291, 293–95, 302, 304–9, 310, 327–28

Porter, John T. 109, 116–17, 123

Powell, Congressman Adam Clayton, Jr. 59, 72, 139–40, 219

Powers, Georgia Davis 327
PPC *see* Poor Peoples Campaign
Prayer Pilgrimage (1957) 59
Price, Cecil 253
Prince Edward County, Virginia 68
Pritchett, Sherriff Laurie 91, 94,
   95–102, 110, 117, 137, 186, 227,
   306, 346

Raby, Al 219, 222, 228, 235–36,
   238, 242
Rainbow Coalition 328
Ramparts (magazine) 269
Randolph, A. Philip 18, 31, 34, 52,
   61, 72, 93, 256; and March on
   Washington 142–43, 146–47,
   151, 155; *see also* organized labor
Ray, James Earl 296, 302–4, 347–48
Readers' Digest (magazine) 274–75
Reagan, Ronald 7, 143, 320–22; and
   King Holiday bill 323–24
Reeb, James 201–2, 206, 211
Reese, Frederick 183, 191–92
Reuther, Walter 151, 155, 235,
   260, 270
Reynolds, William Bradford 320
Rhodesia 313
Ribicoff, Senator Abraham 268
Richmond, David 67
Ricks, Willie 253
Riverside Church, New York 2, 5,
   271–75, 278
Robertson, Carol 157–58
Robinson, Chester 242, 244
Robinson, Cleveland 265
Robinson, Jackie 76, 173
Robinson, Jo Ann 34–35, 36, 40–41,
   50, 345
Robinson, Ruby Doris Smith 351
Roche, John 273–74
Rochester, New York 216
Rock Hill, South Carolina 57,
   78, 79
Rockwell, George Lincoln 188
Roosevelt, Franklin D. 16, 19, 73
Rowan, Carl 46, 274

Rowe, Gary 206
Rush, Congressman Bobby 331
Rusk, Dean 276
Russell, Senator Richard 144–45
Rustin, Bayard 48–49, 51, 56–57,
   61, 70, 72, 178, 184, 199, 208,
   214, 217–18, 256, 351; and
   March on Washington 142, 149,
   150, 152, 155, 163; opposes
   Chicago campaign 215, 221, 224,
   227, 245; opposes King on
   Vietnam 268, 282, 287, 337; and
   PPC 307–8
Rutherford, William 280, 289

St. Augustine, Florida 167–76, 192,
   211, 248, 347
St, John the Divine Cathedral, New
   York 52
Salinger, Pierre 139. 160
Savannah, Georgia 156, 170
Schools: desegregation of 28, 66, 68,
   155, 156–57, 229; de facto
   segregation of 213–15, 222, 224
Schwerner, Michael 176–77
SCLC *see* Southern Christian
   Leadership Conference
SCOPE *see* Summer Community
   Organization and Political
   Education
Scott, Coretta *see* King family:
   Coretta
Seale, Bobby *see* Black Panther Party
Seay, Solomon 34, 71
Seigenthaler, John 81
Sellers, Clyde 36, 42–43, 45–46,
   54, 61
Selma, Alabama: 5–6, 25, 31, 135,
   223; 1965 campaign 186–207
Shabazz, Betty 316
Sharpton, Al 326, 329
Sherrod, Charles 78, 90, 91
Shiloh Baptist Church, Albany 90
Shuttlesworth, Fred 56–57, 62, 71,
   174, 179, 346; and Freedom Rides
   78, 80–83; and Birmingham

campaign 105–12, 115–18; 121, 123–24; 127–34, 136, 139, 147, 157, 162, 169
Simpson, Judge Bryan 170–71, 174
Six Day War (Arab_Israeli) 277
Sixteenth Street Baptist Church, Birmingham 124–26, 130; bombing of 157–59
Smathers, Senator George 170, 172
Smiley, Glenn 48–49, 50, 56, 57
Smith, Congressman Howard 166
Smith v *Allwright* (1944) 16
Smitherman, Mayor Joseph 186, 211
Smyer, Sidney 107, 108, 118, 128, 130, 136, 162
SNCC *see* Student Nonviolent Coordinating Committee
Social Gospel 12, 18, 22, 35, 217
Solidarity Day 307–8
South Africa 53, 125–26, 178, 313
Southern Christian Leadership Conference (SCLC): formation of 56–57; initial difficulties 58, 60, 61, 62–63, 65, 68; Crusade for Citizenship 59–61; rivalry with NAACP 69–70; and Ella Baker 60–62, 68, 83; organizational weaknesses; financial position 78, 223, 291; and Wyatt Walker 71, 89, 95, 97, 103; and Freedom Rides 79, 83; and Albany 95–103; rivalry with SNCC 103; and Birmingham 111–33; and St Augustine 167–75; and Selma 186–207; and Chicago 218–36; and SCOPE 208–9, 215, 223, 261, 262; and Memphis 290–303; and PPC 279–87, 304–9; under Ralph Abernathy 304–9, 327; *see also* Citizenship Schools; Operation Breadbasket; and individual campaigns
Southern Conference for Human Welfare (SCHW) 32
Southern Manifesto 52, 164
Southern Regional Council 88

Spock, Benjamin 265, 270, 271, 281
Spring Mobilization (1967) 261, 270; *see also* Vietnam
Steele, C.K. 54, 56
Steele, Shelby 153
Stokes, Mayor Carl 219, 278
Stoner, J.B. 157, 172, 301
Student Nonviolent Coordinating Committee (SNCC): Atlanta 73–74, 78–79, 165; Nashville 78, 81, 83; formation 68; Freedom Rides 81–83; jail not bail 78; voter registration 88–89; Albany 90, 95, 96–97, 98, 100, 102–3; March on Washington 149, 150–51; Mississippi Freedom Summer 166–67, 176–77; MFDP 177–79, 211; Selma 167, 183, 187, 189, 192, 194–95, 198, 200–202, 203; Black Power 231, 248–49, 253–56, 259, 337; expulsion of whites 256; Vietnam 266–68, 275; rivalry with SCLC 102–3, 142, 203; see also Stokely Carmichael; James Forman; John Lewis; Robert Moses
Summer Community Organizing and Political Education 208–9, 215, 223, 261, 262

Tallahassee, Florida 53–54, 56, 57
Talmadge, Governor Herman 75
Television 41, 51, 95, 98, 140, 143, 151–52, 154, 187, 194, 196, 202, 203, 234, 335–36
Thomas, Judge Daniel 189, 190, 191
Thomas, Norman 269
Thurmond, Strom 31, 275, 305, 325
Till, Emmett 38, 105,
Tilley, John 61–62
Time [magazine] 58–59, 96, 165,
Trenholm. H.C. 40
Truman, Harry S.: desegregation of armed forces 23, 31; and Dixiecrat revolt 31–32, 106; and Red Scare 31, 32, 247–48

Turner, Albert 193
Tuscaloosa, Alabama 49, 140,
Tuskegee, Alabama 157, 350
Tuttle, Judge Elbert 100, 136
TWO, *see* Woodlawn Organization,
  The,

Unemployment 19, 142, 214, 216,
  228, 249, 263, 269, 278, 321;
  see also employment discrimination
Union to End Slums 225
Unions *see* organized labor
United Church of Christ 260
Urban Progress Centers 228

Vandiver, Governor Ernest 66,
  75–76
Vann, David 107, 125, 127, 130,
  133 315
Voter Education Project (VEP) 88,
  97, 114, 182
Voter registration 13, 15, 19, 34, 37,
  57–58, 60, 63, 69–70, 86, 88–90,
  102, 109, 150, 160–61, 167,
  181–82, 187–88, 191, 207, 215,
  223, 245, 250, 252–53, 262, 337;
  see also Crusade for Citizenship;
  Citizenship Education Program
  (CEP); Summer Community
  Organizing and Political
  Education (SCOPE) and Voter
  Education Project (VEP)
Voting Rights Act (1965) 2, 5,
  141, 192, 197, 201–2, 207–8,
  210–11, 217, 224, 252, 305,
  310, 353

Wachtel, Harry 265, 274, 275, 276
Wagner, Mayor Robert 178
Walker, Wyatt T. 71, 75, 83, 88,
  89, 95, 97, 102–3, 109–10,
  112–15, 117, 119–21, 123–24,
  126–27, 129, 135, 161, 165, 169,
  172, 179
Walk Against Fear *see* Meredith
  March

Wall Street Project 328–29
Wallace, Governor George 6–7, 107,
  143, 145, 147, 153, 160, 166–67,
  176, 216, 296, 305, 321; and
  Birmingham 117, 120, 129, 135,
  138–39, 157–58; and Selma 187,
  193–99, 201–2, 205, 207
Wallace, Henry 31, 32
Walton, Norman 45
War on Poverty 5, 141, 177, 204,
  216, 218, 223, 225–26, 228, 252,
  269, 322
Ware, J.L. 116
Washington, Mayor Harold 245
Washington, DC: disturbances after
  King's death 301–2; *see also* March
  on Washington; and Poor People's
  Campaign (PPC)
Watters, Pat 93, 167–68, 346
Watts disturbances 217–18, 220,
  232, 251–52, 258–59, 265, 321
Webb, Sheyann 197, 347
Wesley, Cynthia 158
White, Lee 189
Wilkins, Roy 29, 44, 61, 143–44,
  150, 179, 252, 352; rivalry with
  King 59, 69, 142, 149, 175, 256;
  and Lyndon Johnson 165, 178,
  274, 337; *see also* National
  Association for the Advancement
  of Colored People (NAACP)
Willard Hotel, Washington, DC
  184–85
Williams, A.D. *see* King family
Williams, Alberta *see* King family
Williams, Hosea 170, 172–73, 179,
  195–97, 208, 215, 223, 261, 262,
  295, 299, 328, 337
Williams, Robert 69, 83, 89,
  168, 345
Williams, Willis *see* King family
Willis, Benjamin 222, 224
Wingate, Livingston 178
Wofford, Harris 73, 74–75
Women's Political Council
  (Montgomery) 34, 36, 40–41

Wonder, Stevie 323
Woodlawn Organization, The
   (TWO) 86, 225
Wright, Fielding 31
Wright, Jeremiah 333
Wright, Marian (Edelman) 278

Yorty, Mayor Sam 217
Young, Andrew: 99, 114, 119, 127,
   142, 163, 171, 185–86, 255, 297,
   328, 332, 344; joins Citizenship
   Education Program 87–88;
   Birmingham negotiations 130,
   133; as executive director 172,
179, 208, 229, 260–62, 267; in
Selma 189–90, 192, 196–97, 205;
and Chicago 217–18, 228, 234,
236; and Vietnam 265; and PPC
279–80, 283, 291; and King's
assassination 302; as UN
ambassador 315, 317; *see also*
King: relationships: Young; and
Southern Christian Leadership
Conference (SCLC)
Young, Whitney 143, 165, 178,
   252, 256, 274, 287–88 353
Youth March for Integrated Schools
   (1959) 62

9 781138 781634